ISRAEL BETWEEN EAST AND WEST

"From the East will I bring thy seed
And from the West will I gather thee."

Isaiah 43.5

ISRAEL BETWEEN EAST AND WEST

A STUDY IN HUMAN RELATIONS

BY RAPHAEL PATAI

Second edition with
Supplementary Notes and a New Postscript
by the Author

GREENWOOD PUBLISHING CORPORATION
WESTPORT, CONNECTICUT

Library of Congress Catalog Card Number: 70-98711

SBN: 8371-3719-5

Greenwood Publishing Corporation
51 Riverside Avenue, Westport, Conn. 06880

Greenwood Publishers Ltd.
42 Hanway Street, London, W.1., England

Printed in the United States of America

Contents

11. Challenge and Outlook

Preface to the Second Edition

The extent and magnitude of the developments characterizing the recent history of Israel since the publication of the first edition of *Israel Between East and West* were forcefully brought home to me when I reread the book seventeen years after I had written it in order to decide what updatings were required for the second edition. Throughout the intervening years I have been in close touch with developments in Israel, visiting the country frequently (annually since 1961), continuing to study it and write about it, and, since 1964, working on the *Encyclopedia of Zionism and Israel* (to be published in 1970). In the light of all the new developments, which I thus continuously observed and absorbed, the original edition of *Israel Between East and West* as a whole made on me the impression of a historical document, describing, analyzing and interpreting the phenomena of a bygone era.

This being the case, a new edition of the book should, ideally, have contained a completely rewritten and updated text. Unfortunately, an extremely tight schedule of other commitments made it impossible to follow this course. The alternative, that of issuing an unchanged reprint of the first edition, seemed unacceptable because readers of a book on Israel published in 1970 would be justified in expecting to find in it at least some information on recent developments and on the effect the fateful events of 1967 have had on the life of Israel's population. Therefore, I settled on a compromise. The text of the 1953 edition is reprinted without changes, but marginal asterisks next to specific passages call attention to additional comments related to the subjects dealt with and found at the end of the book. In this manner, the text of the book retains whatever historical value it has as a contemporary record and analysis of Israel in 1952, while the social and cultural developments of the last 17 years are also indicated. Following these supplementary notes, there is a Postscript 1969, dealing in its entirety with the problem of the Oriental Jewish culture within the modern Ashkenazi culture of Israel.

RAPHAEL PATAI

Forest Hills, N.Y.
March 1969

From the Preface to the First Edition

In the spring of 1933, when I arrived in Jerusalem, the city as well as the country as a whole still had much of their centuries-old Oriental flavor. My first home was in an old Arab house which has since been torn down and replaced by a modern motion picture theater. It was here that I received my first impressions of the Middle East. I remember distinctly the piece of string which hung from the ceiling of the narrow hallway. Through a hole in the ceiling it was connected to a wooden block which swam in a tin water barrel below the roof. This piece of string was our lifeline: the less cord visible, the lower the level of the remaining water in the barrel and the less of the precious fluid we were allowed to use. Once a week the municipal water-works opened their tight-fisted plenty, and then a full length of cord dangled merrily in the windy passage indicating that a sparing shower might be in order.

Soon after my arrival, Dr. Noah Braun of the Hebrew University introduced me to Sheikh Ahmed F. Alkinani, a young teacher in one of the Government schools in Jerusalem, and for the next fifteen years Ahmed and I met—circumstances allowing—at least once a week. At first he taught me Arabic and I taught him Hebrew; later we conversed alternatingly in these two languages.

I shall never forget my first visit to the bazaar in the Old City of Jerusalem with Ahmed as my guide. It was what Ali Baba must have felt when he first pronounced the magic words and found himself in a world of precious stones and fascination. Soon I knew the labyrinthine Old City so well that I could guide others not only through its winding alleys, but also into many of its homes on whose hospitality I and my friends could always count.

As usually happens when one lives in one place year after year, the circle of my friends and acquaintances grew steadily and included Jews, Christians and Moslems. On many a Ramadhan-night I sat among friends in the cafés of the Old City listening to the animated performances of famous story-tellers from Cairo or Damascus.

In 1936, when the more sanguinary elements among the Arabs began their riotings which were to end only in 1939 with the outbreak of World War II, several of my Arab friends offered me the protection of their homes—in the event the situation got out of hand.

While, on the one hand, I thus obtained a first-hand and deepening insight into the social and cultural life of the Arabs of Palestine, I was equally drawn to the Oriental Jews whose *shekhunot* encircled the center of the New City like a necklace of multi-colored beads. On Sabbaths and holidays I sat on the floor-cushions in the synagogues of the Yemenite Jews, and on weekdays I went to their homes to talk to them and to take notes of whatever I heard and observed. After Ahmed had taken me to an Arab soothsayer from Baghdad, I sought out a Yemenite *Mori* and found that the methods employed by both showed surprising similarity. Many of my Moroccan, Iraqi and Bokharan friends revealed musical talent, and for some of these I arranged programs to be broadcast from the studios of the P. B. S. (the Palestine Broadcasting Service). Work on the completion of Dr. Erich Brauer's manuscript on the ethnology of the Jews of Kurdistan brought me in close contact with the Kurdish community and their *Hakhams*. My own landlord for many years was a Jew from Meshhed, Iran, and through him I became friendly with the leaders of this Marrano community to which I devoted several studies. Five minutes' walk took me from Meshhed to the heart of central Asia, the quarter of the Jews from Afghanistan.

As time went on I became more and more fascinated by the underlying similarities which I discovered existed beneath the apparent diversity of the more overt cultural manifestations. I was thus empirically led to the awareness of that cultural substratum which is common to Arabs and to Oriental Jews and which clearly differentiates all Middle Eastern population groups from the Jews of Europe, and especially of non-Mediterranean Europe.

To this observation was added the realization that in the inevitable clash between the Middle Eastern culture, represented by Oriental Jews and Arabs, and Western culture represented by the European Jewish immigrants and the small but influential British personnel in the country, in almost every instance Middle Eastern culture succumbed. Gradually it became clear to me that the degree and rate of Oriental assimilation depended on a number of factors, such as the relative numerical strength of the two groups, the intensity of contact between them, the degree of prestige enjoyed by each group in the eyes of the other, and the practical usefulness of the traits offered by the exponents of Western culture. Some preliminary observations on this subject I incorporated into a small monograph on the working of culture contact in modern Palestine.

Continued study of the traditional cultural forms and functions among the Middle Eastern and Western population groups in Palestine, as well as of the processes of change evinced by them under the impact of intensive culture contact, convinced me at an early date that here was a research-field of overwhelming magnitude and importance which could be attacked with some promise of success only by a group of scholars working in concert. However, after the untimely death of my friend, Dr. Brauer, in 1942, I found myself the only student of ethnology in the country. When prolonged efforts to persuade the Hebrew University to introduce the teaching of the subject (with special emphasis on the Jews and the Middle East) proved of no avail, I decided to make an independent effort. With the help of a handful of friends I founded the Palestine Institute of Folklore and Ethnology in 1944. In 1945 we launched a publishing program which was quite considerable for local conditions. In the short period of three years the Institute published three volumes of the quarterly *Edoth* (in Hebrew and English), five volumes of a library called "Studies in Folklore and Ethnology," and two volumes of another series called "Social Studies." All this was done with very little institutional support.

In the fall of 1947, when I received a fellowship from the Viking Fund (now The Wenner-Gren Foundation for Anthropological Research, Inc.) with an invitation to the United States, I left with the hope that the work would be carried on by others. That this was not the case, and that the Institute together with its publications and other activities became a casualty of the War of Liberation, will always remain one of the great disappointments of my life.

To this day, five years after the foundation of the State of Israel, in a country literally teeming with anthropological problems and opportunities, there is not a single anthropologist employed by any public or private body, although anthropologists elsewhere have splendidly demonstrated their usefulness in solving practical problems arising out of contacts between peoples and population groups. The only anthropologists working in Israel today are American students of the field who go there occasionally on a temporary basis and are supported by divers American funds.

After the establishment of Israel, the contact phenomena between the rapidly increasing Oriental sector of the population and the percentually diminishing European Jews offered new material daily for study and analysis. In 1949 and 1951 I returned to observe and search for any changes in the familiar trends. The results of these studies are laid before the reader in this book. Its central themes are the background, the unfolding, the phenomenology, the critical aspects, and the outcome of the problems created by the presence in Israel of two major groups of population elements basically differing in cultural characteristics. A proper understanding of these problems and of their repercussions on the nascent culture of Israel is imperative for any appraisal of its socio-cultural development.

RAPHAEL PATAI

The Faces of Israel

Oriental Jews

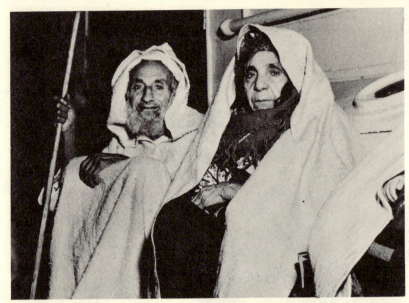

From Morocco

From Morocco

From Algeria

From Tripoli

From Egypt

From Yemen

From Egypt

From Yemen

From Hadhramaut

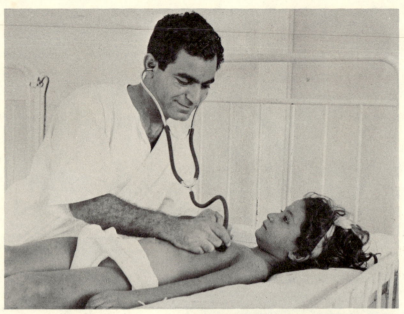

From Iraq

From Kurdistan

From Kurdistan

From Iran

From Burma

From India

From India

Sephardi Jews

From Turkey

From Bulgaria

From Turkey

From Turkey

From Bulgaria

Ashkenazi Jews

From Rumania

From Rumania

From Poland

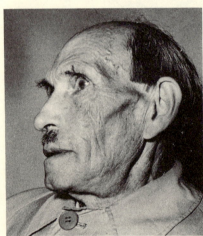

From Poland

From Poland

From Hungary

From the U.S.S.R.

From Hungary

From Czechoslovakia

From the U.S.S.R.

From Austria

From Germany

From Belgium

From France

From the United States and Canada

ISRAEL BETWEEN EAST AND WEST

Introduction

Israel's quest for a cultural physiognomy of its own, which can be regarded as a pilot project of utmost relevance to the problem of world understanding, hinges upon the possibility of reconciliation between the two cultural archetypes of the East and the West.

The Middle East as a whole, in whose hub Israel is located, is an extensive area of interpenetration between Eastern and Western culture. It has by now become a commonplace among students of the Middle East to speak of the "Westernization" of this important world area. As a result of the cultural, social and economic contacts between the Western world and the countries of the Middle East, the latter have come increasingly under the influence of the West, absorbing—often indiscriminately—Western technical equipment, Western methods of production and administration, as well as Western ideas, outlook and fashions. This, in brief, is what is meant by the "Westernization" of the Middle East.

The processes of Westernization, in most Middle Eastern countries are, to be sure, still in their very beginnings. They have affected to an appreciable extent only the life of the upper class, and to a lesser degree that of the middle class, in the big urban centers, such as Istanbul, Beirut, Damascus, Baghdad, Teheran, Cairo, Alexandria, Tunis or Algiers. These big cities in their turn are only now becoming secondary centers for the dissemination of Western influences across their respective hinterlands.

The most Westernized country in the entire Middle East today is Israel. Israel, as a matter of fact, is part of the Middle East only geographically. Its socio-cultural structure is alien to the area, a European growth transplanted by the European Jewish immigrants who came to the country during the three decades of the British Mandatory period. The laying of the foundations—economic, social, cultural and political—the investment of skills and capital, the widely ramified preparations for statehood—all this was done mainly or exclusively by Jews who came from the Western world.

3

During World War II, however, the human reserves of Western Jewry were suddenly and catastrophically depleted. By the time the goal of independence was reached, and the British-blocked road of immigration could be cleared at the Israeli receiving end, the potential flow of immigrants was cut off at its European source. The young and powerful American branch of Western Jewry was ready to stand by with large-scale financial support. But what the new State needed at least as much as economic aid was human material, and this was not forthcoming from America.

Such was the situation when Oriental Jewry appeared on the scene. Its existence had been all but forgotten; yet here was a solid block of a million Jews, concentrated in a dozen Middle Eastern countries, practically unscathed by the deluge of blood which swept away six millions of their brethren in Europe, ready to go to Israel, in fact clamoring to return to the re-established homeland.

Thus it happened that soon after the gates of Israel were thrown open, Oriental Jews became the major immigrant group. At the time of this writing, their numbers in the total Jewish population of Israel itself have reached the halfway mark.

If one looks into the future, one must envisage the balance between the Eastern and the Western population elements in Israel as rapidly reaching the proportions which prevail in the world as a whole. Two-thirds—tending to become three-fourths—of the human species is characterized by what Sir John Russell calls "Eastern rates of population increase." These rates of increase are several times higher than the corresponding Western rates found in the remaining one-third to one-fourth of the world's population. In Israel, on a scale reduced a thousand times, a similar ratio will soon exist between the Oriental elements with their high rate of increase and the European Jews who belong, in this respect as in many others, to the West.

Students of population have long pointed to the organic and causal connection between the under-privileged status of peoples and their over-multiplication. Uncontrolled and very high fertility, counterbalanced, it is true, to some extent by equally uncontrolled and very high infant, child and general mortality; poverty and disease; suffering and squalor; ignorance and backwardness—these are some of the inseparable characteristics of the under-privileged two-thirds of humanity. In Israel, with the influx of the Oriental Jewish masses, there is an acute danger that a similar pattern will develop. The slums in the Palestine of the Mandatory period were populated almost exclusively either by Arabs or by Oriental Jews. Today in Israel, very much against the wishes of the Government, Oriental

Jews constitute the overwhelming majority of those who live in substandard conditions. More often than not, the Oriental Jewish immigrants come from slums or slum-like ghettos, *mellahs* or *haras*, and when they are settled in Israel in overcrowded quarters they cannot help re-creating a semblance of the slums in which they spent their entire lives. The poverty which was their lot in the old countries becomes even more pronounced in Israel where they arrive literally without anything they can call their own. Even under the best circumstances it will take a long time until they are enabled to earn enough to eat and dress adequately. It will take even longer until they and their children are redeemed from oppressive ignorance which is one of the main obstacles in their way to economic betterment.

There is only one sphere in which immediately effective help is given to them, and in which considerable improvement can be observed soon after their arrival in Israel. This is the sphere of sanitation and medical care. The sick are treated in hospitals and clinics; and, though reluctant at first, they soon learn to trust the medical services put at their disposal by the authorities without charge and to make use of them with increasing frequency. The result is a rapid amelioration of the health situation; infectious diseases are brought under control and their spread is effectively prevented. In one of the immigrants camps, for example, trachoma was reduced within four months from an incidence of 98% to 20%.

One important outcome of these medical efforts is the considerable reduction of infant and child mortality which under traditional circumstances in Middle Eastern countries is as appallingly high among Oriental Jews as it is among Arabs (reaching 600 per thousand of live births during the first five years of life). The number of births shows no immediate corresponding decline. This can be expected to set in only several years later as one of the end results of the economic and socio-cultural adaptation to the new conditions. Consequently, for the next 10 or 15 years the rate of natural increase of the Oriental Jews in Israel must be expected to grow considerably and become several times higher than that of the Ashkenazi (European) Jews. Thus a half-European and half-Oriental Israel in 1953 will become, in all probability, by 1975 one-third or one-fourth European and two-thirds or three-fourths Oriental. Whether this will mean a pronounced approximation in Israel of that socio-cultural level which prevails in most Middle Eastern states, or whether it will mean merely the presence of Oriental Jewish genes in the biological makeup of the majority with an undiminished transmittance of all the Western achievements of the country, will depend chiefly on the educational and cultural policies of its leadership in the coming most crucial years.

This situation will clearly give rise to a race between the rate at which the population groups of Oriental extraction in Israel will multiply, and the rate at which the institutions of the state will be able to supply them with a Western-type cultural equipment and instill in them the values of their own Western-type culture. In the final analysis, therefore, the question is whether the *successful acculturation* of the Oriental population groups can be accomplished by the Western element in Israel before it becomes numerically too weak to impress its own imprint on the Oriental parts of the population.

Successful acculturation, however, does not mean the desirability or advisability of imposing upon the Oriental Jewish segment a purely Western character. The wholesale imposition of an alien culture on a population can easily lead to deculturation instead of acculturation. Wise and planned acculturation will rather entail a careful selection of indisputably desirable complexes as focal points for the acculturative process, with the retention of as much of the traditional cultural texture of Oriental communities as possible. This has to be done not only in order to facilitate the acceptance of Western culture by tradition-bound Oriental Jewish groups, but also with a view to the enrichment of the nascent culture of Israel as a whole.

The West has concentrated its attention on economic and material advancement, on social security and physical health. These attainments have been established in Palestine (Israel) by the European Jewish immigrants and have become basic and focal complexes in the socio-cultural structure erected in the old-new homeland. It is self-evident to those who are responsible for the planning of a better future for the young Jewish State that an equalization must be effected between the European and the Oriental elements in the country with regard to a decent minimum standard of nutrition and health, of housing and comfort, of social security and educational opportunities. But it should be equally self-evident that not only people coming from an Eastern cultural background can benefit by learning from the culture of the West; the West too has much to learn from the East. Students of culture know only too well that by concentrating on economics, social security, material benefits and physical health, the West has narrowed down its field of vision, growing blinders to shut out from view everything but the road it traverses. As Julian Huxley so aptly put it, "Our new view of human destiny insists that emotional and intellectual and spiritual satisfactions must also be taken into account . . . new kinds of potential experience—in aesthetic perception, for instance, or in intellectual understanding—should be realized in actual achievement, and new levels of possibility, such as telepathy and so called mystical experience, should be explored . . ."[*]

These achievements, mentioned as examples of desiderata in Western culture, may be present in other cultures outside the Euroamerican sphere. The Oriental Jews who arrive in tens of thousands in Israel are the carriers of such a non-Western culture: the traditional culture of the Middle East. Wise statesmanship in Israel should be on the lookout for the possible presence in the culture brought along by the Oriental Jews of some of these desiderata lacking in Western culture. The incorporation of these into the nascent culture of Israel could immensely enrich it.

To accomplish this, the objective contents of traditional Middle Eastern culture—of which the culture of the Oriental Jews is a part —must first of all be understood, analyzed and made available in its main components for eventual utilization. The "Wisdom of the East," handed down in Oriental imagery, must be translated into Western terms before the Western mind can attempt to enrich itself by it. The traditional ways of the Orient, which are but the external and everyday manifestations of its doctrines, outlooks and attitudes, must be studied in the context of the totality of Oriental culture which alone makes it possible properly to evaluate the meaning of single cultural elements for the peoples of the Orient themselves.

Planned selection of cultural traits or complexes for inclusion into another culture is a most difficult task, in the execution of which one cannot as yet lean on scientifically validated methods. But it is possible to delineate the differences between two cultures, to point out the differential emphases in each, and thus, by grasping the essentials in both, to reach an understanding of the processes of change taking place as a result of the interaction between the carriers of the two cultures. Once one understands a cultural process, its motives, its mechanisms and its results, one can try to direct it, or at least to facilitate its motion in one direction while impeding it in another.

In this manner the cultures of the modern West and the traditional East which today meet and impinge on each other in Israel, could, to some extent at least, be led to a constructive confluence. Instead of mechanical "Westernization" with its everpresent danger of Levantinization, a synthesis could be reached in which neither of the

[*] Cf. Julian Huxley, "Population and Human Destiny," *Harper's Magazine*, New York, September, 1950, p. 45.

two population elements would slavishly ape the other, but in which both would contribute what is valuable in their own culture, and lacking in the other, to a new, doubly enriched cultural configuration. For Israel, this outcome would mean all the difference between crisis and resolution, between defeat and victory. For the world at large, still struggling futilely along isolated and rival paths, it would provide a small-scale but dynamic example which can be turned into a blueprint for global understanding.

Chapter One

Chronicles of the People

1. Origins

For more than two thousand years the history of the Jewish people was unfolded in the Middle East, or, more precisely, in a few countries located in its very center: Palestine, Egypt and Mesopotamia. It was somewhere between Babylonia and Canaan that the first families arose which were called by the name *Ibrim*, or Hebrews, denoting either the children of Eber, their eponymous ancestor, or people coming from *eber*, that is, beyond, the River. The Patriarchal Age of the Hebrews—beginning with the immigration of Abram or Abraham from Ur of the Chaldees to Canaan, the Land of Promise, and ending with the emigration of his grandson, Jacob, also called Israel, from a starving Canaan to abundant Egypt—is vividly depicted in the stories of Genesis which are veritable masterpieces of the ancient Oriental art of narration. Historically, however, this early age is a very elusive one, the difficulties starting with the exact setting of the time-span of the period and ending with the problem of the historicity of the principal figures themselves, who at times seem to be projections of entire tribes rather than individual characters.

Then comes the servitude in Egypt which is corroborated by historical data, but the duration and exact time of which are highly problematical. Tradition, incorporated in the biblical narrative, puts it at four hundred years, but regards the entire Egyptian sojourn as a mere episode of trial conceived and staged by the inscrutable Divine Will. The Hebrews suffering in slavery in Egypt were sustained, according to tradition, by the belief that redemption was nigh, redemption, that is, return, to the Promised Land of their fathers. The hope of return thus animated and fired the Hebrews even before they became a people, and when it was accomplished, the Exodus from Egypt remained the everlasting symbol of their birth as a nation as well as a religious community. The great hand of God was seen in everything: it was He who inspired their un-equalled master, Moses, who led them out of Egypt amidst miracles and portents; who made them wander for forty years in the Desert; who placed on them the yoke of the Law at Mount Sinai; and who gave them victory over thirty kings of Canaan.

After the conquest of Canaan under Joshua, the disciple of Moses, there followed a long epoch of some six centuries in which the entire Hebrew nation lived in the Land of Israel, first under the leadership of local headmen; called Judges, then under the rule of kings. The first three kings, Saul, David and Solomon, reigned over the entire country; but their successors had to be content with either the King-dom of Judah in the south, or with the Kingdom of Israel in the north. In this period, commonly referred to as the "Days of the First Temple,"—the temple built by Solomon in Jerusalem—the Hebrew tribes were welded together to form one nation which fought, con-quered or was beaten by neighboring peoples and kings, eventually establishing peaceful contact with them, interbreeding with them and assimilating important aspects of their culture.

The culture which the Hebrews themselves developed was merely a special variant of the cultures of the ancient Near East, containing the same basic elements, but in a somewhat different proportion and combination. As the centuries moved on, greater and greater em-phasis was placed on monotheistic and centralized worship and on the moralistic and ethical components in religion. The initial tribal monotheism of the conquerors of Canaan, which held that the God worshipped by Israel was the only God of Israel and was the God of Israel alone while other tribes and peoples may have had their own god or gods, was supplanted by a universal ethical monotheism pro-claiming the belief that the God worshipped by Israel was the only God existing. This religious development, which was the greatest cultural achievement of the Hebrews, reached its peak, towards the end of the Days of the First Temple, in the teachings of the great Hebrew prophets, the first three of whom, Amos, Hosea and Isaiah, appear to us today as giant figures of spiritual revolutionaries.

In 721 B. C. E., Israel, the northern kingdom, fell to the Assyrians, and in 586 B. C. E., Judea, the southern, Davidic, state was captured by the Babylonians and the ancient Temple of Solomon in Jerusalem sacked and destroyed. The major part of the population of the coun-try was exiled to Babylonia; some managed to flee to Egypt, taking with them Jeremiah, the great prophet of a tragic age. Only the poor of the land were left behind. From this time on, and down to our present days, throughout two and a half millennia, only a minor part of the Jewish people lived in the Land of Israel, or Palestine (meaning Land of the Philistines) as it was called by the Greeks and the Romans. The majority remained abroad and continued to settle in several foreign lands. But the idea that the People of Israel and the Land of Israel belonged to one another remained ingrained in the hearts of the Jews wherever they lived and wherever they were able to keep their traditions alive.

In every land and in every epoch this idea, which became a basic tenet of Jewish religion and tradition, actuated some of the Children of Israel to return to the Land of Israel. Sometimes only a few, sometimes many were able to satisfy their impulse. The first time this desire became manifest in a movement was in the generation which followed that of the exile. Political changes for the better, the conquest of Babylonia by the Persians and the rule of a benevolent tyrant, Cyrus, enabled a group of about 40,000 men, under the leadership of Zerubbabel, to return to the Land of Israel and to start rebuilding their desolate country, its capital city of Jerusalem and its religious center, the Temple. This was the opening of the era of the Second Temple, which ended another six hundred years later when Titus captured Jerusalem, in 70 C. E.

Numerically, throughout this long epoch, only an increasingly smaller minority of the Jewish people lived in the Land of Israel, while the ever-growing majority lived in Babylonia and in Egypt, and from these two major centers set out to settle also in countries contiguous to them, like Syria, Persia, North Africa, Arabia and the southern outskirts of Egypt. Towards the end of this period large Jewish communities were found also in Greece (including Asia Minor), on the islands of the Mediterranean and in Rome.

Spiritually, however, throughout this period the Jews of Palestine retained the hegemony. Practically all the literary documents which survive from this epoch, and which are the repositories of Jewish creativeness, derive from the soil of Palestine. It was this age which saw the collection and canonization in Palestine of the twenty-four books of the Hebrew Bible. The Apocrypha and other religious literary works, not admitted to the Canon but preserved in original or in translations to this day, were for the most part written in Palestine. Most of the books and writings included in the New Testament were written in Palestine. The first sages whose religious and ethical ideas are incorporated in the Mishna lived towards the end of this period in Palestine, where also the first versions and the final form of the Mishna itself were shaped in the following century. The first Jewish historian to write in Greek, who witnessed and described the siege of Jerusalem and the destruction of the Temple by Titus, was a Palestinian Jewish priest, Josephus Flavius.

This is not the place to recount the many political vicissitudes which befell the Second Jewish Commonwealth in its independent periods or while under Persian, Greek (Ptolemaic and Seleucid) and finally Roman overlordship. What is relevant to our purpose is the fact that after nearly two thousand years of recorded history, during which the People of Israel lived only in Palestine and in surrounding Near Eastern countries and were exposed to Oriental cultural influences only, towards the end of the days of the Second Temple an increasingly numerous section of the Jewish people already lived in the West, and came under Western cultural influences. In the first century C. E., considerable cultural differences existed between the Jews who for a number of generations had lived in Rome, and the Jews whose home had been in Babylonia for five centuries. In other words, after the Jews had been an Eastern people for two millennia, they now grew a new, Western, branch. This is the first intimation of a bifurcation of the Jewish people into a Western and an Eastern division.

2. The Oriental Environment

The beginning of the next epoch was marked by the disappearance of the last vestiges of Jewish suzerainty in Palestine; the added importance gained by the synagogues as the only remaining places of Jewish religious worship after the destruction of the Temple of Jerusalem; and the increased emphasis placed on the study of the Law. Spiritual and cultural hegemony was retained for well over a century by the Jews of Palestine, whose religious and temporal leader, Rabbi Yehuda haNasi, codified about 200 C. E. the Mishna, the most important Jewish religious source-book after the Bible.

From the 3rd century onward the cultural ascendance of the Jews of Babylonia became more and more pronounced, and their collective *magnum opus*, the Babylonian Talmud, which was codified about 500 C. E., soon gained primacy over the contemporaneous effort of the Palestinian sages laid down in the much smaller Jerusalem Talmud. Though the Babylonian Jews of this period were more learned than their Palestinian brethren, and were also much more numerous, powerful and well-to-do, and could look back to a local history of about a thousand years, they never ceased—at least in principle—to regard themselves as exiles from the Land of Israel; they called their leader *Resh Gelutha*, or Head of the Diaspora; and they repeatedly expressed in their Talmud their feeling that it was ideally the religious duty of every Jew to return to Palestine. Taxes, and later voluntary donations, continued to flow from Babylonia to Israel, and caravans plying between the two countries kept personal contacts alive.

The relationship of other diasporas to Israel was largely similar, with the one difference, however, that, while Israel remained· their Holy Land, the land of their fathers and the direction of their prayers, they felt dependent also on Babylonia because of the latter's supremacy in religious learning. With the Roman conquest of the eastern Mediterranean, two powerful and rich diasporas, the Roman and the Alexandrian, were drawn into a single orbit, though the culture of the latter continued to remain Greek. Of the cultural attainments of the Jewish communities within the Roman Empire, however, very little has survived and is known. Religiously, so much is clear, the life of all the Jewish diasporas was centered on Jerusalem; their synagogues contained pictorial representations of sacred objects from the destroyed Temple, such as the Ark, the Pitcher, the Menorah, the Altar; and their prayers, which in this period assumed the form familiar to us today, frequently expressed the hope and the wish for a return to Palestine and a re-establishment of the Temple service.

When the Roman Empire extended its limits to the west and to the north, to include parts of what are today England, France, Spain, Germany, Austria, Hungary and Rumania, Jews also went along with the conquering armies or in their wake, and scattered tombstones testify to this day of their presence in many a Roman army camp, station or colony. The decline and fall of the Roman Empire brought about the severance of the connections among these dispersed Jewish communities and a further differentiation between the Western and the Eastern division of the Jewish people. Eastern Jewry weathered the Byzantine period in the eastern Balkans and in Asia Minor, while elsewhere in the Middle East it changed overlords when the Arabs started on their conquests in the century following the appearance of Mohammed (570-632).

Just as the expansion of the Roman Empire facilitated the dispersion of the Jews over Central and Western Europe, the Arab expansion enabled them to settle in all the countries which fell to Islam. In the west, the Moslem conquest of North Africa as far as the Atlantic coast brought a new wave of Jews into these lands, numerically much stronger than the Jewish groups already there since Roman times, and opened up the gates of the Iberian Peninsula to a Jewish element which was destined to play a leading role in Jewish history for several centuries to come. In the south, Jews penetrated

Ethiopia, either through Upper Egypt or through Southern Arabia. In the east, they moved from Babylonia into mountainous Kurdistan and into Persia, and thence into the Caucasus, Bokhara, Turkistan, Afghanistan, India and China. Babylonia, however, remained the major center of the Jewish people approximately to the 11th century.

From the outgoing ancient times onward the Jews began to share more and more fully the cultural fate of the countries in which they settled. In spite of voluntary or imposed isolation, which was in many cases sufficient to establish a tenacious barrier against the penetration of concrete cultural content from the non-Jewish environment into the life of the Jewish communities, the general tenor of non-Jewish culture deeply impressed itself on them. Cultural ascendancy on the part of the non-Jewish environment was accompanied by a similar phenomenon among the Jews; and cultural decadence among the first was paralleled among the latter. The Moslem cultural zenith in the Middle Ages was the time when the Jews in Moslem countries reached the height of their cultural development, culminating in the Golden Age of Hebrew poetry, philosophy and religious literature in Spain, in North Africa, in Egypt, in Baghdad and in Persia. From the 11th century onward the cultural hegemony passed from the Babylonian to the Spanish Jews, who in the course of the 12th to the 15th centuries adopted Spanish as their everyday tongue. The descendants of these medieval Spanish Jews are to this day identified as Sephardi Jews. The Sephardi Jews lived, both before and after their expulsion from Spain (1492), within the Islamic orbit in North Africa and the Ottoman Empire; the emergence of Sufism, the mystical trend in Islam, in the 10th and 11th centuries, was paralleled by a powerful impetus given by Sephardi and Oriental Jews to the Jewish movement of mysticism, the Cabala.

During this period Christian Europe was submerged in scholasticism, and correspondingly the main Jewish intellectual effort, too, centered on the scholastic exegesis of the Bible, the Mishna and the Talmud. The great figures of Franco-German Jewry were the commentator Rabbi Shelomo ben Yitzhaq (Rashi, 1040-1105) of Troyes and his followers, the super-commentators known under the collective name of Tosafists.

The decline of Arab culture from the 15th and 16th century onward marked also the decline of Jewish cultural creativity in the Moslem countries. Religious literature, and in the first place compendia of religious codes, persisted somewhat longer after the disappearance of other branches of intellectual activity. While up to the 17th century the great majority of the Jewish religious authors, whose works are to this day the authoritative sources of Jewish religious law, emanated from the Eastern sector of the Jewish people, from that time on the balance shifted to Europe where the rapidly expanding Jewish communities began to produce spiritual leaders of their own. The codification of the Law especially was the forte of the Sephardi Jews, the last of the codes produced by them being the *Shulhan Arukh,* the great Jewish *corpus juris,* written by Rabbi Joseph Qaro (1488-1575) in Palestine. The intellectual independence reached by the East European Jews about this time was manifested in the fact that, still in the lifetime of its author, the *Shulhan Arukh* was glossed, annotated and emended by a Polish rabbinical authority, Moshe Isserles (1525-1572, Cracow), and that whenever a difference of opinion was evident between Qaro and Isserles, the Polish and other European Jews adhered to the emendations of Isserles, while the Sephardi Jews accepted the decisions of Joseph Qaro in unchanged form. This is the corporealization of the religious differences between the Sephardi and the Ashkenazi (East and Central European) Jews.

3. Dispersion and Assimilation

The origins of the Ashkenazi division of the Jewish people go back to a twofold migratory movement. Probably soon after the destruction of the Second Jewish Commonwealth (70 C. E.) Jews moved northward through Asia Minor to the port cities of the Black Sea, and eventually penetrated into the interior of Russia. As early as the 8th century Jews were found in the city of Kiev. These Jews spoke Slavic languages.

The second Jewish migratory movement reached Central and Eastern Europe from the West. Excluding the few early Jewish settlers in the Roman colonies, and the isolated data testifying to the presence in the 4th century of Jewish communities in a few townships such as Cologne, the existence of Jewish settlements in the Frankish Empire is well documented from the end of the 8th century. Jews first appeared in the cities along the Rhine and the Moselle, and a century later they are found also on the banks of the Danube. From the 11th century the Jews of France and Germany were called in Hebrew literature *Ashkenazim,* as distinguished from the Sephardi Jews who lived in Spain and the Provence. After the expulsion of the Jews from France in 1306, Germany became the undisputed center of Ashkenazi Jewry which by that time included communities of German Jewish emigrants in Bohemia, Hungary, Italy and Poland. The persecution of the Jews in German lands had as its consequence a further shift to the east. In the 16th century tens of thousands of Ashkenazi Jewish families settled in Poland, Lithuania, Russia and Wolhynia. Here they merged with the older Jewish communities, whose Slavic languages were replaced by Yiddish, or Judeo-German, brought along by the Jews from the German lands. By the middle of the 17th century, in the wake of the atrocities perpetrated by Chmielnicki in the Ukraine, a reverse migratory current set in, from east to west, which was continued for the following three hundred years.

While Oriental and Sephardi Jewry continued to decline or to lead an existence of passive resignation, Ashkenazi Jewry produced in the 18th century a number of vital movements the outcomes of which are felt to the present day. The first was the Hasidic movement, created by the Polish rabbi, Israel Baal-Shem-Tob (1699-1760). The essence of the Hasidic teachings is that man must serve God with faith, love and joy, with singing and dancing, and with complete devotion to the Divine Will, rather than by an overly rigorous observance of all the minutiae of the practical commandments and an unrelenting study of the Law as laid down in the Talmud and the Codes. For Hasidism, the Land of Israel is the center of the universe, and the *Zaddik*, the miracle-working rabbi, is the center of Israel.

The second movement was the Jewish counterpart of the general trend towards enlightenment which spread in the middle of the 18th century in Central and Western Europe. Its initiator was the German Jewish philosopher, Moses Mendelssohn (1729-1786) under whose influence a considerable part of German and other Ashkenazi Jews began to seek secular education, familiarize themselves with the culture of Europe and first of all with that of contemporary Germany, and free themselves from the bonds of the spiritual ghetto in which they had lived. Towards the end of the century this movement resulted in a Jewish spiritual revival, called *Haskala* (enlightenment), and an increasing use of the Hebrew language as a means of secular literary expression.

Orthodox Judaism, faithful to talmudic learning, rallied around Rabbi Elijah of Wilna (1720-1797) in its opposition to Hasidism and Haskala alike. This movement became known under the name of *Mitnagdim* (Opposers).

The last of these popular movements which demonstrated the great vitality of Ashkenazi Jewry both before and after its emancipation and liberation from the ghettos, was the *Hibbat Zion* (Love of Zion) movement, the forerunner of political Zionism founded by Theodor Herzl (1860-1904).

Throughout the long period sketched above, whatever the movement or the trend which swept the Jewish communities, whether in the Orient or in the Occident, religious tradition kept alive the idea of the Return to Zion. The Talmud written in Babylonia, the poems and philosophical treatises of the great Jewish minds of the Spanish period, the biblical and talmudic commentaries of the traditional masters of Western, Central and Eastern Europe, the *corpora juris* of the great Sephardi codifiers of Jewish religious law, the pronunciamentos of the false messiahs, the teachings of the Hasidim in Eastern Europe, the literary efforts of the *Haskala* authors—all abound in references to the Holy Land and in expressions of the hope that God will grant His people to return to Zion. Often in these writings it is stated expressly that life in Palestine is superior to that in any other country, that many religious duties incumbent upon every tradition-keeping Jew can be fulfilled only in the Holy Land, and that the Return to Zion itself is a supreme religious duty.

Material considerations kept most of the Jews from translating this ideal into reality. But a small number of them, from all corners of the world, following up these convictions, went to settle in Palestine. Some went to live and to work there, others—in old age in order to be buried in the hallowed soil of the Holy Land. Some of the greatest figures of Judaism, like Jehuda haLevi the poet-philosopher, Maimonides the philosopher-codifier-physician, Joseph Qaro author of the *Shulhan Arukh*, Rabbi Jehuda heHasid with his followers (in 1700), and many others throughout the centuries, followed this path. The messianic movements from the 12th to the 18th centuries, arising as far east as Kurdistan and Persia and as far west as Italy and Spain, always could secure an enthusiastic following with the one magical phrase, "Return to Zion." The great leaders of the Hasidic movement, beginning with the Baal-Shem himself, endeavored to settle in Palestine, though only a few of them were able to do so. In 1777 three Hasidic leaders, together with more than three hundred of their flock, actually settled in Palestine. Others, who were prevented from going, felt it their duty to support the poor of the Holy Land. However far the dispersion, however long the exile, Palestine, the Holy Land, symbolized by Zion and Jerusalem, remained the great focus of spiritual life, the powerful center of religious orientation.

Emancipation, enlightenment and assimilation transformed the Ashkenazi Jews, and especially those of Western and Central Europe, within a relatively short period from an isolated and dispersed foreign group in the body of the European peoples into an integral part of the economic, political, social and cultural life of the countries in which they lived. It was inevitable that in the course of the merging processes which ensued much of the original cultural idiosyncrasies of the Jewish people should get lost. Religion was usually the last remaining bond, but in the assimilatory maelstrom this too was at times given up and in this manner total fusion with the neighboring gentiles actually or reputedly achieved. But even when religion, and with it a certain congregational identification, were retained, the Jewish communities of Europe most thoroughly approximated in several other cultural and demographic aspects the non-Jewish majority groups among whom they lived.

A similar process took place in the Oriental countries, though here the particular circumstances were different. The association with the host peoples extended here over a much longer period of time. Assimilation in every other respect but religion was an accomplished fact long before the emancipation of Ashkenazi Jewry. The way of life, the language spoken, the clothing worn, the food eaten, and many other cultural traits, had long become practically identical among Jews and Moslems. Demographical characteristics, such as birthrate, deathrate, life expectancy, incidence of and proneness to diseases, all these had become almost identical between the two. Here was a Jewry, which, as a 19th century observer put it, was in Arab lands "Arab in all but religion"; in Persia it was Persian in all but religion. Religion, however, remained the great separating force, true to the universality of its power and influence over Middle Eastern life. In general, Islam was characterized by a certain amount of tolerance toward the Jews which stood in sharp contrast to the intolerant attitude of Christianity in Europe up to the onset of the liberal trends which led to the emancipation of the Jews in one European country after the other in the course of the 19th century. Before the emancipation, therefore, the position of the Jews was decidedly better in Islamic countries than in Christian Europe; after the emancipation the positions became, broadly speaking, reversed. Christian Europe ostensibly accepted the Jews as parts of its nations and enabled them to assimilate; in Islamic countries the Jews remained, as before, a tolerated but despised foreign body on account of the indelible difference in religion. "Arab in all but religion," meant still a great distance between Jew and Moslem, while the German Jew who became Germanized in every respect but religion, sincerely believed that the religious difference between him and a Catholic German was not greater than the difference between a Catholic and a Protestant German.

4. The Great Migration

In the 19th century great new changes occurred in the geographical distribution as well as the cultural and linguistic characteristics of Ashkenazi Jewry. The first of these changes took place within the European continent itself. In the beginning of the century practically all the Ashkenazi Jews—numbering at the time about 1,500,000—spoke Yiddish and were concentrated primarily in Eastern Europe. Toward the end of the century, as a result of the enlightenment and the emancipation, a considerable percentage of Ashkenazi Jews had already exchanged the Yiddish mother-tongue for the languages of the countries in which they lived and were well advanced on the road to cultural assimilation. Their numbers had increased more than sixfold, to about 9,550,000, and though their majority still lived in Russia (5,200,000 in 1897), the east-to-west movement among them assumed gigantic proportions. From all the countries east of Germany the Jews began to move to Austria (mostly to the capital, Vienna), to Germany, Belgium, France and England. No statistical data are available to show the extent of this migration in the course of the 19th century, but it is known that its continuation from 1900 to 1930 brought nearly half a million Jews from Eastern Europe into the five countries enumerated above, in some cases doubling their Jewish population.

In the last two decades of the 19th century the great migration began of East-European Jews across the seas. The main countries from which the stream of emigrants came were Russia (including Poland), Galicia and Rumania; and their goal was the United States of America. Other overseas countries, such as Canada, Argentina, Palestine, South Africa, Brazil, Uruguay, Mexico, Cuba, Egypt, Australia and New Zealand, served as secondary and tertiary places of absorption.

In 1880 the Jews in the United States numbered about 230,000. From 1880 to 1900, about 632,000 Jewish immigrants were added to this number, followed in the period from 1901 to 1929 by another 1,795,000. Eighty per cent of all these came from Eastern Europe (including Austria and Hungary).

The result of this great migration—numerically the largest ever in the long history of the Jewish people—was a wide and new distribution of Ashkenazi Jews over the Anglo-Saxon countries and the rest of the New World. The countries which admitted them afforded to immigrants in general better economic opportunities than they had had in the old countries, as well as better political conditions; and these favorable circumstances resulted demographically in a considerable natural increase, while culturally and linguistically they led to a relatively speedy assimilation to the new environment. Both points are best illustrated by the United States. This country had 230,000 Jews in 1880, admitted another 2,427,000 from 1880 to 1929, making a total of 2,657,000. Yet in 1929 the number of Jews in the United States was 4,350,000. As far as cultural assimilation is concerned, it is known that the children of immigrants who were brought up or born in the United States as a rule do not speak any longer the language brought along from the Old World by their parents (usually Yiddish), but only English. The same phenomenon can be observed in the other Anglo-Saxon countries, while in Latin America it is the local Spanish or Portuguese tongues which supplant the old language with equal rapidity. The assimilation of Ashkenazi Jewry to Western culture, began in the 19th century in the Old World, thus became an accomplished fact in the 20th century both in the Old and the New Worlds.

No commensurate migratory movement took place in the 19th and the first third of the 20th century among the Oriental and the Sephardi Jews. Oriental Jews, that is, those who during the period of the Second Jewish Commonwealth moved from Babylonia and Egypt, or from Palestine itself, to other Asiatic and African countries, spread slowly and successively, but never in large numbers, across Central and Southern Asia as far east as China, and across North Africa to Morocco in the west. Towards the end of the Middle Ages this division of the Jewish people became more or less stationary, and remained so until the beginning of the 20th century, when about 50,000 Oriental (and Sephardi) Jews immigrated to the New World. Up to the penetration of Europeans into the Middle East in the 19th century, Oriental Jews never had any first-hand contact with European peoples or cultures. They lived in an all-Oriental cultural atmosphere and ethnic environment, and as the centuries passed they became more and more saturated with the traditional culture of the Middle East of which Jewish culture originally was a variant and which, therefore, was similar to their own at the very outset of their long sojourn in Islamic lands.

As already mentioned, in the 11th century one branch of this Oriental Jewry reached Spain, then under Arab rule, and this offshoot became the ancestors of the Sephardi division of the Jewish people. After four centuries of sojourn in Spain, during which period Spanish Jewry achieved the undisputed cultural leadership of the Jewish people, the decline of the Spanish Caliphate and the rise of Christian power in the Iberian Peninsula, with the inquisition and persecutions as its concomitants, caused the Spanish Jews to disperse over many countries in Europe, Asia and Africa. The important migrations of the Sephardi Jews began in the 15th century and continued on to the 18th century. In the course of these four hundred years Sephardi Jews settled in France, Holland and England in

Western Europe; in Italy and the Balkans in Southern Europe; in the countries of North Africa from Morocco in the west to Egypt in the east; in Turkey, Syria and Palestine in Asia; and finally in Mexico, the United States and South American countries in the New World. The four centuries in Spain stamped the Sephardi Jews with definite cultural characteristics of their own, one of the most outstanding and persistent of which was the use of the Spaniolic (Sephardi or Judeo-Spanish) language which they retained in most cases to the present day.

Relatively little contact took place between Ashkenazi and Sephardi Jews apart from such marginal and numerically unimportant areas as the Provence in the Middle Ages, and Holland and England from the 15th century onward. Ashkenazi Jews and Oriental Jews were cut off from each other to an even greater extent. Sephardi and Oriental Jews, however, repeatedly met, in the course of the last five hundred years, mixed and interbred, and influenced each other culturally. After the expulsion of the Jews from Spain (1492), their great majority settled in Moslem lands all of which contained old Oriental Jewish communities. In many cases the result of the arrival of the Spanish Jews, with their prestige, superior learning and great emphasis on nobility of lineage, was a partial or complete assimilation of the Oriental Jews to them. Arabic thus was replaced by Spaniolic in several Oriental Jewish communities, and their progeny began to reckon itself as belonging to the Sephardi division of the people. In other places the fusion was not so complete, and the Oriental Jews retained their separate identity, their language and their culture; in these cases intermarriage between Oriental and Sephardi Jews was often frowned upon by both sides. Again, in some communities, where the influx of Spanish Jews was slight, it was they who became assimilated to the Oriental Jews in language and custom. In some places, even without the presence of a considerable local Jewish community, the exiled Spanish Jews adopted the language of the country and in this manner they were set apart from the rest of Sephardi Jewry. This happened, for instance, in Italy where the Sephardi Jews adopted Italian soon after their arrival from Spain, and where they continued to constitute a separate branch of Sephardi Jewry down to the present day.

Numerically, the Ashkenazi division of the Jewish people evinced a phenomenal increase since the beginning of the 19th century. The Ashkenazi Jews, who numbered about 1,500,000 in 1800, increased to 3,600,000 in 1840, to 5,200,000 in 1860, to 9,550,000 in 1900, and to 14,600,000 in 1930. As against this, the number of the Sephardi and Oriental Jews remained almost stationary during the entire 19th century, as was the case also with the Moslem peoples of the Middle East, numbering about 1,000,000 in 1800; 900,000 in 1840; 800,000 in 1860; and 950,000 in 1900. In the 20th century, together with the onset of numerical increase among the Moslem peoples, the Jews living among them also began to increase, reaching by 1930 the figure of 1,300,000.

As a consequence of this shift in the numerical balance, the overwhelming majority of the Jewish people in 1930 belonged to the Ashkenazi division (92.8%), while only 8.2% of them belonged jointly to the Sephardi and the Oriental Jewish divisions.

In 1930 the Jewish people, Ashkenazim, Sephardim and Oriental Jews together, numbered 15,900,000. By 1939 they showed a further increase to 16,633,000, and in that year the division between Ashkenazi and non-Ashkenazi Jews was approximately 14,930,000 or 89.2% Ashkenazi Jews as against 1,700,000, or 10.2% Sephardi and Oriental Jews.[*]

During the decade 1939-1949 the most drastic and tragic changes occurred in the ethnic and continental distribution of the Jewish people. The Nazi massacre reduced the number of the Jews in Europe from 9,639,000 (in 1939) to 3,679,000 (in 1949). At the same time the number of Jews in America increased by nearly 300,000, and in Asia and Africa by about 400,000. The changes in numbers can be summarized in the following table.

NUMBER OF JEWS IN THE FIVE CONTINENTS IN 1939 AND 1949[1]

Continent	Number in 1939	Number in 1949
Europe (incl. Asiatic USSR)	9,639,000	3,679,000
America	5,480,000	5,778,000
Asia	871,000	1,130,000
Africa	610,000	745,000
Australia and New Zealand	33,000	44,000
Total	16,633,000	11,376,000

[1] *American Jewish Year Book,* vol. 50, p. 692, with slight modifications.

Although 5,800,000 Jews were massacred in the Nazi onslought in the early 1940s, thus diminishing the number of European Jews by 60%, the Nazi carnage did not achieve its goal, the total extermination of the Jews in the countries under German domination. In all the countries which were the homes of Jewish communities in the 1930s, fragments of the Jewish population survived. At the

[*] Figures based on Leon Shapiro and Boris Sapir, "Jewish Population of the World," *American Jewish Year Book,* vol. 50, Philadelphia, 1949, pp. 691 ff.

same time, Jews penetrated into new overseas countries, and their numbers showed increases in others.

5. Race and Language

Corresponding to the great dispersion of the Jews among the peoples of the East and the West, in five continents and nearly a hundred countries, profound differences developed among the various Jewish communities with regard to physical features and languages spoken, as well as cultures carried by them.

There is only one general rule which can be laid down as to the Jewish physical types: the majority of the Jews in each country strongly approximates, but does not equal completely, the physical character of the gentile population. Concretely this means that, for example, the Jews of Eastern Europe resemble their non-Jewish neighbors in physical features such as: a strong Alpinoid strain, characterized by medium stature, squat and heavily set frame, brunet pigmentation, round-headedness, relatively short and broad face, and nose of medium length and breadth with "blobby nasal tips which are often inclined in an upward direction."[*] Other strains present in both the Jews and the non-Jews in Eastern Europe are Nordic, and to a smaller extent also Dinaric, East Baltic and Mediterranean stocks.

The Sephardi Jews are more homogeneous in their physical features. They are on the whole Mediterranean, and in this strongly resemble the gentiles among whom they live. The Mediterranean racial type is characterized by short to medium stature, slender body-build, skin color varying from very light brown to darker olive shades, eyes generally dark brown, hair brown to black and curly or wavy. The head is long and narrow, with a protruding occiput and a high and well-rounded forehead. The face is small, oval, without strong, rugged or bony outlines. The nose is mostly long and thin with a very high bridge. This kind of face makes an "aristocratic" impression.

Oriental Jews have approximated the physical type of their gentile neighbors in a more narrowly localized sense. Persian Jews look like Persians, Yemenite Jews like Yemenite Arabs, Bokharan Jews like Bokharan Tajiks and other Turkestan peoples. This means that, whenever in these gentile groups the Alpine and Iranian Plateau elements with their broad-headed and heavier types predominate, the same physical type is found to characterize also the Jews; on the other hand, where the Mediterranean type is the more usual one,

[*] Carl Seltzer, "The Jew—His Racial Status," in Earl W. Count (ed.), *This Is Race*, New York, 1950, p. 616.

the same is usual also among the Jews, the Yemenite Jews being the best example of the latter.

Lamentably few anthropometrical measurements have to date been undertaken in Jewish groups. However, even the few data which are at our disposal suffice to indicate that the Jews of different countries, and, more generally, the Jewish groups of the three main divisions of the Jewish people—Ashkenazim, Sephardim and Orientals—greatly differ from one another in easily observable characteristics, such as the color of the skin, the eyes and the hair, as well as in other physical traits which can be ascertained by exact measurements only and to which physical anthropologists as a rule attribute greater significance than to coloring, such as head form (cephalic index) and blood-group percentages. The impression is thus gained that *the Jews do not belong to a single homogeneous racial group.*

As to the languages of the Jews, one must differentiate between the old traditional tongues and the new European languages acquired by the Jews in the post-emancipation period. To these latter belong German, English, French, Russian, Polish and other Slavic languages, Rumanian, Hungarian, etc.

Up to the emancipation, and to a large extent up to a generation ago, the predominating traditional language of the Ashkenazi Jews was Yiddish, or Judeo-German. Since Yiddish was the language of the Ashkenazi Jews, it was until recently also the colloquial of the great majority of the Jewish people in general. Yiddish is a language with a fine and rich literature and a well-established literary history going back many hundreds of years, and with numerous but closely related and mutually understandable dialects. The main constituent element in Yiddish is German, more precisely a "frozen" substratum of the German spoken in the Middle Ages. German words constitute about 70% of the vocabulary of the Yiddish language, to which is added another element of about 30% of Hebrew words or roots. In addition to differences in pronunciation, the various Yiddish dialects differ from one another in their youngest and slightest element which is derived from the languages spoken by the neighbors of the Yiddish-speaking Jewish groups: Russian in Russia, Polish in Poland, English in North America, Spanish in Latin America.

Second in importance is Ladino (Judeo-Spanish), the old tongue of the Sephardi Jews. Ladino shows in many respects a development analogous to Yiddish: it too has an admixture of Hebrew

---

* Anthropometrical data concerning the Ashkenazi, Sephardi and Oriental Jewish communities are collected in R. Patai, *The Science of Man* (Hebrew). Jerusalem, 1947, vol. I.

words to approximately the same extent as Yiddish; it too is based on a medieval form of a European tongue, Spanish; and it too is spoken by Jewish groups who left Spain several hundred years ago, just as Yiddish is spoken by Jews who left Germany several hundreds of years ago. Both Yiddish and Ladino have always been written in Hebrew characters; Ladino too has developed a literature of its own, though not comparable in richness with Yiddish literature. The Ladino-speaking Jews were always much less numerous than the Yiddish-speaking ones, and they lived in relative proximity to one another, the great majority of them never leaving the countries flanking the shores of the Mediterranean. Ladino therefore has not developed so many and such different dialects as Yiddish has. Another difference between the two is that, while Yiddish is the *only* traditional Jewish language of the Ashkenazi Jews, Ladino is the Jewish tongue of only the majority of the Sephardi Jews. A small group of Sephardi Jews, who immigrated in the Middle Ages from Spain to Italy, very soon adopted there the Italian language, so that Italian is the second traditional Jewish tongue spoken by Sephardi Jews. No comparable loss of the original, that is, medieval, language can be found among the Ashkenazi Jews.*

In the Oriental Jewish communities there are three languages in which specifically Jewish dialects developed: Arabic, Persian and Aramaic. Special Jewish-Arabic dialects are spoken by several Jewish communities in North Africa and in Yemen. Some of these possess a literature of their own, parts of which have been committed in writing in a phonetical form, in Hebrew characters. Judeo-Persian dialects are spoken by the Jews of Persia, of Afghanistan, of Bokhara and the Caucasus. Very little is known of these dialects, the investigation of which is one of the urgent tasks of Jewish ethnology.§ Neo-Aramaic is a modern version of the Aramaic language which was once the *lingua franca* as well as the language of diplomatic contact all over the ancient Near East. Today it is spoken only by small and isolated communities, such as a few villages in Syria, and the Nestorian Christians and the Jewish groups in Kurdistan. The Neo-Aramaic spoken by the Jews of Kurdistan is divided into various dialects. The remnant of an Aramaic dialect mixed with Arabic and spoken by Jews was reported also from Libya in North Africa.

* Here is the place to mention also a small Jewish group which up to the Nazi catastrophe lived in the very midst of the proudest Sephardi Jewish community although it was not a Sephardi group at all: the Jews of three towns in Greece: Ioannina, Larisa and Arta, who spoke Greek as their mother tongue.

§ Cf. Raphael Patai, "Problems and Tasks of Jewish Folklore and Ethnology," in *Journal of American Folklore*, January-March 1946, pp. 25-39.

In addition to these more important Jewish languages, there are quite a number of other languages spoken by peripheral or exotic Jewish communities, such as the Falashas (the Jews of Abyssinia), the Jews of India, the Krimchaks (ancient Jewish inhabitants of the Crimea), the Karaites of the Crimea, etc. These splinter-languages, however, need not concern us here.

The Jewish people in the 20th century thus appear as consisting of a great number of separate groups, each one of which is characterized by a close approximation to the Gentile environment in physical features, in languages spoken, in demographical traits exhibited, as well as in the great majority of the elements, traits, complexes and activities of the material and mental-spiritual equipment the totality of which is called culture. The distinctness of the Jews from the Gentiles in each country hinges upon a minor part of the cultural materials in every place which is peculiar to the Jews alone. Religious, historical and cultural tradition, a belief in the genetic continuity from the days of Abraham, and a sentimental attachment to Palestine, the Land of Israel, are, generally speaking, the main features in this specifically Jewish cultural component. After a continued fragmentation for two and a half millennia into many separate communities scattered over the five continents of the world, these specific elements, rooted ultimately in the ancient Palestinian history of the Hebrews and the Jews, still constitute the common bases of the varied manifestations of Jewish culture in the Ashkenazi, Sephardi and Oriental divisions, and fill the Jewish people with a keen awareness of their community of fate.

Political Zionism, which achieved its aim when the State of Israel was founded in 1948, would not have been possible without the Haskala movement which brought the Jews of Europe into close contact with Western culture and thus enabled them to adopt, when the need arose, Western political forms and methods. Without the persistance of the historical and sentimental attachment to Palestine the response of the Jewish masses to Zionist slogans would have been as negative as their reception of other colonization plans which called for the settlement of Jews in Uganda, Argentina, Crimea or Birobidjan. But in the ultimate analysis, it was the enduring sense of the community of fate, of the indivisibility, even in the 20th century, of the scattered tribes of Israel, which enabled the numerically insignificant group of Jewish pioneers whom Herzl met when he visited Palestine in 1902 to grow within half a century into a Jewish state with a population of more than a million and a half.

Chapter Two

Eastern and Western Culture

1. "Fellah"-Peoples?

What is there in the traditional cultural heritage of the Middle East, brought along to Israel by the Oriental Jews, which the developing new culture of the country can absorb to its advantage? And, conversely, what is there in it which must be regarded as sufficiently harmful to warrant a mobilization of the state's legislative, administrative and educational apparatus against it?

The old-fashioned and shortsighted view, which unfortunately is expressed only too often both orally and in writing in Israel, holds summarily that the Oriental Jews are in need of a complete re-education, that their entire being and thinking must be re-shaped in the European Jewish image, and that, where this cannot be achieved by suasion and example, the situation calls for legislative measures.

This viewpoint was typical of the approach of the colonial powers to their subject peoples, the "natives" of their colonies, in past centuries. It has wrought unspeakable harm, causing the cultural and physical disintegration of numerous healthy and virile non-European peoples.* The modern anthropological concept termed "cultural relativism,"§ came too late for most colonial peoples to derive much actual benefit from it.¶ In Israel, however, it would be a crime both against the new State and against the Oriental Jewish communities to repeat the mistakes of 19th-century colonialism and

---

* Cf. Raymond Kennedy, "The Colonial Crisis and the Future," in R. Linton (ed.), *The Science of Man in the World Crisis*, New York 1945, pp. 306 ff.

§ Cf. Melville J. Herskovits, *Man and His Works*, New York, 1948, pp. 61 ff.

¶ As to the actual role of anthropology in modern colonial policy and administration, cf. Felix M. Keesing, "Applied Anthropology in Colonial Administration," in R. Linton (ed.), *The Science of Man in the World Crisis*, pp. 373 ff.

not to utilize the insights gained in recent years into the nature of culture and the mechanisms of culture contact and culture change.

The offhand negative answer to the question concerning the value of Middle Eastern culture for Israel is often the outcome of insufficient familiarity with the cultural heritage of the Middle East. A more considered reply will therefore have to be based on a study, or at least a survey, of the main characteristics of Middle Eastern culture of which the immigrating Oriental Jews are as much a part as any other population group in the area.* Before an attempt is made to isolate these main characteristics, it must, however, be emphasized that the difficulties of such an undertaking are numerous and serious. Our knowledge of Middle Eastern culture is, to say the least, limited. This will become apparent as soon as we try —as will be done in the following pages—to compare the main complexes of Western culture, made predominant in Israel by the Ashkenazi Jews, with corresponding or equivalent features in Middle Eastern culture.

Western culture, or Western civilization as some students prefer to call it, has been made the object of numerous scientific studies; it has been described, analyzed and interpreted. Its features have been systematized, its meaning has been questioned and scrutinized, its values and shortcomings pointed up. Students of Western culture, themselves Westerners and thus possessing the prerequisites of a thorough inside familiarity with their own cultural environment, devoted lifetimes to painstaking studies of its problems and achievements. The philosophical, historical and sociological study of Western culture actually has become one of the characteristic features of Western culture itself.

No such trait developed within the culture of the Middle East. What we know of Middle Eastern culture is mostly the result of studies conducted by Western students. These studies, however, were devoted up to the present time almost exclusively to historical aspects. The original impetus for them was given by the religious interest in the Bible, the book which sprang from the ancient Near East and so profoundly influenced the cultural development of the West. The entire Middle East, which was the locale for the histories related in the Bible, came to be designated as "Bible Lands," and the ancient history of these lands, their archaeology, their languages, religions, as well as their geography and to a lesser extent also the "manners and customs" of their modern inhabitants, were studied with a view to reaching a better understanding of the

* Cf. R. Patai, "The Middle East as a Culture Area," in *The Middle East Journal*, Winter 1952, pp. 1-21.

Bible.* It was in this way that the great ancient cultures of the Middle East began to be studied; and thus incomparably more attention was focused on the ancient Near East with its splendor and its high civilizational attainments at the very "dawn of history" than on the present-day inhabitants of the same world area, who appeared in comparison with their great predecessors as poor "fellah-peoples"§ vegetating in poverty and destitution in the shadow of the magnificent monuments of their remote past.

Since the development of modern anthropological science, the approach to the cultures of non-European peoples in general has undergone a decisive change. This shift in approach was soon followed by the beginnings of a more serious study of modern Middle Eastern culture. Nevertheless, the culture of the modern Middle East is still one of the least known in the world, and in view of the great strides Westernization is making in most countries of the area, there is very little likelihood that its traditional cultural patterns will ever be studied adequately before they are replaced by new developments. Thus the culture of the contemporary Middle East in its traditional forms will in all probability never be known with anything approximating our knowledge of Western culture.

2. Cultural Foci

Western culture, as exemplified by the cultural developments of the last two centuries in Western Europe and in the United States of America, is focused on the two main and interconnected themes of technical development and mass benefits. The development of motive power, of the modern factory system with its mass-production, of soil-chemistry, scientific packing, storage and distribution of food, banking and insurance, communications, transportation and the like, are all expressions of a special kind of achievement made possible by the common denominator of technical development. Mass education, universal suffrage, sanitation and hygiene, safety systems, postal service, newspapers, periodicals and books, the motion pictures, radio and television, the mass production of visual and vocal arts in highly standardized forms, sports and athletics, are all available, not to just a few privileged individuals, but to the masses of the population as a whole; but while aiming thus

* Cf. Raphael Patai, "A Survey of Near Eastern Anthropology," in *Transactions of the New York Academy of Sciences*, April, 1948, pp. 200-209.

§ The expression (*Fellachenvoelker*) is that of Oswald Spengler, who in his *Decline of the West* (*Untergang des Abendlandes*, London, 1937) painted a sombre picture of the present-day heirs to what he termed the "magian culture" of the Middle East.

at mass benefits, or at least at mass consumption, they too are the outcomes of technical development. The outstanding social, ethical and economic doctrines of Western civilization are also mass-oriented, and the philosophies of democracy, of socialism and of group-interests, as well as religious doctrine and ethics, are all made to serve and benefit every man, or at least large groups within the population.*

Ever since their emancipation in the 19th century, Jews of the Western world have been among the most ardent exponents of progress in many of the cultural fields in which the West has most intensely engaged. It was therefore only to be expected that the culture which the builders of the Jewish homeland—the vast majority of them Western Jews—should foster would be Western in all its essentials, with the addition of such specifically Jewish features as the Hebrew language, the Jewish religion, and the Jewish historical, national and intellectual tradition. From the very onset of the Zionist homebuilding activity, it was clear that a new Jewish village or town in Palestine meant the transplantation of a piece of the West into the midst of the Middle East. In the beginning, when the number of settlers from Europe was relatively small, it was inevitable that local Eastern cultural influence should make itself felt; but as soon as the immigration of Ashkenazi Jews increased, a definite shift in the cultural balance became noticeable, and not only Western cultural elements, but a Western type of cultural configuration as a whole became predominant.§

It has been observed that the Jews tend to assimilate to their environment in relation to the cultural enticement it offers to them. German Jews, for instance, were a more assimilated group than the Polish, because German culture had more to offer to them than Polish culture. Actually, this is but the specifically Jewish variant of a general tendency observable in culture contact situations: it is the higher type of culture which is more readily absorbed by those originally partaking of a culture which they feel to be of a lower type. In accordance with this general observation, the Jews in the Moslem world began to participate most actively in Arab culture as soon as the latter reached a high degree of development, which was almost simultaneous with the spread of Islam. In the Middle Ages we find the Jews as much a part of the Moslem-Arab culture of the Middle East and Spain, as they were several centuries later,

* On the total pattern of Western civilization cf. O. W. Junek, *American Anthropologist,* 1946, pp. 397-406.

§ R. Patai, *On Culture Contact and Its Working in Modern Palestine,* American Anthropological Association, Memoir No. 67, 1947.

after their emancipation, in the Christian countries of the West. When the decline in Moslem cultural prominence set in after the Middle Ages, it carried down with it also the Jewish communities. However, the close ties between Moslem and Jewish culture in the Middle East have persisted down to the present time, so that the Oriental Jewish element in Israel today represents the folk-ways, the mores and the mode of life, in brief, the culture which is the heritage of the Middle East as a whole, and of which the Arab, Druze and other minorities in Israel are equally typical representatives.

Middle Eastern culture must not be conceived of as possessing any greater uniformity or homogeneity than Western culture. Like the term "Western culture," it is a generalized concept, an abstraction reached when the basic similarity of a number of separately definable cultures is recognized. "Western culture" actually comprises a considerable number of subdivisions, each of which shows local differences and deviations from the generalized concept of Western culture. Polish, German, French, English and American cultures are all component parts of Western culture, yet each is different from all the others. Exactly the same is true of Middle Eastern culture. It also is composed of a number of subdivisions, the more important of which are the Turkish, Iranian, North African and Arabian cultures, the last mentioned being again divided into several sections. To the same extent to which these cultures differ from one another, the cultures of the Oriental Jews immigrating from them into Israel also differ from one another.   ✳

Notwithstanding these local variations, there are, just as in the case of Western culture, a number of basic characteristics which hold good for the cultures of the entire area called the Middle East. The simplest way of isolating these basic characteristics is to attempt a comparison between Western and Eastern culture. In this context the concept of *cultural focus* can serve as a useful analytical instrument. It has been found that cultures are as a rule oriented towards certain *foci*; in other words, certain cultural elements, or certain combinations of such elements, are chosen by each culture and are made *foci* or centers of attention. As every culture has a tendency "to exhibit greater complexity, greater variation in the institutions of some of its aspects than in others,"✳ these focal aspects can advantageously be used for the characterization of entire cultures. A comparison, therefore, of the most highly and intensely developed cultural complexes in Western civilization with the corresponding forms found in the culture of the Middle East will at

✳ Cf. Melville J. Herskovits, *Man and His Works*, New York, 1948, pp. 542 ff.

once make us aware of significant differences in emphasis and orientation characterizing the two cultures.

The total pattern of Western civilization was analyzed by Dr. O. W. Junek[*] and his observations can largely be followed as far as the focal complexes of Western civilization are concerned; to them will be appended brief statements concerning their Middle Eastern equivalents or counterparts. For the sake of brevity, the Middle East will be referred to in the following pages simply as the East; moreover, when speaking of Eastern culture as contraposited to Western culture, only the traditional, locally developed culture of the Middle East will be meant, omitting from consideration those developments which have come about lately as a result of Western cultural infiltration.

3. The Western Pattern

One of the basic main complexes, on which a vast amount of attention has been focused in Western civilization, is *motive power*, derived from steam, electricity and internal combustion. Of all this Eastern culture knows nothing. Motive power is still derived from the traditional age-old sources of animal and human muscle only. Just as in the days of Samson, blind laborers are still to be seen occasionally in the depths of vaults in the bazaars of the old Eastern towns turning the big wheel of a grinding stone; and everywhere in the East, in the towns as well as in the villages, one finds animals, such as donkeys, mules, oxen and camels, harnessed to wheel-handles or otherwise employed to supply motive power. Animal and man power are employed for all kinds of work, whether of the locomobile or the locomotive variety, for which in the West a great number of specialized machines are used.

Another basic focal complex of the West, that of the *modern factory system* involving the mass-production of merchandise, is also utterly foreign to the East, where individual human hands equipped with a few simple tools are the only instruments of production, whether the products are pieces of practical utility such as garments, furniture, tools, or objects of art like sculptures, pictures, gems, and ornaments. Individual achievement, valued today in Western civilization only in the narrowly delimited fields of art, still renders precious in the East such a diversity of products as a shoe, a carpet, a vessel, a saddle or a sword, in addition to what we are used to regard as actual *objets d'art*.

The East lacks equally all the concomitants of Western mass pro-

[*] Cf. O. W. Junek, "The Total Pattern of Western Civilization," in *American Anthropologist*, 1946, pp. 397-406.

duction and factory system, like organized distribution and sale, and labor unions. In the East, artisanship and tradesmanship, often practiced by the same person, are highly individual, independent and competitive occupations; though those specializing in the same field show a predilection for congregating in close quarters. Cobblers, cloth-merchants, coppersmiths, butchers, each have their separate streets in the bazaars of Oriental towns, a custom going back to the most ancient times and occasionally taking such pronounced forms as among the Jews of Alexandria some two thousand years ago who, in their great synagogue, sat also in separate professional groups; or among the Indians whose caste-division often coincides with occupational specialization.

The next points to be considered in the total pattern of Western civilization are *mass education* (enforced by law) and *universal suffrage*, with all that these involve in accordance with the democratic principle of equal rights and duties of every citizen. Both are lacking in Eastern culture, but not to an equal degree. The very idea of elections is totally unheard of in the East, where every vacancy less than a throne is filled by appointment. Schooling and education, on the other hand, play a considerable role, though they are neither general nor compulsory. A child has to be educated— this is the consensus of opinion; but taught what, when, how and by whom?—all this is left for the father to decide and for nobody else. If it is a male child, the father may think it desirable that he learn, in some sort of school, at least the rudiments of reading and writing and as much of the Holy Books and other traditional literature by rote as possible. Two or three years of this kind of religious-literary education will be regarded in most cases as sufficient; and even this rudimentary schooling is limited as a rule to townsfolk or certain social classes. If it is a girl, she will be spared even this and kept at home to learn from her mother and older female relatives the practical arts and crafts, considered indispensable for women, the number of which is often astonishingly great. The practical education of boys, begun before school age, is continued after the two or three years' interruption spent at school.

Sanitation and hygiene, playing an increasingly important role in Western civilization, are almost unknown in Eastern culture. Medicine, it is true, exists everywhere in a traditional form, mostly as a mixture of empirical knowledge and magical practice. Age-old medical theories still hold their own; diseases are still believed to be possessed of either a "hot" or a "cold" nature, corresponding to which "hot" or "cold," "dry" or "wet" substances have to be used as antidote and medicament. Although practitioners in this traditional medical art abound, there goes, hand in hand with the trust in the magico-natural efficacy of medicine and its materials, the belief in the predestined course and inevitable outcome of every single case of illness. Needless to say, the idea that the state or any other public body should assume responsibility for the health of individual persons is utterly foreign to a culture whose views on health and sickness—and on life and death for that matter—rest on such foundations.

Safety systems, that is, armed and other forces, yet another important complex in Western civilization, not only have their counterpart in Eastern culture, but existed in the East in a fully developed form a long time before the rise of Western culture itself. Eastern safety systems, it is true, were not and still are not public, for they are controlled, not by representatives of an elected body, but by an absolute ruler or his appointed deputies. Moreover, sovereignty and direct control of the armed forces are one and the same thing in the East, and numerous examples in nearly every Eastern land show that the shortest way to the throne often leads through the control of the army. In internal rule, that is, apart from the traditionally all-important task of subduing the peripheries of the realm, the forces in Eastern culture are maintained with a view to fulfilling a double role: first, to secure the rule of the monarch who always leans heavily on the loyalty of his army; and second, to secure the safety of his subjects in the face of external or internal attacks, thereby increasing their attachment to the monarch. The "protection racket" of American notoriety has its ancient counterpart in the East: one of the main sources of income for every petty chieftain in Eastern lands have been the taxes he levied on merchants and travelers passing through the territory under his control in exchange for his protection against robbery and armed assault. In addition to cavalry and other formations of armed forces capable of being raised all over the land on the shortest notice due to the feudal system, there exists a permanent police force in the form of guards and watchmen of gates and palaces, and a network of spies whose silent menace is more conducive to "peaceful" behavior than its most efficient Western counterpart.

The complexes of *soil chemistry and conservation* and of *scientific packing, storage and distribution of food*, are perhaps the most recent in Western civilization and are distinctly scientific achievements. Of these complexes, we find in the East soil conservation only, and even this exists today in most cases merely in a rudimentary form. In ancient days it was a main governmental duty to keep the great rivers, such as the Nile and the twin rivers of Mesopotamia, well regulated, the canals in good repair and the adjoining territories adequately irrigated. The neglect of such public works in Eastern countries followed upon a loss of power by the central government and led in its turn to a general cultural decline. Small-scale irrigation, terracing, crop-rotation and resting the land once every so many years have been practiced in the East ever since the emergence of agriculture, several thousands of years ago, and are today the only means of safeguarding the fertility of the soil apart from the more occasional use of manure. In the East, with its vast deserts and comparatively small stretches of fertile land, the people have always come to value and to guard the soil that could yield crops. The proverbial barrenness of the Middle East, with its wastage, disappearance of the forests, denudation of the topsoil and increase of aridity, has been due mainly to the constant wars which throughout history have again and again destroyed its towns and villages and laid waste its fields and forests.

In place of the Western complexes of *banking and insurance*, we find in the East moneylending and charity. A season of drought or the failure of crops for any other reason are sufficient to render the need for money imperative, if not desperate. A fellah in need of money falls inevitably into the hands of moneylenders and is easily ruined altogether by their usury.

Commercial insurance, though appearing in ancient Babylonia,* vanished long ago from the context of traditional Oriental commerce. Social insurance is likewise unknown, but its place is more or less filled by organized or private charity, both religious in their character. Religious charitable foundations, the so-called *waqfs*, in the lands of the East are highly complex affairs and it is impossible to give here even the roughest sketch of their variety and working. In passing it is sufficient to mention that a very considerable proportion of the destitute in every Eastern land—in addition to many who are not poor at all, but enjoy benefits by dint of being the descendants of the founder—are cared for by these foundations, while others, less fortunate, nevertheless succeed in soliciting charity from private persons. To give alms to the poor is considered a great religious duty in the East, one of the "Five Pillars of Faith" in Islam; and to be a beggar is, far from being shameful, equivalent to having attained a definite, though somewhat limited religious status.

The purely technical achievements of *communications, telephone, telegraph, teletype and wirephoto services* are, of course, lacking in

---

* Cf. Raphael Patai, *Jewish Seafaring in Ancient Times* (Hebrew), Jerusalem, 1938, pp. 91 f.

the East, which also lacks the technical development but not the essence of *postal service* and of *newspapers, periodicals and books*. The rich in the East have sent their mail for thousands of years by private couriers, while the less well-to-do have had to content themselves with employing the services of an occasional traveler. News as a rule traveled much faster by word of mouth, or was broadcast over fairly elaborate signalling systems, such as fire-signals. Newsprint and magazines are again a definitely Western invention, but books came from the East where, in the untouched outlying districts, volumes copied by hand still hold their own against the cheaper but uglier Oriental prints.

Radio and cinema in the West go back, at least in one of their aspects, to theatrical art which was very much at home in the East before the emergence of the Greek drama. Dramatic performance was bound up with religious ritual and as such we shall refer to it again later.

Transportation, highly mechanized and variegated in the West, largely retains in the East its age-old traditional forms which have given way only slowly to modern vehicles introduced from the West. On land, it is the back of an animal or, less frequently, the wheel-cart; on water, the small craft propelled by oar or sail, or perhaps carried down by the flow of swift rivers and then again towed up along the shore with the help of ropes. Roads are not built but tramped out by men and animals who follow a path once proved advantageous; rivers are rarely bridged, more frequently forded; mountains, not pierced by tunnels, but passed. All these technical inadequacies notwithstanding, there exist in the East, and have existed for thousands of years, transportation systems, caravan routes and sea paths, which have spanned distances never heard of in the West until modern times. The products of India and China reached Arabia and Africa regularly; and it was due to these world-wide commercial connections that the world view of the East was never as narrow as that of the European Middle Ages. The annual *Hajj*, the great religious pilgrimage to the holy cities of Mecca and Medina in Arabia—another of the "Five Pillars of Faith"—has been conducted until lately on the traditional pattern of commercial caravans, though on a vastly larger scale, involving the transporta-tion of many thousands of pilgrims together with their baggage, on horses and camels, over distances such as those between Turk-estan or Afghanistan and the west coast of Arabia. Doughty, in the 1870s, still witnessed the march of the enormous caravan down the pilgrim road, and in his classic *Arabia Deserta* gave a colorful description of the *Hajj* which reminded him of the desert wander-

ings of the "thousands of Israel."* Yet, while from the days of Moses
to the days of Doughty the ways and methods of crossing the desert
changed but little, soon after Doughty's visit to Arabia the processes
of change set in, wiping almost completely away the traditional
forms of the *Hajj*, and leaving also elsewhere in the East only scanty
traces of the traditional methods of transportation. Today an ever
larger group of pilgrims prefers the railroad, the automobile, the
steamship, and even the airplane, to the camel.

Sports and athletics, though well known in Eastern culture, occupy a very different position than in Western civilization. In the
West, although there are large groups of vicarious sportsmen, it is
generally expected that everyone will indulge in his own particular
fancy; in fact, the development of personal skills in sports and
gymnastics are part and parcel of the general compulsory educational scheme. In the East the situation is different. Individual active participation in a sport for its own sake is known only in Persia.
In the countries inhabited by Arabic-speaking peoples the only
traditional forms of sport are hunting and racing, the mount being
either the horse or the camel. Great spectacular popular festivals
are always religious, but sports play little or no role in them, with
the exception again of Persia where the traditional *Nauruz*, or New
Year festival, is the occasion for a great sportive display. This Persian predilection for gymnastics and sports is the last surviving
remnant of the Hellenistic love of athletics which was introduced
by the Greek conquerors wherever they passed. During the centuries of Roman rule in the East, participation by the people in
games and sports was adjudged a sign of assimilation to the culture
of the overlords. Later Byzantium, the Rome of the East, continued
alone in this old tradition and passed it on to the Persians, while
all the other countries in the East have long since forgotten that
sports once were a fashionable pastime.

The complex of *esthetics* occupies a relatively minor place in
Western culture. Esthetic enjoyment, it is true, has been made
available to the masses in the West in a highly mechanized, mass-
produced and standardized form. Yet here we have a clear example
of a culture complex which occupies a much more focal position in
the East than in the West; a fact which, though from another angle,
was only recently pointed up by Northrop.§ In the West, the products of visual and vocal arts have been relegated to the role of

* Cf. Charles M. Doughty, *Travels in Arabia Deserta*, Cambridge, 1888, vol.
I, pp. 7 ff.
§ Cf. F. S. C. Northrop, *The Meeting of East and West*, New York, 1947,
pp. 375 ff.

recreational agents, to be enjoyed in the few hours of rest and leisure, and more often than not they constitute merely one of the varieties of social functions. During the daily seven to nine hours of work, during the time spent commuting to and from work, while pursuing all the by-the-way and incidental activity which fills up the rest of the day, any esthetic flavor is absent, and the twin stars of efficiency and comfort are the ruling constellation in the sky.

In traditional Eastern culture all this is vastly different. Almost every branch of everyday's work is permeated with esthetic considerations. A Damascene blade has to be, not only sharp and resilient, but also beautiful in form, finish and proportion. The beauty of objects everywhere intrudes into, or, better, complements, their practicality and utility. Art is called in to embellish everything. The richer a man the more time he spends at the enjoyment and practice of art. But the significant thing is that the poor as well, the great masses of the simple people, live a life in which esthetics plays a considerable role.

Religious ritual, though performable everywhere, was always and still is preferably bound to temples and shrines which are highly esthetic *foci* of visual and vocal arts all over the East. Annually recurrent festivals, which are great events in the life of Eastern peoples, are esthetic-religious-emotional affairs rich in pageantry. Entertainment in Moslem countries on the nights of the fast-month Ramadhan is provided by story-tellers who, though bound by certain general traditional lines, nevertheless combine the arts of the poet, the novelist and the actor, and very often also those of the composer and instrumental performer. Poetry is so much a part of everyday living that the ambulant vendors in the streets of Oriental towns praise their wares in rhymed ditties rhythmically recited to a special tone or melody. School children in Iran compete with one another in composing poems by way of a pastime, while elsewhere, in Arab lands, literacy itself is no prerequisite for versification, which is indulged in by people in all walks of life. Music, the most mechanized and most mass-produced of Western arts, is perhaps the most individualistic in the East. Not only will two performers never give the same interpretation of a traditional musical piece, but the same musician will only very rarely play or sing the same song twice in exactly the same manner. The rule is that the performer is also his own composer, and even when playing a well-known tune, he will inevitably introduce variations and changes of his own, under the spur of the moment's mood. Moreover, the Eastern musician, as a rule, also builds his own musical instrument; his musical training as an apprentice to a master begins with his learning

how to make for himself an instrument of his own.* In the shadow-
theatre, a favorite traditional pastime in the lands of the East, the
master of the theatre makes his own figures, writes his own plays,
directs the performance and plays the main roles.§ Tradition in the
various branches of art fixes only the frame, which can be filled in
varying ways in accordance with the talents and inclinations of the
individual artist. The distinction, so sharply drawn in the West,
between creative artist and performer, simply does not exist in the
East where every performance involves at least the creation of a
new variation on the original theme.

4. Religion

Closely bound up with esthetic tradition in the East is religious
tradition. Religion is such a great, all-pervasive power there that no
proper understanding of the cultural differences between the East
and the West is possible without a closer scrutiny of the role played
by religion in each of the two cultures. Such an examination, however, is made more difficult than the comparison of other cultural
complexes of the West and the East because of the fact that the
present-day ruling religion of the West, Christianity, had originally
penetrated the Western world from the East. Although religion
must be counted among the outstanding social, ethical and economic doctrines now commonplace in Western civilization,¶ it has
at best a rather narrowly delimited field of its own, and, at least as
far as institutional ritualistic forms are concerned, is somewhat out
of touch with the focal economic and technological complexes of
Western civilization.

The role of religion in Eastern culture is profoundly different.
Religion in the East has no field of its own because the whole of life
is its domain and is permeated with it. In the unadulterated strongholds of tradition-bound Eastern life, as among the bedouin of
Arabia, or in the out-of-the-way villages of the settled parts, religion holds supreme sway. Just as in the West the first question
when meeting a stranger concerns his nationality, in the East it is
his religion, for the significance of citizenship or nationality is less

* Cf. Edith Gerson-Kiwi, "The Musicians of the Orient: Their Character and
Development," in *Edoth, A Quarterly for Folklore and Ethnology* (Hebrew),
ed. R. Patai and J. J. Rivlin, Jerusalem, July, 1946, pp. 227-233.

§ Cf. J. M. Landau, "Shadow Plays in the Near East," in *Edoth*, Oct.
1947-January 1948, pp. xxiii-xliv (in English) and pp. 33-72 (in Hebrew).

¶ The most important of these are the Madisonian philosophy of interests,
the Jeffersonian philosophy of democracy, the philosophy of socialism, the
Marxian philosophy of communism, and the Judeo-Christian religion and
ethics; Cf. Junek, *op. cit.* pp. 404-405.

than secondary compared with the importance of religious affiliation. There are "no nations in Islam," says an Arabic proverb. The brotherhood of Sunnite or of Shi'ite Islam transcends political boundaries, while, on the other hand, the belonging to a common country or political unit is a far from adequate bond with which to bridge the gulf separating the adherents of the numerous religious denominations of the East and often makes for overt animosity among them.

The name of God is always on the lips of the people of the East and is one of the most frequently used words in every conversation, serious or casual, reflecting the psychological omnipresence and everpresence of God and the religious consciousness of the people. The will of God, as manifested in the form of religious precept, narrowly circumscribes every step of day-to-day life by positive and negative commandments. Some of these commandments, like, for instance, that of the five daily prayers—another of the "Five Pillars of Faith"—cannot be put off whenever their hour arrives, so that the Moslem can feel no ostentation at all in performing his prayers with the prescribed number of prostrations in public, on any wayside or busy thoroughfare.

Another highly characteristic trait of all the religions which originated in the Middle East is their distinctly dual aspect of materialism on the one hand and spiritualism on the other. Eastern religion, beginning with the most ancient Egyptians and Mesopotamians, and down to the most recent trends in Islamic sectarianism, has always had two main concerns: physical well-being in this world and spiritual welfare after the death of the body. The ways and means of securing this double aim remained practically unchanged through centuries and millennia. The often changing names of the great gods or goddesses, easily adopted and frequently syncretized, came to designate always the same type of deity whose main dual function remained throughout the ages that of dispensing material blessings to his people in this life, while compensating the miserable but righteous with a blend of material and spiritual pleasures in the afterlife. Eastern ritual, especially of the popular kind, also remained practically unchanged throughout the ages, although the deity in whose honor, or to propitiate whom, it was being performed came to be called by many different names. The preoccupation with the soul and salvation, a characteristic of Eastern religion in its varied manifestations, is the complementary side of the picture, the basic features remaining always the same in spite of the often revolutionary changes which swept the surface of the religious palimpsest. Early in the religion of ancient Egypt we find a typical example of this trend in the so-called "Negative Confession" in which the dead, standing before the bench of Osiris, the Judge of the Nether World, enumerated a long list of sins and crimes and offenses of which he was *not* guilty during his lifetime. The idea of ultimate judgment, and the underlying notion of an ideal morality, to aspire to which is incumbent upon every mortal, has remained a dominant feature in every Middle Eastern religion. Hence the supreme value in Middle Eastern religions of righteousness, of a pure soul, which is regarded as the only real achievement of man in contradistinction to all earthly wealth which is viewed as empty vanity. In traditional Oriental thinking the supreme good that man can acquire for himself is of a moral quality. What this doctrine has meant to this day in the everyday life of the East, only those can appreciate who are familiar with the unthinkable extremes and inequalities found in the distribution of wealth and all the comfort, ease, pleasures and luxuries that can be bought with it. The traditional situation which has prevailed in the East for thousands of years, and which is still encountered there, is that of a few fabulously rich as against great masses of the very poor among whom many live in a poverty quite unknown in the West of today. It is certainly no exaggeration to say that, for the poor, religion, with its moralistic and spiritualistic tenets and with its great promise of future reward, is the last foothold without which they would inevitably fall into utter misery and despair, but sustained by which they can even feel superior to the "idle rich."

Another point must be mentioned here, however briefly. The religions of the Middle East cannot imagine the salvation of the soul without the most meticulous observance of ritual injunctions, both positive and negative; their moralism is always inclusive of ritualism, though to Western ideology the two lie on two quite separate planes.

Yet another characteristic of Middle Eastern religions is the absence of a formally ordained priestly class or group which in the later developments of Christianity came to play the role of exclusive mediators between the common lay folk and the deity. With the partial exception of the Eastern Christian Churches, Middle Eastern religions recognize no official mediation between the common man and God, the very idea of the need for any flesh-and-blood spokesman to act as a go-between between man and God being utterly foreign and even abhorrent to them. The distinction between lay folk and priesthood being unknown in Middle Eastern religions, every man is, so to speak, his own priest, in the sense that the direct personal appeal to God, or, in the more popular forms of religion, to the manifestations of supernatural powers localized in sacred stones, wells, trees and shrines, is equally accessible to everybody. Hence the emphasis on the knowledge of the religious law and lore, both in its ritualistic and doctrinal aspects; for, if the paths are open to all, one had better know which ones to choose and how to tread upon them. In the ultimate analysis, therefore, Middle Eastern religions are an expression of a greater reliance on man the individual, with greater emphasis on his personal spiritual potentialities.

Apart from these doctrinal aspects, there are several obvious differences which even a casual observer would notice about the role of religion in the East and in the West. The first of these is that in the West the great majority of the people are not religious; that many have practically no contact whatsoever with religion, their official adherence to a church, synagogue or other congregation being a less than nominal one, a matter usually regarded indifferently. For those not religious, and to a somewhat lesser extent also for the religious element, morality is quite divorced from religion and is an ideal for its own sake, while ritualism is scorned or ridiculed.

In the East, on the other hand, the great majority of the people is religious. The observance of the traditional forms and rites of religion is an important and integral part of their everyday life. Religion not expressed in formal ritual and observance is unthinkable. But more than that: Religion is the central force which moves, motivates and rules all phases and aspects of culture, and has its say in practically every act and moment of life. Reference has been made above to the fact that every simple and commonplace conversation in the East is frequently interspersed with the name of God and is therefore something quite definitely stamped with the mark of religion. Morality always appears in the guise of religion and is merely one of the aspects of religion; a moral law dissociated from religion cannot even be conceived of by these people steeped in Middle East culture.

Art is unquestionably a handmaiden of religion; its scope is closely determined by religious precepts. The representation of the human figure is almost entirely excluded, and that of animals largely so. Decorative art and architecture, in which the Middle Eastern artistic genius most fully expresses itself, are even more closely connected with religion—the richly decorated mosques and the prayer-rugs being the examples which most readily suggest themselves. But even in its secular aspects, decorative art is not free of religious motifs as exemplified by the ever recurring use of the name of Allah or of Koranic passages as decorative inscription-gar-lands on every conceivable object—trays, lamps, daggers, saucers and the like—made of such diverse materials as glass, china, clay, wood and various precious or common metals.

Articles of clothing, such as headgears, mantles, belts, sandals, and so forth, are in their forms, cuts, colors and decorations closely dependent upon custom fixed by age-old traditions which allow the individual artistic talents or inclinations expression only in relatively minor variations; and all custom and tradition is basically religious, for whatever is old and customary and traditional is hallowed by religion, which in itself is mainly tradition and custom and to a small extent only doctrine and law.

The entire field of custom—wide and infinitely ramified in its permeation of everyday life—is incapable of being divorced from religion either in theory or in practice. Whatever man does in his waking or sleeping hours, during his entire lifetime on this earth, and also what is done to him at his birth and after his death, or what he is imagined to do in his prenatal and *post mortem* existence, all these always conform to custom, tradition and religion. These three—religion, tradition and custom—are the pivotal points on which Middle Eastern life rests in its entirety.

A small minority of irreligious persons can be found, to be sure, in Middle Eastern social groupings. But apart from the big cities where Western influences are increasingly felt and where consequently irreligious Easterners can feel free to talk and act as they please, the irreligious individual generally is cautious and retreating, and is regarded by the religious majority as an asocial being, a person who does not live up to expectations and must therefore be looked upon as one whose value for the community is severely impaired.

5. Oriental *Weltanschauung*

The sway religion holds over performance and the grooves it cuts into thinking, deeply influence one's entire appraisal of life. Middle Eastern man knows that he has to work and to exert himself in order to make a living; but although work is recommended by religiously hallowed traditions, and the praise of labor is expressed in many proverbs and *Hadith*-sentences supposedly handed down from the mouth of the Prophet Muhammed, there is no love for labor, no pride in industriousness, no work for its own sake. Work for most of the mortals is an inevitable burden, a necessary evil, the curse of Adam, and the less one needs of it the better. Material goods are, of course, desired, but if they cannot be had in some easy way, it is better to put up with more privation than to burden oneself with more work. The old rabbinical saying, "Who is rich? He who contents himself with his allotted share," epitomizes the general attitude of the great majority of Middle Eastern peoples to this day. Privations caused by one's own unwillingness to make exertions, blows dealt by external agents, human or natural, avoidable or uncontrollable, are all borne with an equanimity quite unusual in the West. For all this the influence of religion is largely responsible. Religion, with its great promise of reward in the Other World, with its lure of pleasures just around the corner behind the door of death—which thus actually becomes but a door to Paradise —creates in the believer a state of mind which is to him an infinitely greater asset in making his way through this world than any physical comfort, plumbing and hot water, medical service and social security ever could be.

An old Arabic proverb admirably sums up this attitude towards life here and life in the Beyond: "Labor for This World of yours as if you were to live forever; and labor for the Other World of yours as if you were to die tomorrow," though the laboring referred to does not have to be understood as meaning overly vigorous exertions in either of the two directions indicated. Doctrines such as these, however, inculcated from earliest childhood, make for a balanced attitude towards all the vicissitudes of life which, consequently, are viewed from a wider angle, a long-range perspective, in which life on earth with all its possible gains and losses appears as a mere lower and lesser half of a great totality of existence, the essentials and ultimates of which lie in the Beyond. Spiritual outlook thus moves along a higher plane, beyond the reaches of discomfort, pain, anguish and privation; hence that composure, that peace of mind preserved even in the face of great adversity, which ever and again gives rise to great wonderment in the Western observer. Religious systems which can give *this* to their followers, almost inevitably exercise a powerful hold on them, a factor which, on the other hand, also creates intolerance, fanaticism and cleavage along narrow sectarian lines.

The remarkable thing, however, is that every one of the religious sects in the Middle East—and there are a great number of them— although differing in actual details as to ritual and belief, holds the same sway over its adherents and is capable of imparting to them the same detachment and tranquility; the same contentment stemming from a disregard of small shortcomings, even of great misery; and the same deep conviction of being in possession of the only existing key to the gates of the desirable Beyond. The various Moslem and semi-Moslem sects, the Christian Churches of the East, and the Jewish communities, while opposing, fighting and often despising one another for the more obvious surface differences in ritual and belief, all share these ultimate essentials of Middle Eastern religion. Orthodox Jewry, which has conserved a great deal of the ancient traditional content of Jewish religion in its undiluted Oriental form, has remained in this respect very near the other Middle Eastern religions. Here one might look for one of the reasons which make for rapprochement between the religious parties and the Sephardi and Oriental Jews in Israel.

The mental outlook which we find characterizing Middle Eastern religions today is an ancient Asiatic heritage.

"In ancient Asia," says Kurt Singer,* "the idea of a universal order constituting the unity of our world and guaranteeing the undisturbed flow of events, human and non-human within this cosmic frame, . . . does not admit of conflict proper . . . Where clashes actually occur they appear to these men as mere ripples in a sea of serene peace swayed by a light cosmic tide. They may be suffered, tolerated, overlooked like minor misdeeds of inferiors to which no Oriental man of breeding would ever pay serious attention. The measure of oppression, arrogance and cruelty has probably never been smaller in Asiatic countries than in the west; but the Oriental mind prefers to disregard such facts, which seem to matter as little in his cosmic image as details of election finance in western theories of universal suffrage, or as intrigues between staff members in disquisitions on the idea of a university.

"It is thus not necessarily a case of cant if Orientals claim that in spite of all social injustice and moral defects the westerner is prone to note in Asia, life in the Orient is happier and more harmonious than in the west where, not only as a matter of dire fact, but almost on principle, everybody stands arrayed against everybody, except on Sundays, at coronation ceremonies and other legacies of ancient ritual. Oriental harmony is not a statistical phenomenon and cannot be measured in terms of abstention from violence and quarrelling; it is a mood in which Oriental man accepts both peace and strife as he accepts the change from light to darkness, summer and autumn, life and death. We might say that to him it is an *a priori* condition of emotional experience, indifferent to personal pain or pleasure, and therefore not to be invalidated by any amount of empirical evidence about the frequencies of battles, enslavements and tortures. To the Oriental

* Cf. Kurt Singer, *The Idea of Conflict*, Melbourne, 1949, pp. 50-52.

the true reality dwells beyond the sphere in which such incidents and details can be still perceived. To a man initiated into the mystery of being, their relevance is of so low an order of magnitude that it can safely be neglected, or, at the most, turned into an additional urge to leave this world of suffering and change. It is a basic tendency of the Asiatic mind to keep aloof from every thought that hinders him in his great movement of withdrawal from the world, an illusory veil to be cast off by him who is awakened, a tiny shore which must be left in order to reach the infinite expanses of the Great Void."

To regard this world as one of "suffering and change," as "a tiny shore which must be left" in an urge to reach "the infinite expanses of the Great Void," is not typical of the whole of the Orient but only of South Asian culture, as exemplified by Hinduism, its most ancient and most constant religion. In Hinduism human life is regarded as but a brief episode in a long chain of transmigrations, and the attitude to earthly existence is consequently negative or indifferent. Middle Eastern culture has avoided this extreme just as it has avoided the other, that of Western culture, with its concentration on technical, material and other this-wordly achievements only. In Western culture the emphasis is definitely on existence in this world; South Asian culture, equally definitely, negates this world and emphasizes the desirability of leaving it. Middle Eastern culture —situated also spatially between the Western and the South Asian spheres—steers clear of both these courses and takes the path of the golden mean: it keeps what it feels to be the proper balance between equal shares in the material enjoyments of this world and in the spiritual rewards (also conceived in a material image) of the Other World. It is focussed on the human individual in the dual aspect of his existence in This World and in the Great Beyond.

6. What the East Must Learn

An evaluation of the differences emerging from the comparison between the main complexes of Western and Eastern cultures is made difficult because of the fact that there exists no general yardstick which would be equally applicable to all component parts of both cultures. As Herskovits put it, "With the possible exception of the technological aspects of life, the proposition that one way of thought or action is better than another is exceedingly difficult to establish on the grounds of any universally acceptable criteria."* And as far as technological developments are concerned, our survey

* Cf. Herskovits, *op. cit.*, p. 70.

showed that practically all of those technological traits which occupy positions of focal interest in Western culture are almost entirely absent from the context of traditional Eastern culture. The East has no modern factory system, no mass production, no sanitation and hygiene, no soil chemistry, no mechanized communications, services and transportation. In some instances at least it has been recognized also that a trend is increasingly evidenced by Eastern peoples to borrow technological features from the West. This trend is accompanied by corollary adjustments within their own traditional culture necessary for a successful adaptation of the Western traits and complexes. The willingness, and often eagerness, on the part of Eastern peoples to adopt these traits means that they themselves recognize the superiority of Western culture at least with respect to technological development. It does not mean, however, that traditional Eastern culture has developed no cultural responses of its own to the needs which in the West gave the impetus to the development of these focal complexes. The East, too, has reached definite, and for many centuries satisfactory, solutions for the problems posed by these needs, although its responses lay in directions other than those which have determined the developmental trends in the West.

The lack of mechanical motive power in the East, for instance, actually means that the power of human and animal muscle, which has been replaced in the West by mechanical contrivances, is still utilized here, and that true to its tradition-abiding nature, Eastern culture found this source of motive power sufficient for its needs up to the present times.

The absence of mass production and of the factory system, and the corresponding prevalence of individual work for individual use, mean a greater reliance on individual skill and dexterity, on the ability and the talent of the individual artisan to plan and execute a piece of work in accordance with the requirements of the highly developed taste of individual customers. Products of individual artisanship executed by hand and not by machine are still sought by connoisseurs and people of special refinement in the West, and favorite catchwords of advertising mass-produced merchandise are "individualized" and "personalized." The execution of a piece of work, whether it be a shoe, a chair, a water-pipe, a brass tray, a rug, a lamp, a camel-litter, a basket, or an earthenware jug, from its inception to its completion, gives the artisan a deep sense of satisfaction and an interest in his work sorely missed by the Western factory worker who for eight solid hours a day is tied to his place along the assembly line, repeating in endless monotony one single movement the significance of which in relation to the finished product he is as a rule unable to recognize. While in the West a worker is thus frequently reduced to fulfilling the role of a living machine, in the East most of the artisans are actually artists whose esthetic judgment plays an important role in their work. Esthetics thus are an integral part of everyday life to an extent quite unknown in Western civilization.

In perhaps no other field is the immediate advantage accruing to the individual from the adoption of Western achievements so obvious as in that of medicine. The high incidence of infectious diseases in the Middle East, cutting down life expectancy to a very low average, is too well known to need elaboration. The epidemics which had decimated the peoples of the Middle East with a frightening frequency, were brought under control in the course of the last few decades only thanks to the application of Western medical experience; endemic diseases continue to undermine the health of entire populations and to contribute to their misery. If there is a field of Western cultural achievement which without question it is urgently necessary to incorporate into Eastern life, this is undoubtedly medicine. Yet even in the field of medicine, traditional Middle Eastern culture is far from lacking developments of its own, as has been indicated above (p. 33). In Middle Eastern medicine an empirical and a psychological component can be discerned, the empirical being based on a great familiarity with the physical properties of *materia medica* taken from the animal, vegetable and mineral kingdoms; while the psychological component is characterized by a greater reliance on mental and spiritual powers for healing purposes than is the case in Western academic medicine. Traditional Middle Eastern medicine can best be described as magico-natural, the magical element working psychologically, while the natural ingredients administered alleviate pain and occasionally at least actually help the healing processes physiologically or chemically.

Illiteracy, too, is a condition which must change. The remarkable thing about Oriental illiteracy is that for four or five thousand years it has characterized the overwhelming majority of the populations; and yet, during this whole long period, literacy has been an ideal, carried great prestige and served as one of the surest paths leading to elevated positions in society. But the circumstances of life have been such, from the early days of dynastic Egypt and the Sumerians to the present times, that only a very few could afford to acquire the skills of reading and writing, and thus literacy became yet another of those possessions which have set off the privileged few against the great masses of the poor and simple folk. Still, Middle Eastern illiteracy does not mean a complete lack of familiarity either with the mental and spiritual products of preceding generations or with the events of the contemporary world. Illiterate people usually possess a rich store of "oral literature," consisting of folk-stories and legends, poetry and songs, riddles, sayings and proverbs; and this is certainly the case with the illiterates of the Middle East whose oral literature is heir to the age-old and famous "Wisdom of the East." And as to the events of the contemporary world, the grapevine of the bazaars, cafes, markets and caravanserais does ever and again surprise the Western observer with its rapidity, efficiency and penetration, though not always with its accuracy. The astonishing amount of oral literature and knowledge of contemporary events, as well as the great variety of orally transmitted folk-science, stored in the head of an average person, creates the impression that illiteracy is accompanied by a greater reliance on human memory, and this can be taken as yet another positive characteristic of Middle Eastern culture.

Illiteracy is closely tied up with the lack of free, general and compulsory elementary education. Though in the more advanced of the Middle Eastern countries education bills have been passed in recent years, in practice none of them succeeded in more than slowly increasing the percentage of children (boys mainly) actually attending schools. However, institutionalized education on a scale found in Egypt today, with its *ilzamiya* (compulsory) schools, though still very far from encompassing all the school-age population of the country, is a great step towards Westernization in the sense of making at least the rudiments of elementary education available to a great part of the young generation.

With regard to the technological aspects of culture, the basic difference between Western and Eastern culture can now be stated in general terms. Both the West and the East rely in these phases of life on tools which are the product of the human mind, on the one hand, and on man himself, on the other. In the West the reliance on the mechanical products of the human mind is so great that, compared with it, the role man himself plays must seem insignificant. Between man and the end-product of his work there is the machine, the excessive use of which is both a reality and an ideal. Man no longer does directly and immediately what he aims to do; he manipulates a machine and makes it do the thing for him. He does not walk where he wants to, he sits in a car and drives it. He does not fashion a pot or a jar with his hands, he serves a machine which molds it. He does not even like to write any more with his own hand, but prefers to push the keys of a typewriter instead.

In the traditional East, on the other hand, there is still a much greater reliance on man himself, on his individual skills and on his personal abilities, with a correspondingly much lesser degree of utilization of tools, not to speak of machines and mechanical equipment, in manufacturing processes or other labors and jobs. The mainstays of work and production in the Middle East are physical endurance, muscular power, manual dexterity and familiarity with materials and their processing acquired under the tutorship of a master craftsman in the course of a long and patient apprenticeship. In addition to these developmental divergencies in the working methods themselves, significant differences exist between Eastern and Western culture with regard to the purposive orientation in the trends of technological development. In the West the main purpose of all technological development is utilitarian, practical, functional; in the East technology reached a high perfection whenever it served esthetic ends, but remained primitive, backward and undeveloped when yoked to utilitarian purposes.

Summarizing these differences in technological development, and recalling the certainly much more significant differences in mental orientation and spiritual outlook between the West and the East, Middle Eastern culture as a whole is found to have concentrated its attention on *foci* very different from those which played the central role in the development of Western civilization since the close of the Middle Ages. Instead of technical achievement, organizational advancement and social services—activities occupying focal positions of great emphases in Western culture—Middle Eastern culture was, and is in its present-day traditional form, focussed on arts, on esthetics and spiritual values, and is generically characterized by an all-pervasive religious outlook.

7. Eastern Social Structure

A brief chapter like this on Eastern and Western culture cannot endeavor to give more than the highlights of a few of the main characteristics distinguishing the two cultures. Yet even so the social aspects cannot be left out of account. In this connection, structure and functioning of the family in both Eastern and Western culture have to be considered first of all. In modern Western society the typical family is composed of the parents, that is husband and wife, and their minor children. Such a family resides together; the father, and in many cases also the mother, works away from home, thus providing for the family expenditure, while the children, who rarely number more than two, undergo a lengthy process of preparation for the same tasks by institutionalized schooling and less formal socialization. When the children finish their studies and are able to fend for themselves, they usually leave the home of their parents and set up separate residence, marry and thus become founders of new families. Contact is kept alive with the parents, but it becomes considerably loosened, and the primary interest with all its manifold implications becomes centered in the reciprocal relationship between husband and wife and in that between them and their children, if and when these arrive on the scene. The parent-child relationship thus is a relatively short one; and the parents, knowing that their children will become independent of them soon after they grow up, prepare them for this independence by educating them for the making of their own decisions and by heeding their wishes increasingly as they mature. At an early age efforts are made to inculcate a sense of responsibility into the developing minds of the children, so that as greater freedom is given to them they are better equipped to use it in a considered manner and to substitute their own judgment for parental authority.

In traditional Middle Eastern society the family consists as a rule of the parents—that is, husband and wife, or, rarely nowadays, more than one wife—their unmarried daughters, their unmarried and married sons as well as the wives and children of the latter. Sometimes it includes also married grandsons and their wives and children and a few lateral relatives of the oldest male member of the family. All these reside together under one single roof; or, in the case of nomadic peoples, in a cluster of neighboring tents. Thus, while in modern Western society the typical family is the *immediate family*, in traditional Middle Eastern society the typical family is an *extended family*, usually including the members of three generations in the male line.

Economically, too, the extended family is the basic unit in the Middle East. Whether the means of livelihood are derived from agricultural activities—as is the case with some 70% of all Middle Eastern families—or from other occupations; whether the earners of the family work jointly, as is mostly the case among the Fellahin, or, what is more prevalent in the towns, each at his separate work and source of income; the rule is that the earnings are pooled and the expenses of the household are defrayed from a common purse. The women, if their husbands work land they own or rent, may help in the fields; otherwise, their place is in the home and their main task is to make the meager earnings of the men go a long way by working hard and economizing tightly, sharing the household chores or taking turns in performing them.

The number of children is large, though not as great as one would expect, for the very high birthrate is counteracted by a very high rate of infant and child mortality which cuts life expectancy down to appallingly low averages. Institutionalized schooling, as has been pointed out above (pp. 33 and 38), is more the exception than the rule and is rudimentary; social conditioning is achieved mainly in the course of informal processes of education and socialization taking place within the family circle. The children begin at an early age to participate in the work of their parents, whereby a differentiation between the sexes appears immediately, the boys being introduced into male occupations by their father or elder brothers, and the girls into those of women by their mother or elder sisters. Girls, when they marry—which occurs at a very early age—are whisked away from the parental home, and the relationship between them and their parents becomes from then on even looser and more remote than that which obtains between a married woman and her parents in Western society. This is due not only to the fact that up to the tenth or twelfth year of life, when the girl-child is usually given away in marriage, no such close emotional tie and attachment can develop as those which exist between a twenty or twenty-five-year-old bride and her parents in modern Western society. Another, probably even more decisive factor is the circumstance that the Middle Eastern bride actually marries not only her husband but also his entire family; she becomes absorbed into the new household most effectively, and very often has not the physical possibility of visiting her own parents. From the stern tutelage of her own mother, the young bride goes to the more rigid one of her mother-in-law, and only many years later, after she has given birth to children, and especially to sons, and these are on their way to manhood, can she begin to assert herself as a *mater familias* in her own right.[*]

The achievement of a status of independence and self-determination comes as late in the life of a son as of a daughter. He gets a wife when his father decides that he can spare the bride-price, and after being duly married he continues to live within the extended family of which his father is either the head or a senior member. Age is an asset in Middle Eastern outlook, and the older the son becomes—the smaller the number of members in the extended family older than himself and the greater the number of those

[*] Cf. R. Patai, "Relationship Patterns among the Arabs," in *Middle Eastern Affairs*, New York, May 1951, pp. 180-185.

younger than he—the more he grows in esteem, the more weight his opinion carries, and the more he can live after his own will.

In this order of family life no attempt is made on the part of the parents to educate their children towards independence in the sense in which this is regarded as essential in modern Western society. The parent-child relationship is in the case of a daughter very short, but as soon as it ends—with the wedding of the daughter—its place is assumed by the mother-in-law–daughter-in-law relationship which in many respects is an even more stringent one for the young bride, and in which there is neither need nor chance for independent thinking, judgment or volition by the young woman. In the case of a son, the parent-child relationship, on the other hand, is a very protracted one; it actually lasts in an unbroken and only slowly-changing succession as long as the father is alive. The daughter, having to submit to her elders in the house of her future husband, is therefore taught obedience already in the house of her own parents. The son, whose role will remain subordinate to his father as long as the latter lives, is also taught from childhood on to obey and honor his parents and other elder members of the extended family. The importance of the individual, and especially of the younger individual, remains always secondary in the Middle East compared with that of the family-group as a whole. He is inculcated, it is true, with a sense of responsibility not unlike his Western brother, but here it is a responsibility not based on a gradually widening and deepening personal knowledge of what is good and bad in accordance with a maturing judgment, but a responsibility stemming from a superimposed authority of the elders and directed toward the chief goal of ameliorating the position of the family and contributing a share to the increase of whatever material or imponderable good the family wishes to obtain.

The personality type most likely to develop, and most likely to achieve a satisfactory degree of adjustment in such a socio-cultural setting, is characterized by such traits as obedience and subordination to parental and group-authority, tending with the advance of age and status to become transformed into a self-assertive authoritarianism in the traditionally sanctioned sense; tradition-abiding conservatism; inclination to follow established patterns in both thought and action; a preoccupation with the past, the "good old days when men were men"; an ingrained veneration of old age which is regarded as synonymous with wisdom, experience and influence; a capacity for self-effacement and group-identification; a habit of thinking in terms of "We" rather than "I"; and a tendency to reject innovations and to distrust anything new and unknown.

The well-adjusted modal personality in the Middle Eastern family will, of course, also be religious, and the self-assurance derived from religious belief (cf. above, pp. 39 ff.) merges imperceptibly with the confidence drawn from the more manifest source of family unity and family strength.

As to social groupings larger than the family, significant differences will disclose themselves here, too, even to a most cursory glance into modern Western and traditional Middle Eastern social structure. In the West, kinship groups larger than the immediate family play at best a very subordinate role. Cousins or second cousins will in most cases be practically strangers to one another, and a large family group of distant relatives will meet only at weddings or funerals. Local groups, such as the village or the urban neighborhood, are usually not composed of families related by blood to one another, and the coherence in such groups is weak. Individuals in modern Western society usually belong also to a considerable number of groups based on cultural interests—such as clubs, corporations, labor unions, "societies," etc.—and the participation in such groups cuts across family ties and frequently makes for a weakening of them.

In traditional Middle Eastern society, participation in social groups larger than the extended family is a family affair and not that of individuals. This can be considered as the second most important difference between the Middle East and the modern West with regard to social structure. The family as a whole is always part of a larger unit and this larger unit is in most cases composed of a number of extended families related to one another by common descent, which is either actually traceable or traditionally assumed. This is especially true of the nomadic peoples of the Middle East, the most typical of whom are the bedouin of the Arabian and Syrian deserts, but also among the settled agriculturists—kinship groups larger than the extended family constitute the most prevalent social setting. In many villages traditions are preserved which tell of a group of people, consisting of one or more related families, who several generations back came from the same place, occupied the site of the village and settled there. Preferred marriage in the Middle East being that between cousins, or, failing this, between more removed relatives, within a few generations all the families of such a village became closely related to one another, and came to regard themselves as branches of a single big family group. The individual, therefore, whether in nomadic or in settled society, is a member of larger social units not in his individual capacity, but as a part of his own family. Participation in such larger social groups can never cut across family ties. (It would be inconceivable for the father to vote Democratic and the son Republican; both will vote as they are told to by the head of the larger group to which their family belongs.) On the contrary, the fact that the family belongs to a larger social group will only strengthen the family unity, for the stronger the family as a whole the greater its weight within the larger unit. These additional circumstances tend to reinforce the development of those character-traits which make up the typical modal personality in Middle Eastern society.* The strength of the individual lies in the family; the strength of the family lies in the larger social unit to which it belongs, and so forth. Therefore: if you wish to be strong, help to strengthen the family and the larger units, and help to preserve the traditional social order.

Five crucial focal complexes of traditional Oriental culture have been discerned in the foregoing brief discussion. In relation to the corresponding traits in Western culture they can be characterized in summary as follows:

1. A greater permeation of everyday life by the esthetic element.
2. An all-pervasive religiosity, including the elements of belief, ritual and morality.
3. A broader outlook on human existence accompanied by a greater detachment from material benefits.
4. The primary importance of the extended family as the basic economic and social unit and the subordination of the individual to it.
5. The composition of larger social units not of individuals but of (extended) families.

It is with these complexes as focal concerns in their cultural equipment that the Oriental Jews come to Israel. In them, if anywhere, will be found those features of Oriental Jewish life which modern Israel can utilize for the enrichment of its nascent culture.

* Cf. above, p. 53.

Chapter Three

Currents of Immigration

1. From *Halukka* to *Bilu*

The political independence of the Jews in Palestine came to an end—after twelve centuries of national existence—when Jerusalem was destroyed by Titus. During the nineteen centuries that followed, the rule of the country passed from the Romans to the Byzantines, to the Arabs, to the Turks, and finally to the British; but throughout, Jewish groups, tolerated or oppressed, welcomed or hunted, favored or persecuted, continued to live in the Holy Land of their forefathers in communities of fluctuating sizes, scattered here and there in the towns and villages of the country. Their numbers were augmented from time to time by a thin trickle of immigrants. From the Middle Ages onward they were concentrated mainly in the four Holy Cities of Jerusalem, Hebron, Tiberias and Safed. Here, the great majority of them lived in utter poverty, in ghetto-like quarters, dedicated to religious observance and to the study of the Talmud, that inexhaustible storehouse of ancient Jewish law and lore.

In the 15th century, we find the Jews of German descent in Palestine supported by an institution called *Halukka*, or "distribution," the funds for which were acquired through donations made by Jews in Europe. Soon afterwards, a similar institution was established for the benefit of Jews of Spanish origin, with the result that in the 16th century the Ashkenazi (German) Jews, and the Sephardi (Spanish) Jews are found to constitute two distinct groups. Their fund-collectors, called *shlihim*, emissaries, systematically made the rounds of the home communities of their respective groups, and in this manner ensured, not only the steady flow of funds sufficient to keep body and soul together, but also the continuing interest of Jews all over the world in the Holy Land. As early as 1759 the first emissary of the *Halukka* arrived in America, and thenceforward the share of American Jewry in providing for the remnants of Israel in their ancient homeland constantly increased.

It was in this milieu of a small Jewish microcosm dedicated to religion and tradition, removed from any worldly interest, that the idea originated which was destined to provide the animating force in the upbuilding of a new Palestine by its returning sons. The plan was first conceived by a group primarily of Hungarian Jews in Jerusalem who subsisted on donations granted them by their own *Halukka* system. It was briefly, the idea of the Return to the Soil. In 1878, when the total number of Jews in Palestine was about 20,000, they made an attempt to translate the idea into practice; they bought a plot of land from the inhabitants of the Arab village of Mulabbes, some eight miles to the northeast of Jaffa, and founded a colony there to which they gave the biblical name of symbolic content, Petah Tikva, "Door of Hope."*

Their attempt, like many a first experiment, was not successful. The new settlers succumbed to malaria spread by the mosquitoes of the nearby swamps and were forced to abandon the settlement. But the news that Palestinian Jews had made an effort to settle on the land reached Eastern Europe, where very soon thereafter a new movement was founded, called *Hovevei Zion*, "Lovers of Zion." Members of this movement who immigrated to Palestine were called *Biluim*, a name composed of the initials of the biblical verse, *Beit Yaakov lekhu wenelkha* (Isa. 2.5)—"O house of Jacob, come ye, and let us walk . . ." When the first *Bilu* immigrants reached Palestine, in 1882, some of them reopened the Door of Hope, while others founded the new colonies of Rishon Lezion, Nes Zionah, Zikhron Yaakov and Rosh Pina. Petah Tikva, now fondly given the epithet "Mother of the Colonies," is today (1952) a bustling town of some 35,000 inhabitants.   *

In 1882, the number of the Jews in Palestine was about 24,000. The so-called "First *Aliya*," or first wave of immigration which reached Palestine between 1882 and 1903, brought into the country another 25,000 Jews, and ever since that time the development of Jewish Palestine has been determined by the quality, the endeavor, the vision and the achievements of successive waves of immigrants.

The First *Aliya* succeeded in converting the position of the old, religious *Yishuv* (settlement) in Palestine into a numerical minority. The newcomers were a human element basically different from the old *Yishuv*; they were, in fact, in most respects diametrically op-

* By that time the agricultural school of Mikwe Yisrael, founded by the French-Jewish Alliance Israélite Universelle in 1869, was ten years old, but its alumni had made no attempt as yet to found an agricultural settlement.

posed to the older group. Their aspirations were national, their attitude in many cases decidedly anti-religious, while the old *Yishuv* was practically without exception a deeply religious group to whom nationalism was an unknown entity. The ideal of the old *Yishuv* was to live a life dedicated to religion and to the study of religious lore; it was their conviction that the Jews all over the world were in duty bound to support them in return for the incomparably greater service they were rendering world Jewry in pursuing a God-fearing life in the Holy Land, and thus playing the role of hallowed intercessors, or at least intermediaries, between God and His people. On the other hand, the new immigrants were imbued with the conviction that they could rebuild their own lives only by rebuilding the land of their ancestors, by leaving behind in Europe the traditional ways of Jewish religious life as well as the customary Jewish occupations, and by laying the foundations in Palestine for an independent, healthy agrarian economy. As a final striking difference, it must be remarked that the old *Yishuv* was in its majority Sephardi and Oriental, while the new immigrants of the First *Aliya* were exclusively Ashkenazi Jews from Russia and Rumania.

The First *Aliya*, greatly aided by Baron Edmond de Rothschild of Paris and later by the Palestine Jewish Colonization Association, introduced into Palestine that type of rural agricultural settlement which is known to this day by the name of *moshava*, "colony," or more correctly, settlement. The *moshava* was, and is, an agricultural settlement, very much like the villages in European agricultural countries. The land, either privately owned by each settler, or apportioned to him by the P. I. C. A., was (and is) privately worked, with the help of hired hands who, for several decades after the establishment of the first villages, were Arabs in practically every instance. The Jewish settlers, or "colonists," were gentlemen-farmers who merely supervised the work of others, instead of actually tilling the soil with their own hands. It remained for the Second *Aliya* to establish in Palestine a type of agricultural village which constituted a most radical departure from any agricultural settlement form existing in those days and which is perhaps the most outstanding feature of the social experimentation in Israel to this very day.

2. The Second *Aliya*

The Second *Aliya*, too, came almost exclusively from Russia and brought into the country within a decade, from 1904 to the eve of World War I, about 40,000 Jewish immigrants. This wave of immigration, which started soon after the organization of political Zionism by Theodor Herzl (1860-1904), was composed mainly of young working people who were both politically and nationally more self-conscious than their predecessors of the First *Aliya*. Moreover, they shared the ideal of self-labor and were opposed to exploiting the labor of others in order to make their personal lives more comfortable.

The immigrants who entered the country with the Second *Aliya* launched into a bitter struggle for what was termed "the conquest of labor" (*kibbush ha'avoda*), that is, the replacement of the Arab hired hands by Jewish agricultural laborers in the older Jewish colonies which had been established toward the end of the 19th century. They also fought for the "conquest of watching," that is, the employment of Jewish watchmen, *shomrim*, in place of the Arabs. The headway they made against the stiff resistance of the "colonists" was slow but persistent, and it was due to the belated but well-earned fruit of their efforts that, in 1936, when the Arabs of Palestine organized their general boycott against the Jews, there were relatively few Arabs left in Jewish employ who now could be called upon by the Arab leadership to leave their jobs.

The other memorable achievement of the Second *Aliya* was the development of the communal agricultural settlement, the so-called *kvutza* or *kibbutz*. The first *kvutza* was founded in 1909 on the shores of Lake Tiberias. Today, this *kvutza*, called Daganya, can boast of a middle-aged second generation and a growing third one.

Much has been written about the *kvutza* which is the most thoroughly studied form of rural settlement developed in new Palestine.[*] It will therefore suffice to summarize here very briefly the main principles of the *kvutza* as first developed in Daganya and adopted by the entire *kibbutz*-movement. These include the basic idea "from each according to his ability, to each according to his needs"; and the principles of all-pervasive communal living, of self-labor only, of complete democracy in the management of affairs, of the absolute absence of private property within the *kvutza*, the equal status of the sexes, the emphasis on agricultural occupations, and voluntary membership. Yet withal, the *kvutza* as a whole is a strongly capitalistic enterprise which works for profit and endeavors to increase its property and wealth. Just as the principles of communal living and working apply only within the *kvutza* itself, so does the complementary principle involving the absence of private property.

These principles, however, did not appeal to all the members of

[*] Cf. Henrik F. Infield, *Cooperative Living in Palestine*, London, 1946; Edwin Samuel, *Handbook of the Communal Villages in Palestine*, Jerusalem, 1945. ✳

the Second *Aliya*. Some of them preferred a combination of traits taken from the *kvutza*, on the one hand, and the old-fashioned European-type of private village, on the other. The name given to this type of village is *Moshav*, or Smallholders' Settlement.

The *moshav* consists of individual farms, whose land is as a rule owned by the Jewish National Fund (*Keren Kayemet*) which was founded as far back as 1901. Each farm is just big enough so that a farmer family can work it without outside help, as most of them actually do, although there is no prohibition against hired labor. Mixed farming is typical of the *moshav*. Each settler grows vegetables, has some poultry, a few cows, and in this manner utilizes most intensively the relatively small plot of land apportioned to him. Almost all the farmers in the *moshavim* are members of village-cooperatives for marketing and purchasing, for water supply, for credit and the like. A new member can join the *moshav* only if the management of the *moshav*, the landowners and the settling institutions give their consent.

These three developments, the "conquest of labor" and the emergence of two entirely new types of agricultural settlements, the *kvutza* and the *moshav*, were the great achievements of the Second *Aliya* within the "Return to the Soil" movement. At the outbreak of World War I, when the Second *Aliya* came to an abrupt end, the number of Jews in Palestine was estimated at about 85,000, of whom some 12,000 lived in 47 rural settlements of different types. The Hebrew language had begun by that time to make headway against the diaspora-tongues brought along by the new immigrants and still spoken by the Old *Yishuv*, and the foundations were laid for a national Hebrew educational system.

The years of World War I were years of suffering and privation for the young Jewish population of Palestine. Large numbers of them were deported by the Turkish authorities to Syria, and especially to Damascus; others fell victim to epidemics; and at the termination of the war, in 1918, the number of the Jews in Palestine had decreased to 56,000.

It was towards the end of World War I that a historic document was issued in England which became a cornerstone in the legal foundations of the Jewish Return to Palestine movement. On November 2, 1917, in the Balfour Declaration, the British Government undertook to support ("facilitate") "the establishment in Palestine of a national home for the Jewish people."

This was followed by the occupation of Palestine, which had been for exactly four hundred years (1517-1917) under Turkish rule, by the forces under the command of General Allenby; the establish-

ment of a civil administration; and by the League of Nations' con-
ferring, in 1922, of the Mandate over Palestine upon Britain. Thus,
while the First and the Second *Aliyot* came to Turkish Palestine by
sufferance, the Third *Aliya*, which started soon after the end of
World War I, came by the right granted in an instrument of international law.

3. The Third and Fourth *Aliyot*

The Third *Aliya* was not so productive in the development of new
rural settlement-forms as had been the Second *Aliya*. The only new
form of agricultural settlement to spread during the Third *Aliya*
period was that of the *moshav ovdim*, the Workers' Smallholders'
Settlement, the beginnings of which went back to the years preceding World War I, that is, to the times of the Second *Aliya*. After the
inception of the Third *Aliya*, in the years 1920-21, the *moshav ovdim*
idea was put into practice with the establishment of the first two
such settlements, Nahalal and Kfar Yehezkel. In the course of a few
years, the *moshav ovdim* became a very popular form of rural settlement, and by 1946 there were in Palestine no less than 68 such
settlements, with a population totalling 18,400.

The idea of the *moshav ovdim* sprang from the same discontent
with existing rural settlement and life-forms which had given the
primary impetus also to the *kvutza* and the *moshav*. The immigrants
of the Second *Aliya* felt that the position of the Jewish agricultural
settlement, as they found it in Palestine, was unsatisfactory both
from an economical and from a socio-national viewpoint. Economically the agriculture of the *moshavot* was based on monoculture,
on plantations in the plains of the seashore, and on unirrigated field-
crops (the *falha*) in the Galilee. They also felt that the employment
of Arab workers in the *moshavot* endangered the socio-national position of the small agricultural sector of the *Yishuv* in general. Farming based on monoculture is in constant danger of being ruined due
to such causes as failure of crops, pests, decline in marketability,
and the like. Mixed farming was therefore adopted by all the new
rural farm-forms developed or conceived by the Second *Aliya,
kvutzot, moshavim* and *moshve ovdim* alike. Mixed farming consists
of several products which complement one another and thus make
for additional safety in the economy of the farm, also enabling all
the members of the family or *kibbutz* to work in it each in accordance with his strength, ability or inclinations. Especially with respect to the Smallholders' and the Workers' Smallholders' Settlements, mixed farming can supply the family with most of its needs,

and the surplus can be sold to feed the town population and to provide the necessary cash for the farming family.

A separate mixed farm for each settler is the first of the five principles on which the Workers' Smallholders' Settlement is based. The other four principles are as follows: national land; self-labor; selling and buying only through the settlement's institutions; mutual help and responsibility. National land and self-labor are principles which exist also in the *kibbutz* movement. The first stems from the endeavor to remove the land, which is the basis of the agriculturist's existence, from the sphere of privately purchasable or alienable property. The second, self-labor, is a characteristic expression of the socialist outlook of the Second *Aliya* which ever since has characterized the working sector of the *Yishuv* in Palestine. This same principle underlies the largest single organization in Israel to this day, the General Federation of Labor, or *Histadrut.** In the Workers' Smallholders' Settlements, the principle of self-labor also prevents, to a large extent, the formation of sharp social extremes based on the differences between the status of the employers who live on the work of others and that of the employees, the hired laborers, who have no land, no property, no standing in the community. The principle of selling and buying through the village institutions only grew out of the practical considerations for the increase of the settlement's economic strength, to prevent waste of energy and effort by the individual farmer, and to eliminate the middleman and his profits whose existence would mean a corresponding loss for the farmer. And lastly, the principle of mutual help and responsibility is the result of the endeavors of the settlers to increase the security of the individual within the framework of the community and to prevent sudden and catastrophic deterioration in the economic position of a member afflicted with family ills or stricken in his farm by the capricious whims of nature.

By the time the Fourth *Aliya* came to a close in 1931, the Jewish population of Palestine numbered 174,610, of whom 136,160 lived in 19 urban settlements, while 38,450 were scattered all over the country in no less than 110 rural settlements. Within the rural sector itself, the first postwar decade showed clearly that the tendency was towards cooperative and communal forms of settlement, compared with which the relative numbers of both the private villages and their inhabitants showed a slow but constant decrease.

As to the numerical relationship between the Ashkenazi and the Sephardi-Oriental Jews in Palestine, upon which we touched briefly

---

* Cf. below, pp. 160 ff. and 330-2.

in the beginning of this chapter, the year 1918 provides us with the first more or less reliable data. In that year, 33,000, or 58.9%, of the *Yishuv* were Ashkenazi Jews, that is, Jews mainly of Eastern and Central European extraction; 11,000, or 19.6%, were Sephardi Jews, that is, Jews who reached Palestine from Spain via Turkish lands or North Africa or Italy, and some of whom proudly maintained the tradition that their ancestors came to Palestine directly from Spain after the expulsion of the Jews from that country at the end of the 15th century; and 12,000, or 21.5%, were Oriental Jews, that is, Jews whose ancestors never lived in Europe but settled in the countries of the Near and Middle East many hundreds and even thousands of years ago when the political vicissitudes and catastrophes which befell Palestine made it impossible for most of its inhabitants to hold on to their old habitats. The Sephardi and Oriental Jews together numbered 23,000, or 41.1%, and the largest single homogeneous group within them was that of the Yemenites, with 4,400 souls, or 7.9% of the total Jewish population.*

4. Oriental Influences

The presence of such considerable number of Oriental and semi-Oriental (Sephardi) Jewish groups in the country became a decisive factor in the cultural developments of the first postwar years, and especially during the periods of the Third and Fourth *Aliyot*, the first of which extended from 1919 to 1923, the second from 1924 to 1931, and which brought into the country 35,000 and 82,000 respectively, the overwhelming majority of whom were Ashkenazi Jews. The traditional forms of life pursued by these Oriental and Sephardi Jews differed very little from those of any other urban community within the wide bounds of the prewar Turkish Empire. The new immigrants, therefore, who came from Eastern Europe principally, found in Palestine a local variety of Oriental culture in which a comparatively well-established Jewish group participated in the most lively manner. The result of the contacts which developed between the newcomers, on the one hand, and the Palestinian Arabs and Oriental Jews, on the other, was that quite a number of local Arab-Jewish cultural traits were taken over by the new immigrants.

The great majority of the Jewish people has always been ready, in every country, to assimilate to higher standards of living. In Palestine, what the Oriental way of life lacked in higher economic-material standards was made up for, in the eyes of the newcomers,

* Cf. below, pp. 189 and 194.

by the romantic admiration they nurtured for the indigenous population of their much-coveted ancient homeland. Thus, as long as the number of the European Jews arriving in Palestine was relatively small, there was a marked, though perhaps in some cases unconscious, tendency towards the emulation of certain traits in the local culture.

The red fez, for instance, the uniform Turkish headdress of three continents, was adopted by the immigrant Jews and their sons. So was the *qaftan* (also a Turkish word), the long robe with a waist girdle, above which the more "modern" people wore a short European jacket. That housing had to conform to traditional Oriental fashion will become understandable if we consider that the first immigrants had to rent houses built by Arabs; later, when they wished to build houses, they had to employ Arab builders; and still later, when they themselves built their houses, they built them according to the familiar Arab pattern. The accommodation of families within the houses was conditioned by the existing form of the housing. Oriental houses (both Arab and Jewish) were built for an "extended family," that is, for a man and his wife and for their married sons and their families. Furnishings and kitchenware, too, were purchased in the local market, and many of these have succeeded in holding their own to this very day—for instance, the porous earthenware jar (*jara*) which cools water without ice or electricity almost as well as any icebox or refrigerator; ceramics, rugs (from Gaza), various types of basket, wickerwork chairs, inlaid Damascene furniture and boxes, lace and embroidery (also as personal adornment), wooden house-shoes, and the like.

The food-habits of the immigrant European Jews were also influenced by prevailing local tradition. They would, for example, prepare sour milk at home in Oriental fashion in large open earthenware pots. They learned to eat and even to enjoy the bitter salted olives, the eggplant, and many other fruit and vegetable species quite unknown to them in Europe. Oriental ways of cooking, too, were adopted, such as the frying of meat or vegetables first in oil and then cooking them in tomato or some other juice, or the grilling of meat. Oriental hot and cold drinks became popular: Turkish coffee, and all sorts of lemonades given the generic name *gazoz*, an Arabicized form of the French (*eau*) *gazeuse*.

Oriental influence made deeper inroads than merely in the fields of material culture. Oriental music, equally dear to Arab and Oriental Jew, became appreciated also by the European Jewish immigrant. The folk-songs which were composed and became popular among them in the first "romantic" period show the distinct influence of Oriental scale and rhythm. The first Jewish shepherds took over from the Arab shepherds, along with Arab garments, also the flute and its melodies. The Jewish mounted watchmen, the *shomrim*, emulated the *fantaziya* performances of the Arabs, a sort of Oriental torchlight tattoo.

In the beginning, some seventy years ago, when the first Jewish agricultural settlements were founded in Palestine, the inexperienced settlers took over much of what they found among the Arab fellahin. Their farms were held individually; for the most part Arab laborers were employed, extensive cultivation was practiced, or citrus groves were planted, all according to Arab example.

Until the end of Turkish rule in Palestine (1917), the only officially recognized religious authority of the Jews was that of the Sephardi rabbis, headed by the Sephardi Chief Rabbi of the entire province of Palestine whose proud traditional title was (and is to this day) *Rishon leZion*, that is, The First One in Zion. The Ashkenazi Jewish community in Jerusalem, organized in 1812 and split into two factions, or *Kolelim*, one called Hasidic and the other, opposing them, named *P'rushim*, "seceders" (the name in its original use meant Pharisees), was subject to the Sephardi community in matters of ritual slaughtering of livestock, burial and the payment of taxes to the Turkish government. Only after the Western powers, especially Germany, Austria and Russia, had set up their consulates in Palestine, were the Jewish subjects of these countries who resided in Palestine exempted from the payment of the head-tax in accordance with the Turkish "capitulations." The struggle of the Ashkenazi Jews to free themselves from the yoke of the Sephardi supervision of interment and *shehita* (ritual slaughtering) continued for several decades, in spite of the energetic assistance rendered them also in this matter by the consuls of their European home-countries.

Considering the institutional advantages enjoyed by the Sephardi Jews, and the higher status accorded them by the Ottoman authorities, as well as their prestige as older inhabitants of the country and their numerical preponderance, it will be understandable that their influence on the first Jewish immigrants from Ashkenazi countries was considerable. In fact, intermarriage with them was favored by the European Jewish immigrants, especially in Jerusalem and Safed, which were the main Sephardi strongholds, and cases are known in which Ashkenazi Jewish immigrants came to be regarded, and regarded themselves after one or two generations, as Sephardi Jews.

In these and many other ways, the Oriental (Arab-Jewish) culture, developed in Palestine during the four centuries of Turkish rule, influenced the culture of the first small waves of European Jewish immigrants. As long as the newly arrived groups were small, they had to live, at least in the towns, in close contact with the larger groups of Oriental Jews whom they found in the country, and consequently their mode of life had to be patterned, willy-nilly, after the prevailing common traits of Oriental Arab-Jewish culture.*

5. The Fifth *Aliya:* Westernization

With the arrival of larger waves of Jewish immigrants from Europe, in the years that followed the Balfour Declaration the situation began to change. The Third and Fourth *Aliyot* jointly brought into the country more than 116,000 Jewish immigrants (from 1919 to 1931) of whom 102,000, or 88% were Ashkenazi Jews, while the combined total of the Sephardi and Oriental Jewish immigrants reached only 14,000 in absolute figures, or 12%. In spite of the much greater natural increase exhibited by the Oriental and Sephardi Jews,§ this overwhelmingly Ashkenazi immigration resulted, by 1928, in a reduction of the relative numbers of the Sephardi and Oriental Jewish element in the country to 29% as against the 41.1% of a decade earlier.

The results of the large-scale Ashkenazi immigration soon began to be felt on the cultural scene. As the numbers of the new *Yishuv* became greater, its increasing settlements began to be permeated with a cultural atmosphere of their own. The rapidly growing new *Yishuv* had to rely and indeed wished to rely, more and more on its own labor, products, economy, society, language and culture. As these developed they evolved new phases, in which the role of the older Arab-Jewish Oriental elements steadily decreased. On the other hand, the developing culture of the new *Yishuv* began to make itself felt in the life of the older inhabitants of the country.

This process of "Westernization" in Palestine reached a new high with the onset of the Fifth *Aliya*, which brought into the country in the course of eight years (1932-1939) about 225,000 Jews, of whom 170,000 were Ashkenazim, among them a considerable number German (36,000) and Central European (about 12,000). It was this immigration that, superimposed upon the already existing majority of East European Jews, gave the final stamp of Western character to the new *Yishuv* of Palestine. On the eve of World War II, the Ashkenazi element in Palestine reached a new high of 77.5%.

* Cf. Raphael Patai, *On Culture Contact and Its Working in Modern Palestine,* American Anthropological Association, Memoir No. 67, October, 1947, pp. 19-20, 32.
§ Cf. The following chapter, pp. 85 and 87.

In view of the overwhelmingly and increasingly Ashkenazi character of the *Yishuv*, no serious consideration was given to the possibility that a Jewish state, if it were ever achieved, would be anything but a predominantly Western country with a socio-cultural structure which—apart from a few specifically Hebrew and Jewish cultural elements—would essentially resemble a small West-European state, such as Switzerland or Belgium.

No appreciable change occurred in this situation during the years of World War II. True, the percentage of Sephardi and Oriental Jewish immigrants jumped to 26.3% in the period from 1939 to 1945; but as a consequence of the British White Paper policy, introduced in 1939, the total Jewish immigration into Palestine during these years was so small (some 81,000) that the increase of the non-Ashkenazi element among the immigrants did not effect any change in the ethnic composition of the Jewish population of the country as a whole.

To sum up the numerical relationship between the Ashkenazi and the Sephardi-Oriental elements in the *Yishuv* during the thirty-year period which preceded the establishment of the State of Israel: The Sephardi-Oriental element decreased during the first twenty years of Zionist settlement work (1918-1939) from somewhat over two-fifths to somewhat over one-fifth, and then, for the next seven or eight years, remained at approximately the same level.

6. The Oriental *Aliya*

A sudden change of unprecedented magnitude occurred in the second half of the year 1948, when, with the establishment of the Jewish state, the gates of Israel were thrown wide open to unrestricted immigration. It was only then that the effects of the catastrophic events which had taken place during the war years in Hitler's "Fortress Europe" were fully felt.

With the European massacre of six million Jews, the ethnic balance of world Jewry as a whole underwent a tragic change. The victims of the Nazi inferno were, with very few exceptions, Ashkenazi Jews. Consequently, the numbers of the Sephardi and Oriental Jews in relation to the Jews of the globe as a whole increased by some 40 to 45%. The numbers of potential immigrants to Israel from the Sephardi and Oriental communities, however, increased by many times the above figure. Only a few hundred thousand Jews who survived on the European continent outside the Russian sphere were left after the war as potential immigrants to Israel. From Russia itself there was no Jewish immigration; and from its satellite countries, whence immigration could have flowed in a steady stream, it was allowed only to trickle. The predominantly Ashkenazi Jews of the Anglo-Saxon orbit were too deeply anchored in their countries of residence to yield considerable numbers of immigrants. This left approximately one million Jews in the Moslem lands as the largest reservoir for potential immigration to Israel.

The Jewish communities in the Moslem countries until World War II supplied proportionately few immigrants to Palestine. The official bodies of the *Yishuv* neglected these diasporas in the years when it would have been possible to send *shlihim*, emissaries, and thus to create a movement for Palestine, as was being done in Poland and in other East European countries. On the other hand, Zionist propaganda and organizational activities were frowned upon by the governments and peoples of the Middle Eastern countries, which professed to a certain solidarity with the Palestinian Arabs. As long as the social and economic position of the Jews was tolerable, the leaders of the Jewish communities themselves discouraged, often very actively, any Zionist activity. This attitude was conditioned primarily by a well-founded fear that participation in the Zionist movement would focus the attention of the Moslem governments and their people upon the existing link between the local Jewry and Palestinian Jewry—who were after all considered to be the enemies of the Arabs—thus creating identification of the one group with the other. However, as has happened several times in the long history of the Jewish people, the Jews of the Diaspora had to suffer again for events which took place between the Jews of Palestine and their non-Jewish neighbors. The Jews of Palestine—now the young state of Israel—had to resort to force in self-defense against armed aggression launched by several of the Arab states; and, while the outcome of the ensuing war was victory for the Jews of Israel, the Jews of the Arab East had to bear the brunt of the wrath which could find no satisfaction on the battlefield.

The result was a rapid and disastrous deterioration of the position of the Jewish communities in the Arab states. During the crucial months when Israel fought for its birth and existence, the Jews of the Middle East were not even given an opportunity to deny their allegiance to Israel and to affirm their identity with the countries of their respective citizenships. They were singled out from the very beginning of the hostilities as helpless scapegoats, and though the persecutions even at their peak never did approximate the genocidal mass-slaughter of the Nazis, they were cruel and vicious enough to make untenable the position of considerable parts of the Jewish communities in the Arab countries. The result was just the opposite of what the Arab countries wished to achieve: instead of setting up a barrier between their own Jewish citizens and the new Jewish state, they actually drove them towards its open gates.

While emphasizing the political repercussions of the establishment of the State of Israel on the Jews of the Middle East as a decisive factor in the increase of immigration from this area to Israel, we must not overlook the psychological effect which the rise of Israel has had on the Jewish communities of these countries. In Yemen and in North Africa, the two Moslem territories from which Jewish immigrants in large numbers arrived in Israel immediately upon the establishment of the Jewish state, a movement, almost Messianic in its emotional intensity, began to spread with phenomenal speed. It soon reached dimensions which surpassed many times what the authorities in Israel and the immigration offices of the Jewish Agency were prepared for. Notwithstanding hardships and sufferings, even actual danger to their liberty and their very lives, the Jews of these countries sold whatever possessions they had and hid themselves or trekked hundreds of miles through roadless countries in order to reach the port of exit where they hoped to be shipped to Israel. According to eyewitnesses, this spontaneous mass-exodus from mountain villages, from cave-dwellings and desert-bound oases, was like a great tidal wave breaking through a dam which had held it back for centuries. Emotional upheaval, on the one hand, and political pressure, on the other, whipped these ancient and tradition-bound Jewish groups into a sudden movement, into an unparalleled outbreak.

As to the two great non-Arab states of the Middle East, Turkey and Iran, the impetus there for immigration into Israel must be related to an even greater extent to psychological motivations rather than to a deterioration in the political and the socio-economic position. While the situation of the Jews in these countries was never too comfortable, the effect of the Israeli-Arab war was felt here less than could have been anticipated. Neither the Turks who ruled all the Arab nations for centuries, nor the Iranians who are separated from them by history, language, and the religious schism of the Sunnite-Shi'ite cleavage, have any real sympathy for the Arabs, and especially not for the Arabs of that backward former Turkish province, Palestine. Lip service, of course, was amply paid to the cause of the Palestinian Arabs also in Turkey and Iran, but retaliatory measures, such as every Arab state felt duty bound to put into effect against its own Jews, were taken by neither of these two countries. The early official recognition of Israel (in March 1950) by these two states was an additional blow to Arab hopes for a united Moslem front against the new Jewish state. It is therefore not so much the actual or potential deterioration in their positions, as the outcropping of Jewish religio-nationalistic enthusiasm in the wake of the establishment of the State of Israel and the victories of the Jewish forces over the Arabs—news of which found its way everywhere—which has to be regarded as chiefly responsible for the greatly increased Jewish immigration into Israel from Turkey and Iran. This religio-nationalistic enthusiasm was more easily fanned to a white flame in these countries, since a religiously motivated nationalism is the characteristic form taken by awakening political consciousness in every Middle Eastern state. Having been prevented by their minority status from sharing in the religious-nationalistic endeavors of the countries of their citizenship, the Jews of the Middle East found an outlet for these feelings and attitudes—highly fashionable in their socio-cultural environment—in an emotional focussing on the new, and already successful and victorious State of Israel in which they hoped they would become full and equal members.

The combined effect of these two factors—the socio-economic pressure and the religious-national enthusiasm—resulted in a desperate wish to emigrate to Israel, and in a succession of overt or covert efforts to translate the wish into reality. Overt—in places where the governments were willing to release their Jews, as a rule for a ransom consisting of their entire fortune; and covert—where no passports or permits were issued to Jews, and where to leave the country was an almost capital offense.

Yet, in spite of the sacrifices required and the all but insurmountable difficulties, the immigration from the Middle Eastern countries started in full force soon after the establishment of the State of Israel and has been on the increase ever since. In the course of the four years which elapsed since the independence of Israel, the bulk of the Middle Eastern Jewish immigration came from Yemen, Iraq, North Africa (including Egypt) and Turkey. Yemen and Iraq were practically emptied of their Jews, supplying jointly some 170,000 immigrants to Israel; in Turkey about half of the Jews were left behind; in North Africa their numbers were diminished by about one tenth. Statistics are a rare thing in Middle Eastern lands, and the total number of the Jews in any of these countries can only be given in a rough estimate which is likely to err by tens of thousands on either side. It is, nevertheless, clear that in 1952 the Middle East still contained a potential immigrant-reservoir of some three-quarters of ✳ a million Jews.

7. New Settlement Forms

Just as the periods of the earlier waves of immigration were characterized by the establishment of new rural settlement forms, so also the great wave of immigrants which reached the shores of the independent Israel occasioned the development of new types of rural aggregates. The First *Aliya* (1882-1903) created the *moshava*, the traditional village with the land privately owned and individually worked. The Second *Aliya* (1904-1914) brought the *kibbutz*, the collective settlement, and the *moshav*, the cooperative smallholders' settlement. The days of the Third *Aliya* (1919-1923) saw the spread of the *moshav ovdim*, the workers' smallholders' settlement, in which cooperation and mutual aid received a greater emphasis than in the *moshav*. The Fourth *Aliya* (1924-1931) was the period in which several more modern *moshavot*, private villages, were founded, in addition to workers' smallholders' settlements and *kibbutzim*. The Fifth *Aliya* (1932-1939) established the modern (mainly German) *moshavim*, and saw the inception of the *moshav shitufi*, the collective smallholders' settlement, and the *kfar shitufi*, the collective village.

During the decade from 1939 to 1948, when immigration was at a low ebb, the only rural settlement form which showed any considerable growth was the *kibbutz*. In 1936 there were altogether 47 *kibbutzim* in Palestine; in 1941—87; in May 1948—149.

With the onset of the mass immigration during and after the War of Independence, the first arrivals were settled in the abandoned Arab towns and villages which were converted into smallholders' cooperatives. When these were filled up, and the number of newcomers in the immigrants' reception camps continued to grow—reaching the 100,000 figure in the summer of 1949—new and rapid absorptive measures had to be developed. In response to the critical situation among the immigrants, two new settlement forms were evolved: the *ma'abara*, and the *kfar avoda*; and by the end of 1952 the immigrants' tent cities practically disappeared from the Israel landscape.

The *ma'abara*, or transit village, is a camp of tents, huts and barracks, set up in places where work is immediately available or can be provided through public work schemes. The inmates of the *ma'abarot* receive housing free of charge, but must support themselves from the wages they earn. By December 1951, more than 175,000 immigrants lived in *ma'abarot*. The *kfar avoda*, or work village, differs from the *ma'abara* only to the extent that it is set up on cultivable land on which the immigrants are set to work in reclamation, afforestation, and the like. In both types of village the tendency is to improve the housing conditions and to make the site ✳ suitable for more permanent settlement.

The immigrants to Israel since the establishment of the State preferred in most cases to settle in cities and towns, in urban settlements or even in *ma'abarot* on the outskirts of towns, rather than go into agricultural areas. It is difficult to obtain unequivocal statistical data, but there can be no doubt that a considerably smaller percentage of the immigrants settled in villages and took up agriculture than would be desirable for the economy of the country. Those who were prepared to engage in agriculture, whether European or Oriental Jews, preferred the *moshav ovdim,* the cooperative village, to all other forms of settlement. The European immigrants were averse to the *kibbutz* because they spent many years of their lives in concentration camps, displaced persons camps, and immigrants camps, and yearned for the privacy of their own four walls. The Oriental immigrants were, as a rule, too tradition-bound to understand the ideological basis of communal *kibbutz* life.

This resulted in a sudden increase of the *moshav* type of village as against a much slower growth of the *kibbutz* movement. From May 15, 1948, to March 31, 1951, only 71 new *kibbutzim* were founded as against 189 new cooperative settlements, of which 123 belonged to the workers' smallholders' settlement type. Taking a longer period, it is found that of the 301 settlements established from January, 1947, to July, 1951, only 92 were *kibbutzim,* the rest (209) being cooperative settlements. During the 12 months of 1950, only 3 new *kibbutzim* were founded bringing their total number up to 214 and increasing their population from 63,000 to 67,500. The number of the private and cooperative villages, on the other hand, increased in the same year from 237 to 319, and their population from 94,890 to 153,515. If this trend continues, as it apparently will, the *kibbutzim,* which in the mandatory period were the agricultural backbone of the *Yishuv,* will play a secondary role in the future rural economy of Israel.

The *kibbutz* form of settlement also proved unable to expand rapidly enough to allow it to absorb large numbers of newcomers. During the first three years of the State, of the 600,000 new immigrants only 10,000 were absorbed by the existing *kibbutzim.*✳ At the same time ideological differences of long standing became so pronounced in the *kibbutzim* belonging to the Kibbutz haMeuhad organization that they resulted in an open breach between the Mapai and Mapam parties within them, causing a breakup of the entire

✳ Cf. *Israel Government Yearbook,* 5712, p. 168.

organization, an exodus of the minority groups from the individual *kibbutzim*, and, finally, in November 1951, a merger of those with a Mapai majority (3 settlements) with the Hever haKvutzot organization (40 settlements) whose membership belongs to the Mapai in its entirety.   ✳

It is a significant phenomenon that, among the new immigrants who established most of the rural settlements since independence, the share of the Sephardi and Oriental Jews was considerably greater than their proportion among the other immigrants. In the period from January 1947 to July 1951, less than 50% of the immigrants were Sephardi and Oriental Jews. Of the 231 settlements, however, founded by new immigrants in this period, 136, or 59% were established by Sephardi and Oriental Jews, and only 95, or 41%, by Ashkenazi Jews. (67 additional settlements were set up by Israelis, and 3 more by immigrants of "miscellaneous" origin.) Among the Oriental Jews, the share of the Yemenites was especially great in the establishment of new rural settlements. The 45,000 Yemenite Jews who came to the country in the period in question, constituted only 7.5% of the total number of immigrants. Yet of the 234 new settlements established by the new immigrants, 57, or 24.3%, were set up by Yemenites. North African Jews, with 35 settlements, held the second place, and Iraqi Jews, with 15, the third.✶

8. The Changing Ethnic Composition

The awakening desire of the Oriental Jews to migrate to the independent Jewish State has already wrought a decisive change in the ethnic composition of the immigration current. From the end of World War I to the end of World War II, 86% of the immigrants to Palestine were Ashkenazim and only 14% Sephardim and Oriental Jews. In 1948 the change set in: of the 118,912 immigrants who reached the shores of Israel in that year 32.8% were Sephardi and Oriental Jews. In 1949 the immigration showed, for the first time in the history of modern Palestine and Israel, a non-Ashkenazi majority: 57.7% of the immigrants were Sephardi and Oriental Jews. In 1950 their percentage sank to 50.6, but in 1951 it rose to 72.3.

The influx of the Sephardi and Oriental Jews soon began to be felt in the percentage level of their communities in the ethnic composition of Israel. By December 31, 1948, the number of the Sephardi and Oriental Jews in Israel rose to 23.7%. By March 1, 1949, it reached 24.4%. By July 1 of the same year it increased to 27.2%, and on December 31, 1949, it constituted 31 per cent of the Jewish popu-

✶ Cf. *The Jewish Agency's Digest*, Aug. 31, 1951, vol. III, no. 50.

JEWISH IMMIGRATION TO PALESTINE AND ISRAEL, 1882-1952[1]

Years	Total	Ashkenazi Jews	Per cent[2]	Sephardi & Oriental Jews	Per cent[2]	Of Unkown Origin
1882-1903[3]	25,000	24,000	96	1,000	4	—
1904-1913[3]	40,000	38,000	95	2,000	5	—
1919-1923	35,183	29,000	92.4	2,400	7.6	3,783
1924-1931	81,613	64,000	86.7	9,800	13.3	7,813
1932-1939	224,785	170,000	91.6	15,600	8.4	39,185
1940-1945	54,109	25,000	61.7	15,500	38.3	13,609
1946	17,760	6,138	78.4	1,695	21.6	9,927[4]
1947	21,542	18,168	93.2	1,340	6.8	2,034
1948[5]	118,912	69,517	67.2	33,813	32.8	15,582
1949	239,141	99,112	42.3	134,824	57.7	5,205
1950	169,405	82,983	49.4	84,940	50.6	1,482
1951	173,901	48,197	27.7	125,456	72.3	248
1952[6]	14,920	4,949	33.2	9,971	66.8	—

[1] Sources: *Statistical Handbook of Jewish Palestine, Jerusalem,* 1947; *Statistical Bulletin of Israel.*

[2] The percentage of the Ashkenazi and of the Sephardi and Oriental Jewish immigrants was calculated on the basis of the sum total of only those immigrants whose country of birth was known.

[3] Unofficial estimates.

[4] Presumably the majority of these were European Ashkenazi Jews.

[5] From May 15, 1948 (the date of the independence of Israel) to Dec. 31, 1948, there were 101,828 immigrants.

[6] First half of the year only.

lation. With the arrival of 120,000 Iraqi Jews in 1950-51, the percentage of Sephardi and Oriental Jews in Israel reached about 40% by the end of 1951. Their numbers are bound to show additional increase in the next few years due to continued immigration from the Middle East.

As long as the Jewish community of Palestine was a minority group within a larger aggregate of peoples under the mandatory regime of Britain, it constituted a separate entity with a narrowly drawn socio-political horizon. The Arabs of Palestine stood beyond the pale, and although social, economic and cultural contact between them and the *Yishuv* existed, they were not, and could not be, felt as part of the totality of Jewish life in Palestine. With the establishment of Israel, however, the situation changed radically. Israel is now a state and, as such, it is responsible for all the peoples living within its boundaries, including the non-Jewish population groups, the Moslem and Christian Arabs, the Druzes, and all the other minorities.* As it happens, practically all of these minority groups

* Cf. Chapter VIII: The Non-Jewish Minorities.

ETHNIC COMPOSITION OF THE JEWISH POPULATION OF
PALESTINE AND ISRAEL FROM 1936 to 1952[1]

Year	Total	Ashkenazi Jews	Per cent	Sephardi and Oriental Jews	Per cent
1936	404,000	315,000	76.7	94,000	23.3
1939	445,000	345,000	77.5	100,000	22.5
1943	533,000	423,000	79.4	110,000	20.6
1945	592,000	460,000	77.7	132,000	22.3
1946	622,000	483,000	77.7	139,000	22.3
1947	641,000	501,000	78.1	140,000	21.9
1948[2]	759,000	579,000	76.3	180,000	23.7
1949[2]	1,014,000	691,000	69	323,000	31
1950[2]	1,203,000	787,000	65.5	416,000	34.5
1951[2]	1,405,000	853,000	60.7	552,000	39.3
1952[3]	1,430,000	862,000	60.3	568,000	39.7 ✳

[1] Calculations based on data contained in the sources mentioned in the previous table.
[2] From 1948 to 1951 provisional figures.
[3] Provisional figures, as of July 1, 1952.

in Israel are Oriental peoples. Culturally, therefore, they are closely related to the Oriental Jews. If their numbers (about 180,000) are added to that of the Sephardi and Oriental Jews, it is found that already in 1952 over 50% of the total population of Israel consisted of non-Western elements.

9. Capital and Labor

Of the total number of immigrants who reached Palestine from the end of World War I to the end of World War II, almost 23% (taking earners and dependents together) were capitalists, that is, people with limited but sufficient means to establish business enterprises in the country. For a number of years the minimum amount required of an immigrant family to qualify for a special immigration visa as a capitalist was 1,000 Palestinian Pounds which was the equivalent of $5,000, but had in pre-war years a considerably higher purchasing power. Most of these so-called capitalists invested their limited capital in small business enterprises which enabled them to make a living only because, in addition to employing others, they invested their own labor as well. More than 47% of the total were laborers, and almost 19% were dependants of residents in Palestine. The rest, about 11%, were juveniles without families or people of unspecified occupations.

It was the very high percentage of capitalists and laborers together (about 70%) that determined the socio-economic structure of Jewish Palestine. The numerical relationship between the two groups was fortunate: for every two laborers one capitalist immigrated, thus creating a steady demand for working hands. One of the most significant differences between the traditional Middle Eastern social structure and that of the modern West is the absence in the Middle East of anything comparable to the solidly-entrenched and numerically-significant middle class, which is characteristic of advanced countries. With the immigration of about 84,000 small capitalists (including dependents) there came into being in Palestine a middle class on the European model, sharply differentiating the entire social structure of the Jewish sector of the country from that of the Arab sector as well as from that of other Arab states.

The influx of capital together with the immigration of large numbers of predominantly young people resulted in a marked economic development in Jewish Palestine based on industry on a scale approximating that of Western Europe. Of the total number of earners (125,000) who immigrated from 1919 to 1945, 33.4% were originally workers in industry and handicrafts, 13.6% were unskilled laborers, 6.6% worked in building and construction, and 1.2% in transport and communications. The occupational structure of the immigrants thus closely resembled that which characterizes Western Europe and the United States, and differed widely from the typical Middle Eastern occupational pattern.

The entrenchment of this Western-type society was largely accomplished when the State gained its independence. Following the oft-voiced demand for the opening of the gates of Palestine to all Jews, the Israeli Government announced an open door policy for all Jewish immigrants. Had the immigrants who subsequently began to arrive in unprecedented numbers been of the same or similar character as those who came up to 1947, the hardships of the first few years of Israel's existence would have been considerably mitigated. The Western-type life established in the country by the immigrants who came from the West would have continued to receive reinforcements from the same quarters.

But the post-independence immigration was profoundly different in many respects. The changes in the ethnic composition were dealt with above. The occupational structure of the immigrants who have come to Israel since independence also showed a considerable disparity when compared with the immigration during the Mandatory period. The most significant difference between the two immigrations is the marked decrease in the percentage of the gainfully occupied (or economically active) population in relation to the total number of immigrants. In the 1919-1945 period, 31.6% of the immigrants had been economically active abroad prior to their immigration, which means that the number of dependents per earner was somewhat more than two. In the years 1949 to 1951, only 23.7% were economically active prior to their immigration, that is, each earner had an average of more than three dependants.

Significant changes can be observed also in the percentage of the various occupations among those gainfully employed prior to their immigration. (Cf. table below.) Compared with the corresponding figures in Mandatory times, one notes first of all a decrease by more than two thirds in the number of those engaged in agricultural pursuits. The average of those engaged in industry and construction in the three years 1949-51 is somewhat lower than the 1919-1945 figure, and, in addition, one suspects that the proportion of the unskilled laborers must have been considerably higher in 1949-51. The increase in transport and communications workers is due to the fact that many Oriental Jewish immigrants gave porterage as their occupation abroad which was included under this heading. Persons engaged in public administration and professions also show a decrease which, coupled with the generally lower percentage of the economically active sector, was sufficient to create an acute

OCCUPATIONAL STRUCTURE OF THE JEWISH IMMIGRANTS TO PALESTINE IN 1919-1945 AND TO ISRAEL IN 1949-1951.[1]

Occupations	1919-1945 Number	%	1949 Number	%	1950 Number	%	1951 Number	%
Agriculture and Primary Product.	19,491	15.6	2,134	5.1	2,444	4.9	2,663	5.7
Industry, Constr. & Unskilled Lab.	66,898	53.6	24,353	58.0	23,713	48.3	20,177	43.0
Transport and Communications	1,449	1.2	2,057	4.9	1,352	2.7	1,164	2.4
Commerce	16,693	13.3	5,234	12.5	7,777	15.7	10,631	22.6
Public Administr. and Professions	14,544	11.6	3,922	9.4	4,737	9.6	3,500	7.4
Domestic, Personal Service and Clerical Work	5,284	4.2	4,122	9.9	9,041	18.3	8,842	18.9
Total Gainfully Occupied	125,019		41,842		49,404		46,977	
Total Number of Immigrants	394,683		239,141		169,405		173,901	
% of Gainfully Occupied in Total	31.6		17.5		29.3		27.0	

[1] Calculated on the basis of data contained in the *Statistical Handbook of Jewish Palestine*, Jerusalem, 1947; *Statistical Bulletin of Israel*, March-April, 1950 and April-September, 1951; *Alon Listatistiqa* of the Histadrut, Tel Aviv, March, 1952.

shortage in professionally skilled peoples, such as doctors, teachers and technicians. The increase in the category of domestic and personal service and clerical work was due to the relatively large number of people who claimed clerical work as their occupation.

This general deterioration of the immigrant population in the matter of skills possessed has had different causes in the two major groupings into which the post-independence immigrants fell: the Oriental and the European Jews. As to the Oriental Jews, their occupational structure reflects the special place they occupied within the backward economies of the Middle Eastern countries. They were mainly engaged in commerce on a small scale, and in handicraft, often on the traditional Middle Eastern level where no sharp distinction can be made between the two. Many Yemenite Jews, for instance, were silversmiths, manufacturing as well as selling ornamental jewelry, and thus being both craftsmen and merchants at the same time.

While the general character of the human material which came from the Oriental countries after the independence of Israel remained much the same as during the Mandatory period, a marked change occurred in the composition of the immigrants who came from the West. The First *Aliya* (1882-1903) was composed of idealists who came from Russia and established "colonies" in Palestine. The Second and Third *Aliyot* (1903-1913 and 1919-1923 respectively) brought a pioneering element from Eastern Europe who created new forms of rural settlements. The Fourth *Aliya* (1924-1931) was composed of pioneers as well as middle class people who settled mostly in the towns. The Fifth *Aliya* (1932-1939) consisted of a large number of Eastern and Central European Jews (among the latter many from Germany) who brought with them a good deal of capital and developed industry, trade and agriculture on a large scale. Immigration from the beginning of World War II to the foundation of Israel (1940-1947) was on a relatively small scale and its weight was barely felt within the population as a whole. The huge post-independence immigration from Europe (about 300,000 from 1948 to 1951) brought to the country the remnants of concentration, labor and extermination camps, displaced and uprooted persons, many of them penniless and destitute, and a young generation which grew up without family and school. The skills which were needed by these in order to survive were not such as would enable them to find their place in the expanding economy of Israel. A difficult process of adjustment, although of a different nature and of a more limited scope, was therefore required in their case as much as it was in the case of the immigrants from the Middle East.

Chapter Four

Demographic Highlights

1. The Growth of Jerusalem

The true significance of the changes in the immigration currents surveyed in the previous chapter will become evident only after a demonstration of the great cultural differences which separate the various Jewish communities from one another. First, however, it seems advisable to adduce certain demographic considerations. Demography deals with the statistical study of populations as to births, marriages, mortality, health and so forth, and is usually restricted to physical conditions and vital statistics.

It has been the finding of students of Jewish demography that the demographic picture of the Jews in every country shows a marked similarity to that of the non-Jewish population of the same country. There were always, to be sure, certain differences between the demographic data of a Jewish and of a non-Jewish group of a given locality, but these differences were insignificant when compared with those shown by the Jewish community of one country against the Jews of another country.

Reliable and accurate demographic data as to both Jews and non-Jews exist mainly in Western countries only, that is, in Central and Western Europe and in America. But also the less reliable and less accurate data, which are to be found in Eastern Europe and in the countries of the Middle East, show that the demographic resemblance between the Jewish and non-Jewish population exists there as well.

Consequently, the various Jewish communities in Israel, composed as they are of a majority of immigrants and only of a minority of Palestinian-born persons (the so-called *sabras*), show a wide range of variation in demographic characteristics. Unfortunately, the demographic study of the Jewish ethnic groups in Israel is in its very infancy, and the data at our disposal are insufficient for more than the barest outline of the country's demographic structure. The situation is somewhat better as to Jerusalem which has been studied more thoroughly and which, incidentally, is the most fascinating of all the landmarks of Israel with its unique, mosaic-like ethnic configuration.

Pre-partition Jerusalem had a total population of about 167,000 (in 1947), of which over 100,000 were Jews and the rest mainly Arabs. In a rough estimate, the non-Jewish population of Jerusalem was divided equally between Moslems and Christians. Of this segment of the population we shall have more to say in the chapter dealing with the non-Jewish minorities in Israel.

As to the Jewish population of Jerusalem, up to about 30 years ago this was Oriental in its overwhelming majority. During four hundred years of Turkish rule over Palestine the country was one of the provinces of the Ottoman Turkish Empire. To migrate from the Balkans —also under Turkish rule—from Anatolia, from Egypt, or from Southern Arabia to Palestine was a relatively simple matter, apart from the technical difficulties in transportation, something like moving from one state to another in the United States. As late as 1856, over 70% of the Jews of Jerusalem belonged to the Sephardi and Oriental communities, and it was only in the 1920's that the number of the Ashkenazi Jews caught up with that of the Sephardi-Orientals. The following table shows the development of the two main sectors of Jewish Jerusalem from the middle of the 19th century to 1939.

THE ASHKENAZIC AND SEPHARDIC-ORIENTAL JEWISH
POPULATION OF JERUSALEM FROM 1856 TO 1939*

Year	Total No. Jews	Ashkenazim	Sephardim & Orientals	In % Ashken.	Orient.
1856	5,700	1,700	4,000	30	70
1880	13,920	6,660	7,260	47	53
1890	25,300	13,600	11,700	54	46
1899	28,228	15,180	13,048	54	46
1913	50,000	25,000	25,000	50	50
1916	26,605	13,125	13,480	49	51
1939	80,850	42,576	38,274	52.7	47.3

* Based on Gurevich, *The Jews of Jerusalem*, Jerusalem, 1940, p. 22.

Until 1812 officially all the Jews of Jerusalem belonged to the Sephardi community. This community included a thin substratum of Jews whose tradition maintained that their ancestors had never left Palestine at all, but had continued to live there ever since the destruction of Jerusalem by Titus (70 C. E.), and who were therefore called by the Arabic name *"musta'rabin,"* that is "Arabicized ones." In addition to these, the descendents of Jews who returned to Jerusalem from North Africa and Europe before the Crusades and were amalgamated with the local Jews, together with the Jews who came from Iraq, the Yemen and other Middle Eastern countries, counted themselves as members of the Sephardi community after the more considerable immigration of genuine Sephardi Jews reached Jerusalem following their expulsion from Spain in 1492.

In the beginning of the 19th century, the growth of the non-Sephardi groups among the Jews of Jerusalem provided the impetus for one group after another to secede from the Sephardi community organization and to set up communities of their own. The first to do so were the Ashkenazi Jews, who in 1812 organized their own community. They were followed in 1854 by the Jews from North Africa, mainly Moroccans, called *Mughrabim* in Arabic (with the Hebrew plural suffix appended), or *Ma'aravim* in Hebrew, meaning "Westerners" (i.e., West Africans). In 1863 the Georgian Jews (called *Gurjim*) followed suit, while 1868 saw the foundation of the Bokharan Jewish community in Jerusalem. In 1883 the Yemenite Jewish community was founded and in 1902 that of the Urfalis, the Jews who came from Urfa, a town in Turkey near the Syrian border.

The foundations of the Ashkenazi community in Jerusalem in 1812 were laid by the followers of the Gaon of Vilna who four years previously had settled in Safed and later moved to Jerusalem. This was the beginning of the so-called "old *Yishuv*" in Jerusalem, consisting of extremely orthodox Jews organized into several *Kolelim*, or communities, each with a *Halukka* system (cf. above, pp. 56-7) of its own. A hundred years later this old *Yishuv* numbered about 10,000, and this approximately is their number to this day, due to the effects of desertion from their ranks which neutralizes both their considerable natural increase and the smaller increment of their numbers due to immigration.

THE DIVISION OF THE OLD *YISHUV* IN 1916 ACCORDING TO *KOLELIM*.

Russian *Kolelim* ....7,000 persons

Of these, in *Kolel* Vilna 1,400
Of these, in *Kolel* Warsaw 1,400
Of these, in *Kolel* Grodno 1,100
Of these, in *Kolel* Wolhynia 1,000

Austro-Hungarian *Kolelim* ....3,500 persons

Of these, in *Kolel* Ungarn 1,800
Of these, in *Kolel* Galicia 1,000

Source: Gurevich, *The Jews of Jerusalem*, 1940, p. 21.

We have a clearer picture of the ethnic composition of Jewish Jerusalem than of any other place in Israel or the country as a whole due to the statistical study made in 1939 by the late Dr. David Gurevich, chief statistician of the Jewish Agency for Palestine in Jerusalem. However, even in this internal Jewish census, which was the most detailed enumeration ever made in Palestine up to that time, the various Ashkenazi Jewish communities are treated as one homogeneous population group. For instance, no answer can be found in the study to such a simple question as, how many Russian or Polish or German Jews were in Jerusalem at the time of the enumeration. The only data which give us any idea, if not of the number of Jews belonging to the various Ashkenazi communities, at least of the number and identity of the countries whence they came to Palestine, are those which enumerate the Jews of Jerusalem according to places of birth. Here we find that of 75,150 Jews of Jerusalem in September 1939 who consented to cooperate in the census (5,700 refused, bringing the grand total to 80,850), 34,171 were Palestinian born, and 40,979 were born abroad. A mere enumeration of the countries from which these immigrants came to settle in Jerusalem will give us some idea of the mosaic-like ethnic composition of the city. The Ashkenazi Jews came from Poland, Germany, Russia, Austria, Rumania, Hungary, U. S. A., Lithuania, England, Czechoslovakia, Latvia, France, Holland and several more European and American countries. The Sephardi Jews came from Turkey, Yugoslavia, Greece, Italy and Bulgaria. The Oriental Jews showed the greatest fragmentation, as can be seen from the following list of the Oriental Jewish community organizations (*kehillot*) in Jerusalem, with the date of their foundation or registration with the District Commissioner's Office:

Moghrebites (from North Africa, mainly Morocco)	1844
Gruzinim (or Gurjim, from Georgia in the Caucasus)	1863
Bokharans	1868
Persians	1877
Halabim (from Aleppo, a city in North Syria)	1880
Yemenites	1883
Daghestanim (from Daghestan, a district in the Caucasus)	1887
Bavlim (from Bavel, i.e., Baghdad, Iraq)	1888
Afghans	1900
Urfalim (from Urfa, a town on the southern border of Turkey)	1902
Crimeans	1909
Hararim (i.e., mountaineers, from the Caucasus)	1912
Jarmuklim (from Cermik, a town in Turkey)	1920
Sviriklim (from Siverek, a town in Turkey)	1922
Urmiyim (from Urmia a town in Iranian Kurdistan)	1923
Damaskim (from Damascus in Syria)	1925
Meshhedim (from Meshed, Khorasan, N. E. Iran)	1928

Iranim (a separate community from the Persians)	1931
Kurdim (Kurds, mainly from Amadiya, Dehok etc., in Iraqi Kurdistan)	1931
Targum (another group of Kurdish Jews)	1932
Arbelim (from Arbel, a town in Iraqi Kurdistan)	1936
Diarbekrim (from Diar Bekr, a town in Turkish Kurdistan)	1936
Asshurim (i.e., Assyrians, mainly from Mosul, N. Iraq)	1938
Zakhoim (from Zakho, a town in Iraqi Kurdistan)	1938
Nesibin and Kamishlu (from the twin towns, Nusaybin in Turkey and Kamechlie in Syria)	1938
Adenim (from Aden Colony)	1938

2. Vital Statistics

One of the most significant demographic characteristics of a population is the *birthrate*.* In general terms it has already been stated that the Ashkenazi Jews have low birthrates, like the European peoples, while the Oriental Jews have high birthrates, like the other peoples of the Middle East. Birthrate is usually calculated by the annual births per thousand of the population. The significance of the differences in birthrate becomes, however, more easily comprehensible if, instead of relying on the crude annual birthrate figures, one calculates the average number of female children born to women of the various ethnic groups in question during their entire lifetime. This is called the *gross rate of reproduction*. This calculation was done by Bachi, based on the statistics of 1938-1940 in Palestine, and the results he arrived at are very significant.§ Taking the mothers' countries of birth as the basis of classification, the Jewish communities of Palestine fell into three distinct groups, each with a characteristic range of its own in the average numbers of children (or rate of reproduction), and accurately corresponding to the threefold division of the Jews into Ashkenazi, Sephardi and Oriental communities. There is no overlapping among the three ranges of rates, and, what is even more significant, there is a definite gap between the maximum of each lower range and the minimum of the next higher one. The average number of children of both sexes born to Ashkenazi mothers during their entire lifetime begins with a minimum of 1.32 (women born in Austria) and ends with a maximum of 1.83 (women born in all American countries taken together). The corresponding figures for Sephardi mothers begin with a minimum of 2.12 (Bulgaria) and reach a maximum of 3.55 (Turkey). The Oriental Jewish women lead with a minimum of 4.63 (Syria and the Lebanon) and a maximum of 7.28 (Yemenites).

* Cf. the Table on p. 84.

§ Cf. R. Bachi, "Population Problems of the Yishuv in Palestine" (Hebrew), in *Ahdut Haavoda, Meassef Mifleget Poale Eretz Yisrael, Meassef R'vi'i, Middot Q'lita*, Tel Aviv, 1946, p. 297.

CRUDE RATES OF BIRTHS, DEATHS, INFANT MORTALITY AND
NATURAL INCREASE OF THE JEWISH POPULATION OF PALESTINE
AND ISRAEL FROM 1922 TO 1952.[1]

Year	Birth Rate	Death Rate	Infant Mortality[2]	Natural Increase
1922	31.67	12.37	144.30	19.30
1923	36.46	14.70	126.03	21.76
1924	38.16	12.65	105.71	25.51
1925	32.65	14.89	132.11	17.76
1926	35.51	11.93	107.93	23.58
1927	34.60	13.26	115.38	21.34
1928	34.93	11.90	96.06	23.03
1929	33.63	11.60	89.68	22.03
1930	32.97	9.45	69.01	23.52
1931	32.20	9.58	81.59	22.62
1932	29.06	9.60	85.76	19.46
1933	29.02	9.21	80.48	19.81
1934	30.03	9.47	77.96	20.56
1935	30.64	8.53	64.15	22.11
1936	29.67	8.81	68.85	20.86
1937	26.47	7.72	57.20	18.75
1938	26.26	8.11	58.51	18.15
1939	23.02	7.57	54.00	15.45
1940	23.72	8.18	49.07	15.54
1941	20.67	7.89	55.59	12.78
1942	22.73	8.60	57.98	14.13
1943	29.04	7.72	44.14	21.32
1944	30.22	7.14	36.12	23.08
1945	30.3	6.7	35.8	23.6
1946	29.12	6.35	31.54	22.77
1947	31.09	6.48	29.22	24.52
1948	25.58	6.40	35.98[3]	19.18
1949	29.94	6.48	51.71[3]	23.11
1950	32.64[4]	6.48	46.58[3]	26.16[4]
1951	32.72[4]	6.41	39.02[3]	26.32[4]
✳ 1952[5]	31.10	6.60	37.16	24.50

[1] Sources: *Statistical Abstract of Palestine 1944-45*; *Statistical Handbook of Jewish Palestine*, Jerusalem, 1947; *Statistical Bulletin of Israel*.

[2] Per 1,000 of live births.

[3] The rise in infant mortality in 1948 and 1949 is due to the influx of Oriental Jewish immigrants. From 1950 on the situation was being increasingly controlled and infant mortality reduced. In 1949, infant mortality among the immigrants was 157. By 1951, this had been reduced to 82. In the *kibbutzim*, as a result of excellent infant care, it was 16.5. Cf. *The Jewish Agency's Digest*, Nov. 28, 1952, p. 176.

[4] The rise in birthrate and natural increase in 1950 and 1951 is due to the increasing percentage of Oriental Jews in the population.

[5] First half of the year only.

The following table shows the rates of reproduction in 28 Jewish ethnic groups:

AVERAGE NUMBER OF CHILDREN BORN TO JEWISH MOTHERS IN PALESTINE GROUPED ACCORDING TO THE MOTHERS' COUNTRIES OF BIRTH. BASED ON STATISTICAL DATA FROM 1938-1940.*

Mother's Country of Birth	Average No. of children	Average No. of girls (gross rate of repro- duction)	Net rate of repro- duction
Ashkenazi Communities			
Austria	1.32	0.64	0.60
Germany	1.47	0.71	0.66
Czechoslovakia	1.49	0.72	0.67
Latvia	1.56	0.76	0.71
Rumania	1.58	0.77	0.71
Poland	1.64	0.80	0.75
Lithuania	1.66	0.80	0.75
Hungary	1.66	0.81	0.75
Great Britain	1.66	0.81	0.75
Other European Countries	1.72	0.84	0.78
All American Countries	1.83	0.89	0.83
U.S.S.R. (exceptional)	2.46	1.19	1.11
Sephardi Communities			
Bulgaria	2.12	1.03	0.90
Other Asiatic Countries[1]	2.46	1.19	0.99
Italy	2.75	1.33	1.24
Other African Countries[2]	2.91	1.41	1.17
Egypt[3]	2.93	1.42	1.18
Greece	3.03	1.47	1.28
Palestine (mixed)	3.40	1.68	1.50
Yugoslavia	3.54	1.72	1.50
Turkey[4]	3.55	1.72	1.42
Oriental Jewish Communities			
Syria and Lebanon	4.63	2.25	1.86
Aden (Arabia)	5.11	2.48	2.05
Afghanistan	5.70	2.77	2.29
Iraq	5.79	2.81	2.32
Iran	6.41	3.11	2.57
Morocco	7.04	3.41	2.82
Yemen	7.28	3.53	2.92 ✳
Average for the *Yishuv*	2.16	1.05	0.98

* Source: R. Bachi, *Marriage and Fertility in the Various Classes of the Jewish Population of Palestine* (Hebrew), Jerusalem, 1944, pp. 159, 223-4.

[1] Including Oriental countries like Bokhara and the Caucasus. Based on 66 births only.

[2] Partly Oriental and partly Sephardi groups. Based on 12 births only.

[3] Mixed group of Oriental, Sephardi and European Jews.

[4] Mixed group of Oriental and Sephardi Jews.

The significance of the figures contained in the foregoing table lies in the following considerations: In order to keep a population on a constant level, the net rate of female reproduction, that is, the average number of female children born to a mother during her entire lifetime and remaining alive up to their 15th year, must be one. The net rate of reproduction for Ashkenazi mothers, according to the table, ranges from 0.60 to 0.83; it is therefore far below the required minimum for a stable population, and it actually shows that, if the indicated trend continues, the Ashkenazi population is bound to decrease by 17% to 40% in one generation. While all the Ashkenazi communities seem thus to be heading towards natural decrease, most of the Sephardi communities show a slight natural increase (ranging from 0.90 to 1.50). The net rate of reproduction of the Oriental Jewish communities ranges from 1.86 to 2.92. This is a considerable rate of natural increase which, at its upper limits, can almost treble the population within one generation.

A comparison of the gross and net reproduction rates gives us some ideas as to the extent of the infant and child mortality. In the Ashkenazi communities the difference between the two rates is slight (4-6 points), indicating a very low infant and child mortality. In the Sephardi group it is higher (13-30 points), and in the Oriental group very high (39-61 points), showing a moderately high and a very high infant and child mortality respectively. As a matter of fact, it is known that, in 1935-36, of every thousand children born to Ashkenazi families 32 died before reaching their first birthday; the corresponding figure among the Oriental Jews was 76. By 1945-46, the Ashkenazi infant mortality was reduced to 12, while the Oriental Jewish figure decreased to 26. The average Jewish infant mortality rate in 1947 was 28. With the great influx of Oriental Jews into Israel, an increase of the average infant mortality rate was inevitable, reaching a high of 51.71 in 1949. Energetic health and sanitary measures again reduced the rate to 46.58 in 1950, and to 39.02 in 1951, in spite of the continued mass immigration of Oriental Jews.[*]

Still another fact can be deduced from a scrutiny of the table on p. 85. Although the distinction between Ashkenazi and Sephardi Jewish communities is an old and traditional one, the distinction between the Sephardi and the Oriental Jews is overlooked at times. The Sephardi Jews themselves are inclined, for reasons of political expediency, to include under the Sephardi denominator also the

[*] Cf. *Palestine's Health in Figures.* Compiled by the Vaad Leumi . . . for the information of the U.N. Spec. Committee on Palestine. Pamphlet, n.d. *Statistical Bulletin of Israel.*

Oriental Jewish communities of Africa and Asia. The table shows that, at least so far as this particular demographic characteristic is concerned, the inclusion of the Oriental Jewish communities into the Sephardi group is not justified. Actually, the difference in the net rate of reproduction is greater between the Sephardi Jews and the Oriental Jews than between the Sephardi Jews and the Ashkenazi Jews. And the rate of reproduction is, as is well known, not a single, isolated phenomenon, but merely one of the most easily recognizable and demonstrable manifestations of a total way of life and cultural tradition.

These figures show that, barring changes in the trend of natural increase, and not counting the effects of additional immigration, there will remain within one generation, in place of a hundred Austrian Jewish women, only 60 in the country, while in place of a hundred Yemenite Jewish women, there will be 292. The Ashkenazi element thus will become relatively smaller, while the Oriental (and to a lesser extent also the Sephardi) element will go on increasing. The final effect of this will be to turn Israel into a country with a growing majority of Oriental population.   *

Similar results are obtained when the actual number of surviving children in families belonging to different ethnic groups is studied. The actual sizes of families in Jerusalem in 1939 was found to be as follows:

SIZE OF FAMILIES AMONG THE JEWS OF JERUSALEM IN 1939

	Families	Persons	Aver. Size of Fam.
Total Number	16,247	67,794	4.27
Ashkenazim	9,181	32,687	3.56
Bokharans	394	1,782	4.52
Sephardim	1,963	9,268	4.72
Yemenites	745	3,520	4.73
Georgians	197	958	4.86
Syrians	364	1,790	4.92
Moroccans	467	2,310	4.95
Persians	1,050	5,433	5.17
Iraqis	1,038	5,535	5.33
Kurds	799	4,318	5.40
Various & Unknown	49	193	3.94

*

The general trends shown by this table tally very well with those of the table on p. 85. The Ashkenazi Jews lead at the lower end of the list, the middle part is occupied by the Sephardi Jews (here undifferentiated), and the higher brackets are reserved for the Oriental Jews. The only exception here is that of the Bokharan

Jewish community which stands below the Sephardi. This can have two reasons: first, there might be an error in the small figure, as this survey included only 394 Bokharan Jewish families; and second, the small average of the Bokharans could be caused by the fact that this community, more than any other Oriental Jewish group, contains a high percentage of well-to-do merchants and businessmen, and their higher economic level might have influenced the average size of the families in this group.

In this connection yet another demographic fact has to be taken into consideration, namely, that in the Sephardi and Oriental Jewish communities the percentage of the young people is much higher than among the Ashkenazim. As the advanced hygienic and health services in Israel tend to equalize the originally considerable differences in life expectancy, this means that in a decade or two the surviving members of the Ashkenazi division of the Jewish people in the country will be relatively fewer than those of the other two divisions. The age structure of the various Jewish communities in Palestine in 1946 is shown in the table on page 89.

The significance of these figures will become more evident if we consider the percentage of those under the age of twenty in the four groups analyzed above.

PERCENTAGE OF THOSE AGED 0-19 IN THE VARIOUS
JEWISH COMMUNITIES IN PALESTINE IN 1946

Ashkenazi Jews	34.70
Sephardi Jews	47.51
Yemenite Jews	57.26
Other Oriental Jews	49.93

Based on these data of the reproduction rate, and presupposing that the population trends they show will remain constant for some time at least, one could easily calculate how many years it will take for the Sephardi and Oriental Jewish element to become the absolute majority in Israel, even in the event that additional immigration does not enter the picture. But immigration was the decisive factor in the ethnic composition of the *Yishuv* in the three decades preceding the establishment of the Jewish state, and it will remain at least one of the decisive factors in the years to come. We have seen (above, Chapter III) that up to World War II the immigration was heavily weighted in favor of the Ashkenazi element. Since the end of the war, and especially since the establishment of the Jewish State, however, the immigration balance has shown a steady shift towards a Sephardi-Oriental majority. The trend in immigration therefore, when combined with the superior natural increase of the Sephardi-

AGE STRUCTURE OF THE VARIOUS JEWISH COMMUNITIES
IN PALESTINE IN 1946 IN PERCENTAGE[*]

	0-4.9	5-9	10-14	15-19	20-24	25-29	30-34	35-39	40-44	45-49	50+	Unknown
Ashkenazim	10.93	8.74	6.70	8.33	7.19	15.45	13.10	9.42	5.75	3.12	10.49	0.78
Sephardim	13.84	12.47	10.98	10.52	7.71	10.85	9.37	6.66	4.97	2.84	9.64	0.45
Yemenites	19.07	16.40	12.21	9.58	7.13	8.21	6.35	5.23	4.44	2.69	7.70	0.66
Other Oriental Jewish Comm.-s	13.51	14.43	12.04	9.95	6.66	7.19	5.92	4.87	3.95	2.76	8.99	9.73

[*] Source: Gurevich and Gerz, *Agriculture and Jewish Agricultural Settlement in Palestine* (Hebrew), Jerusalem, 1947, p. 23.

Oriental Jewish communities, makes it even more evident that, barring some unforeseen change in the near future, Israel will very soon have a majority of Sephardi and Oriental Jews.

3. Occupational Structure

Significant differences are found to exist also in the occupational structure between the Ashkenazi sector of the population and the Sephardi and Oriental divisions. The Ashkenazi Jews surpass the Sephardi and Oriental Jews in technical skills, and their percentage is several times higher than that of the latter also in the professions, in banking and in clerical occupations. The percentage of Oriental Jews is higher in the trades and industry, in quarries, transportation (porters) and in the ownership of shops (small stores). The differences in the occupational structure of the women are even more outstanding: three-quarters of the Ashkenazi female earners work in fields such as the clothing industry, commerce, clerical work, medical and teaching professions etc., and only one-fourth of them work as household helpers; as against this, over two-thirds of the Oriental Jewish women who work outside their own houses are in domestic service. Taking the percentage of the Ashkenazi Jews in the various occupations as the basis (100%), the following occupa-

OCCUPATIONAL STRUCTURE OF JEWISH ETHNIC GROUPS IN JERUSALEM IN 1939.[1]

Occupations	Ashkenazi Jews	All Sephardi & Oriental Jews Together	Sephardi Jews	Yemenite Jews	North African Jews	Syrian Jews	Iraqi Jews	Kurdish Jews	Persian Jews	Bokharan Jews	Georgian Jews
Industry and Trades	100	148	168	135	206	177	133	144	146	88	95
Building, Construction and Public Works	100	164	79	289	—	—	172	217	198	—	—
Transport and Porterage	100	263	224	—	—	—	308	575	249	—	—
Finance	100	83	110	94	—	—	75	—	62	198	—
Commerce	100	123	125	66	94	168	166	77	155	143	140
Religion	100	65	51	—	—	—	—	—	—	—	—
Professions	100	14	32	—	—	—	—	—	—	—	—
Clerical Work	100	51	88	49	60	38	34	28	23	—	—
Domestic Service	100	256	152	353	255	182	252	392	296	295	214

[1] Source: Gurevich, *The Jews of Jerusalem*, Jerusalem, 1940.

tional structure is found among the Sephardi and Oriental Jews in Jerusalem. (See the table on page 90. Where the number of earners in a given occupation is less than 50, the percentage was not calculated and the space is left blank.)

A clearer picture will emerge if we compare the actual number of earners and their distribution among the various occupations in a characteristically Western and in an equally characteristic Middle Eastern Jewish community. If we multiply the number of Moroccan Jewish earners in Jerusalem by five, we get almost exactly the number of the German Jewish earners in the same city. The occupational structure of the two communities can then easily be compared and the striking differences noted.

OCCUPATIONAL STRUCTURE OF GERMAN AND MOROCCAN
JEWS IN JERUSALEM IN 1939.

(Number of Moroccans Jews multiplied by five. Based on Gurevich, *op. cit.*)

Occupations	German Jews			Moroccan Jews		
	Total	Males	Females	Total	Males	Females
Total number of earners	3,629	2,361	1,268	3,710	2,635	1,075
Agriculture	62	45	17	10	10	—
Industry and trade	511	354	157	1,260	1,065	195
Building and Public Works	73	72	1	275	270	5
Transportation and Traffic	66	66	—	115	115	—
Finance and Investments	312	224	88	105	70	35
Commerce	539	415	124	485	405	80
Religion	33	32	1	205	200	5
Professions	936	621	315	35	25	10
Clerical Work	459	313	146	365	305	60
Domestic Service	277	183	94	855	185	670
Supported and Unproductive (incl. students)	390	203	187	565	195	370

The most striking single instance of difference is that of the professions: the Germans have about 27 times as many professional people as the Moroccans (936 against 35). Of the 936 German Jewish professionals 653 were physicians, engineers, architects, lawyers, teachers, university teachers, or scientific workers. The category "Domestic Service" includes also private service and insufficiently described occupations, and this explains the figure 277 in the German group, while in the Moroccan group most of the 855 persons in this category, and certainly all the 670 women, worked as house-hold helpers. Also, the figures in the category "Industry and Trade" do not give the true picture unless we qualify them by stating that, of the 511 German Jews in these occupations, the majority worked in skilled trades and therefore earned a considerably higher income than the overwhelmingly unskilled Moroccan industrial laborers. Remarkable is the fact that over six times as many Moroccans were in religious professions as Germans; the explanation, of course, lies in the traditionally determined greater preoccupation of the Moroc-can Jews (like all the other Oriental Jews) with religion. The fact that three times as many German Jews as Moroccans were in the "Finance and Investment" category, reflects the higher percentage of wealthy people among the former. Finally, it is worth mentioning that in the German group the participation of women in earning a living in general was about 20% higher than among the Moroccans, and that 65% of the Moroccan women who worked for an income were employed in domestic service, while 25% of the German women worked in the professions. The general and unmistakable impression one gains after comparing the occupational structure of the two communities is that the Germans show a definite trend to concen-trate in the "higher" occupational brackets, while the Moroccans are characterized by a strong preponderance of the "lower" occupations; which, however, is but the Western way of stating that each of the two groups shows in its occupational structure a high degree of conformity to the occupational patterns prevalent in their respective home countries.

In recent years the Oriental and Sephardi Jews have taken a larger share in the establishment of new agricultural settlements than their percentage among the immigrants. In the period between January 1, 1947 and May 31, 1951, the number of Ashkenazi immi-grants, on the one hand, and of Sephardi and Oriental Jewish immigrants on the other, was equal, each group numbering about 320,000. Yet of the 231 agricultural settlements established in this period by the newcomers, 136, or 59%, were settled by Sephardi and Oriental Jews, and only 95, or 41%, by Ashkenazim. The breakdown by countries of origin is shown in the table on page 93.

4. Residential Segregation

The fact that the Ashkenazi Jewish communities, on the one hand, and the Sephardi and Oriental Jews, on the other, possess demo-graphically and culturally significant different characteristics, is demonstrated also by their tendency to settle in separate quarters. The city of Tel Aviv as well as the smaller towns (or larger *mosha-*

vot) have separate quarters inhabited mainly by Oriental Jews. Yemenite quarters, for instance, exist adjoining Petah Tikva, Rehovot, Rishon Lezion, etc. However, the place in which both the spatial segregation and the fusion of the largest number of different Jewish communities can best be studied is Jerusalem.

AGRICULTURAL SETTLEMENTS ESTABLISHED IN ISRAEL FROM JAN. 1, 1947, TO MAY 31, 1951 BY COUNTRY OF ORIGIN OF THE SETTLERS.*

Oriental Jews		Sephardi Jews		Ashkenazi Jews	
Country	No.	Country	No.	Country	No.
Yemen	57	Bulgaria	8	Central and Eastern	
North Africa	35	Turkey	5	Europe	82
Iraq	15	Yugoslavia	4	Anglo-Saxon	
Iran	8	Greece	2	Countries	9
India	2			South America	4
Total	117	Total	19	Total	95

* Cf. *The Jewish Agency's Digest*, August 31, 1951, p. 1937. In addition to the above, in the same period 67 settlements were established by Jews of Palestinian origin, and 3 by others.

In 1939 Jerusalem had 80,850 Jewish inhabitants (in 1950 they numbered about 120,000). The concentration of certain communities ✳ in certain quarters of the city was in several cases due to historical facts, as has been indicated in the beginning of this chapter. Once a concentration of a certain community in a certain quarter came into existence, the later immigrants belonging to the same community tended to settle in the same quarter, thus increasing the density of the population in the quarter; or they settled in its immediate vicinity, thus making it expand spatially. This was especially the case among the members of the Old *Yishuv*, on the one hand, and of the Oriental Jewish communities, on the other. Thus, while no such thing as a Russian Jewish, or Polish Jewish, or German Jewish quarter exists in Jerusalem, *Botei Ungarn* or *Botei Warsha* (Hungarian houses, Warsaw houses) are closely delimited quarters inhabited by people of the Old *Yishuv*, as are the Bokharan, Yemenite, Kurdish, etc., quarters inhabited by immigrants from Bokhara, Yemen, Kurdistan and their descendents. However—and this is a very important characteristic of the Oriental Jewish quarters—in the great majority of cases a given quarter is inhabited by Jews belonging to two or more Oriental communities, as well as by a small percentage of Ashkenazi Jews. As an illustration for this, let us take the Nahlat Zion and Knesset quarters which, in the 1939 census of

Jewish Jerusalem, were treated as a single unit (no. xvi) of enumeration. In this quarter, 4,473 persons were enumerated, of whom 3,111 were Oriental Jews, 1,092 were Sephardim and 270 Ashkenazim. Of the Oriental Jews, 1,190 belonged to the Persian Jewish community, 390 were Iraqi Jews, 382 were Aleppo (Syria) Jews, and 319 Moroccan Jews.

The distribution of the Ashkenazi, Sephardi and Oriental Jews in the 22 census-districts of Jerusalem (including the Old City and the outlying suburbs) in 1939 is shown in the table on page 95.

The most important general observation which can be based on this table is that the segregation of the Ashkenazi and the Oriental communities from each other is greater than that of either of them from the Sephardi group. More than three-fourths of all the Ashkenazi Jews in Jerusalem lived in quarters (eleven census districts) which had an Ashkenazi majority ranging from 97% to 64%; and less than one-fourth of the Ashkenazim lived in quarters with a combined Sephardi-Oriental majority. The Oriental Jews were even more confined to their own quarters: 87% of them lived in quarters with a combined Sephardi-Oriental majority ranging from 98% to 57%. Out of the eleven census districts which had a combined Sephardi-Oriental majority, seven had an Oriental absolute majority as against the combined total of the Ashkenazim and the Sephardim, three had a combined Sephardi-Oriental majority, and only one small quarter had a Sephardi absolute majority. Only 13% of the Oriental Jews lived in quarters with an Ashkenazi majority.

The Sephardi Jews occupied an intermediary position between the Ashkenazim and the Orientals. Thirty-two per cent of them lived in those quarters of the city which had an absolute Ashkenazi majority; another 32% in those quarters in which there was an absolute Oriental majority; and the remaining 36% lived in quarters in which they held the balance between the Ashkenazim and the Oriental Jews. We shall see later that also in several other demographic characteristics the Sephardim hold a similarly intermediary position between the other two, more fundamentally different divisions of the Jewish people in Jerusalem, as well as in Israel as a whole.

A second important observation concerns the limited nature or relativity of the sectional segregation. There exists no single quarter in which only members of one of the three main divisions would live. The most purely Ashkenazi quarter, Rehavia (not counting Mount Scopus which was no real residential section but the seat of the Hadassah Hospital and the Hebrew University), had 6% Sephardi and Oriental Jewish residents, while the most purely Oriental section, census district xv, had 2% Ashkenazim and another 15% Se-

THE JEWISH POPULATION OF JERUSALEM BY COMMUNITIES AND CENSUS DISTRICTS IN 1939

(Source: D. Gurevich, *The Jews of Jerusalem*, Jerusalem, 1940.)

Census Distr.	Quarters	Ashkenazim Persons	%	Sephardim Persons	%	Orientals Persons	Seph.-Orient. %	Total Persons
I	Jaffa Road, St. of Prophets	1,965	74	390		293	26	2,648
II	King George Ave., Ben Yehuda St., Bezalel St.	4,543	80	503		607	20	5,653
III	Zikhron Moshe, Ruhama	2,107	43	1,369		1,382	57	4,848
IV	Ahwa; Yegi'a Kapayim	2,031	72	317		425	28	2,773
V	Meqor Barukh, Romema	2,699	66	985		390	34	4,074
VI	Geula, Kerem, Abraham, Tel Arza	6,031	87	216		651	13	6,898
VII	Bokharan Qtr., Mahanayim, Sanhedriya	581	12	214		4,069	88	4,864
VIII	Mea Shearim, Hungarian Houses, Warsaw Houses	5,163	89	200		426	11	5,789
IX	Old Beit Yisrael	2,127	41	181		2,842	59	5,150
X	New Beit Yisrael, Nahlat Yitzhaq	1,706	36	326		2,496	62	4,528
XI	Rehavia	5,376	94	278		82	6	5,736
XII	Newei Bezalel, Shaarei Hesed, Nahlat Zadoq	1,257	87	50		131	13	1,438
XIII	Mahanei Yehuda, Even Yisrael	833	33	1,302		720	67	2,857
XIV	Sukkat Shalom, Mishkenot	728	35	599		761	65	2,088
XV	Zikhron Yosef, Nahlat Zion	97	2	603		4,090	98	4,790
XVI	Nahlat Zion, Knesset	270	6	1,092		3,111	94	4,473
XVII	Nahlat Ahim, Zikhron Ahim	1,063	22	395		3,274	78	4,732
XVIII	Yemin Moshe	191	19	551		266	81	1,008
XIX	Beit Hakerem, Qiryat Moshe, Bait weGan	2,063	64	421		561	36	3,045
XX	Talpiyot	1,150	93	63		24	7	1,237
XXI	Mount Scopus	149	97	3		2	3	154
XXII	Old City	446	22	527		1,084	78	2,057
	Total in Quarters with Ashkenazi Majority	32,427	76	3,426 (32%)		3,592 (13%)	18	39,445
	Total in Quarters with Sephard.-Or. Majority	10,149	24	7,161 (68%)		24,095 (87%)	82	41,405
	Grand Total	42,576	52.6	10,587		27,687	47.4	80,850

phardim. The tendency towards segregation, or, more precisely, towards concentration in separate residential areas, is conditioned by economic factors (higher rentals in the modern Ashkenazi sectors of the city, which only a very few of the Sephardi and Oriental Jews can afford to pay); by a predilection especially prevalent among the Oriental Jews to reside amongst others of their own community; and by the fact that the residential quarters inhabited by Oriental Jews have often a slum-like character (high density, low cleanliness, etc.) which makes them undesirable in the eyes of the great majority of the Ashkenazi Jews. However, there has never been in any of these quarters, nor in any other locality in Israel, an attempt on the part of the residents of an area to exclude from their neighborhood members of any community, Ashkenazi, Sephardi or Oriental. The majority of the Jews of Jerusalem lived (and continue to live to this day) in mixed quarters, and even if there are in some areas a few small blocks occupied only by members of a single community, they imperceptibly merge into blocks in which members of another community live or which are inhabited by members of several communities. The so-called "quarters" (*shekhunot*) of Jerusalem are thus places in which old community traditions can easily be preserved, but which can also serve as a day-to-day meeting ground for people hailing from different communities and thus an excellent locale for mutual cultural influences.

This is especially the case with the Oriental communities among themselves. In most of the census districts showing an Oriental Jewish majority, considerable groups of two or more such communities were found to live either closely side by side or in a mosaic-like mixture. In the Bokharan quarter (popularly called *Bukharaliyya*) and adjoining areas, about 1,000 Bokharan Jews lived side by side with about 1,500 Persian Jews, as well as several hundred Afghan Jews. In the Nahlat Ahim and Zikhron Ahim quarters (together with the neighboring Nahlat Zion quarter popularly called "the *Nahlaot*"), the 2,500 Oriental Jewish residents belonged to four communities: that of the Urfali, Yemenite, Kurdish and Aleppan Jews. The other side of the picture was that none of the communities was entirely concentrated within one single quarter. Frequently immigrants from the same country settled in two or more quarters, often at quite a distance from one another. In addition to the 812 Yemenites in the *Nahlaot*, 666 Yemenites lived in the Old Beit Yisrael quarter near the opposite end of the city. Considerable Persian Jewish concentrations were found, in addition to the Bokharan quarter, also in the nearby New Beit Yisrael and Nahlat Yitzhaq quarters, but also in the distant Nahlat Zion and Knesset quarters. About half of the

Oriental Jewish residents of the Old City of Jerusalem were Moroccan Jews (479 persons); other large groups of Moroccan Jews were
found in the western sections of the new city.

After the establishment of the State and the conquest of practically all of new Jerusalem by the Jews, the residential segregation of
the Ashkenazi, Sephardi and Oriental Jewish communities nevertheless continued. Many of the new immigrants were either settled by
the Jewish authorities in the houses deserted by the Arabs, or else
they themselves took the law into their own hands and, without
waiting for official authorization or allocation of lodgings, "invaded"
the empty houses and were later confirmed by the authorities in
their possession of an apartment, or, more frequently, of a part of it.
Those sections of southern Jerusalem which were formerly known
under the names of Katamon or Greek Colony, German Colony,
Upper and Lower Baqa, and which were populated by Moslem and
Christian Arabs as well as by highly Arabicized Greeks, Germans,
Armenians, and some Englishmen, became settled almost overnight
by Jewish immigrants. Occasionally it happened that people with the
most different cultural and ethnic backgrounds were placed in one
single house or even in one single apartment in which several families were given one room each, with a share in the kitchen and other
facilities. The general situation, however, was that immigrant groups
tended to settle in closed clusters which preserved at least a semblance of the character of their old social environment.   ✳

5. "Mixed" Marriages

In the foregoing discussion we have several times referred to
the Sephardi and Oriental divisions of the Jewish population as one
single element. It should be clearly understood that this was done
for the sole purpose of facilitating over-all classification and for
pointing up the basic demographic differences existing between the
Ashkenazi division as a whole, on the one hand, and the Sephardi-
Oriental divisions as a whole, on the other. There is no intention to
neglect or to minimize the differences which exist between the
Sephardi Jewish division and the Oriental Jewish division, or between any two of the numerous communities belonging to the latter.
In later chapters we shall have occasion to deal with some of the
most important Oriental Jewish communities separately and to
discuss the specific characteristics not shared with others.

There is, however, at least one demographic characteristic which
seems to justify a lumping together of all the Oriental Jewish communities—a proceeding which, in the case of the various Ashkenazi
communities is regularly and unquestioningly resorted to by every

student of the Israeli scene. This characteristic is the frequency of intermarriage which has been found to be several times higher among members belonging to the Sephardi and Oriental divisions than among the Ashkenazi Jews. A study of the intermarriages between members of the various Jewish communities is very interesting and instructive also for an evaluation of the status differences existing among these communities.

The statistical returns for Jerusalem in 1939 showed that, of the 16,247 married men enumerated, 1,233, or some 7.5%, married outside their own community; however, one must not lose sight of the fact that the census took all the Ashkenazi communities as one single group, and all the Sephardi Jews as another single group. In other words, if a Russian Jew married a German Jewish woman, this was not counted as intermarriage between two communities, both being Ashkenazim; neither was the marriage of a Turkish Jew and a Bulgarian Jewess, both being counted as Sephardim. But if an Urfali Jew married a Kurdish Jewess, or even if a Jew from Damascus married a Jewess from Aleppo, this was counted as an intermarriage between members of two different communities.

Therefore, if the returns show that, of 9,181 Ashkenazi married men, only 139 have intermarried with other communities, this merely means that 139 Ashkenazi men married non-Ashkenazi women, but leaves us in the dark as to the number of Ashkenazi men who married outside their own more narrowly circumscribed community. Similarly, the returns contain information only as to the marriages entered into by Sephardi men with non-Sephardi women, but are silent as to the intermarriages among the various Sephardi communities among themselves. For this reason, the intermarriages between the various Oriental Jewish communities among themselves, which are enumerated in the returns, are not comparable to the intermarriages enumerated with regard to Ashkenazi and Sephardi husbands. To find the comparable data, we have to calculate all the Oriental Jewish communities together, and to take into account only those intermarriages in which the spouses were not of another Oriental community but from either an Ashkenazi or a Sephardi community. The results of these calculations can be summarized in two tables, one taking the husbands as a basis, the other the wives.

These tables show that the least frequent are marriages outside one's own ethnic division among the Ashkenazi men and women, each of whom has chosen a non-Ashkenazi spouse only in 1.5% of the cases. Both Ashkenazi men and women, who married outside their own division, preferred Sephardi spouses to Orientals, though this preference was somewhat more pronounced in the case of men

INTERMARRIAGES BETWEEN MEMBERS OF THE THREE DIVISIONS IN JERUSALEM IN 1939. I.

Community	Total Number	Husbands — Of Them Inter-married Number	%	Ashkenazim Number	% of all Inter-marriages	Sephardim Number	% of all Inter-marriages	Orientals Number	% of all Inter-marriages
Ashkenazi	9,181	139	1.5	—	—	101	72.7	38	27.3
Sephardi	1,963	214	10.9	98	45.8	—	—	116	54.2
Oriental	5,054	385	7.6	45	11.6	340	88.4	—	—
Total	16,198	738	4.5	143		441		154	

INTERMARRIAGES BETWEEN MEMBERS OF THE THREE DIVISIONS IN JERUSALEM IN 1939. II.

Community	Total Number	Wives — Of Them Inter-married Number	%	Ashkenazim Number	% of all Inter-marriages	Sephardim Number	% of all Inter-marriages	Orientals Number	% of all Inter-marriages
Ashkenazi	9,185	143	1.5	—	—	98	68.6	45	31.4
Sephardi	2,190	441	20.1	101	22.9	—	—	340	77.1
Oriental	4,823	154	3.2	38	24.7	116	75.3	—	—
Total	16,198	738	4.5	139		214		385	

(72.7%) than in the case of women (68.6%). Marriages between Oriental Jewish men and non-Oriental Jewish women were about five times as frequent as out-of-division marriages of Ashkenazi men. Almost nine-tenths of those Oriental Jewish men who married outside their own division took Sephardi women as wives, and only a little more than one-tenth of them married Ashkenazi women. Very different was the situation with regard to the Oriental women. The frequency of marriages between Oriental Jewish women and non-Oriental Jewish men was only about twice as high as that between Ashkenazi men and non-Ashkenazi women, and less than half as frequent as between Oriental men and non-Oriental women. Of the Oriental Jewish women who married non-Oriental men only three-quarters were married to Sephardi men while one-quarter married Ashkenazi men.

The Sephardi division as a whole shows the highest rate of intermarriage. Over one-tenth of the Sephardi men and over one-fifth of the Sephardi women married non-Sephardi spouses. Among the Sephardi men who married outside their own division no decisive preference could be observed as to either Ashkenazi or Oriental women, though somewhat more than half of them married Oriental women, and somewhat less than half Ashkenazi women. The Sephardi women, on the other hand, who married non-Sephardi husbands, married mostly Oriental men (77.1%), while only a small minority of them (22.9%) married Ashkenazi husbands.

Taking both men and women together, the following results are obtained:

INTERMARRIAGES BETWEEN MEMBERS OF THE THREE
DIVISIONS IN JERUSALEM IN 1939. III.

Division	Number of Married Persons	Of Them Inter-marriages	In %
Ashkenazim	18,366	282	1.5
Sephardim	4,153	655	15.7
Orientals	9,897	539	5.4
Total	32,416	1,476	4.6

The extremely high percentage of intermarriage in the Sephardi division, where every sixth person married otuside the division, can be taken as yet another indication of the intermediary position which this division holds between the Ashkenazi and the Oriental ones. The more educated and economically better-off persons (the two usually go hand in hand) among the Sephardim are in cultural as well as social standing very near the average Ashkenazim, while the less educated ones, who are in most cases also economically on a lower level, approximate the average of the Oriental groups. Members of both the Ashkenazi and the Oriental divisions can therefore find suitable spouses in this division to a much greater extent than is the case in the Ashkenazi and the Oriental groups between themselves.

Let us now turn to intermarriage within the Oriental division itself, a study of which might give a clue to the relative affinity prevalent among the various communities belonging to this division. For this purpose let us first consider the frequency of exogamous marriages in the communities making up this division.

INTERMARRIAGES WITHIN ORIENTAL JEWISH COMMUNITIES IN JERUSALEM IN 1939

Community	Number of Married Men	Of Them Outgroup Marriage	In %
Damascans	(44)	15	34.1
North Africans	467	135	28.9
Aleppans	(320)	69	21.5
Georgians	197	41	20.8
Kurds	799	140	20.0
Yemenites	745	137	18.4
Persians	1,050	149	14.2
Iraqis	748	82	10.9
Afghans	(?)	3	—
Indians	(?)	1	—
Unspecified	(?)	2	—
Proselytes	(?)	4	—
Total	4,370	778	17.8

In the following table the exogamous marriages of the Oriental Jewish communities are broken down according to preferred spouses, beginning with the community in which the highest preference can be found for Oriental communities and ending with those in which this preference is the lowest. (See the table on page 102.)

The sum-total of the results of these two tables is as follows: about 82% of all the Oriental men marry women of their own communities, that is, Persian Jewish men marry Persian Jewish women, Aleppan Jewish men Aleppan Jewish women, etc. Of the remaining 18%, over half (56%) marry women from other Oriental Jewish communities; less than two-fifths (38.7%) marry Sephardi Jewish women, and only a fraction (5.3%) marry Ashkenazi Jewish women. There is thus a considerable amalgamation, first of all in the various

Oriental Jewish communities among themselves; then a less intensive confluence between the Oriental division, on the one hand, and the Sephardi division, on the other; and finally, a still less pronounced merging process can be observed between the Oriental Jewish division and the Ashkenazi division.

OUTGROUP MARRIAGES AMONG THE ORIENTAL JEWS IN JERUSALEM IN 1939 ACCORDING TO PREFERRED COMMUNITIES

Community of the Husbands	Total Number of Outgroup Marriages		Oriental Wives		Sephardi Wives		Ashkenazi Wives	
	Husbands	%	Wives	%	Wives	%	Wives	%
Afghans	3	100	3	100	—	—	—	—
Urfalis	42	100	33	78.6	8	19.0	1	2.4
Kurds	140	100	101	72.1	38	27.1	1	0.8
Damascans	15	100	10	66.6	4	26.8	1	6.6
Persians	149	100	93	62.4	49	32.3	7	5.3
Iraqis	82	100	48	58.8	29	35.3	5	5.9
Aleppans	69	100	39	56.5	29	42.1	1	1.4
Bokharans	60	100	33	55.0	20	33.3	7	11.7
Yemenites	137	100	75	54.7	58	43.7	4	2.9
North Africans	135	100	45	33.3	80	56.3	10	7.4
Georgians	41	100	10	24.4	23	56.1	8	19.5
Indians	1	100	—	—	1	100.0	—	—
Unspecified	2	100	—	—	1	50.0	1	50.0
Proselytes	4	100	3	75.0	1	25.0	—	—
Total	880	100	493	56.0	341	38.7	46	5.3

According to our tables, it is mainly the Sephardi Jewish division which is affected by these processes of "race" mixture: every ninth Sephardi man married a non-Sephardi woman and therefore had children of mixed descent; while the same situation prevailed in the case of every fifth Sephardi woman. The positive side of the picture is that the Sephardi division thus fulfils the role of a connecting link between the two more different divisions of the Jewish people, the Ashkenazim and the Oriental communities.

Least affected by the "racial" admixture were the Ashkenazim, according to these data. Only one out of sixty Ashkenazi men married non-Ashkenazi women, and the same ratio was found among the Ashkenazi women. The few intermarriages which did occur took place between Ashkenazi and Sephardi spouses, while the incidence of Ashkenazi-Oriental intermarriages was quite negligible.

It remains to be seen what the effects will be of the greatly increased Sephardi and Oriental Jewish immigration to Israel on the incidence of intermarriage between them and the Ashkenazi Jews, ✳ as well as among themselves. As to the intermarriages in the Oriental Jewish communities among themselves, their high frequency seems to warrant the conclusion that there is a definite tendency towards racial amalgamation in these communites. A similar tendency can be observed—though this has not yet been statistically verified—in the Ashkenazi division of Israel. Long range prediction, therefore, would visualize the development in Israel of two distinct and separate population elements, each with a growing cultural homogeneity and with a trend towards a stabilized range of variation in physical type. The one will be Ashkenazi, that is European-Jewish, into which the "upper classes" of the Sephardi division will have been absorbed, and which will show less and less inside differentiation among groups with East European, Central European and Anglo-Saxon background. This group will constitute the majority in the professions, in management, in finance, in skilled labor, and in the communal and cooperative forms of the rural sector. Its relative numbers, however, as against the other population element, will decrease, and it will have to fight hard in order to retain the leadership in the country. The second population element will be an Oriental one, into which will have been absorbed the "lower" strata of the Sephardi division, and which will also become rapidly less and less differentiated with regard to surviving traces of ethnic background, showing a generalized Middle Eastern substratum with a superimposed but not deeply penetrating Westernization. This element will constitute the majority in urban labor, especially in the unskilled occupations, such as building work, transportation and porterage, in domestic service, in the private and moderately cooperative forms of the rural sector. Its relative numbers as against the Ashkenazi element will constantly increase, though at a probably decreasing rate, and it will soon feel strong enough to make its first bid for the conquest of political leadership.

Only two eventualities can at present be foreseen, either of which could prevent the fission of the Israeli social cell along lines indicated above. One of them, new aggression on the part of the Arab states or some other external enemy, would be so disastrous that the beneficial effect of becoming united for the duration in the face of a common danger would be many times offset by the destruction it would wreak in the body of the state as a whole. The other would involve a wise, prescient and selfless political and cultural leadership of a stature never yet attained by any government, whether based on a single party or on a coalition system, in any state known to us from the past or in the present.

6. Juvenile Delinquency

Yet another demographic characteristic of the Jewish communities in Israel, in which a considerable difference can be found between the Ashkenazi and the Sephardi-Oriental divisions, is that of criminality. No statistics have been published to date as to the over-all distribution of the criminal cases among the various ethnic groups; with regard to juvenile delinquency, however, this has been done, especially since the establishment of the State of Israel. In the course of one year (from May 15, 1948 to May 15, 1949), 1,450 delinquents were tried before the Juvenile Courts in the three cities of Jerusalem, Tel Aviv and Haifa. Of these, 1,195 were charged with theft, housebreaking, attempted theft or possession of stolen property. From 56 to 10 (in diminishing order) juveniles were brought up on the following charges: assault, battery, quarrelling, vandalism, possession of arms and ammunition, vagabondage, violation of law and order, flight from detention or from arrest, criminal trespass, indecent behavior and membership in illegal organizations. These offenses all together accounted for 206 cases. The remaining 48 cases included traffic offenses, criminal neglect, gambling, rape or attempted rape, distribution of leaflets, fishing by means of explosives, participation in committing a crime, manslaughter, solicitation for immoral purposes, keeping a brothel, fraud, forging of documents, murder, being found in suspicious circumstances, and desertion. The *Statistical Bulletin* of Israel (no. 4, Nov.-Dec., 1949), from which these data are taken, does not enumerate the part of the various ethnic groups in relation to each of these offenses. But it gives the distribution of the total cases tried among the various communities.

JUVENILE DELINQUENTS (AGED 9-16) IN
1948-49 ACCORDING TO COMMUNITIES

Ashkenazim	290
Sephardim	524
Yemen & Aden	228
Kurdish	121
Persian	69
Urfa (Southern Turkey)	53
Iraq	52
Morocco	45
Syria	24
Bokhara	22
Caucasus	21
India	1
Total	1,450

The distribution of the juvenile delinquents between the two main divisions of the Jewish people of Israel, and the ratio of juvenile delinquency to the percentage of each division in the Jewish youths of the 9-16 age-group can be shown in the following table:

JUVENILE DELINQUENCY IN THE TWO MAIN DIVISIONS
IN ISRAEL IN 1948-49

| | Ashkenazim | | Sephardim-Orientals | |
	Number	%	Number	%
A. Number of Juvenile Delinquents	290	20	1,160	80
B. Number of All Youths	60,000	66.6	30,000	33.3
Ratio A:B	1:207	0.3	1:26	2.4

According to these figures the juvenile delinquency rate among the Sephardi-Oriental divisions in 1948-49 was eight times higher than among the Ashkenazim.

✻

The figures giving the distribution among the communities of the inmates of the Jerusalem Detention House for Boys (aged 11-16) show a similar picture. Of the 32 boys detained in 1949 only three, or 9.4%, were Ashkenazi, while 29, or 90.6%, belonged to the Sephardi or Oriental communities.

It is the experience of those who studied juvenile delinquency that, in localities where young people of different ethnic or social groups have ample opportunity to consort, their delinquency rates show a tendency to approximate one another. In Israel, Jerusalem is such a place, where larger numbers of youths of more communities have more occasion for contact than in any other part of the country. Accordingly, one would expect in Jerusalem a diminished differential between the juvenile delinquency rate of the Ashkenazi and the Oriental Jewish communities as against the exceedingly pronounced differential found in the country as a whole. That this actually happens to be the case can be shown by calculating the juvenile delinquency rates among the various Jewish communities in Jerusalem. (See the table on page 106.)

These figures show that in Jerusalem the delinquency rate of the Sephardi-Oriental youth is only four times as high as that of the Ashkenazi youth, as against an eight-times higher rate in the whole of the country. What is more interesting in this table, however, is the very wide range of juvenile delinquency rates shown by the various Oriental Jewish communities among themselves. The Persian and Afghan rate is only slightly higher than the Ashkenazi one (0.50 as against 0.36), while at the other end of the scale the North African (Moroccan) rate is almost eleven times as high as the

DELINQUENT AND NEGLECTED YOUTH IN THE VARIOUS JEWISH COMMUNITIES IN JERUSALEM. AVERAGES FOR 1936-1945.
(Modified after Frankenstein, *Neglected Youth*, p. 204.)*

	Ashken.	Persians & Afghans	Sephard.	Iraqi	Caucas. & Georgia	Bokhar.	Yemen.	Aleppo	Urfa	Kurds	N. Afr.	Aver. of all Orient.
A. Percentage of the Juvenile Delinquents	14.4	5.6	13.1	7.6	1.7	3.1	7.4	5.5	7.2	20.3	14.1	85.6
B. Percentage of All the Jewish Youths	40.2	11.2	15.8	7.4	1.5	2.4	5.3	3.3	2.8	6.4	3.7	59.8
Ratio A:B	0.36	0.50	0.83	1.02	1.13	1.29	1.39	1.66	2.57	3.18	3.81	1.43
C. Percentage of the Neglected Youth	9.0	5.6	14.6	9.1	4.0	3.4	10.2	4.0	5.6	16.4	18.1	91.0
Ratio C:B	0.22	0.50	0.93	1.23	2.66	1.42	1.92	1.22	2.00	2.56	4.89	1.52

* The table shows that, for example, of all the juvenile delinquents 14.4% were Ashkenazim, while of all the Jewish youth 40.2% were Ashkenazim. The Ashkenazim therefore had a lower juvenile delinquency rate (Ratio A:B) than the other communities.

Ashkenazi one and almost eight times as high as the Persian-Afghan rate. An even wider range of variation is shown by the rates of neglect in the youth of the Oriental Jewish communities, where the Moroccan rate is almost ten times as high as the Persian-Afghan one.

As juvenile delinquency is one of the overt manifestations of social unrest and cultural crisis in the entire community-group to which the delinquent juveniles belong (see below), the wide range of variations in the rate can be taken as an indication of the differential degree of resistance shown by the various Oriental Jewish communities to the disintegrating effect of the socio-cultural contact between them and the dominant Western element in the country.

One does not have to seek far for the causes of the higher rate of juvenile delinquency among the Sephardi and Oriental Jewish divisions. Despite their great appreciation of learning and of education, there have been families among these communities whose economic position was such as to preclude them from sending their children to school. The main economic preventive was not the moderate tuition fee which had to be paid by the parents of the children in most of the Jewish schools in Palestine, but the earnings of the children themselves which the families would have lost if the children had been sent to school. In the summer of 1949, when the Education Bill came up before the Knesset, establishing general free and compulsory elementary education, there were in Israel about 8,000 children of the Sephardi and Oriental communities, of them over 3,000 in Jerusalem who had never before gone to school.*

PERCENTAGE OF PUPILS WITHIN THE SCHOOL AGE POPULATION AMONG THE ASHKENAZI AND SEPHARDI-ORIENTAL JEWS IN JERUSALEM IN 1939.[1]

Age Group in Years	Ashkenazi Jews			Shephardi & Oriental Jews		
	Boys	Girls	Total	Boys	Girls	Total
5- 9.9	86.8	84.7	85.8	78.6	63.2	71.2
10-14.9	94.6	92.5	93.6	77.0	66.4	71.8

[1] Source: D. Gurevich, *The Jews of Jerusalem*, Jerusalem, 1940, p. 23.

Most of these children spent their days, as well as part of the nights, in the streets, earning a few piasters daily by selling newspapers, shoelaces, boxes of matches, or working as shoeshines on streetcorners, in cafes, barbershops, restaurants. It was this group of children who furnished a major part of the juvenile delinquents. Of the 1,450 juvenile delinquents in 1948-49, 827 were either working, perma-

* Ten years previously the situation was considerably worse in Jerusalem, as shown by the table.

nently or temporarily, or were without work but unaffiliated with any educational institution; while of the remaining 623 only part were pupils of schools, others were educated in families, on farms, or in other places with insufficient supervision.

Another reason for the higher rate of juvenile delinquency of the Sephardi and Oriental Jewish youth is the generally greater poverty prevailing in their families and the incredibly crowded living conditions in their homes. Many of these children live with six, eight or more brothers and sisters and their parents in one single room, inadequately lighted and aired, with insufficient furniture and facilities, in the most unsanitary conditions. For these children, even if they spent part of their day in school, it is difficult, often almost impossible, to stay at home in the afternoon hours, and it is hard even to return home for the night's rest. In the mild climate of Palestine it is possible and even pleasant to spend many hours outdoors all the year round; and the habit of loitering, easily acquired by the children and the adolescents, creates a favorable atmosphere for delinquency.

A third factor is the breakdown of the paternal authority. In the traditional Sephardi and Oriental families the authority of the father is supreme, for he is the head of the family not only figuratively but most effectually. As long as the family remains in a traditional atmosphere, even in Israel, the strength of paternal authority is sufficient to act as a deterrent against any unruly behavior on the part of the children. Whether they go to school or not, they know that the father's word is law for them and it is a relatively rare occurrence for him to have to support his verbal command with his stick.

In most places in Israel, however, the Oriental or Sephardi Jewish families do not live isolated from the Ashkenazi Jews. The young people especially have frequent occasion to meet and to consort with others of their age-group from Ashkenazi communities, and they learn from them what is most attractive for young people to emulate —their bearing of greater freedom and independence. Rebellion against paternal authority then becomes the order of the day, either openly and defiantly, or more frequently surreptitiously, by keeping up appearances at home and finding compensation in unrestrained behavior away from parental supervision.

The breakdown of paternal authority is most eloquently shown by a study made recently among Yemenite graduates of elementary schools in Tel Aviv. A comparison with the general Israeli youth of the same age-group, also graduates of the elementary schools in the city, demonstrated the relatively much lower incidence among the

Yemenite boys of the image of the father as an ideal. The most highly esteemed persons among the Yemenite and non-Yemenite Jewish boys studied showed the following order of precedence in diminishing frequency:*

Order of Frequency	Yemenites	Order of Frequency	Non-Yemenites
1	A National Hero	1	The Father
2	A Friend	2	Edison
3	A Teacher	3	An Instructor[1]
4	An Instructor*	4	A Teacher
5	A Writer	5	Jabotinsky
6	The Father	6	Herzl
7	A Hero of Fiction	7	Trumpeldor

[1] Hebrew *madrikh*, a group-leader in the youth movements which are recreational in intent and usually organized by a political party.

The father's place among the Yemenite youth is taken by a national hero, who occupies in the mental world of the non-Yemenite youth the fifth, sixth and seventh places only. It would be very interesting to find out whether "A Friend," whose image as an ideal among the Yemenites comes immediately after the National Hero, is in most cases a Yemenite boy, or an Ashkenazi boy, and it is a pity that the study referred to did not contemplate this distinction.

The breakdown of paternal authority is in many cases caused by the subordinated social and economic position in which the father finds himself after he settles in a society which is predominantly Western. Once this happens, the entire family, whose traditional relationship-patterns were based on paternal authority and female subordination, finds itself in close daily contact with Western people and Western cultural patterns, a circumstance which causes grave disturbances in its equilibrium. The juveniles of the family, who meet Western (Ashkenazi) friends of their own age in school or in the streets, soon recognize that their father has to content himself with an "inferior" occupation which does not yield an adequate income to provide for the family because he is too religious, or too old-fashioned, or simply not clever enough to make good. We would say that the father is insufficiently prepared to take his place in the Westernized and highly competitive urban society in Israel.

Maternal authority never amounted to much in Oriental society, in which the subordination of women is a traditional characteristic of social and family life. Yet, in the patriarchal social organization

* Cf. Shoshana Baklyar-Alon, "Affective and Intellectual Characteristics of the Yemenite Youth," (Hebrew), in *Hahinukh*, Tel Aviv, 1950, no. 3, pp. 300-323.

of the Oriental village or of tribal society, women attained a status and fulfilled roles marked by a certain stability and a sufficiently widely circumscribed course to enable them to live a full and satisfactory life within the general social dynamics of the family and the larger unit. The mother was constantly with her children—with the boys in their tender years, with the girls until their marriage—and though her authority over her children was only a derived one, upheld by that of the father, it was still sufficient to enable her to influence their education and the development of their character. In the contact-situation amidst a Westernized society the mother is even less prepared than the father to find her place in a social order based on the full participation of women and practically equal opportunities for making a living for both sexes. She is nevertheless forced only too often to contribute her earnings, and having no choice in the matter must seek employment where she can find it, which in the great majority of the cases means domestic service. As a consequence of her spending the major part of the day away from her own home, she has to give up even the modest position she has occupied in the circle of her own family. The effect of this situation on the children is nothing short of disastrous. The father completely loses control over them, the mother is not around to take care of them; and what is worse, neither of them is prepared to substitute any other relationship for that of the authoritative father to his submissive children, so that after paternal authority is gone, literally no channels remain open through which the father (or the mother) can influence his children.

Criminality is a social phenomenon confined predominantly to males among both adults and juveniles. Nevertheless, there were 129 girls in Israel in 1948-49 among the 1,450 juvenile delinquents,

JUVENILE OFFENDERS BY SEX
Jews and Arabs, 1940-49

| | Jews | | | | Arabs | | | |
| | Boys | | Girls | | Boys | | Girls | |
Year	Number	Per cent	Number	Per cent	Number	Per cent	Number	Per cent
1940	359	89.5	42	10.5	1,607	95.6	74	4.4
1941	298	89	37	11	1,690	95.2	84	4.8
1942	341	89.1	42	10.9	1,875	95.3	92	4.7
1943	361	87.9	50	12.1	1,832	95.8	80	4.2
1944	430	85.2	75	14.8	2,408	93.9	156	6.1
1948-9	1,321	91.1	129	8.9				
* 1949*	1,751	92.3	146	7.7	355	93.9	23	6.1

* Up to and including 17 years of age.

which is a considerably lower ratio of girls to boys than the one which obtained from 1940 to 1944.

These figures show that in Mandatory years the percentage of the girls among the Jewish juvenile delinquents was more than twice as high as among the Arabs. The segregation of sexes in Arab urban society, the strict enforcement of a rigid sexual code with regard to the female members of the family and the high percentage of girls who were virtually never let out of sight of the mother or some other older female relative, contributed to keeping the percentage of Arab female juvenile delinquency at a very low rate.

Among the Ashkenazi Jewish families there are no such deterrents at work, and as to the Sephardi-Oriental Jewish families, even in the most tradition-bound situation, the position of women is a much freer one than among the Arabs. Moreover, while among the Arabs (especially the Moslems) the traditional code of behavior imposed upon women was strong enough to resist any changes the occurrence of which would be expected as a result of the contact-situation in Palestine, the less restricted Oriental Jewish women (and especially the young generation) soon succumbed to the Western examples forcefully brought to their attention in their much closer contact with Ashkenazi elements. In general, the effect of this situation was an accelerated emancipation of Oriental Jewish women of the younger age-brackets; but in certain cases undesirable concomitant phenomena were also noticeable. Especially in the poorer classes of the Sephardi and Oriental Jewish communities, where girls are sent to Ashkenazi or other better-off families to do housework at a very early age (often when they are nine or ten years old), and where the meager earnings of such a girl-child can mean a lot to the very limited budget of her parents, the fact that she becomes an important economic asset to the family causes her to resent the continued attempts of her father (and mother) to assert his authority over her. In such cases the breakdown of paternal authority results also from the girl's becoming closely acquainted with the customs, habits and standards of the well-to-do Ashkenazi family for whom she works. The difference between these and what she sees at home invites comparison which works to the detriment of her own family, and this in turn gives the impetus to objections, disobedience, and an often frustrated desire for a change "for the better."

Dr. K. Frankenstein, Director of the Henrietta Szold Institute for Child and Youth Care in Jerusalem, who studied criminal and neglected youth in Palestine, summarizes the background of juvenile delinquency among the Oriental Jews in Palestine by referring to the tension which is often found to exist in the various Oriental

Jewish communities among themselves, as well as the tension which at times reaches a degree of hatred between the Oriental and Sephardi Jews, on the one hand, and the Ashkenazim, on the other. The groups differ from one another in language and custom, the women particularly preserving the special characteristics which separate their communities. The social position of the Oriental Jews cannot be compared at all with that of the Ashkenazim; the overwhelming majority of the Jews living in the poorer quarters of Jerusalem are Oriental Jews, and they do not always incline to improve their housing conditions even when the means required stand at their disposal. Only a relatively small number of the Oriental Jews succeed in advancing in their occupations and in fulfilling more complicated tasks. Often the family does not function as a unit. The oppression of women and the lack of appreciation toward them as individuals cause, at times, protest and embitterment and consequent disturbances in the relationship between parents and children. The fathers are frequently characterized by a lack of responsibility and educational understanding, by excitability and affectivity; and sometimes these traits can be found also among parents who make conscious efforts to understand their children and to care for them. There exists a seemingly unbridgeable contrast between Western civilization, with the many enticements it offers, and the dark atmosphere of the parental home with its tensions, in which the father sternly continues to demand blind obedience and unquestioning submission from all members of his family, or else withdraws altogether into indifference often bordering on apathy. The youth feels compelled to protest against his parents' lack of understanding of everything which excites and moves him, against the religious formalism which has been emptied of its content, against the burden of early work, against the primitive observance of antiquated norms which do not fit the new reality around him. On the other hand, he finds himself unable to adapt to this reality, intellectually and socially, to understand its ideas, to take part in it productively, and actually even to exist outside of the body of the family against which he rebels. A grave disturbing factor is the segregation and isolation of the various ethnic groups, each with its specific characteristics, inclinations, talents, as well as shortcomings and feelings of inferiority. Also, there is an inclination among the Oriental Jewish communities toward indifference and lethargy, on the one hand, and excitability and exaggerated emotionalism, on the other, and a tendency to take a negative stand towards the demands of collective responsibility with which they find themselves confronted in the Westernized society. These are the factors in the situation in Palestine which, according to Frankenstein, have to be kept in mind in order to reach an understanding of the high incidence of juvenile delinquency in the Oriental Jewish communities there.*

7. General Criminality

A disquieting phenomenon is the considerable increase in the rate of both juvenile delinquency and general criminality among the Jews of Israel as compared with the Mandatory period. The following table gives the findings in the years 1940-49 with regard to juvenile delinquency:

INCIDENCE OF JUVENILE DELINQUENCY IN PALESTINE-ISRAEL

Year	Jews Number of Juvenile Delinquents	Incidence per 1,000 of those aged 9-16	Arabs Number of Juvenile Delinquents	Incidence per 1,000 of those aged 9-16
1940	401	7.16	1,681	7.85
1941	335	5.77	1,774	8.07
1942	383	6.49	1,967	8.74
1943	411	6.63	1,912	8.24
1944	505	7.77	2,564	10.68
1945			3,261	12.46
1948-49	1,450	12.08		

An increase similar to that of juvenile delinquency can be found in general criminality since the establishment of the State of Israel. The following table contains the most essential figures:

GENERAL CRIMINALITY OF THE JEWS IN PALESTINE AND ISRAEL FROM 1941 TO 1951 AS SHOWN BY NUMBER OF PERSONS TRIED AND SENTENCED IN ALL THE COURTS.[1]

Year	Population in the country[2]	No. of persons sentenced	Incidence per 1,000
1941	504,000	19,307	38.3
1943	539,000	19,748	36.6
1944	565,000	16,402	29.2
1948	867,000[3]	28,112	32.4
1949	1,164,000[4]	55,858	48.0
1950	1,370,000[5]	77,289	56.4
1951	1,578,000[6]	89,000	56.4

[1] Data based on figures published in the *Statistical Abstracts of Palestine,* 1942 and 1944-45, and the *Statistical Bulletin of Israel.*

[2] For the years 1941-44 the Jewish population of Palestine; for 1948-51 the total population of Israel.

[3] Includes 108,000 Arabs and other non-Jews.

[4] Includes 150,000 Arabs and other non-Jews.

[5] Includes 167,000 Arabs and other non-Jews.

[6] Includes 173,000 Arabs and other non-Jews.

* Cf. K. Frankenstein, *Neglected Youth* (in Hebrew), Jerusalem, 1947, pp. 144-5, 147.

Let us compare with these figures the criminality rates of the Arab (Moslem and Christian) population of Palestine in the years 1941-44:

GENERAL CRIMINALITY OF THE ARABS IN PALESTINE FROM 1941-44 AS SHOWN BY NUMBER OF PERSONS TRIED AND SENTENCED IN ALL THE COURTS

Year	No. of Arabs in Palestine	No. of persons sentenced	Incidence per 1,000
1941	1,098,000	39,071	36
1943	1,160,000	44,158	38
1944	1,197,000	45,107	38

The data concerning the general criminality rates, both those supplied by the Department of Statistics of the British Mandatory Government of Palestine and covering the years 1941-44, and those published by the Central Bureau of Statistics of the Government of Israel and covering the years 1948-51, treat the Jews of the country as an undivided entity, and contain therefore no clue as to the distribution of the criminal cases among the various Jewish communities. Nevertheless, the conclusion seems to follow that, just as in the case of juvenile delinquency so also in general criminality the Oriental Jewish element rates higher than its numerical proportion in the population. The post-independence increase in the percentage of Oriental Jews in Israel would therefore seem to account for the increase in general criminality as well. One has, however, to take into account also the circumstances of the European Jewish immigration. Dr. K. Frankenstein, in the course of an interview in Jerusalem in the summer of 1951, confirmed the impression gained by the author that not only has the incidence of juvenile and adult criminality increased in Israel, but that the character of criminal activity has undergone a change for the worse. In Mandatory years, Jewish criminality, and especially juvenile delinquency in Palestine, was of the unplanned kind, of the type which makes use, mostly under the spur of the moment, of an unexpected opportunity to misappropriate something or to commit some other misdemeanor. Since the establishment of the State, the number of carefully planned and expertly executed criminal acts has increased. The explanation, according to Dr. Frankenstein, lies in the fact that the unscreened mass immigration has brought a number of expert criminals into the country, especially from Poland, Rumania and Morocco. These "high class" criminals, with whom the Israeli police is practically unable to cope, find it easy to recruit helpers from among the neglected, maladjusted and dissatisfied youth, mainly of Oriental Jewish background for whom delinquency is an outlet and a satisfaction. The activities of these professional criminals thus transform the character of juvenile delinquency from relatively harmless, haphazard, grab-and-run affairs into serious and dangerous, organized criminal acts.

The eradication of criminality is a task for the police. If screening processes were introduced before admission to Israel is granted to any group or individual, they could prevent the further arrival of criminals from any country. But it is up to the social welfare agencies, the immigrants' settling authorities, and in general the established population of Israel as a whole, to create an atmosphere for the Oriental Jewish communities which in itself should give the children and youths a resistance to criminal enticements.

We have chosen but a few demographic characteristics in order to illustrate the differences between the Ashkenazi and the Sephardi-Oriental division in Israel. A complete demographic survey would have to include many more aspects of vital statistics and physical conditions—such as the marriage rates, marriage ages, incidence of disease and types of diseases, death rates and the figures of life expectancy—and all this, not only with regard to the three main divisions of the Jewish population, but to each of their major component communities. Only such a study would reveal all the implications of the compelling demographic fact that the Jewish population of Israel is composed of a large number of different ethnic groups hailing from the four corners of the world and, for the time being at least, continuing in Israel in their wonted ways and traditional mores shaped to a large extent by the local cultures of their respective countries of birth. Yet even the examples to which the present chapter was confined were sufficient to show that definite differences exist between the Jewish groups coming from the Western world and those arriving from the East in constantly increasing numbers. What these differences consist of in terms of cultural traits will be considered in the next chapter.

Chapter Five
The Cultural Mosaic

1. Substratum and Variants

Each Jewish ethnic group in Israel has brought along its culture from the country of its origin. In the old countries the culture of the Jewish population, as it existed in the lifetime of the generation which ultimately migrated to Israel, was the result of prolonged and complicated cultural processes which varied considerably from place to place. The main common features which appeared in the processes of cultural development in every country of the Jewish Diaspora were as follows:

The basis of the Jewish cultural configuration was in each place the traditional Jewish cultural substratum brought along by the ancestors of the group when settling in the country in question, and ultimately going back to an ancient Palestinian-Jewish cultural heritage. Superimposed upon this ancient component was the influence of the local non-Jewish culture, the extent of which depended on such factors as the socio-economic position attained by members of the Jewish group; the willingness of the non-Jewish population to permit the Jews to adopt traits from their culture and to participate in it, and vice versa; and the relative level of the non-Jewish culture compared to the culture developed by the Jews themselves, and its degree of attraction for the Jewish group. The attraction of a non-Jewish culture depended on the intrinsic and extrinsic enticements it could offer, and on its evaluation by the Jews in relation to their own traditional culture. The acculturation of Jews to German culture, for instance, was considerable only since the Haskala movement, for ever since the Haskala period German culture was regarded by Jews both within the German orbit and on its peripheries as the highest achievement of the culture of Europe.

The extent of the influence of the local non-Jewish cultures on that of the Jewish groups depended also on still another factor: the original compatibility between the traditional Jewish substratum and the actual non-Jewish culture prevalent in the locality. Whenever and wherever the compatibility between the two was great, or they evidenced a considerable degree of affinity, cultural borrowing on the part of the Jewish group soon after its arrival on the scene was facilitated and eventually reached a high intensity. The best example of this process is that of the Jews in the lands of the Middle East, where the traditional Jewish culture, itself Oriental in flavor and tone, met with other, not essentially different versions of Oriental culture. The initial affinity between the two greatly facilitated the acculturation of the smaller Jewish groups to the larger Moslem populations. Another, less patent but still very instructive example is that of the differential rate of acculturation of the Ashkenazi and the Sephardi Jewish immigrants in the countries of Latin America. The acculturative processes of the Ladino-speaking Sephardi Jews to the Spanish-speaking environment were easier, smoother and more rapid than those of their Ashkenazi brethren for whom Spanish was a totally new language. An example of the retardatory effect of the absence of initial affinity between the two cultures can be found in Central Europe where cultural borrowing by the Jews set in late, and became considerable in volume and intensity only after an almost complete break with the traditional Jewish cultural heritage.

A third factor in the cultural processes, the end result of which was the present-day culture of the Jews in their lands of dispersion, was the amount of contact between a given Jewish community and Jews in other countries. Wherever such contacts were frequent and intense, the lines of cultural development did not diverge to too great a degree; wherever contacts were scarce or non-existent, the isolation resulted in specific, unrelated developments.

These theoretical considerations in themselves will suffice to make us expect to find only a small part of the culture of any given Jewish group shared by the other Jewish communities. Also historically speaking, it would be too much to expect that a common cultural heritage of more than two thousand years should be able to hold its own on several fronts in the face of cultural influences pouring in from all sides. Even a purely numerical consideration will make us aware of the fact that the chances for old, original Jewish cultural traits to survive in unchanged forms in widely scattered localities are very slight indeed; for it can be shown that, other things being equal, the numerical relationship between two groups in contact is a very potent factor in their influencing of each other: the numerically larger group exerts a greater influence on the smaller one than the other way round, and the extent of the influence seems to be determined, among other factors, also by a coefficient derived from this numerical relationship.*

After these preliminary clarifications, and knowing more or less what to expect, methodical procedure would now call for a comparison, trait by trait and complex by complex, between the culture of a sufficient number of representative Jewish communities and the culture of their respective non-Jewish environments. The cultural materials of two or three typical Ashkenazi Jewish communities, like American Jewry, German Jewry and Polish Jewry, should be carefully compared with American, German and Polish cultures respectively. The same should then be done with respect to a few Sephardi Jewish communities, such as Italian, Greek and Turkish Jewry. And finally the same survey and comparison should be repeated in a larger number of Oriental Jewish communities—larger in view of their greater diversity and fragmentation—such as the Kurdish, Persian, Iraqi, Yemenite and Moroccan Jewish communities. The cultural differences between all or most of these Jewish communities and their non-Jewish neighbors could thereupon be taken as the constituent elements of a specifically Jewish culture, and the same findings would also give us a more concrete idea as to the common features in the culture of the various Jewish communities among themselves.

In order to proceed in this methodical manner, however, one would need a requisite number of reliable and adequate surveys of the cultures of both the Jewish communities and the non-Jewish peoples amongst whom they live. Such surveys on the large majority of the Jewish communities, unfortunately do not exist nor are they always available with respect to the non-Jewish peoples.§ For this regrettable reason, nothing in the way of a systematic summation of findings can be given at the present time, but only a very general and provisional statement can be made.

The bulk of the distinctly Jewish cultural traits in every Jewish group is found to lie within the intellectual and religious fields. Even in situations of advanced acculturation the Jewish group in a given country tends to retain its somewhat different intellectual equip-

* Cf. R. Patai, *On Culture Contact and Its Working in Modern Palestine*, pp. 19, 20, 21.

§ Of the Oriental Jewish communities, only two have been fully studied ethnologically; cf. Erich Brauer, *Ethnologie der Jemenitischen Juden*, Heidelberg, 1934; and E. Brauer (ed. R. Patai), *The Jews of Kurdistan* (Hebrew), Jerusalem, 1947. The only anthropological study of Jewish life in the pre-World War II East-European small town is *Life Is with People* by M. Zborovsky and E. Herzog, New York, 1952.

ment and orientation and its more clearly distinct religious beliefs, practices and organization. It would appear, therefore, that the ultimate and residual distinguishing trait of a Jewish group anywhere in the world is the consciousness of being heirs to an old tradition composed of several distinct yet interwoven and inseparable aspects: historical, national, "racial" and religious. This tradition manifests itself mainly in mental orientation, in a knowledge and awareness of an historical past different from that of the non-Jewish environment. All the tangible expressions of Jewish cultural life are derived from this single source of group-consciousness; it is this awareness of tradition which is the motive power behind such cultural phenomena as the community organization, the synagogue and its services, and is the driving force towards self-perpetuation achievable only by establishing and maintaining the proper mechanisms of cultural transmission in the form of educational institutions and of other, less formal processes of socialization.

It has been recognized by every Jewish community that the only way to secure its continued existence is to hand down the Jewish cultural tradition to the next generation. Historical experience has shown that Jewish communities which were not successful in this respect, became extinct almost immediately. A case in point is that of the Jews of Kaifeng-Fu: Soon after the knowledge of Hebrew was lost among them, they became assimilated to their Chinese environment and ceased to exist as Jews. Another example is that of the Persian Jews who, in several townships, were forced to adopt Islam, which made it impossible for them to continue to teach their children how to read and understand the Hebrew Bible, prayers and the like. The result was that the very next generation became actually Moslemized despite the fervent determination of the parent-generation to adhere in secret to the Jewish faith. Only in the city of Meshed, where the forcibly converted *Jedid al-Islam* (new Moslems) succeeded in establishing secretly a Hebrew school for their children, did the subsequent generations preserve their Jewish faith clandestinely.*

The complementary positive side to this picture of paucity in specifically Jewish, and therefore basically common, traits in the cultural make-up of the various Jewish communities all over the world, is the great diversity shown by the majority of their cultural traits. Even the traits enumerated above, though they may be specially Jewish, or at least show a specifically Jewish tinge, do not

* Cf. Raphael Patai, "The Hebrew Education in the Marrano Jewish Community of Meshed" (Hebrew), in *Edoth*, July 1946, pp. 213-226.

necessarily appear in identical forms in the various Jewish communities. Jews may have, for instance, in each country in which the institution of newsprint exists among the non-Jews, a Jewish press of their own which in content, endeavor, aim, style and form may differ to varying degrees from the non-Jewish press. This, however, does not mean that the Jewish press, in America and in Egypt for instance, must be similar to each other. As a matter of fact, this example goes a long way towards showing that, whenever we compare a cultural trait found among the Jews of different countries, we have to take into account also the similarities and the differences evidenced by the trait in question as it appears among the Jews of a given country when compared with the corresponding trait of the non-Jews in the same country.

If specifically Jewish cultural traits are characterized by variations from one Jewish group to another, how much more so will be the case with those traits which originated among the various Jewish groups as a result of cultural borrowing from their respective non-Jewish neighbors. The great majority of cultural traits and complexes belonging to the manifold fields of material equipment and their use will be found in this category, as a glance at the great diversity of dwellings and other structures used by Jews in the various countries, of clothing worn by them, of food eaten, of occupations engaged in, and the like, will demonstrate. But even such "non-material" traits as language, social stratification and personal relations, family, kinship and other organizations, as well as components of mental and spiritual equipment like religious beliefs, ideas about nature and man, extent and trends in exact knowledge, will be found to differ greatly from one Jewish community to another.

It is the realization and contemplation of these cultural differences which justifies our calling the cultural situation in Israel of today a "cultural mosaic." Each immigrant group tends to carry in Israel its own cultural "ballast" for a considerable time, either because it consciously wishes to do so or out of sheer inertia. The retention or discarding of the old cultural traits depends, of course, also on a number of external circumstances, one of the most decisive of which is the locality in which the family or the group takes residence. If this happens to be a village settled only by people from the old country of the newcomers, the old cultural traits will tend to persist longer after due adjustments have been made to the new physical environment. A village, even in a small country like Israel, lives in relative isolation, and if such a village is settled by members of one single ethnic group only, cultural traits imported can easily survive. A few examples will serve to illustrate this point.

2. Iraqis, Americans and Rumanians

In 1950-51 some 125,000 Iraqi Jews were brought to Israel by "Operation Ali Baba," an airlift dwarfing in size its more famous predecessor, "Operation Magic Carpet" of the Yemenite Jews. The transplantation of the Iraqi Jews to Israel entailed many changes in the external circumstances of their lives. In Iraq, most of the Jews had been city dwellers, and their typical occupations had been those of small shopkeepers and tradesmen, craftsmen like masons and carpenters, domestic servants, or, in the middle class brackets, small bankers, retailers, agents, merchants, civil servants, clerks, as well as members of the professions. Agriculture was practised only by the Jews of Iraqi Kurdistan, especially in the Amadiyya district.

All of these arrived in Israel completely penniless and destitute, since all their property had been left behind in Iraq. After their arrival at Lydda Airport, they were carried off either to immigrants' camps, or directly to *ma'abarot*, transit villages. In general, there was much less inclination to engage in agriculture evidenced by the Iraqi Jews, of whom 90% had lived in the big city of Baghdad, than by the Yemenite Jews. Fifty thousand Yemenite immigrants established 57 agricultural settlements, while 125,000 Iraqis set up only 15. Both in their agricultural settlements and in the closely packed suburban quarters where the Iraqi Jews settled, the continuing influence of their popular traditions and folkways remained much in evidence. By and large, they set about recreating a semblance of the life they had led in Iraq as far as the changed circumstances permitted it. Dissatisfaction with available jobs, which were in most cases not identical with or even similar to those they used to hold in Iraq, was rife. Those who were prepared, or could be persuaded, to settle in villages, established *moshavim*, cooperative settlements, in which, however, few of the customary cooperative *moshav* institutions were set up. Their religious bent predisposed them to agree to affiliation with the Hapoel Hamizrahi movement, as was the case with three *moshavim* established by them in the Beisan Valley in September 1951. Even in Arab Nazareth, impressing itself as Oriental and colorful upon those driving over from industrious Haifa, the Iraqi Jews, who came in from their new settlements in the neighborhood and were seen resting in the shade under the awnings of the bazaar, appeared in their fantastic costumes as figures come to life from the pages of the Arabian Nights.   *

Predilections brought along from the home country and persisting mental dispositions lent a very different shape to the life which settlers from the Western world carved out for themselves in Israel.

In Upper Galilee, for instance, the deserted Arab village of Sasa was given to members of a Hashomer Hatzair *kibbutz* (originally called Kibbutz America Hé), comprising 98 adults and 12 children, all English-speaking, mainly from the United States and Canada. New Sasa is purportedly an agricultural settlement, but the American fondness for mechanization and industrialization, brought along by the young American pioneers, asserted itself from the very beginning. Almost all the settlers had had technical training in America and they were attracted to technical occupations also in Israel. They had brought along with them advanced mechanical equipment and a typically American efficiency in using it, and within less than a year after they had settled in Sasa (which was in January 1949), they had already set up a carpentry and a metal-workshop and engaged in transporting water for the settlements in their vicinity with their four trucks. They served the neighborhood also with their four tractors, and several of the members of the *kibbutz* joined the Shahar Transportation Cooperative, the headquarters of which are in Haifa. As one of the settlers stated with unconcealed pride: "Because of our superior machinery and trained men we have become the repair and servicing center of the area, a sort of Chicago of central Galilee."* Four thousand dunams (c. 1,000 acres) of forest lands in the vicinity of their village, which belong to the Jewish National Fund, were given to them to care for, and they also worked a vineyard of some 40 dunams (10 acres). They took up the cultivation of fig and olive trees which had belonged to the village, as well as some *falha*. Intensive agriculture has but little chance for developing, because the village lacks sufficient water for irrigation. The idea of supplementing the income derived from agriculture with industrial enterprises is not new in the *kibbutzim* of Israel, but these American settlers have reversed the order of priority by relying mainly on industry and services, and only secondarily on agriculture. The village will probably become a prototype of an industrial rural settlement and thus constitute a new development in the constant experimentation
✱ characteristic of rural Israel.§

There are, of course, considerable differences within the various groups of Ashkenazi immigrants themselves. Near Sasa is another deserted village called Tarshiha, in which over a hundred families from Rumania were settled. The plan for Tarshiha was not to make it a *kibbutz*, a communal settlement, but a *moshav ovdim*, or

* Cf. *The Launching: Sasa's First Year* (pamphlet), Zionist Organization Youth and Hechalutz Department, 1951, p. 61.

§ Cf. J. Ayit, "Workers' Settlements and Communal Settlements in Deserted Villages," *Haaretz* (Hebrew daily), Tel Aviv, Dec. 23, 1949.

workers' smallholders' settlement, with small but intensively cultivated, independent but cooperatively worked farm units. But a few
months after the group was settled in the village, it began to look
very doubtful whether these Rumanian families would be able to
adjust themselves to the life-form and working conditions of this
type of settlement. Much bitterness could be noticed everywhere,
and the people were full of complaints over lack of work and livelihood. Little initiative was shown by them and, temporarily at least,
the main source of income was seasonal work in the olive-harvest of
the neighboring villages and employment as day-laborers in certain
public works, such as roadbuilding, carried out by the Government
in the vicinity of the village. What form of life and organization is
likely to develop in this village is difficult to foretell; but the personality traits and culture patterns of its present inhabitants make it
most unlikely that it will grow into a well organized *moshav ovdim*
with the high degree of cooperation characteristic of this type of ✳
agricultural settlement.✳

3. Beit Dagon

The situation is quite different when immigrants from several
countries and continents are thrown together by the settling authorities into one village. Such a place is Beit Dagon, which was until
the Israeli-Arab war an Arab village called Beit Dajan, with some
3,000 inhabitants and about 16,000 dunams (4,000 acres) of good
land, some five miles to the southeast of Tel Aviv. Externally, in the
summer of 1951, Beit Dagon still looked very much like the Arab
village it had been until 1948. Almost no new buildings have been
erected, and in many places structures and entire blocks demolished
by shellfire testified to the fierceness of the fighting which took place
here during the war. The streets of the village were called by the
letters of the Hebrew alphabet, and the houses were numbered. But
the streets themselves were the same unpaved streets, dusty and
sandy in the summer and muddy in the winter, and the houses the
same old and dilapidated Arab structures.

Very soon after the cessation of the hostilities (in the fall of 1948),
the first Jew appeared in the completely abandoned village. He was
a Polish immigrant, and he held the fort for two weeks without any
help from the Jewish Agency or any other authority. Then the
settling authorities started to direct new immigrants to Beit Dagon,
and very soon the village was like a small-scale model of the "Ingathering of the Exiles." First came 130 Bulgarian families, and

✳ Cf. J. Ayit, *ibid.*

after them groups of Algerian and Tunisian Jews (20 families, among them 6 Karaite families from Tunisia); Egyptian Jews (20 families); Turkish Jews (30 families); Rumanian Jews (100 families); Polish Jews (100 families); and finally Yemenite Jews (100 families). A few families from Italy, Hungary, Yugoslavia and Czechoslovakia also settled in Beit Dagon, as well as three families who came to Israel after several years' sojourn in China. The sum total in the summer of 1951 was over 500 families comprising nearly 2,000 members.

The plan of the settling authorities was to make Beit Dagon a *moshav*, a smallholders' settlement; but actually agriculture played an insignificant role in the economy of the village. Every family which expressed the wish, was given a small plot of land, varying in size from half a dunam to three dunams (0.125 to 0.75 acre), and most of the families availed themselves of this opportunity to get land on which to grow vegetables and keep some livestock, to supplement their otherwise very meager rationed diet. Thus, the new settlement of Beit Dagon did not need all the land which belonged to the Arab village of Beit Dajan; the plan now is to allocate part of the land to two additional settlements to be established in the near future.

An attempt was made to allocate also the available rooms in a just and equitable manner. A rapid survey sufficed to establish that none of the habitable buildings in the village contained rooms which would rate as Category A. A few were found to rate as Category B, while most rooms were assigned to Category C. The monthly rent paid by the people to the local council of Beit Dagon, and transferred by the latter to the Custodian of Abandoned Property pending the final settlement of the Arab property problems, was 2.500 Israel Pounds ($7.00) for a B room, and £.I. 1.500 ($4.20) for a C room. Several families had more than one room, while most of them had kitchens attached, built of corrugated iron sheets.

Unemployment was never a serious problem in Beit Dagon, in the course of its three years' existence. In 1951, several dozens of workers were still being employed temporarily in cleaning up the ruins of demolished houses. Others were paving two streets within the village, which in its Arab days had not a single road suitable for wheeled traffic. Many of the workers went outside the village to find labor. Some thirty of them worked in the storehouses and garages of the army depot in the immediate vicinity of the village. About sixty were employed in the Tirza furniture factory near Rishon Lezion which had taken up also the manufacture of small wooden barracks. Several were commuting to Tel Aviv, some went as far as Beer Sheba in the Negev. The average daily wages earned by skilled laborers were four to five Israel Pounds ($11.20-14.00). The unskilled laborers, mostly recruited from the Yemenite group, worked in the nearby orange groves or in roadbuilding, and earned £.I.1.800 to 2.500 daily ($5.04 to 7.00).

Several industrial ventures were initiated by the immigrants. Eight men set up a cooperative for the manufacture of concrete building blocks, but their work was greatly impeded by the unavailability of raw materials. Seven banded together into a cooperative for automobile repairs and iron work. Two brothers, with three workers employed by them, set up a roof tile factory. There was also a cooperative bakery, and a small factory for pickled peppers. All in all there were about ten workshops in the village.

In relation to the economic importance of industry, agriculture as a basis of livelihood was insignificant. Vegetable gardening was seriously handicapped by a lack of water for irrigation. It was easier for the people to take to small scale chicken farming, which was facilitated by an instructor sent to the village by the settling authorities together with a donation of about one thousand hens.

The sanitary and health conditions in the village were far from satisfactory, though even as much as there was of health services was much more than most of the immigrants had ever before experienced. The *Kuppat Holim* (Sick Fund) of the *Histadrut* opened a clinic in the village staffed with a single, sorely overworked physician. Especially among the children coming from Oriental countries, there was initially a very high incidence of eye and skin diseases which were rapidly brought under control. One of the settlers, a Bulgarian woman dentist, started private practice in the village, but few of the villagers were financially able to avail themselves of her services.

Over two years had to pass until the village was able to have telephone service installed. In the summer of 1951, there were three telephones, one at the post office, one at the labor exchange, and one at the Council. The installation of electricity was still awaited.

The party affiliations of the villagers were reflected in the composition of the eleven-man Village Council which was elected on March 26, 1950: Mapai—5; Mapam—3; Hapoel Hamizrahi—1; Freedom Party—1; Communists—1.

There were two schools and three kindergartens in the village: an elementary school belonging to the Labor trend, with about 120 pupils and 8 teachers; and a Mizrahi school conducted along the traditional lines of the Tora-schools, with about 40 pupils. To the same two trends belonged the kindergartens: two, with about 75-80 children in them, were affiliated with the *Histadrut* system, and a third, with about 30 children, with the Mizrahi system. For lack of suitable accommodation, all the teachers of the schools lived outside the village.

Much less satisfactory was the situation with regard to adult education and cultural activities. These were conducted partly by the State's Department of Education and Culture, and partly by the Cultural Center of the *Histadrut*. Evening classes for Hebrew were opened at an early stage in the history of Jewish Beit Dagon, but attendance remained sporadic, confined mainly to women. The men were too exhausted by their work to attend. Once or twice a month social evenings were organized, in the summer outdoors, in the yard of the Council House (which also was the locale for an open-air cinema); in the winter at the *Histadrut* Hall in the center of the village. These gatherings featured lectures as well as musical and theatrical performances—in the form characteristic of organized cultural activity everywhere in Israel—combining entertainment with education. These meetings, as well as the weekly excursions and hikes in the neighboring countryside, were generally well attended.

While the party affiliations cut across the ethnic groupings, countries of origin remained the basis for religious life. Among the Ashkenazi Jews only a few were religious, and their synagogue could barely gather the daily *minyan* (ten male adults) necessary for communal prayer. They had a *shohet* (ritual slaughterer), but he had practically nothing to do, since very few people could afford the luxury of slaughtering a chicken, and of these even less were prepared to pay him the fee of 50 pruta (14 cents). The Sephardi Jews (mainly Bulgarians) had a synagogue of their own, as had the Yemenite Jews; these two, especially the synagogue of the Yemenites, were more frequented, on weekdays as well as on Saturdays and holidays.

Marriages tended to be contracted only within one single ethnic group. During the three-year life span of Beit Dagon only two "mixed" marriages took place: one between a Yugoslav man and a Bulgarian woman; the other between a North African man and a Bulgarian woman.

The relationship among the various ethnic groups in the village seemed to be good, at least as far as day-to-day personal contact was concerned. That there was nevertheless a latent animus between people belonging to different groups, could be observed on such occasions as when two persons who had a quarrel happened to belong to two different ethnic groups. In such a case, the compatriots of each would take, as a matter of course, the side of their own fellow countryman. Such occurrences, however, were rare, and did not seriously disturb the generally friendly atmosphere prevailing in the village.*

A mixed village like Beit Dagon would seem to be the best way found as yet to bring about a speedy and relatively frictionless cultural amalgamation among different Jewish ethnic groups. All the people finding themselves side by side in the village are newcomers; they all have the same or largely similar problems to cope with and difficulties to overcome; they work together, or at least in close proximity with one another; and the only common language through which they can communicate is Hebrew. Mutual adjustment is facilitated by the very presence in the village of *several* different ethnic elements, a situation in which no single group is able to achieve a status of prominence or predominance and create a feeling of isolation and discrimination in a smaller group.

The population of Beit Dagon consisted of four Ashkenazi groups (Polish, Rumanian, Hungarian and Czechoslovakian Jews), one highly Westernized Sephardi group (the Italian Jews), two less Westernized Sephardi groups (the Bulgarian and Yugoslovian Jews), yet another typically Eastern Sephardi group (the Turkish Jews), and three Oriental Jewish groups very different from one another (Algerians-Tunisians, Egyptians and Yemenites), altogether eleven groups, each with a distinct cultural heritage of its own. The *a priori* prognostication that such a multiple group has a better chance for mutual adjustment seems to be borne out by the actual developments in Beit Dagon.

The difficulties encountered by a small group of newcomers, when it is received into an older settlement with a more or less crystallized and homogenized individuality of its own, can be illustrated by the example of 45 Bulgarian Jews who upon their arrival in Israel were settled in a *kibbutz,* a communal settlement, with some 300 older members. The Bulgarian immigrants remained a separate entity

* The above account of life in Beit Dagon is based on field notes taken in July, 1951, in the course of an interview with the vice-chairman of the Village Council of Beit Dagon, Mr. Jacob Oberweis, who also acted as secretary of the Council. It may be of interest to mention here the opinion of Mr. Oberweis—himself a Polish Jew who came to Israel, via Germany, in January 1949—as to the qualities of three main groups of people whom he knew from prolonged first-hand contact in Beit Dagon. According to him, "the best element among the immigrants are unquestionably the Yemenite Jews. They are satisfied with what they have and what they get; they are disciplined and love to work. Much worse than the Yemenites are the European immigrants, who are full of caprices, are dissatisfied, are not used to labor, and for whom life in Israel is strange. Worst of all, however, are the North Africans, who definitely dislike to work, and who are devoid of both religious and secular culture."

within the *kibbutz*. The whole group was lodged together in a separate part of the *kibbutz*, they went to work as a group and took their meals in the communal dining hall as a group apart from the others. After supper they again repaired as a group to the separate *beit tarbut*, culture house, which was set up for them. There they found entertainment by listening to the phonograph or dancing to jazz music.

The other members of the *kibbutz* showed the attitude of sympathetic tolerance and politeness characteristic of "broadminded" people when encountering customs and behavior patterns different from their own. But no one tried to take part in their social life or to spend his hours of leisure with them. It was clearly evident that, apart from one or two members of the *kibbutz* whose assigned task it was to talk to the newcomers and convince them that the ways of the *kibbutz* were good and preferable as a permanent form of life, the rank and file did not care too much what the Bulgarians did, felt or thought. Thus, in spite of the fact that in every objectively measurable aspect the Bulgarians enjoyed complete equality with the older members of the *kibbutz*, they were unable to take root, to acquire that at-home feeling which is so essential, especially when living in a small community. As one of them put it, they felt like strangers who are guests in a hospitable house, which, however, is superior to them socially. Not many months passed before 40 out of the 45 Bulgarians left the *kibbutz*.[*]

A comparison of the case of these 45 Bulgarian immigrants with that of Beit Dagon indicates that the importance of the social and cultural conditions can in certain cases outweigh that of the economic situation. The 45 Bulgarian immigrants were economically in a completely satisfactory position; having been received by the *kibbutz* as members, they were freed from any economic or financial worry and obtained an economic and material status equal to that of the old *kibbutz* members. Yet 88.8% of them chose to face the economic vicissitudes which awaited them outside the *kibbutz* rather than put up with a socially and culturally unsatisfactory situation. In Beit Dagon, on the other hand, a socially and culturally satisfactory situation more than made up for what the new immigrants of the eleven different communities lacked economically.

Of course, the degree of success in adjustment to a new environment depends not only on the latter's social configuration but, at least to the same extent, also on the cultural heritage and back-

[*] Cf. D. R. Elston, "The Duty of the Citizens in the Absorption of Immigrants" (Hebrew), in *Haaretz*, Tel Aviv, March 3, 1950.

ground of the group seeking adjustment. Differences in cultural background come to the fore especially when a group settles in a separate village, and one can compare it with groups with different cultural backgrounds settled in other separate villages. The developments in a village settled only by Iraqi Jews, in a second village settled only by American Jews, and in a third village settled only by Rumanian Jews, sketched above in a few brief sentences, demonstrate most eloquently the decisive influence of the differential cultural backgrounds invisibly accompanying each immigrant group in addition to the visible, material equipment brought along by them.

4. A Tel Aviv Slum

In Mandatory times, the majority of the Jewish slum-inhabitants were Sephardi and Oriental Jews, and the same ethnic elements fill the slums in Israel today.

A typical slum is the Hatiqwa Quarter between Jaffa and Tel Aviv, inhabited in 1950 (together with two adjoining slum areas) by about 35-40,000 persons, 87% of whom were Sephardi and Oriental Jews.* The Hatiqwa Quarter had belonged to Jaffa, and its growth and development into one of the worst slums in the country took place while it was under the jurisdiction of the Arab municipality of Jaffa. But even since its incorporation into the municipal area of Tel-Aviv no changes have occurred (up to 1950), no public works have been initiated and no sanitary or other improvements made.

The residents of the Hatiqwa Quarter belong to 12 separate community groups and hail from twice as many countries. Percentually they are distributed according to countries of origin as follows:

Country	%	Country	%	Country	%
Yemen	25	Tripoli	6	Other Countries	8
Syria	12	Palestine	6	Europe	13
Turkey	11	Persia	4	Total	100
N. Africa	11	Egypt	4		

The average number of years passed since the immigration of the adult residents was 12 in 1950, and about 22% of the heads of families had been in the country for more than 20 years. These people, therefore, were "old Palestinians," most of whom had lived through the Arab riots of 1936-39, the difficult period of World War

* The following is based on the results of a survey carried out by Dr. M. Levital and Arye Globerson, and published in three articles, in *Al Hamishmar*, Tel Aviv, May 17, 23 and 25, 1950 (in Hebrew).

II, the subsequent civic strife with the Mandatory power, and the Arab-Jewish war, together with the rest of the *Yishuv*.

A considerable proportion of the earners also underwent those changes of occupation which were characteristic for every immigrant group whether it came from the East or from the West, and the most outstanding single feature of which is the decrease in the number of merchants and increase in that of laborers in relation to the *status quo* in the home countries. The following brief table gives a comparison (in percentages) between the occupations of the residents of the Hatiqwa Quarter in 1950 and their occupational structure before their immigration to Palestine:

Occupation	Abroad	In Israel
Merchants	46	10
Laborers	7	54
Artisans	21	21
Pedlars	8	5
Silversmiths and Ritual Slaughterers	8	1
Others	10	9
Total	100	100

Some 25% were unemployed at the time the survey was conducted, most of them chronically so, and in general this was explained as being the result of discrimination practiced against the Oriental Jews by the rest of the *Yishuv*.

The average number of children (alive) per family was 4.5. The children attended school for a maximum of only four years, and at the age of ten or eleven they began to work. The teachers complained of the difficulties they encountered in trying—mostly in vain —to counteract the influence of the home and of the street. When the ten-year-old boy or girl would leave school and start working, he (or she) would be directed by his own choice and the influence of the parents to an occupation which would give the highest income at the earliest date; hence in most cases the children learned no trade or other skill which in the long run would enable them to obtain a permanent position with adequate wages. A large number of the boys went into various services (unskilled labor), and most of the girls became household helpers. The young generation was thus channeled into the same path traversed before them by their parents leading to a perpetuation of the slum-conditions and of the underprivileged status of the people.

In general, the population of the Hatiqwa Quarter was rather conservative. They took no proper interest in the social and cultural

life of Israel, and the members of the various communities lived in more or less closed and isolated groups with little outside contacts. After twelve or more years' residence in the country, most or all of which time was spent in the same quarter in very close proximity with other Oriental Jewish communities, 78% of the marriages were still contracted within the same community; marriages where the husband and wife belonged to two different Oriental Jewish communities were entered into only by 22% of the married couples.*
Marriages between Oriental Jews and Ashkenazim were very rare, and, true to the conservative outlook, divorce was regarded as shameful.

Conservatism and isolation were responsible for the fact that in spite of the 12 or more years which had passed since the immigration of these Oriental Jews to Palestine, about four-fifths of them still used in everyday life the language brought from the old home countries. The languages used were as follows in percentages:

Language	%	Language	%	Language	%
Arabic	45	Turkish	7.5	Bulgarian	3.8
Hebrew	20.5	Yiddish	7.5	Others	3.7
Ladino	7.5	French	4.5	Total	100.0

Arabic was spoken by the Jews of Yemen and the majority of those coming from North Africa, Syria and Egypt. Ladino was spoken by those coming from Turkey mainly, though some Sephardi Jews from North Africa, Egypt and Syria also retained Ladino as their conversational medium. French was spoken by some of the North African Jews.

The housing situation in the quarter was even worse than it had been several years previously among the poor Oriental Jews in Jerusalem. There the average density was 5.5 persons per room,§ whereas in the Hatiqwa Quarter in 1950 it was 6.1. Ten per cent of the Quarter's residents lived in the almost incredibly overcrowded conditions of 10-13 persons per room. Only one-fifth of the families had two-room apartments, the rest lived in one room, lacking in most cases kitchens or bathrooms. There was no sewerage in the Quarter so that the streets were full of sewage, dirt and stench. In the narrow lanes heaps of garbage accumulated with no one caring. As a consequence of the unsanitary conditions, contagious diseases (including

---

* This proportion, however, is somewhat higher than the proportion of marriages between members of different Oriental Jewish communities in Jerusalem in 1939; cf. above, p. 101.
§ Cf. below, p. 136.

tuberculosis, skin-diseases, intestinal infections, venereal diseases, eye diseases and children's diseases) had a much higher incidence than in neighboring Tel Aviv. Many of the older people objected to entering a hospital, even when seriously ill, for they believed that a person who entered a hospital thereby greatly diminished his chances of recovery. Most of the women still preferred to give birth to their children at home, with the help of a midwife from their own community. It was the people from this and similar quarters who as late as May 1950, on the occasion of the traditional *Lag baOmer* pilgrimage to the tomb of Rabbi Shimon bar Yohai in Meron in the Galilee, filled the rooms and caves of the holy place and spent the night there in ecstatic supplication for recovery from incurable or criminally neglected diseases, or for the opening of sterile wombs, and for the passing of other miseries.[*]

The majority of the residents of the Hatiqwa Quarter were keenly conscious of the inadequacy of their living quarters and wished for an improvement. The question, "Are you satisfied with your lodgings?" was answered by 69% in the negative. The 31% who answered affirmatively were mostly Yemenites who lived even within the Hatiqwa Quarter in the most crowded conditions, but whose traditional modesty is unparalleled among the other Jewish communities.

In general, the opinion in the Hatiqwa Quarter was that they were discriminated against because they were Oriental Jews. The pertinent question, "Does discrimination exist against the Oriental Jews?" was answered 75% with an unhesitating "Yes," by 13% with "No," and by 12% with an emphatic "No." Those who answered in the affirmative felt that the discrimination extended into practically all phases of life: settlement and housing, employment, education, public services and so forth. There was a great embitterment against the official authorities of the State, the city of Tel Aviv, the Jewish Agency. One of the few civic actions for which the people of the Quarter were able to rally unitedly, was to refuse the payment of the municipal taxes to Tel Aviv in protest over the lack of any activity on behalf of the municipality in their Quarter.

5. Measurable Differences

Very often, even if the more tangible, overall material frame of existence is similar or even identical in two or more groups, differences will be observable which can be explained only in terms of differential cultural heritage. A valuable study on this important subject was made by Dr. Sarah Bergner-Rabinowitz in Jerusalem

[*] Cf. *Davar* (Hebrew daily), Tel Aviv, May 17, 1950.

in 1944-45.* The aim of her study was to find out what differences exist between Ashkenazi and Oriental Jewish groups in points of hygiene, nutrition and education. For this purpose she studied four groups of fifty families each: a group of fifty Kurdish and Persian Jewish families, with a total number of 263 children (5.26 children per family) and with an average per capita monthly income in 1942 of £.P.1.680 ($6.72) which by 1944 increased to £.P.2.703 ($10.81), corresponding to an increment of 64.5%. This group was compared to a correspondingly poor Ashkenazi Jewish group of fifty families, of the most religious element in Jerusalem. The data for this group were: 246 children, or 4.92 children per family; a per capita monthly income in 1942 of £.P.1.630 ($6.52), in 1944 of £.P.2.680 ($10.72), an increase of 63%. Also two family groups of a higher income bracket were studied in the same way: an Oriental Jewish (Persian and Kurdish) group of fifty families with 114 children (2.30 children per family), a per capita monthly income in 1942 of £.P.3.540 (14.16) and in 1944 of £.P.5.980 (23.92), an increase of 69%; and an Ashkenazi Jewish group of fifty families with 106 children (2.12 children per family), a per capita monthly income in 1942 of £.P. 3.830 ($15.32) and in 1944 of £.P.7.500 ($30.00, an increase of 96%). Outwardly, therefore, the two pairs of family groups closely corresponded to each other in number of children as well as per capita monthly income. (To give some idea of the low level of the income-class to which even the two better-off groups belonged, let us mention that in 1942 the average *daily* wage of Jewish laborers in the building trade in Palestine was £.P.0.650 or $2.60, which increased by 1944 to £.P.1.300 or $5.20).

The first outstanding difference between the poor Ashkenazi and the poor Oriental group was that the share of women and children in making a living was twice as great in the Oriental group as in the Ashkenazi group: 13 women (26%) of the Oriental families worked, as against 6 women (12%) of the Ashkenazi families. Of the children between the ages 9-18 in the Oriental families, 26.4% worked, while in the Ashkenazi families only 13%. Moreover, in the Oriental group twice as many girls (22) worked as boys (11), while in the Ashkenazi group there were more boys (7) than girls (5) working.

The greater participation in the Oriental Jewish group of women and children in the family earnings means, of course, that the average earnings of the fathers in these families were correspondingly

* Cf. Dr. Sarah Bergner-Rabinowitz, *Hygiene, Education and Nutrition among Kurdish, Persian and Ashkenazic Jews in Jerusalem* (Hebrew with English Summary). *Social Studies*, vol. I. ed. by Roberto Bachi and Raphael Patai. The Pal. Inst. of Folklore and Ethnology, Jerusalem, 1948, 68 pp.

lower than those of the fathers in the Ashkenazi group. This is explained by the fact that the adult males in the Oriental Jewish group were mostly unskilled laborers whose average daily income was lower than that of the earners in the Ashkenazi group. The Oriental women who worked were occupied in most cases as household helpers away from home; the majority of the working Ashkenazi women, on the other hand, took in sewing and the repair of clothes which they executed in their own homes.

As to the working children, a significant difference is observed as to the age of children entering work: in the Oriental group, of the 33 working children, over half were aged 9 to 12 years, and less than one half from 13 to 18 years of age. In the Ashkenazi group, of the 12 children working, only two were in the lower, the remainder in the higher age-bracket.

This differential in the age of those entering employment makes itself felt in a corresponding difference in the percentage of children leaving school at an early age, or lacking any schooling. The following table contains the relevant figures as to boys and girls aged 5-19 in both groups:

Community and Sex	Now in School	Now in Talmud Tora	Left School after 2 or 3 years	Attends Evening Classes	Never Attended Any School
Oriental M.	26.6	61.7	11.7	—	—
Ashkenazi M.	21.05	76.13	2.82	—	—
Oriental F.	58.3	2.78	8.36	8.36	22.2
Ashkenazi F.	97.3	2.6	—	—	—
Oriental M.-F.	40.3	36.23	10.23	3.62	9.62
Ashkenazi M.-F.	60.0	38.62	1.38	—	—

The most significant differences shown by this table are doubtlessly those pertaining to the education of girls. All the girls of the Ashkenazi group attended school, practically all of them (97.3%) modern schools, and only a negligible percentage (2.6%) *Talmud Tora* schools.* On the other hand, in the Oriental group 22.2%, or more than one-fifth, of the girls never attended any school, another 8.36% attended school only for two or three years and then were made to leave, and yet another 8.36% attended only evening classes— all of which makes a staggering total of 38.92%, or almost two-fifths, who either never attended school or received a less than rudimentary

* The old-fashioned schools in which practically the only subject taught is Bible.

education. If we permit ourselves to generalize* from these figures, and from the data showing the early impressment of girls into remunerative work by the Oriental group, we are driven to the conclusion that in a very considerable percentage of families belonging to the Oriental Jewish communities, it was regarded as unnecessary to give girls any education at all, and the girls were either sent to work at a very early age—mostly as household helpers in better-off families —or were assigned household chores by their own mothers at home. This was fully in accord with the traditional customs of the Oriental Jewish communities brought along by them from their respective countries of residence and continued after their immigration to Palestine and Israel. The Kurdish Jews in Kurdistan, or the Persian Jews in Persia have had no educational facilities of their own for girls, while at the same time 50% to 90% of the boys, the figure varying according to localities, attended *Talmud Tora* schools regularly. The overwhelming majority of the girls, therefore, grew up illiterate, and literate women were found in these communities only exceptionally.§

When viewed against this background, the significance of the percentage of female school attendance in the Oriental communities changes completely. The regular schooling of about three-fifths of the girls from Oriental Jewish families in Jerusalem appears now as a very high figure and as a considerable educational achievement, in view of the fact that the mothers and elder sisters of the same girls never attended any school in their home countries. The fact that three-fifths of the girls were sent to school can also be taken as an indication of the extent of the cultural influence of the new Hebrew environment on these Oriental Jewish groups, and as a gauge of the very significant degree of assimilation evidenced by these notoriously conservative groups to the new cultural atmosphere in Palestine. Instead of regarding it as a disconcerting phenomenon, one will therefore have to view the school attendance by three-fifths of the Oriental Jewish girls as a most encouraging evidence of rapid cultural change which is taking place within these communities. *

As to the types of school preferred by the parents, there is a surprising similarity between the Ashkenazi and the Oriental groups. Both sent practically all of their girls to modern schools while they

* In 1939, of all the Sephardi and Oriental Jewish girls in Jerusalem aged 5-9.9 years, 36.8% did not attend school. In Morocco, the one Oriental country best provided by the Alliance Israélite Universelle with educational facilities for girls, only about half of the Jewish female school-age population attended schools in 1950.

§ Cf. Raphael Patai, "The Hebrew Education in the Marrano Community of Meshhed," (Hebrew), in *Edoth*, Jerusalem, July, 1946, p. 226.

sent the majority of their boys to *Talmud Tora* schools (the Ashkenazi group 76.13%; the Oriental group 61.7%). The explanation of this phenomenon lies in the fact that both groups studied by Dr. Bergner were extremely religious orthodox groups who in their old countries had looked askance at any secular education for their male children, and who have continued to do so after their immigration to Palestine. Hence in Palestine they sent their boys also to the same type of school to which they would have sent them had they remained in Poland or in Hungary, in Persia or in Kurdistan. With the girls the situation was different. Among the Oriental communities these were never sent to any school at all and, compared with the great innovation of sending a girl-child to school, the question as to the type of school to which to send her was quite unimportant. Also, never having had *Talmud Tora* schools for girls, the establishment of such schools in Palestine would have been too much of an organizational innovation. A somewhat similar mentality prevailed among the orthodox Jews from Eastern Europe whose religious tradition too enjoined the religious education of boys only; consequently, it was regarded as permissible to send the girls to the schools established by the Agudat Yisrael (the organization of Jews more orthodox than those in the Mizrahi party), especially for girls from extremely religious homes.

The impression that the choice between an old-fashioned *Talmud Tora* school and a more modern regular elementary school depends at least as much on religious conviction as on ethnic background, can be confirmed by referring to a wider study which gives a general picture as to the educational situation within the Ashkenazi and the Oriental Jewish communities in Palestine in general. This study, made by R. Bachi in 1944[*] shows that of all the Ashkenazi children only 10.5%, and of all the Oriental Jewish children only 42% studied in *Talmud Tora* schools.

HOUSING CONDITIONS OF ORIENTAL AND ASHKENAZI JEWS IN JERUSALEM IN 1944

	Groups of Fifty Families Each			
Average Number of	Oriental Poor	Ashkenazi Poor	Oriental Better Off	Ashkenazi Better Off
Rooms per Family	1.32	1.78	1.62	1.90
Rooms per Capita	0.18	0.26	0.38	0.48
Persons per Room	5.50	3.90	2.64	2.04
Beds per Capita	0.40	0.62	0.92	1.10
Windows per Capita	0.24	0.39	0.55	0.77

[*] Cf. R. Bachi, *Our Children in Numbers* (Hebrew), Jerusalem, 1944.

Significant and interesting culturally-conditioned differences are found to exist between the Ashkenazi and the Oriental groups in such a material trait as housing. The table on page 136 gives a summary of the most relevant data of the four groups studied by Dr. Bergner.

Though the first two groups compared have had approximately the same per capita income and consisted of about the same number of members, nevertheless, in the Oriental group there were considerably more people living in one room and sleeping in one bed than in the corresponding Ashkenazi group. The same can be observed when comparing the two better-off groups. These differences, therefore, cannot be explained by a difference in the income level or in number of persons comprising a family, but must be attributed to the variations in the cultural backgrounds of the groups in question, that is, to the general absence in the Oriental countries of housing standards developed in the West.

A relatively greater difference, however, can be observed between the poor and the better-off Oriental groups than between the poor Oriental and the poor Ashkenazi groups. Between the poor Ashkenazi group and the better-off Ashkenazi group there is also a much greater difference than between any one of these groups and the corresponding Oriental group. This observation leads us to the conclusion that housing standards depend to a greater extent on the economic situation than on the cultural or ethnic background. This conclusion, in its turn, can serve as a basis for practical consideration. In any undertaking which proposes to raise the housing standard of the Oriental Jewish communities, or of any other Oriental groups, the main effort must be directed towards an improvement of the general economic condition, and only secondarily must this be accompanied by a re-educational effort.

Somewhat different results are arrived at when contemplating the sanitary and hygienic conditions in the four groups. These are summarized in a table showing the percentage of families in each group who exhibit certain sanitary and hygienic features (see page 138).

This table indicates that the sanitary and hygienic conditions prevailing in the poor Oriental group are inferior to those found in the poor Ashkenazi group, and that the better-off Orientals show the same relationship to the better-off Ashkenazi group. These results, therefore, confirm the findings based on a statistical scrutiny of the housing situation. A comparison of the poor Orientals with both the poor Ashkenazi group and the better-off Oriental group, however, leads to a different, two-fold conclusion. It appears that those facilities which can be had for an expenditure of money, like electric

SANITARY AND HYGIENIC FEATURES AMONG ASHKENAZI
AND ORIENTAL JEWS IN JERUSALEM IN 1944.

	Percentage of Families in the Groups of Fifty			
Sanitary Features	Oriental Poor	Ashkenazi Poor	Oriental Better-Off	Ashkenazi Better-Off
Street Kept Clean	26	80	72	80
Yard Kept Clean	46	86	90	96
Vicinity of Apartment Kept Clean	60	98	92	100
Apartment Kept Clean	54	94	88	98
Kerosene Lighting	74	40	14	—
Electric Lighting	26	60	86	100
Municipal Water Supply (tap)	64	58	86	100
Cistern Water Used	36	42	14	—
Kitchen Kept Clean	54	92	90	98
Uncovered Kitchen Bin Used	84	24	40	14
Kitchen Bin Kept Covered	16	76	60	86
Bathtub or Shower in House	10	44	68	98
Lavatory without Flushing Facilities	82	62	30	2
Lavatory in the Courtyard	78	60	22	4
Joint Lavatory for 2 or More Families	90	64	56	28
✳ Lavatory Kept Clean	42	78	86	96

lighting, municipally supplied water, a bathtub or shower, a lavatory with water flushing, have been acquired by the better-off Oriental group to a greater extent than by the poor Ashkenazi group. On the other hand, those hygienic attainments which depend on the amount of labor devoted to them by the housewife, like the cleanliness of the street, of the apartment and its vicinity, as well as of the kitchen in particular, including the covering of the kitchen bin, lag in the better-off Oriental group somewhat behind the performance of the poor Ashkenazi group. In this respect, therefore, the practical conclusion will be the reverse of the one reached above concerning the ways of improving the housing situation: should an effort be made to improve the hygienic conditions in the apartments lived in by Oriental Jewish communities, such an effort will have to be first of all educational, and only secondarily will it have to be directed toward an improvement in the economic situation.

Differences in food-habits among the various Jewish communities can be described more easily in terms of foods preferred and methods of preparation than by pointing to inequalities in the amount of calories and nutrients consumed. A knowledge of the foodstuffs preferred or disdained by the Jewish groups from the East and the West is especially useful in a situation when a central station has to provide food for many different groups, such as can be found in the immigrants' reception camp in Israel. Yet the mere fact that each Jewish community has favorite dishes of its own, and that the cuisine of none of them is exactly like that of any other, is too well known to necessitate the adducement of examples. What is of greater significance for an evaluation of the differences in the food habits is an exact measurement of the daily *per capita* food consumption in the various groups broken down according to the main foodstuffs consumed.

DAILY FOOD CONSUMPTION PER CAPITA IN THE FOUR GROUPS (IN GRAMS)

Foodstuffs	Oriental Poor	Ashkenazi Poor	Oriental Better-Off	Ashkenazi Better-Off	Daily Requirement
Bread	413	322	306	332	350
Flour	23	20	19	33	30
Cereals	36	24	48	50	30
Meat & Fish	30	43	62	91	50
Eggs (no.)	0.2	0.4	0.7	1.0	0.5
Margarine	8	14	10	24	25
Fats	27	24	27	27	25
Milk	75	138	205	317	250
Cheese	6	8	12	15	30
Legumes	22	11	14	6	20
Vegetables	280	230	318	408	300
Fruit	380	235	488	572	550
Sugar	27	24	32	35	25 *

A detailed analysis of this table would be too technical and does not seem necessary for our present purpose. In general it can be remarked that the consumption of meat and fish, milk and dairy products, vegetables and fruit is low in both of the poor groups. As to differences between the Orientals and the Ashkenazim, both of the Oriental groups use less meat, fish, milk and cheese, but more bread and legumes than the corresponding Ashkenazi groups. It is also interesting to note that of the 13 kinds of foodstuffs enumerated, there are five (bread, cereals, fats, legumes and sugar) the consumption of which is below the daily requirement in the poor Ashkenazi group, but above it in the poor Oriental group. On the other hand, even those foodstuffs which are consumed in larger quantities by the poor Ashkenazi group than by the poor Oriental group, are still consumed by the former in insufficient quantities. The general impression, therefore, is that the diet of the poor Oriental group, though not quite adequate, is yet more balanced than that of the poor Ashkenazi group. Also in the two better-off groups, the diet of the Oriental group is closer, on the whole, to the daily requirements, while that of the Ashkenazi group shows a considerable excess in many foodstuffs.* While, therefore, the diet of the poor Oriental group leaves much to be desired in certain points, it has more numerous features which the Ashkenazi group could take over to its advantage.

6. Literacy and Languages

Yet another important characteristic of Israel, contributing to the mosaic-like appearance of its cultural picture, is the wide range of variations in the percentage of literates and illiterates among the various Jewish ethnic groups in the country. The average rate of literacy in Israel is high, just as it was high in the *Yishuv* in Mandatory Palestine. According to the 1931 census of Palestine, the literacy rate among the Jewish males reached 93.4%, and among the Jewish females 78.7%. Since that time, the percentage of literates has continued to increase, and with the introduction of compulsory and free education in Israel, the last remnants of illiteracy will soon become a thing of the past.

The fact that in 1931 the literacy rate was *only* as high as it was and to this day has not yet reached 100%, is due to the presence of the Oriental element in Israel's Jewish population. If we were sure that among the Ashkenazim there were absolutely no illiterates, one could calculate the extent of illiteracy among the non-Ashkenazi Jews in Palestine and would reach the following rough percentages: Illiteracy among the Sephardi-Oriental Jewish males: 24.4%; and among the females: 78.8%. These high figures, in themselves staggering, would, of course, be changed considerably by even a small percentage of illiterates among the Ashkenazi Jews. Therefore they can be taken only as the upper limit of possible illiteracy among the Sephardi and Oriental Jews in Palestine according to the 1931 census returns. The highest actual illiteracy rate was shown by the Jews of Jaffa, the great majority of whom in 1931 were Sephardim or Orientals. The figures according to the 1931 census were as follows:

ILLITERACY OF THE JEWS OF JAFFA IN 1931 (IN %)

	Age 7-14	Age 14-21	Age 21 and over	Age 7 and over
Males	23.4	18.0	21.6	21.3
Females	34.1	34.6	51.6	44.8
Both Sexes	28.9	26.6	36.4	33.1

These figures can be regarded as the lowest limit. It can therefore be stated that, in 1931, the percentage of the illiterates among the

* Cf. Sarah Bergner-Rabinowitz, *op. cit.*, pp. 30-2.

Sephardi and Oriental Jewish males in Palestine was between 21.3%
and 24.4%, while that of the females between 44.8% and 78.8%.

Both a high rate of illiteracy and a considerable differential
between the male and the female illiteracy rates, are characteristic
of the Middle Eastern world as a whole. Moreover, the percentage
of illiterates, both male and female, in the Moslem countries is much
higher than among the Sephardi and Oriental Jews. The following ✻
table will illustrate this:

ILLITERACY RATES IN THE MIDDLE EAST (IN %)

Country or Community	Year	Males	Females
Jews of Palestine (5 years and over)	1931	9.7	23.5
Sephardi and Oriental Jews in Palestine (5 years and over)	1931	21.3-24.4	44.8-78.8
Palestinian Christians (5 years and over)	1931	31.7	57.3
Palestinian Moslems (5 years and over)	1931	76.6	96.8
Egyptian Jews (5 years and over)*	1927	18.3	36.0
Egyptian Christians (5 years and over)	1927	53.0	75.1
Egyptian Moslems (5 years and over)	1927	79.7	97.5
Egypt (general; 10 years and over)	1937	76.6	93.9
Turkey (10 years and over)	1935	67.4	89.7
Bulgaria (10 years and over)	1934	19.5	43.3
Greece (10 years and over)	1928	23.3	57.6
Yugoslavia (11 years and over)	1931	32.7	57.1

* The relatively high literacy of the Jews of Egypt is due to the fact that
practically all of them lived in the big cities of Cairo and Alexandria, and that
a considerable proportion of them were of European origin.

Sources: *U.N. Statistical Yearbook 1949-50; Census of Palestine 1931.*

The literacy rates of populations are always calculated on the
basis of their knowing how to read and write *any* language. In
Palestine and Israel, in view of the constant stream of new immigrants, this means the presence of an additional large percentage in
the population which, though literate in its respective languages,
does not know Hebrew and is thus unable to participate in those
cultural fields which use the medium of Hebrew. It is very difficult
to estimate how many in the Jewish population of Palestine-Israel
in any given period knew Hebrew sufficiently well to read a newspaper, a magazine, a book, or to follow a lecture or a theater performance. It would be equally difficult to tell how long it took for
the average immigrant to learn the language. There are those, especially children and people whose work made it imperative, who
have learned to speak Hebrew within a few months; while on the
other end of the scale stand those, mainly older people or women
not in need of making a living, who never learn the language, or at
the most barely manage to make their houseworkers understand

their wishes. Apart from the economic necessity for learning Hebrew, which of course is the strongest incentive in most cases, certain differences seem to exist with regard to the effect of the secondary incentive represented by those aspects of culture which are expressed by written or spoken words. In very general terms, these differences can be said to depend on the relationship between the cultural values accessible to the immigrants through the languages they brought along with them, and the cultural values opened up for them through Hebrew.

The large number of languages brought along by the immigrant groups undoubtedly makes the task of mutual adjustment and the processes of amalgamation more difficult. On the other hand, due to the great diversity of their mother-tongues, the supremacy of Hebrew remains unchallenged. During the thirty-year-old history of Mandatory Palestine, it has looked several times as though the hegemony of Hebrew was being endangered by a large monolingual immigrant group. In the early post-World War I years this rival language was Yiddish. In the 'thirties it was German. During World War II it was English—not on account of a large number of immigrants from English-speaking countries, but because of the presence of great numbers of British soldiers and the great demand for English-speaking Palestinians in all kinds of employment and services. Today, even if tens of thousands of immigrants all speaking the same language arrive in Israel in the course of a single year, they are counterbalanced by tens of thousands of other immigrants speaking a different language. They must learn Hebrew in order to communicate with one another and in order to integrate into the economic, social and cultural life of the country.

It is generally held that the Hebrew language of Israel is spoken in the so-called "Sephardic" accent. It would therefore seem that in this point the Sephardi division of the Jewish people has scored an important victory over the Ashkenazim: it is their Hebrew pronunciation which has been accepted by all and which is the only living, spoken Hebrew today both in Israel and in the Diaspora. In reality, however, this is far from true. The fact of the matter is that *sabra*-Hebrew contains a mixture of Ashkenazi and Sephardi phonemic elements, with a definite preponderance of the Ashkenazi components.

It would be too technical to treat here in detail of the phonological affinities* or to analyze the Eastern and Western influences on the grammar and vocabulary of *sabra* Hebrew. A living language cannot suffer lacunae; since Hebrew is very much alive in Israel, it fills its

---

* This the author intends to do in a separate article elsewhere.

lacunae with great alacrity from the languages brought along by the Jewish immigrants. In one single sentence one may hear Yiddish, Arabic, English and German expressions, words or affixes fused into the Hebrew speech. This fills the purists with despair, but should actually be regarded merely as the normal growing pains of a language.

The differences in linguistic and cultural heritage, brought along by the new immigrants to Israel, are great and overwhelming in the first generation. They are often pronounced enough to make for mutual mistrust and dislike and to give rise to stereotypes heavily weighted on the negative side. The first impression of strangeness and of otherness tends to become the framework determining the approach of one group to another. The history of modern Palestine has shown, however, that in the second generation, or at the utmost in the third, these differences tend to diminish and to disappear altogether, mainly as a result of the common upbringing of the children in the schools and the close contact and interaction between members of the young generation. Among the adult immigrants, however, the differences are not only present but constitute a force to be reckoned with, serving even as a basis for political parties, for economic organizations and for rural settlement groupings. Within the Ashkenazi division itself the belittling attitude of the Russian Jew towards the Polish Jew is well known; similarly, that of both the Polish and the Russian Jews towards the German Jew, the "Jecke," and that of the German Jews towards the East-European Jew, the "Ostjude." Similar group attitudes can easily be discerned within the Oriental Jewish communities, where group solidarity is usually confined to a much smaller unit. The negative stereotype is stamped not only upon the Jews of a neighboring country but on those of the next town. The really "impossible" features will, as a rule, be attributed only to those beyond the state border: the Persian Jews will scorn the Afghan Jews, for example; the Bokharan Jews will deprecate the Persian Jews; the Iraqi Jews will despise the Kurdish Jews, and so forth. And as to the group attitudes of the Sephardi Jews, their conviction that they, and only they, are of the ancient and noblest Jewish blood is too well known to need special mention.

Yet, withal, one must not attribute too great an importance to these differences. The centrifugal force expressed in the negative attitude towards one's neighbor from a different community is more than counterbalanced by the centripetal forces which unite the neighbors when they find themselves confronted by a group more distant and therefore differing even more.

The old Oriental proverb: "I and my tribe against the nation; I and my cousins against the tribe; I and my brothers against my cousins; I against my brothers," could be applied in reverse to the ethnic groupings in Israel: "I against my brothers; I and my brothers against my cousins; I and my cousins against the tribe; I and my tribe against the nation;" and one could add: "I and my nation against other nations." In other words, while there is undoubtedly a keen consciousness of the minor differences between the smallest splinter groups, these differences tend to be disregarded the moment the more significant differences existing between the major ethnic groupings, especially those of the three main divisions of the people, are realized. It should also be emphasized that an awareness of cultural differences between one's own group and other groups, and a concomitant disapproval of these differences, are healthy signs of normal group consciousness and can serve as a basis for constructive contact and cooperation if properly channeled.

Chapter Six
Western Foundations

For a visitor coming from the colder climes of Europe or America, it is difficult at first to comprehend to what degree Israeli culture today is Western in its entire character. One is apt to be misguided by the long and rainless summers, the bright and scorching sun, the spring and autumn *khamsins* which blow the hot dust of the desert across the country; in short, by a climate typifying the arid character of the Middle East. Such external and easily noticeable cultural traits as an architectural style geared to a sunlit climate, a certain nonchalance in dress and a general reduction in the amount of clothing worn, also serve as a constant reminder that one is in a country very different from one's own accustomed environment.

Yet these external features, and others which contribute to the first impression, are misleading. A closer inspection will soon show that the culture of Israel as a whole differs only slightly from the culture of the urbanized West. As a matter of fact, one finds that the difference between the two is merely of the same order of magnitude as the cultural variations of the Western countries and peoples among themselves. There are, of course, outstanding cultural characteristics which are specific to Israel, such as the Hebrew language with all the culture-complexes of which language is the vehicle, Jewish religion with the great cultural heritage it represents, and Jewish national and historical tradition to which a most inspiring chapter has been added with the establishment of Israel. However, the major developments which ensued upon independence, do not lie in these areas. It is in the material, social, intellectual and emotional aspects of life that the young State has experienced unparalleled growth. An analysis of the more recent developments in these areas will uncover the extent to which the culture of modern Israel rests upon Western foundations.

1. The World of Materials

As far as material commodities are concerned, it is a patent and much advertised fact that they are very scarce in Israel; but they are not more inadequate than one would expect if one takes into account the effect of the unprecedented influx of immigrants. Also—and this is the point which should be emphasized here—the commodities and consumers' goods are inadequate only when measured by Western standards, which in point of material equipment are much higher than those of the Middle East. This is most crucially illustrated in the field of housing: when, for instance, Yemenite Jewish immigrants are settled in an abandoned Arab village, this is regarded as an inadequate and merely temporary solution of their housing problem, in spite of the fact that the same houses were regarded as satisfactory by the Arabs who lived in them previously, and that the immigrants themselves lived in Yemen in similar houses or even in inferior ones.

The traditional Arab method of coping with the climate in Palestine (as well as in several other Middle Eastern countries) was to build very thick walls, a few small windows, vaulted ceilings and stone-covered roofs, and thus to insulate the interior of the house from both the heat of the long summer and the cold of the winter nights. Jewish building activity soon discarded this method which could not be employed with multiple-storied houses, and was much too expensive even in small structures because of high wages and building costs. The new style evolved, as typified by the modern houses of Tel Aviv and the other cities of Israel, utilizes a steel or reinforced concrete frame, relatively thin walls, numerous and large windows generally of greater width than height, with upper window sills projecting outward a yard or so in order to cast a shadow over the window during the hottest midday hours, and balconies or terraces often running along the entire front of the house on each floor. The ground plan, which in the case of the traditional Arab houses was arranged around a rectangular central hall, has become in many cases such as to allow for cross-ventilation of the rooms. Central heating has become more and more frequent, especially in the cooler climate of mountain-bound Jerusalem, while a few of the most modern office-buildings in Tel Aviv can boast even of an air-conditioning plant. Electric current is used for lighting, and increasingly also for heating, cooking and refrigeration.

There is feverish house-building activity at present in Israel. Many modern Western innovations in building and construction technique are utilized, and much experimentation goes on continually with time and labor saving devices and machinery, such as the prefabrication of houses or the pouring of an entire house of concrete with the help of a movable mold. But in spite of all these efforts, the rate of construction cannot keep pace with the rate at which the new immigrants arrive in the country. The average daily number of the immigrants during the first three years of Israel's existence was about six hundred. It required almost superhuman effort to provide them with even the most temporary housing, either in abandoned Arab towns and villages, in the tents of immigrants' reception camps, or in the wooden or metal barracks of transit and work villages. *

While speaking of building and housing, mention must be made of the recent shift in the character of the houses put up by the *kvutzot*, the communal villages in Israel. When the first of these were established, it was a matter of both expediency and principle to build living quarters in such a fashion that a married couple, or two or three unmarried persons of the same sex, had one single room in a larger house consisting of several such rooms arranged in rows of four to eight. These houses were, as a rule, long one-story structures and contained neither kitchens, nor bathrooms nor lavatories. The only kitchen in the entire settlement was the one attached to the large communal dining room, while bathrooms—containing only showers and basins—and lavatories were set up in centrally located places so as to be easily accessible from all parts of the settlement. This was expedient, for it reduced building costs and conformed to the strictly interpreted principles of communal living. However, it certainly meant a good deal of discomfort. During World War II the financial position of the *kvutzot* improved considerably. One of the immediate results was a reversion to the more "old-fashioned" style of living, that is, the introduction of certain modest luxuries and amenities. The first innovation was the building of self-contained living quarters for the older and venerated members of the settlements who had had their full share of pioneering life, small bungalows allotted singly to one family only.

While the new immigrants mainly have had to bear the brunt of the housing shortage in Israel, old and new inhabitants alike suffer from the inadequacy of transportation facilities. Yet here again, when we agree with the many in Israel who complain of the shortcomings of transportation, we quite naturally apply Western standards and judgments. It is undoubtedly true that the buses which handle most of the passenger traffic are antiquated, dilapidated, in bad repair, overcrowded and much too few in number; that the taxis * are rare and expensive, and the trains slow and infrequent. Yet it must be remembered that all criticism of this sort tacitly takes it for granted that transportation in Israel must measure up to the Western standard. In the countries of the Middle East, from which half of the present-day Jewish population of Israel has come, there is in many cases no mechanical transportation at all.

It may be mentioned in passing that an improvement in transportation is simply a question of overcoming the dollar shortage. The bus, truck and taxi cooperatives which handle most of the passenger traffic and a considerable proportion of the freight transport in Israel, are prosperous and have enough accumulated funds to renew and replenish their rolling stock. But cars, buses and trucks can be bought only abroad, (the Kaiser-Frazer assembly plant in Haifa works for the time being only for export) and abroad in this case means America.

Nowhere are the austerity measures felt so generally, so immediately and so equally by all sectors of the population as in the field of nutrition. Tight rationing cuts down the amount of food available to any individual, and certain foodstuffs, especially delicacies, are not obtainable at all.

During the British Mandatory regime no strenuous attempts were made either by the government to make the country self-supplying in point of food, nor by the Jewish authorities to achieve the like within the Jewish sector of the population. When the British left Palestine prior to the establishment of the Jewish state, the food imports organized and controlled by them were temporarily disrupted, a circumstance which immediately caused great hardships to the new Jewish state. Increase in local production was soon stimulated, and great efforts were begun to step up vegetable and fruit gardening, dairy production and poultry farming to an extent permitting first the increase and eventually the abolition of rationing. Such staples, however, as flour and meat will have to continue to be imported from abroad. As long as no peace treaty is signed with the neighboring Arab states, which could supply these commodities to Israel, import from abroad means import from overseas, in other words, from countries which accept payment in hard currency only. Expenditure of hard currency for food consumption is a luxury which even old and well-established state economies cannot always permit themselves, and in the case of the infant state of Israel this means a continuation of the austerity program and tight rations for a long time to come. Ideally, if the rationed food were always available, it would no doubt fulfill the minimal requirements. The difficulty lies in the fact that there are long gaps in the supply due to local droughts, transportation breakdowns and other unforeseeable reasons. Food is also very expensive, and, in spite of control and rationing, it cost five to seven times more in 1951 than it did twelve years previously. On the other hand, in 1951 people spent only four times as much on food as they did in 1939, which of course indicates a definite decline in both the quality and the quantity of the food consumed.

However unsatisfactory this situation may be, one must not lose sight of the fact that the rations distributed are fixed so as to approximate the minimum Western requirements of food-consumption which were established in nutritional studies carried out in Europe and America among peoples sharing Western food habits. Whether, however, these ideal standards are applicable everywhere, or whether people brought up in different cultures and consequently having different food habits, have also different nutritional norms as an outcome of their different conditioning, is a problem not yet sufficiently studied. In Israel, no difference is being made in the distribution of rations between people from the West and from the East, although the British Mandatory government of Palestine during World War II set a precedent in this respect by allotting to the Arabs somewhat different rations from those of the Jews in view of the difference in their food habits. Israel regards it as a matter of principle not to differentiate even to this extent between Jew and Jew, or between Arab and Jew. The wisdom of this stand might be questioned in view of the undeniable differences existing in the food habits of the various population elements living in the country. It is a fact, for instance, that one of the main sources of the black market in meat and eggs are the Oriental Jews who are used to consuming even less of these foodstuffs than are rationed out to them and who thus supplement their income by privately selling their meat and egg rations. ✳

A word or two should be said here about the water situation in Israel. Again, when evaluating the adequacy of the water supply, we unthinkingly apply Western standards to a country which geographically lies in the Middle East and which consequently partakes of the arid nature of the area. Canalization and irrigation were always the main concern of Middle Eastern agriculturists; but how to make water available for household purposes,—drinking, cooking, bathing, washing, cleaning—was never seriously contemplated. A single well or spring in the neighborhood of the village, or a cistern under the house or the court to collect rain-water, was regarded as completely satisfactory. A tap in the wall from which water flows as if by magic was an unheard of innovation for Middle Eastern peoples. Yet this innovation was introduced by the Jews everywhere, in villages as well as in towns, and water was made available for home consumption in sufficient quantity and adequate quality, even during the crucial months of the Arab-Jewish war. The only exceptions were those of the localities directly on the front line, like certain villages of the Negev, and hill-bound Jerusalem to which water is piped up across a distance of some forty miles from the sources of Rosh ha'Ayin in the Sharon. The only pumping station along this pipeline which remained in the hands of the Arabs was blown up by them. During the siege of Jerusalem in 1948, people had to line up every day in the streets in order to get their daily gallon from the passing water trucks, in the meantime exposing themselves to the fire of rifles, machine guns, shells and mortars poured by the Arabs indiscriminately into the Jewish quarters of the city. Those days are fortunately passed, and now the 120,000 Jews of Jerusalem again have an adequate water supply. The tanks on the roofs are again being filled from the city's reservoirs, though only once or twice a week, so that housewives have to continue to make use to some extent of the economizing techniques learned during the siege.

Also, the desert-like Negev is being increasingly supplied with water. Deep borings are being made to tap the sub-surface reserves as far as they exist: dams are erected across the beds of *wadis* which are dry for most of the year but fill up for a short while after the rare rainfalls in the area, causing that miracle-like return of the water into the *wadis* which served as a simile for the Psalmist singing of the return of Israel to its land in a long-past age. To supplement these local but not always sufficient sources, pipelines are being laid to bring the life-giving element from the richer central part of Israel to the arid south.

Less shortage is felt in Israel with regard to clothing. This is mainly due to the fact that the climate in the country is warm enough for about eight months of the year to enable people to cut their indoor and outdoor clothing down to a minimum. To reduce clothing as the temperature goes up is—we would scarcely realize this—a specifically Western way of coping with heat. In the Middle East nobody would dream of exposing himself to the fiery rays of the sun. The traditional protection against its heat is to wrap oneself from head to foot in long, loose and flowing garments, as even the most cursory study of Arab apparel will show. The perspiration which develops under the clothing and evaporates due to the access of air, cools the body just as an earthenware jug cools the water it contains by its porousness which steadily permits some water to sweat through its walls and evaporate in the air. One of the most easily acquired external mark of assimilation to the local Israeli scene exhibited especially by youths and young men is the discarding of the clothing brought along from the country of their origin, and the adoption of the uniform apparel of Israeli youth. This is a combination of shorts and shirts, in most cases of the khaki variety. In rural areas shorts and shirts are worn equally by boys and girls, while in the towns the girls replace the shorts with linen skirts. Due to the almost universal adoption—among the young people at least —of this scantier clothing, the expenditure on this item is much lower than in Western countries in general. The cotton, linen and textile factories of Israel can, moreover, produce close to the minimum of the clothing material needed by the people, so that in this respect, though the general standard would undoubtedly strike the Western observer as very low, the shortage is not as painful as in food and housing.*

Most older people show a greater conservatism in clothing and seem to have made no real concessions either to the climate or to the social environment. In general, both Ashkenazi and Sephardi-Oriental Jews of the older age brackets tend to retain their customary clothing. Among the older Oriental Jews one can occasionally observe that they exchange their traditional Oriental garb for a traditional Western tailored suit or parts of it, such as a jacket perhaps or a pair of trousers alone, worn in combination with the major items of the traditional Oriental clothing. Older women among the Oriental Jewish communities are more conservative in this respect than men and often retain their colorful or richly embroidered dresses a long time after their husbands have entirely succumbed to Western garb. Among both the men and the women of the Oriental Jewish communities a tendency can be observed to wear their traditional apparel on Sabbaths and holidays, even though on weekdays they might dress like their Ashkenazi neighbors. ✻

2. The Problem of Absorption

Closely bound up with the field of material goods are the problems of unemployment and the relationship between the cost of living and the income-level, or, in other words, the purchasing power of wages earned. A few words should suffice as to the latter. Were the consumers' goods as amply available as they are in America, the wages earned would prove to be very inadequate. Considering, however, the actual state of affairs, earnings are as a rule sufficient for the purchase of those basic commodities which can be had in the markets. Austerity means a general and planned reduction of living standards, and in Israel the earnings of workers, employes as well as professional men, are more or less in line with the general austerity program. ✻

* On March 20, 1952, most textiles and practically all footwear were taken off rationing. Cf. *The Jewish Agency's Digest*, Nov. 28, 1952, p. 181.

The problem of unemployment in Israel is closely linked to the problem of immigration. The immigration policy of Israel has been very clear from the first moment; as a matter of fact, it was definitively formulated many years before the establishment of the State. It was and is that of an unconditional open-door to every Jew all over the world.

The immigration policy of other countries is often made dependent on the situation in the labor market within the country itself. In Israel, however, the Government and all the political parties have consistently agreed that the gates of the country must be kept open whatever the state of the labor market, thereby reversing the practice common to the rest of the world. The immigrants therefore continue to come and, consequently, employment must be found for them. To find employment for the breadwinners among five hundred to a thousand new immigrants daily can be done only in one way: by expanding the national economy as rapidly as possible. The leaders of the new State consequently have thrown all their resources into the battle for the creation of new sources of employment. One front of expansion is the setting up of new agricultural settlements, especially in those parts of the country which were but sparsely settled by Jews up to the declaration of independence. The new immigrants, however, were but rarely inclined to "go to the land." Only about 14% of those who reached Israel by the end of 1951 chose rural life and were absorbed in new settlements; the rest settled in cities and towns, in suburbs and in such places where they found non-agricultural occupations. In looking for an explanation of this fact we must not forget that these new immigrants, whether from the East or from the West, very rarely experienced a Zionist education. It is true that they wished to come to Israel, and in the majority of cases would have chosen Israel even if other countries had been open to them. But the ideal of "Return to the Soil," which is the backbone of Zionist thinking and education, was largely unknown to them and has remained strange to them even after their arrival

✻ in Israel.

The task of absorbing the immigrants is gigantic. During the first two years after the Independence, the lag between the numbers of those arriving and those absorbed rapidly increased. The "camp population" during 1949 and 1950 varied between 80,000 and 100,000. The established policy towards the immigrants while still in the camps was not to permit them to work outside the camps so as to safeguard the labor market against underbidding. Nevertheless, it was a frequent occurrence that people from the camps secretly "stole" a day's work in the nearby cities or settlements, receiving one-fourth or one-fifth of the wages ordinarily paid to unionized laborers. Officially, however, the immigrants had to wait until they were settled by the authorities outside the camps in permanent quarters, before they could seek employment. This prolonged sojourn in the camps, where the authorities provided food and lodging for them, created fresh problems. Many of them tended to reject employments offered, preferring to wait for white-collar jobs or other work not requiring physical exertion.   ✱

In view of the expected increase in the number of immigrants, the Jewish Agency reversed its policy, in August 1950, and resolved that able-bodied immigrants who had consistently refused work except of the white-collar kind, or who had been content to sit idly in camps for an indefinite period, would not be considered elegible for any of the government's housing projects. About the same time a radical departure was made from the method employed for the reception and absorption of the immigrants. The new policy called for a speedy processing of the immigrants through reception centers and their settling in permanent "points," such as *ma'abarot* and work villages. This meant immediate employment in public works or agriculture. At the same time the new settlers were enabled to spend one or two work-days weekly in starting to develop their own farms or in building permanent homes for themselves. As soon as an immigrant moved into such a transit or work village, he was therefore no longer a public charge; he was now a homesteader.

In spite of the volume of immigration, unemployment in Israel has not assumed significant proportions. In 1951 no more than 20,-000 to 25,000 unemployed were registered monthly in all the labor exchanges; three-fourths of them were unemployed for six days or less during a whole month, and less than 1,000 were unemployed for 19 days or more in a month.   ✱

To sum up: The picture of the material conditions in Israel today is a rather sombre one. It is a country with a very rapidly increasing population, working feverishly at the sisyphean task of providing its people with the barest necessities of life: food, shelter, clothing. The production within cannot, of course, keep pace with the numbers of the population increasing by leaps and bounds. It needs a breathing space of a few years at least to catch up. But the new immigrants have to be fed immediately and, if the serious danger of demoralization is to be avoided, they also have to be provided with a bare minimum of housing and clothing soon thereafter. What then is the solution, if any? The only remedy at present seems to be the importation of commodities on a scale corresponding to the rapidly increasing volume of demand, and the equitable distribution of all that is available among the entire population in fixed rations and at controlled prices. If life in Israel today is hard and bare as far as material commodities are concerned; if the standards of food, housing and clothing are lower today than they were under the British Mandatory regime; this is merely the inevitable consequence of an unparalleled demographical position characterizing this latest epoch in the long series of uncommon situations which make up the history of Israel.

But over and above the purely numerical aspects of immigration, much of the difficulty is caused by the fact that the absorption of immigrants actually means, in the case of the Oriental majority, a simultaneous acclimatization to Western standards and a provision for them, not only of the bare necessities of life to which they were accustomed in the lands of the Middle East, but of a minimum of those commodities which are regarded as indispensable in Western life. It is this double task which taxes so greatly the capacities of the young state: to stretch to the utmost the economic resources of the country so as to absorb the great masses of new immigrants, and at the same time to make a herculean effort to assimilate, or at least to adjust, the Sephardi and Oriental majority to the prevailing Western cultural standards of Israel. In the task of economic absorption Israel is powerfully helped by the financial means put at its disposal by American Jewry through the United Jewish Appeal; in the equally arduous and much more delicate task of cultural absorption it is not, and cannot be, helped by any outside agency but has to rely exclusively upon its own skill, vision and understanding.

3. Family and Community

Just as the dominant features of material culture in modern Israel are essentially Western in their character, also the main traits of the social structure of the country are directly derived from modern Western society. As far as the Ashkenazi majority of the population is concerned, it is self-evident that Jews who came from the cultural orbit of the West brought along with them, among many other material and non-material traits, also the tradition of social structure which was as much theirs as it was that of their non-Jewish neighbors.

The characteristic family of modern Jewish Palestine was the small "immediate" family in which the parent-child relationship became practically dissolved as soon as the children grew up and were able to make their own living, or, at the latest, when they married and thus founded a family of their own. Relationship, though reckoned bilaterally, was a rather weak tie, overshadowed in importance by belonging to groups based on cultural interests of which there were a great many. The Oriental Jews brought along with them to Israel their own typical family structure which differed in no way from the traditional Middle Eastern extended family. But under the impact of close contact with Western families, the Oriental-type family soon suffers a breakdown, or, at least, changes greatly. In a later chapter more details will be given concerning this subject; here, it is sufficient to state that the traditional Oriental Jewish family is undoubtedly losing its character. In the case of the Ashkenazi Jews, a common country of origin did not mean more than it does in other countries of immigration: the presence of a scarcely definable feeling of common origin, of an indistinct and remote kinship which somehow ties together people who in the old country would have had nothing at all in common; a vague coherence created not so much by the actual homogeneity among members of the group as by the realization of the otherness of those who belonged to other groups. A certain number of organizations existed in Palestine (and exists partly to this day in Israel) in which the basis of association was the common country of origin—such as the Associations of German, Polish, Czechoslovakian, Austrian, Hungarian, Rumanian, etc. Immigrants—but the importance of these was secondary and diminished with time, while the importance of other, more primary groupings, based on common cultural interests, was on the increase. Since the forms of social contact in the professional, recreational and other spheres scarcely differed from those which are characteristic of modern Western society, the European Jewish immigrant soon felt at home in Palestine also outside his own circle.

Among the Oriental Jews the situation was different. These, too, brought along to Palestine much of their own Oriental social structure, and, at least as far as the first generation was concerned, tried to retain it unchanged. They were, however, largely unsuccessful in this, due not so much to the social pressure exerted upon them as a minority group by the dominant and prestige-laden Ashkenazi majority, as to the enticements assimilation to the Ashkenazi social forms offered to the members of the younger generation among the Oriental Jewish communities. Nobody cared whether a Kurdish horse-cart driver in Jerusalem continued to wear his traditional Kurdish attire or changed to European workers' clothes; but his son wanted to wear European clothing and wanted to be a truck-driver rather than a horse-cart driver. The crisis which was brought about by the tension between the old generation resisting every change, and the young folks who resented this bitterly, has been discussed already.* In the present context only one thing has to be pointed out, namely, that as long as the Oriental Jews constituted a relatively small minority (about 20%), the internal ferment within their ranks affected but little the social developments in the Jewish community of Palestine as a whole.

All the important institutions in Jewish Palestine, and in Israel today, were Western in origin, concept and function. No traces, or almost none, are left of the traditional Oriental Jewish institutions, such as the shrines of holy men venerated by Jews and Moslems alike especially in North Africa and in Iraq; the weekly markets which played such an important role in the economic life of the Yemenite Jews; or the *Havrāye*, the hard-drinking and powerful men's club of the Jews of Kurdistan. The only significant institution which the Oriental Jews brought along with them and which they succeeded in keeping alive in Palestine (and Israel) was the *kehilla* or *'ēda*, the religious community organization centering around its visible symbol and focus, the synagogue. However, even this could be transplanted from the old country, or could be re-created anew in Palestine, only when and where a sizable group of immigrants settled in close quarters, as was the case in Jerusalem. In Jerusalem, the Oriental Jewish communities have their synagogues and community organizations, the basis of association being the common origin from a country, or frequently from a city. These *'ēdot* (communities) are the Oriental counterpart of the European Immigrants' Organizations with the one significant difference, that, while among the Jews of European extraction the common country of origin served as the basis for a secular association, among the Oriental Jews the common country or city of origin served as the basis for a religious association. The purpose of the various European Immigrants' Organizations was to promote the material welfare of their members by representing their interests in such fields as further immigration, employment and placement, settlement, donations and loans; to help them along culturally and socially by organizing Hebrew language classes and other courses, occasional lectures, meetings, discussions, teas, dance parties and so forth; and by publishing newsletters or newspapers in the language of the home country. The intent of the Oriental Jewish community organizations was, first of all, to provide their members with a synagogue in the manner and tradition of the old country; secondly, to enable them to enjoy the religious services of functionaries from their own home community on such occasion as weddings, circumcisions and fu-

* Cf. above, p. 111 f.

nerals, as well as in connection with such more commonplace religious needs as ritual slaughtering, traditional religious education (in the so-called *Talmud Tora* schools) and the like. The community organization was the framework for charity—in itself an important religious duty—practiced by the few wealthy families in the community and often taking the form of private collections of money, food and clothing. Distribution among the poor of the community was made twice a year, just before New Year in the fall and again just before Passover in the spring. The representation of the community's interests vis-a-vis the British and the general Jewish authorities was only incidental and grew out of the very fact of the existence of these community organizations.

Important differences existed between the immigrants' organizations of European Jews and the community organizations of the Oriental Jews in the way in which they functioned. In the former only those participated who expressed their wish to do so by becoming members and by paying a monthly membership fee (unless exempted owing to unemployment). Non-members who had immigrated from the same country were not represented by the organization and had nothing to do with it. The organization had written statutes, voted on by the general meeting of all members and confirmed by the (British) District Commissioner. The organization was headed by a chairman and a committee, duly elected by the majority of all the members present at a lawfully convened general meeting, for the duration usually of one year. Its income and expenditure was duly registered in books which were controlled by specially elected and accredited comptrollers. In brief, these immigrants' organizations of the European Jews were free and democratic voluntary associations in the best Western tradition.

The community organizations of the Oriental Jews, on the other hand, reflected with equal faithfulness the tradition of the patriarchal clan-organization of Middle Eastern rural and urban society. In the old home country all the Jewish families of a given locality, town or village, regarded themselves as closely related to one another—even if no actual blood or family tie existed among all of them. This feeling of belonging together was carried over in its totality to Palestine and continued to cement together the member-families of the group if they settled in close quarters. All the Jewish families from Herat, Afghanistan, who immigrated to Jerusalem, were therefore members of the community of Afghan Jews in Jerusalem, and it did not occur to anyone to raise the question of membership of a particular individual, or to make membership conditional on a formal declaration of entry and payment of fees.

Just as there was no formal entry, there was also no formal constitution, statute, general meeting, voting, election of officers, book-
keeping and control, membership fees, fixed rights and duties. Thus,
to all legal and formalistic intents and purposes, the community
organization did not exist. But actually not only did it exist, it
wielded considerable power and influence over the members of the
community. It existed and functioned in a typical and traditional
Oriental way. Just as all the immigrants from the locality in question
were unquestioningly members of the 'ēda (community), its leadership was unquestioningly assigned to and assumed by the heads of
the wealthy member-families of the community. The leaders were
never elected, but there was never any doubt about who the "heads
of the community" were, as they were customarily referred to. To
be one of the "heads of the community" meant, of course, enormous
prestige—kavod (honor) in Hebrew—but it also meant heavy obligations and expenditure of money, time and energy. The synagogue was built from funds voluntarily donated by the community,
everyone according to his means, or by one single donor who
wanted in this way to ensure the survival of his name and prestige.
The expenses of the service and of the upkeep of the synagogue
were donated partially by those who were called up week after
week to be honored by reading a part of the weekly portion
(parasha) of the Pentateuch and the Prophets, and partially by the
"heads of the community." If somebody was prompted to donate
something for the poor of the community, he would informally hand
the money or the food or the pieces of clothing to one of the
"heads," who would keep it until the time for distribution arrived.
The "heads" would add their contribution—usually the lion's share
—and would discuss the apportionment of the largess in informal
meetings. The distribution of alms was done in such a manner as
not to offend the susceptibilities of the needy in the community,
and, apart from the "heads," no one knew who received donations
and how much they received. Nobody ever questioned the "heads"
concerning their decisions, or asked them to account for receipts
and expenditures. It was generally known that the "heads" spent
considerable amounts every year out of their own pockets, and thus
the need for accounting did not arise. The heads of the community
were invariably also the heads of the community-synagogue and
participated in the services on Saturdays and holidays. It was they
who decided on the appointment of a rabbi or a cantor, and their
attitude was decisive whether a rabbi or a teacher could open a
Talmud Tora school (which was usually his private undertaking)
for the children of the community.

This patriarchal religious community organization of the Oriental Jews in Israel is no doubt on its way out. In the case of several ✱ Oriental Jewish groups it already has been supplemented by a more modern type of organization closely resembling the immigrants' organizations of European Jews. The best example of this is that of the Yemenite Jews, who, in addition to their traditional religious communities, created also a modern Organization of Yemenite Jews in Palestine as far back as 1923 (see pages 204f). The Committee of Sephardi Jews in Jerusalem also has been created along modern organizational lines. However, the chief difficulty in the way of safeguarding the continued existence of the Oriental Jewish community organizations lies in the very nature of their informal patriarchal structure. In the old countries, the sons of the "heads" automatically succeeded their fathers as time marched on; there the only outlet for persons possessed of a social consciousness lay in the local Jewish community itself. In Israel, however, other, wider interests intrude. The sons of the "heads" grow up together with young people from the Ashkenazi Jewish communities and, if they feel inclined to participate in communal matters, will be more attracted to affairs with a broader political scope than those of their limited and "backward" community. The Oriental Jewish religious communities therefore lose those on whose shoulders leadership would traditionally devolve. They do not possess the organizational preparation for substituting persons who might not automatically assume the role of "heads," but who could be elected or at least acknowledged as such by the community. Eventually, the inevitable consequence is, first, the gradual decrease in the number of "heads" in most communities, then an increasingly acute lack of leadership, and, finally, a breakdown of the entire traditional community organization which originally was based on a common place of origin.

4. Western Institutions

Apart from this singular exception of the traditional religious community organization of Oriental Jews, all the important public institutions in Israel were created by Ashkenazi Jews and patterned after Euroamerican prototypes. Institutions have been created also by Sephardi and Oriental Jews in Palestine after the Western pattern, but these are, as a rule, of secondary importance with regard to size and role. A common characteristic of these Western-type institutions is that their charter, that is, the system of values, programs and principles[*] for the pursuit of which they were organized, was fixed in relation to the totality of the Jewish population of Palestine (and later Israel) without distinguishing (or discriminating) among its constituent communities. This is true, first of all, of the political institutions, such as the government, the Knesset (parliament), the political parties (with the exception of those founded by Sephardi and Oriental Jews, with the express purpose of representing the special interests of these groups), and the municipal and local councils which are the comprehensive institutions of all the residents of given areas. The same is, of course, the case with the so-called "National Institutions" established before or during the Mandatory period. One of these is the *Keren Kayemet* (The Jewish National Fund), the purpose of which is to purchase and to develop land in Palestine (Israel) and to lease it to individuals or groups for usufruct, while keeping the property rights as an inalienable trust of the Jewish people of the country as a whole. The other great national institution, the *Keren Hayesod* (Palestine Foundation Fund), was created to serve as the financial instrument of world Jewry for enabling the Jewish community in Palestine (and now the State of Israel) to engage in large-scale settlement of immigrants and especially in the upbuilding and development of rural areas; that is, this institution, too, serves the Jewish people of the country as a whole.

The economic institutions of the country comprise large sectors of the population along demarcations very different from those of ethnic background. The largest single organization in Israel which falls under this heading is the *Histadrut*, the General Federation of Jewish Labor, whose membership statute says: "Every worker of 18 years of age or more, who lives on his (her) own labor without exploiting the work of others, and who subjects himself (herself) to the discipline of action of the *Histadrut*, can become a member . . ." The criterium for membership is, therefore—apart from the required age-minimum—"self-labor" and discipline of action (but not of conscience), and it goes without saying that ethnic affiliation has nothing to do with it. Thus a Yemenite porter, a Saloniki longshoreman, a Polish lawyers' clerk and a German university assistant, all can, and actually are, members of the *Histadrut*.

As a matter of fact, the Sephardi and Oriental Jewish membership of the *Histadrut* has shown a marked growth, both absolute and relative, since 1939.

[*] Cf. B. Malinowski, *A Scientific Theory of Culture*, Chapel Hill, 1944, pp. 52 and 140.

HISTADRUT MEMBERSHIP ACCORDING TO COMMUNITIES[1]

	1939		1945		1946		1947	
Division	persons	%	persons	%	persons	%	persons	%
Ashkenazim	61,779	92.8	82,164	87.9	93,125	88.5	110,868	87.7
Sephardim & Orientals	4,796	7.2	11,363	12.1	12,093	11.5	15,493	12.3
Total	66,575	100.0	93,529	100.0	105,218	100.0	126,361[2]	100.0

[1] After the year 1947 the breakdown of *Histadrut* membership according to communities was no longer made available.
[2] Plus 1,838 members whose community affiliation was unknown.

Since the establishment of the State the growth of the *Histadrut* became accelerated in direct ratio to the increase of the population.

GROWTH OF THE HISTADRUT, 1947-1951

End of Year	Member-ship	Members and Dependents	Total Jewish Population of Israel	Percentage of Histadrut Population
1947	128,199	275,694	655,000	42.1
1949	177,407	375,042	1,014,000	36.9
1950	238,796	509,469	1,203,000	42.4
1951	309,176	680,988	1,405,000	48.5

*

An interesting change in the relationship in *Histadrut* membership between older inhabitants of the country and new immigrants can be observed since the establishment of the State. Of all the *Histadrut* members in 1947, only 23.6% were new immigrants who joined the ranks of the *Histadrut* within a year after their arrival in Palestine. On the other hand, of the *Histadrut* membership of 1951, 42.1% (or 100.570 in absolute figures) were new immigrants who arrived in Israel since the establishment of the State. An increase in the percentage of new immigrants in the *Histadrut* means an increase of Sephardi and Oriental Jews, since the percentage of the latter among the immigrants, from May 1948 to May 1951, was 52% or 315,000 out of 600,000.*

According to figures published by the Statistical Department of the *Histadrut*, the Ashkenazi earners constituted, in 1951, 43% of the

* Figures for the *Histadrut* taken from *The Histadrut in the Years 1945-1948* (Hebrew), Tel Aviv, 1949; *The Statistical Bulletin* of the *Histadrut* (Hebrew, mimeographed), nos. 14 and 15, Tel Aviv; W. Preuss, *The Histadrut in Figures* (Hebrew, pamphlet), Tel Aviv, 1951; private communication of Dr. W. Preuss of the *Histadrut's* Department of Statistics and Information, Tel Aviv, dated Nov. 13, 1951.

total Ashkenazi division of the population, while the Sephardi and Oriental Jewish earners constituted 36% of the total numbers of their combined divisions.* If this percentual relationship between earners and dependents has remained unchanged since 1947 (and there is no valid reason to suppose that it has not), we can figure that the 15,500 Sephardi and Oriental Jewish members of the *Histadrut* in 1947 represented together with their dependents about 43,000, or more than 30%, of all the Sephardi and Oriental Jews who lived in Palestine at the time (140,000). Thus three out of every ten Sephardi and Oriental Jews were drawn into the orbit of a great and influential social institution of a purely Western type, and through it integrated themselves into the modern economy of the country.

GROWTH OF THE *KUPPAT HOLIM*[1]

End of Year	Members	Members and Dependents	Total Jewish Population	Percentage of *Kuppat Holim* Members
1943	96,814	224,986	539,000	41.7
1944	108,175	250,923	565,000	44.4
1945	120,355	272,321	592,000	46.0
1946	128,904	288,145	625,000	46.1
1947	136,158	304,822	655,000	46.7
1948	152,000	350,000	759,000	46.1
1949	192,125	475,911	1,014,000	46.8
1950	281,000	690,000	1,203,000	57.5
1951	340,000	850,000	1,405,000	60.5

[1] Sources: *The Histadrut in the Years 1945-1948* (Hebrew), Tel Aviv, 1949; *Hiqrei Avoda* (Hebrew), Tel Aviv, August 1951, and December 1951. In 1950 other Sick Funds had 139,000 members.

To belong to the *Histadrut*, however, means much more than mere participation in a labor union active in the economic sphere only. The *Histadrut* has considered its duty the education of its members and their families, including the children of school age, the extension of culturally constructive recreation and entertainment, and the maintenance of health. The statistical figures made public by the *Histadrut* over a number of years show that membership in the *Histadrut*'s Sick Fund (*Kuppat Holim*) has always been several percent higher than membership in the *Histadrut* itself, since it included also members of other labor organizations (such as the Mizrahi Workers, and the Agudat Yisrael Workers). The following figures show the growth of the *Kuppat Holim* since 1943, as well as

* *Statistical Bulletin of the Histadrut* (Hebrew, mimeographed), no. 14; according to the same source, 38% of the total Jewish population of Israel in May 1951, were Sephardi and Oriental Jews.

the percentage of *Kuppat Holim* members in relation to the total Jewish population of Palestine-Israel.

The Sephardi and Oriental Jews are thus found to participate in practically all the institutions set up by the Ashkenazi Jews in Palestine (Israel) proportionately to their numbers and occupational structure. An Iraqi Jewish worker will be a member of the *Histadrut* and its Sick Fund and will, consequently, benefit from such typically modern Western achievements as unemployment compensation, low-interest loans, medical treatment and hospitalization. He will earn his living by working in a factory set up by Ashkenazi Jews according to patterns developed in the West. He will send his children to a school belonging to one of the four recognized trends, all of which were organized by Ashkenazi Jews after having made special adaptations of Western teaching methods and curricula. He will belong to a political party, probably to Mapai or Mapam, or, if he is still religiously inclined, to Hapoel Hamizrahi, all of which have an overwhelmingly Ashkenazi majority and are headed by Ashkenazi leadership. In his recreational activities, as far as these are institutionalized, he will again participate in typically Western forms of recreation, such as movies, ball-games, bathing. To sum up, it can be stated that the institutional aspect of the lives of the majority of the Sephardi and Oriental Jews in Israel has been thoroughly integrated into the network of institutions set up and maintained by Ashkenazi Jews and patterned after Western (Euroamerican) examples.

No corresponding participation of Ashkenazi Jews in the institutions of the Sephardi and Oriental Jews can be observed. While the great majority of Sephardi and Oriental Jews are employed either directly or indirectly by Ashkenazi employers (factories, business enterprises, offices), the relatively few employment opportunities created by Sephardi and Oriental Jewish employers have been filled by Sephardi and Oriental Jewish workers in a much higher percentage than would be warranted by the numerical proportion of these two divisions within the Jewish population as a whole. While many Sephardi and Oriental Jewish parents send their children to schools in which the majority of pupils are Ashkenazim, or which are headed and supervised by Ashkenazim, no Ashkenazi parent would send his child to one of the schools which were established specially for, say, Yemenite children. While the majority of the Sephardi and Oriental Jews in Israel vote for one of the political parties in which the majority are Ashkenazi Jews, no Ashkenazi Jew would affiliate himself with a Sephardi or Oriental Jewish party, which attracts a minority only from their own ranks. In this manner it becomes evident that there is no reciprocal rapprochement between the Ashkenazi and the Sephardi-Oriental Jews: The Ashkenazi Jews, as far as their participation in the institutional network of the country is concerned, move in a purely Ashkenazi environment, while the Sephardi and Oriental Jews, on the other hand, undergo an intensive process of what could be called institutional amalgamation with the Ashkenazi division of the country's Jewish population.

5. Literature

Let us now turn to the third aspect of Israeli culture, that which deals with the esthetic-intellectual life. Literature, poetry, theatrical art, music, dance, the graphic and the plastic arts, the humanities, the social, natural and contemplative sciences can be taken as the main divisions of the esthetic-intellectual culture of any people. A full consideration of the attainments and trends in the esthetic-intellectual culture of Israel should therefore touch upon each one of these fields. But here again we shall have to follow the method adopted in the chapter dealing with "Demographic Highlights," and choose a few examples from the esthetic sphere only. Two considerations seem to point to the propriety of this choice.

First, national and local characteristics are much more readily discernible in the fields of the arts and literature than in those of the sciences. If we think of such terms as "French Literature" or "French Art," with their definite connotations, as compared with the much vaguer meaning of such an expression as "French Science," it will immediately become clear why we prefer to take our examples from the fields of literature and the arts rather than from those of science. Thus even in an *a priori* approach to the new culture of Israel, we will expect to find more definitely Israeli characteristics in fields belonging to the esthetic sphere than in those belonging to the realm of intellectual and scientific activity. Science in Israel, just as in any other country partaking of Western culture, is but an organic outgrowth of that great and invaluable trend of pooling resources and exchanging information which characterizes Western science in our times. Thus, while it would not be easy to discover specifically Israeli traits in the scientific developments of the country—apart from such phenomena well known from other countries as variations and differentials in the application and employment of general principles within the context of the local physical and social environment—the emphasis on science, the reliance on science, the fostering of science, and the role assigned to science in general, constitute most important earmarks stamping Israel quite definitely with the character of a Western country.

The second consideration for choosing our examples from the fields of literature and the arts, rather than from those of science, is the difference in attitude displayed towards Israeli attainments in these two fields. For while the achievements of Israel in the humanities and the sciences are generally well received in professional circles all over the world, one hears only too often the hasty statement that one-third of a century of modern Jewish life in Palestine has failed to produce works of art and literature impressive in their originality, and that consequently the level of esthetic culture in Israel must be low.

This line of approach to Israeli art and literature is taken not only by students and critics from abroad, but, what is even more significant, by the art and literary critics of Israel itself. It is generally not realized that this approach is itself typically and solely Western. It is only in Western (that is, Euroamerican) culture that the traditional limits within which free rein is given to the artistic creative imagination are very wide and loose, and that the more originality and individuality the artist evidences, the more he is acclaimed. Creative originality, however, is by no means the only gauge of values in the world of art. As a matter of fact, as soon as we pass beyond the confines of Euroamerican culture, we find that this specific approach to the evaluation of art is practically unknown. Its place in Eastern culture is taken, for instance, by such evaluative criteria as the truest and most essential expression of traditional forms and ideas; the most harmonious conformity with norms hallowed by time and derived from ancient masterpieces; or the greatest similarity to popular versions well known to the art-loving public and widely acclaimed by it. The emphasis on originality, therefore, shows that the approach to art and the evaluation of art in Israel are themselves dominated by Western ideas.

After having clarified this, we are free to agree or to disagree with those who regard originality as the main or the sole criterion in evaluating Israeli art. If one agrees—as one might be inclined to do in view of the fact that the dominant element in the esthetic culture of Israel is Ashkenazic and therefore imbued with Western cultural tradition—one must, before going any farther, carefully distinguish between two main types of art: one which is primary, or "creative," and one which is secondary, or "interpretive." To the primary or creative arts can be counted the works of novelists, writers, poets, composers, dance choreographers, painters, sculptors. Secondary or interpretive arts are those practised by translators of literary works from one language to another, performers of music in all its varieties (vocal or instrumental), dancers, actors, copyists. Originality is sought for and valued above all in the primary or creative arts only, while in the secondary or interpretive arts the most admired traits are faithfulness in reproducing the original (in translations and copies), deep empathy in expressing the intentions of the authors, or excellence in the interpretation of their work (in music, dance and the theater).

The distinction between primary and secondary arts can serve as a valuable clue in analyzing the artistic production of Israel. First of all, some interesting observations can be made as to the volume of primary artistic creation as compared with the volume of secondary artistic production. To take literature first, it is found that a very high percentage of the books published in the country are translations from foreign languages. Israel has excellent translators. As a matter of fact, many of its authors are also translators, who have by now largely overcome the difficulties inherent in rendering modern English, French, German, Italian or Yiddish literary masterpieces into a medium like Hebrew prose which will be pliable and capable of expressing finer modulations only in the hands of a true master. Partly under the influence of these translations and partly as an outcome of a consciously fostered trend, modern Hebrew literature has come a long way from the flowery and pompous style which characterized the works of the pioneers in new Hebrew literature a generation or two ago. Especially the writings of the younger and youngest generation of Israeli authors exhibit a preference for *sabra*-Hebrew slang which often baffles the older Hebraists. The great interest displayed by the average Israeli reader in the works of foreign authors, which often are read in the original, cannot therefore be attributed to any conscious realization on his part of a higher literary quality in these importations from abroad. Rather, it is due to his twofold interest, divided in equal measure between the literary presentation of his own life and problems, and that of trends and events in the great world of which he feels himself a part.

As to the participation of the Sephardi and Oriental Jewish communities in the literary output of Israel, this is undoubtedly meager. There are many fewer novelists, playwrights and poets among these communities than would correspond to their numerical proportion in the Jewish population of Israel, even taking the ratio of ten years ago as a basis. The reason for this disproportion seems to be the high degree of acculturation obtaining in both Eastern and Western Jewries to their respective cultural environments. In the West, literature is a much respected and highly publicized specialization; consequently the Jews in Western countries took active part in it, and brought this interest along with them to Palestine. Moreover, they succeeded in creating in Palestine a literary atmosphere sufficiently friendly to encourage young people who felt themselves talented. In the lands of the East, on the other hand, literary activity in the modern sense has begun to develop only in the last few years and only in very limited circles. One who devotes himself to literature is a rare phenomenon in the countries of the Middle East. The relative paucity of authors in these countries in general is closely paralleled among the Sephardi and Oriental Jews. But the parallel goes even farther: Just as Arab, Turkish, Persian and other Middle Eastern authors have in recent years adopted Western literary forms for novels, short stories, plays, and other classes of literature taken over from the Western arsenal of *belles lettres,* the Sephardi and Oriental Jewish authors in Israel have also unquestioningly adopted Western literary forms familiar to them either in the European or American originals, or in the Hebrew translations, or at least in the Israeli Hebrew counterparts. It may be that there is a greater preponderance of the Sephardi-Oriental prototype in novels written by Sephardi or Oriental Jewish authors than is found in the novels of the Ashkenazi writers, but this is the only discernible objective difference between the literary crop of the two sectors in the Jewish state.

6. Music, Arts and Crafts

Continuing the observations concerning the difference between primary and secondary art in Israel in other than literary fields, it is interesting to consider next the Israeli contribution to music. It is the consensus of critical opinion that the quality of Israeli performance surpasses that of Israeli composition. It would seem more than a mere coincidence that in the Western world as well the greatest Jewish musicians are not composers but performing artists. Symphonic music and a high degree of instrumental proficiency is an exclusively Western development. Consequently, as we would expect, the Ashkenazi Jews figure predominantly in these fields in Israel. But the love of music, the appreciation of music, and to a lesser degree an active pursuance of some kind of musical endeavor in an amateurish way, is characteristic of the Jews of both West and East. In Western countries it is often pointed out that Jews appear on the concert stage and among the audience in numbers quite out of proportion to their percentage in the populations. Also in Eastern countries Jews play a prominent role in musical life. In Iran, for instance, Jewish musicians are called to play at weddings and other festive occasions in Moslem houses. In other countries of the East, both Jews and Moslems like to accompany every kind of work, every activity and every festivity with special songs, with or without instrumental underlining. A direct outcome of this is that the participation of Sephardi and Oriental Jews in the musical life in Israel is greater than in any other field of artistic activity. Moreover, Israeli music shows a greater Oriental coloring than any other art in Israel. How Oriental music influenced the Ashkenazi Jewish immigrants at the very outset of the Zionist upbuilding work of Palestine has been touched upon in the chapter dealing with "Currents of Immigration." The remarkable difference between the later fate of this influence and that of other cultural influences is that, while in almost every other field, the Oriental influence decreased in proportion to the growth of Ashkenazi immigration, such was not the case with Oriental music which persisted throughout the thirty-year period of Mandatory Palestine and continues unabated to this very day. Oriental musical influences were first felt mainly in the lighter types of music, like popular songs. More recently, however, an "Eastern-Mediterranean" style can be discerned also in the works of the more serious Ashkenazi composers. The lighter side of musical production is most closely bound up with everyday life, and plays in Israel a role comparable to that played by music in other Middle Eastern countries. Many an Oriental melody brought along by the Jewish immigrants from their home countries has been adapted by Western Israeli composers, provided with piano accompaniment and become universally popular. Similarly, Yemenite women-singers are very popular. Their "hits" are usually Oriental melodies sung in most cases in a Western adaptation to be more ingratiating to the Ashkenazi ears brought up in the Western musical tradition. Less popular, and restricted mainly to an Oriental audience, are the Oriental orchestras, of which there are quite a number in Israel and which perform regularly also over Israel's broadcasting stations. The performances of Yemenite dancers are as popular as those of Yemenite singers, though characteristically enough one of the best known of these groups is headed and coached by a Russian Jewish dancer.

A most remarkable development in Israel is the intensive musical life in the rural settlements, especially in the *kibbutzim*, the communal agricultural farms. Many of these have choirs, orchestras and dance groups which meet annually in large country-wide conventions, when also contests among them take place. An important part in furthering these musical activities, as well as the musical interests of the workers in urban areas, is played by the Cultural Center (*Merkaz l'Tarbut*) of the *Histadrut*.

Outstanding in the musical life of Israel on the highest level is the Israel Philharmonic Orchestra founded in 1936 by Bronislaw Huberman. Mention should be made also of the Israeli Opera Company and of the Conservatories of Music.

While the Sephardi and Oriental Jews thus participate most actively in the musical life of Israel and in creating a new musical tradition in the country, they have practically no part at all in the fine arts, that is, in painting, the graphic arts and sculpture. This again can be explained by a reference to their traditional background. In traditional Islam, just as in traditional Judaism, there is a religious prohibition against the pictorial representation of living beings, especially of the human figure. In the West, once the emancipation cut down the barriers between Jew and non-Jew, the former eventually began to enter the fields of the fine arts, although they came later and in smaller numbers. A path to the fine arts was cleared for European Jews when the decline in rigid religious conservatism was followed by a liberal re-interpretation of the biblical commandment, "Thou shalt not make unto thyself any graven image or any likeness . . ." This was now interpreted to mean that the making of statues and pictures is forbidden only if they are to serve idolatrous purposes. In the East, where the Moslem peoples—with the notable exception of Persia—have adhered to the same restriction, the Jews never even conceived of the possibility of re-interpreting this passage of the Second Commandment. Consequently, Jews and Moslems alike eschewed the fine arts and found an outlet for their talents in decorative art only. Painting and sculpture thus remain exclusively Ashkenazi Jewish artistic specializations. ✱

A considerable percentage of the older generation of painters and sculptors are immigrants from Central Europe, especially from Germany.✱ It has been pointed out by art critics that landscape

---

✱ Dr. Karl Schwarz in his book *Modern Jewish Art in Palestine* (Hebrew), Jerusalem, 1941, treats of 96 artists. These were divided according to their countries of birth as follows:

	Central Europe (mainly Germany)	Eastern Europe	Palestine	Total
Architects	6	7		13
Painters and Graphic Artists	23	36	3[1]	62
Sculptors	4	7		11
Industrial Artists	6	3		9
Total	39	59	3	95

[1] Of these, 2 were of Sephardi-Oriental parentage. One additional artist, a painter, was born in England. Many of the artists born in Eastern Europe were educated in Germany and should therefore be credited to the Central European group.

painters coming from a more northern clime with its haze and subdued lighting, struggle often ineffectually with the problems presented by the greater sharpness of contour and brilliant glare characteristic of the Israeli landscape. The work of the younger Palestinian-born painters is as yet too much in the formative stage to enable one to formulate a definite characterization.

As to sculpture, the numbers of artists devoting themselves to this medium of expression is much smaller than that of the painters and graphic artists. Sculpture, too, is an exclusively Ashkenazi Jewish specialization. As late as 1941 there was not a single Palestinian-born sculptor whose work would have been significant enough to warrant his inclusion into the general study on modern Jewish art in Palestine referred to in the footnote above. It is interesting to note that in no public place in the cities, towns or urban Jewish settlements has a single work of sculpture been put up to this very day. Only some of the *kibbutzim* have in recent years commissioned sculptors to make a few statues with the express purpose of setting them up in public, within the confines of the *kibbutz*. It would seem that here the adherence to the old Jewish tradition forbidding the making of "graven images" still interferes. In private homes, however, as well as in museums and libraries, one can find numerous specimens of modern Israeli sculpture.

In contrast to the conspicuous absence of Sephardi and Oriental Jews from the fields of the fine arts, their participation in the decorative arts is decisive, and their influence upon the styles and techniques in certain branches of artcraft is comparable to the role played by them in the development of modern popular music in Israel. Here again, the Yemenites are outstanding, just as they are in music. Yemenite Jews were *the* silversmiths and *the* goldsmiths in Yemen and their skill in these crafts made their work popular in Palestine. Highly artistic necklaces, earrings, bracelets, pendulums, belts, and the like, executed in tasteful silver or gold filigree work, became one of the most sought after embellishments of female apparel in the Ashkenazi sector as well. Even before World War I, several Yemenite industrial artists were drawn by Boris Schatz into the Bezalel School, which he founded in Jerusalem. From 1927 onward their numbers increased, and this led to an improvement in the quality and variety of their work. On the other hand, the Bezalel School as a whole and independently working "Bezalel-artists" of Ashkenazi origin, in an endeavor to profit from the interest of the public in Yemenite work, began to produce pseudo-Yemenite jewelry and objects with artistic decoration, such as vases, Hanukka-lamps, candle-sticks, metal or wooden boxes, brooches, *mezuzot*, and the like, which are to this day sold all over Israel and also exported overseas and which have contributed little to the good name of Israeli art.

Another field in which Yemenite Jewesses attained high perfection, is artistic embroidery. A multi-colored embroidered silk or velvet Yemenite woman's headdress or breastpiece (to be used as the front of a dress) is a work of art which is the end-product of a refined artistic tradition of many generations. The Women's International Zionist Organization (WIZO) set up workshops for Yemenite women (called *Shani*—scarlet) in which their techniques are adapted to modern demands, for instance, to the cut of Western female clothing as accessories, such as shawls, belts, bags, and the like.

A third Yemenite accomplishment is basketry. Baskets, trays, containers and other objects made of straw, raffia and similar materials, colored and artistically patterned, are popular all over Israel, and serve as a favorite decoration in art-loving homes.

This cursory analysis has shown that the participation of Sephardi and Oriental Jews in modern Israeli art is confined to two important fields, mainly that of music and that of decorative art. In both these fields they have contributed something distinctively Oriental and have thus enriched the artistic life of the country otherwise dominated by Ashkenazi artists and by Western artistic trends. Their contribution to a third field, that of literature, is meager and cannot be shown to possess a comparably distinctive character.

As to the dichotomy between primary and secondary arts, this cannot be carried through in the case of Oriental music, where, as we have seen (cf. above, p. 38), the composer is merely an adducer of new variations to traditional and well-known themes, and, moreover composer and performer are usually one and the same person. The question of artistic originality, therefore, cannot be raised at all in connection with the contribution of the Sephardi and Oriental Jews to Israeli musical life. As to their contribution to decorative arts, which are definitely primary and creative arts in the West, here we come up against the difficulty of trying to judge an Oriental artistic achievement by Western artistic standards. In the various branches of decorative art pursued by Oriental (Yemenite) Jews in Israel, there is certainly almost nothing original. They do not endeavor to be original, the very idea of artistic originality is foreign to them, and all their artistic talents are turned in other directions: those of refinement, essential expression of traditional themes and clever but minor variations upon patterns, made "classic" by old and famous masterpieces.

The question as to creative originality is thus found to be applicable in Israel only to the primary arts practiced by Ashkenazi artists and comprising three main branches: those of literature, music and the fine arts. The opinion has been repeatedly expressed that, in these fields, the creative originality of Palestinian (and now Israeli) artists does not compare favorably with that of Jewish artists living outside Israel; that the greatest modern Jewish writers, composers, painters and sculptors are not those living in Israel but those living in other countries.

7. Arts and Pioneering

The comparative evaluation of the artistic merits of two or more groups of artists, or even those of two or more individual artists, is a very delicate and largely subjective undertaking in which the personal taste, preferences and predilections of the critic play a decisive role. It can, however, be stated with a greater claim to objectivity that, in the cultural life of modern Palestine and new Israel, less emphasis has been and is being placed on literary and artistic activities than is the case in the important centers of Jewish life elsewhere. The great preoccupation of the people of Israel with the urgent and immediate problems of their present-day material existence, which has been one of a prolonged emergency for the last thirty years, can explain to a certain extent the relative paucity in the primary, or creative, arts. It is paradoxical, perhaps even tragic, but certainly true that during the three decades of preparation for statehood in Palestine the creative aspects of literature and the arts have played a secondary role compared with the material problems of upbuilding and development, although originally political Zionism itself had been almost exclusively the creation of writers, thinkers and artists. As soon as a beginning was made and idea translated into action, even many of the men of letters themselves became caught in the ever widening maelstrom of practical Zionist work. This, apparently, is what happened to that part of the Jewish people who have become the Israeli equivalent of the American Founding Fathers. Men of intellect by upbringing and choice, whether of the old school which found all its satisfactions in the pursuance of traditional Jewish learning, or of the secular type which tried to vie with its gentile neighbors in modern literary, artistic and intellectual accomplishment, focused their attention on litres of milk instead of literature, on arms instead of arts, and on intelligence of the military kind instead of intellect once they became part of the *Yishuv*. The best brains of the *Yishuv* concentrated on problems which were invariably concerned with the practical issues of the day; incredible amounts of creative energy went into the development of new socio-economic forms whether confined to a single activity like the various urban cooperative enterprises, or all-embracing like the unparalleled experiments of rural cooperative or communal villages. The gradually widening horizon of the National Home in Palestine opened up so many alluring creative possibilities in new fields of achievements which, in addition, were also of immediate value and necessity, that the old and oft-explored fields of esthetic-cultural creativity came to be somewhat neglected. This trend was felt even in everyday style and tone: when there is scarcely enough food to provide the necessary calories, one cannot pay attention to the finesses of the cuisine; when there is no shelter from rain and sun, one cannot tarry to evolve an original and pleasing style of architecture; and when there is barely enough cloth to cover the nakedness of a nation, one cannot waste time on elegance in cut ✳ and tailoring. In many cases, men of letters found that they were needed to satisfy immediate wants in fields of "applied literature," and they became journalists, editors, newsmen; or they were absorbed in the teaching profession. To this day the majority of authors in Israel support themselves by working on the editorial or reportorial staffs of newspapers; others are school teachers or office workers. Of the two greatest modern Hebrew poets, one, Bialik, was part-owner of a publishing house, the other, Tchernichovsky, a school physician. Painters and sculptors are either amateur hobbyists or make a living as art-teachers; musicians are music teachers (with the notable exception of the overworked members of the Israel Philharmonic Orchestra); dancers have dance studios. It is another paradox of the cultural situation in Israel that a population which supports practically no author or artist as such, nevertheless supplies enough art-students to support a considerable number of art teachers. The interest of the people in art and literature is great, but the whole nation is still too small, its means too limited to support directly a class of professional writers and artists.

8. Esthetic Consumption

In the above discussion of the esthetic culture of Israel our attention was focused on artistic production only. Yet, just as in the field of industry a complete picture can be obtained only if both production and consumption are considered, it seems proper that also in the esthetic fields a survey of the cultural production be supplemented with a review of the cultural consumption, that is, the participation of the so-called common people in the esthetic life of the country at the receiving end. The picture of the esthetic life of a country, when regarded from the point of view of the consumer, will, of course, be both similar to and different from the impression gained from a consideration of esthetic production only. The similarities obtain, because there exists a definite and very close correlation between esthetic production and esthetic consumption (just as there exists such a correlation between industrial production and industrial consumption). The differences exist, because esthetic consumption shows the degree of participation of the average person in the various fields of literature and the arts, irrespective of the degree of originality shown by the creative aspects of these fields; and, what is equally important, without even considering whether the single components of these fields are indigenous or are importations from abroad. Again there is a certain analogy here with industrial consumption, which usually relies partly on products or raw materials imported from abroad.

Esthetic consumption seems to be a more reliable yardstick than esthetic production for measuring the standard of cultural life attained by a population in the esthetic fields; an evaluation of esthetic production must needs contain a large proportion of subjective judgment, while the degree of esthetic consumption admits of a more quantitative approach. By focusing attention on esthetic consumption, one can find fairly accurate methods, capable of numerical expression, for comparing the level of one people's cultural standing in the esthetic field with that of others. The number and kind of books an average person reads, the number of theater or opera performances he attends, the number of concerts or dance recitals he follows, the number of exhibitions he visits—all these can be taken as accurate and objective indicators of the esthetic-cultural level attained by the population composed of such average persons, and are comparable to corresponding figures from other countries.

As for esthetic consumption in the literary field, the two primary prerequisites are, of course, literacy and the knowledge of the language.* An almost equally important condition, however, is the *reading-habit*, which is a far cry from the mere ability to read and which can be acquired only in the course of a prolonged process of social conditioning. Reading-habit is a typical form of cultural consumption developed and made popular in the West only recently. The first echoes of this phenomenon are only now beginning to penetrate the Middle East.

The prevalence and intensity of the reading-habit in Israel fully bear out the validity of the name "the People of the Book" given to the Jews. In 1946—the last halfway "normal" year in the life of

* Cf. above, pp. 140 ff.

the *Yishuv*—about one thousand books were printed in Jewish Palestine, that is, one book per every six hundred persons. In 1950—a year of great economic stress—920 books were printed in Israel, or one book per 1,200 persons, including the new immigrants.

In 1952, 323 journals were published in Israel, somewhat less than one-third of them in foreign languages.

Frequency of publication	In Hebrew	In Other Languages	Total
Daily	14	7	21
Twice or more often weekly	3	17	20
Weekly	50	46	96
Monthly	100	16	116
Others	54	16	70
Total	221	102	323

Source: *The Jewish Agency's Digest*, Aug. 8, 1952, vol. IV, no. 45, p. 1513. The newsprint consumption in Israel was, in 1949, 9.25 lbs. per 1,000 of population, as compared to 14.30 lbs. in France.

Perhaps even more significant is the figure reached when calculating the number of books read in one year by the average person. To find this figure, let us leave out of account the children up to the age of ten who make up about one quarter of the total population. For the year 1950 this will leave 825,000 persons, including the new immigrants who had not yet mastered Hebrew. The 920 books published that year averaged 3,000 copies each,* which gives us 2,760,000 copies. If we estimate that a single copy of a book is read on the average by three persons (including books in circulating libraries, school libraries, libraries of *kibbutzim*, etc.), we find that the average person over ten years of age in the Jewish population of Israel in 1950 read nine books. This, of course, is a very approximative figure, for both the number of copies printed and the number of persons reading a single copy is only a rough estimate; but the figures were taken on the low side so that the expected error should be in underestimation rather than overestimation. Also, it has to be taken into account that books printed in previous years were read in 1950 too, thus increasing the average considerably. Nor is this all. It is estimated that in the 1950-51 fiscal year, £.I. 200,000 or almost a quarter-pound per person (over 10 years of age) was expended for the importation of foreign books, and this despite the critical shortage of foreign currency!

* The *Am Oved* (Working People) Publishing House of the *Histadrut* published in ten years (1939-49) 298 books to a total of 1,126,500 copies, which gives an average of 3,778 copies per published book. Actually 900,000 copies were sold; cf. *Davar*, Tel Aviv, March 23, 1950.

Along the same lines one can calculate that the average Israeli attends six to seven theater, opera, concert or dance performances annually; that he spends at least another six to seven evenings listening to lectures, and visits two or three exhibitions of the fine arts or of historical or other instructive character,* and goes 38 times a year to a motion-picture theater. In brief, the cultural consumption of the people of Israel in the esthetic and intellectual fields is rather imposing in its volume, and is certainly entirely Western in its intensity and general distribution.

The Oriental Jewish immigrants who come from a cultural milieu, in which these forms of cultural consumption are as yet in their very beginnings, exhibit a very low participation in the general cultural consumption in Israel. The educational and acculturative task which has to be undertaken here is a much more difficult one than the task of accustoming them to the use of Western material equipment. The use of material equipment can be taught by simply demonstrating a few times its utility and advantages. The participation—even on the receiving end—in the esthetic-intellectual fields of culture, presupposes a mental and psychological equipment which, if not acquired from childhood onward, can be attained only through a protracted and laborious process. Yet, whether difficult or not, it has to be undertaken unless Israel is prepared to resign itself to the continued existence in its midst of a numerically rapid-growing yet culturally alien Jewish group, with all the concomitants of such a situation in stress and strain.

9. The Mental Climate

The fourth aspect of Israeli culture which we now come to consider here is on the psychological plane. The social sciences have recognized for some time that the psychological attunement observable in a population between the individual and his society is independent of either the material or the esthetic-intellectual accomplishments offered by the society to its members, and is, in fact, a group-phenomenon of an order entirely different from them.

The degree of adjustment reached between the individual and his society can be measured quantitatively, by the percentage of well-adjusted individuals in a population, as well as qualitatively, by the degree of emotional satisfaction obtained by individuals from the processes of their enculturative training and from the

---

* According to the figures published by the Tel Aviv Municipality, in the year 5711 (1950/51) 860,000 persons attended the performances of the Habima, Ohel, Matate, and Chamber theaters and the Israel Philharmonic Orchestra and the Israel Opera in Tel Aviv alone.

interplay between their personalities within the range of socially sanctioned behavior.

Personality, again, has been found to be formed and conditioned chiefly by factors other than the material and esthetic-cultural traits and related complexes present in the cultural environment. In every culture there exist certain sets of value-judgments, certain ideals of personality type, of statuses to be achieved and roles to be played, endeavors to be pursued and situations to be avoided. Certain acts are deemed laudable by the consensus of group-opinion, others are regarded as deplorable. Certain ways of behavior, certain personal properties and character traits are considered "good," others "bad." Together with the heritage of material and esthetic-intellectual culture which is handed down by parents and teachers to the younger generation in a prolonged and complex process of socialization and cultural conditioning, of imparting knowledge and developing abilities, certain very definite attitudes are also inculcated from earliest childhood; these become in the course of years a more or less rigid frame of reference into which will have to be fitted all the future value-judgments, ideals and endeavors. From a purely hypothetical, external point of view these attitudes and resulting value-judgments, ideals and endeavors may be condoned or condemned. From the viewpoint of the society itself, they are, as a rule, the only permissible ones. For the individuals who make up the human group, the crucial question is whether their personalities—which are the outcome of such factors as biological, physical-environmental, social and cultural determinants, as well as personal experiences, "accidents," and the like—are in tune with the sets of values, ideals and endeavors prevailing in their society. If the answer is yes, they have every chance of becoming well-adjusted persons, finding satisfaction in their work and life within their group; if not, dissatisfaction and maladjustment will, in all probability, be their lot. The higher the percentage of individuals well-attuned to their society in this sense, the more successful that society can be pronounced in the sphere of psychological achievement.

These theoretical remarks seem necessary for a fuller understanding and a proper appraisal of the emotional-psychological aspect of the culture of new Israel. For if we fail to realize that emotional satisfaction does not depend in the first place on the state of things material or esthetic-intellectual, we should be utterly puzzled by what is encountered in this respect on the modern Israeli scene. We have here an immigrant population practically all of whom suffer hardships and privations for lack of sufficient supplies or primary material commodities; many of whom do not yet understand Hebrew and are thus cut off from most possibilities for intellectual-esthetic satisfaction and full participation in the cultural life of the country; a people which is composed of the remnants of massacres and persecutions and which, barely saved from the Scylla of Europe found itself threatened by the Charybdis of Asia. What we would expect under these circumstances, is a population embittered and frustrated, mourning over past losses, galled by its present privations, and full of anxieties as to its future. But, quite to the contrary, we find nothing of the sort. Isolated cases of nervous disorder, of individual maladjustment, of course, occur; but their incidence is much too small to mar the overall picture which is one of great confidence in the future, a sense of determination and achievement in the present, and a healthy mental scabbification covering up the wounds of the past.

It is of course not intended that the emotional-psychological situation in Israel be painted with undue roseate coloring. The feeling of extraordinary elation which inspired the citizens of the new State during the Arab-Jewish war and in the months immediately following it, is undoubtedly gone. That period was followed by a certain sobering up when it was realized that the true fruits of victory were still far away and that the times ahead would inevitably be full of hardships and privations. The young people who were ready for the supreme sacrifice in "their finest hour" began to show impatience and dissatisfaction when faced with the trying realities of a slow and uninspiring struggle for economic growth.

Yet the great common experience of mortal peril, the communal resolve to stand to the last man and to die fighting, the gradual realization that what all had hoped for, but scarcely dared to believe, had become a reality, welded the people of Israel together into one nation, and created a feeling of brotherhood, of mutual confidence and of a self-reliance formerly not experienced by Jews. The newcomers who arrived after the war, whether from Europe or from North Africa, had no share in this great experience. They came, it was felt, because their position in the lands of the Diaspora had become untenable, and only partially because they, too, wanted to share the free and full Jewish life made possible in Israel by the sacrifices and victories of those who were there before them. Humanitarian considerations, political expediency and strategical calculation made it necessary to help them come; in fact, to bring them into the country urgently and in great masses. The old Jewish tradition of "All Israel are *haverim* (kin)" made them welcome as

brothers among brothers. The unequalled feeling of Jewish solidarity all over the world prepared a modicum of the material
necessities for them. But years will have to pass before the unintentional distinction will have disappeared between those who
fought in Israel and those who came after the fighting; years, even ✱
in the case of those who were unable to come earlier and who went
through experiences in Europe which were a hundredfold worse
than the fiercest battles fought in Israel between Arabs and Jews.
As to the Oriental Jews, it is felt that they could have come but
waited until their social and economic situation became unbearable;
that they are separated from the majority of Israel's defenders by
a wide cultural gulf; and that they resemble the Arab enemy in
several personality traits. All this tends to crystallize the unintentional distinction between the "us" and the "you" into a rigid stereotype fraught with the dangers of social fragmentation. Chapter 10
will be devoted in its entirety to the problems of the cultural crisis
precipitated by this development. Here it can only be stated that,
as a result of this situation, the integration of the Oriental Jewish
immigrants is made more difficult than the cultural differences in
themselves would warrant.

This disturbing phenomenon notwithstanding, the young State of
Israel looks forward to new achievements, like a youth whose period
of parental tutelage has terminated in a frightening and painful
initiation ceremony and who emerges victorious and independent,
capable of taking care of himself and preparing for greater feats.
The dominating mood is still one of pioneering, of girding the loins
for great new tasks, of conquering the new frontiers open to all
initiative within the newly-won boundaries of the State. There is a
sense of meeting a great challenge and of partaking in a great
historical event significant, not only to the Jewish people, but to all
humanity.

The central column upon which the emotional configuration of
new Israel balances is the *sabra*, the Jewish youth born or reared
in Palestine. It was the *sabra* element which, in spite of its numerical
minority, bore a major part of all the vicissitudes which befell
Palestine during the last fifteen years. They had borne arms, in
fact, ever since the Arab uprising of 1936; they went through
strenuous training in the Haganah, the Jewish underground army,
and later served with the British in World War II; so that, when
the crucial test came in the War of Independence, they were ready
for the ultimate stand and the most heroic self-sacrifice.

In molding the modal personality of the *sabra*, the *Yishuv* was un-
commonly lucky and successful. The children born in Palestine, or

educated there from early childhood, exhibited a rare example of high individual attunement to group values, group ideals and group endeavors. After many Jewish generations in all the lands of the Diaspora had been educated in at least the rudiments of dual cultures, they, the *sabras*, were the first Jewish children brought up in one single culture only. It was the culture which had been re-shaped but a generation previously by their own parents to contain elements of which both components of the dual Diaspora cultures were largely devoid: elements of an earthy nature, derived from the ideals of nationhood, soil, and labor. The result was a generation of young people in which the proverbial Jewish nervous uncertainty was replaced by a quiet persistence, intellectual over-agility by a calmer mental dignity, self-ridicule by self-criticism, and hyper-sensitivity by self-confidence.

In the course of the short history of modern Jewish Palestine, the *sabras* have developed yet another characteristic quite unknown in the social world of the Jews outside Palestine, and most valuable for the new-old homeland: an extraordinary capacity for assimilating others to themselves. The importance of this feature cannot be over-emphasized, for it was due to it that immigrants of a relatively young, and hence impressionable and malleable age, have, under their influence, taken over so rapidly many of their characteristics. The author has personally observed numerous young immigrants in their late teens or early twenties arriving in Palestine with all the marks of the East European ghetto in their bearing and personality, then changing rapidly, through intimate contact with *sabras*, and becoming very much "sabraized" themselves within the remarkably short period of a year or two. It is therefore to the *sabras* that Israel must look for the psychological absorption of the younger generation also among the Sephardi and Oriental Jewish immigrants.

In addition to the *sabras*, another population element whose share in the emotional attitudes of the people of Israel is important is the Sephardi-Oriental sector itself, or, to be more accurate, the older residents among them. In the present economic and material crisis in Israel, it has been somewhat easier for both the newcomers and the *sabras* to put up with privations and hardships when contemplating the example of the Sephardi and Oriental Jews in their midst. Here is a large population-group characterized by a traditional attitude of contentment and mental and spiritual peace which they maintain as a rule despite low standards of living and even amidst the most adverse circumstances. Thus the presence of the Oriental Jewish element in the Israeli melting-pot has something of the effect of a tempering and mellowing agent in an otherwise brittle alloy of hard metals. The Oriental attitude of detachment, with its wider outlook on life and its hazards, reasserting itself as soon as it meets with the slightest degree of sympathy and understanding, must be regarded as the greatest asset of Oriental Jewish life and its most significant potential contribution to the mental climate of Israel.

Chapter Seven
The Yemenite Jews

1. Yemen and Its Jews

*   Yemen is a small kingdom in the southwestern corner of the Arabian Peninsula which comprises a territory of some 75,000 square miles. The major part of it is fertile enough, at least when compared with other sections of the Peninsula, to have merited the name of *Arabia Felix* or Happy Arabia. In the west, Yemen is bounded by the Red Sea and its own narrow coastal strip; in the south by the British Crown Colony of Aden; to the east by the great South Arabian Desert, the so-called *Rub' al-Khali* (The Empty Quarter), divided politically between the British Aden Protectorate and the Kingdom of Saudi Arabia; and to the north by what was the Emirate of Asir and is today part of Saudi Arabia. From the coastal plain the mountains rise sharply, reaching in places an elevation of 10,000 feet and receiving enough rain to make cereal and vegetable growing possible. Of the three to four millions of inhabitants of Yemen, the overwhelming majority are cultivators who have terraced large tracts of the Yemenite mountain lands. In ancient times the country was famous for its myrrh and frankincense; later it became known as the great coffee land. In contrast to several other Middle Eastern countries, agriculture is regarded in Yemen as a noble occupation and is reserved for Moslems alone, so that, although non-Moslems can own land, they have been debarred from the actual working of it. In the north of Yemen the population has preserved its ancient tribal structure and the villages in this area serve as permanent tribal bases, though the original occupation, nomadic herdsmanship, has long been given up for settled agriculture. In the east, however, where the mountains merge into the desert, nomadic tribesmen still herd their camels and raise sheep and goats.

  The religion of Yemen is Sunnite Moslem, with the exception of Central Yemen where the prevailing religion is that of the Zaidi sect an offshoot of Shi'ite Islam, established by the Imam Hadi Yahya in 901 C.E. and called after Zaid, a great-grandson of Ali.

The culture of Yemen can be properly evaluated only within the context of Middle Eastern culture as a whole. It is a highly religious culture, in which state and religion are identical to an even higher degree than is the case in other Moslem countries. The ruler, called Imam, is both the religious and the political head of the state. Members of his immediate or extended family fill the highest posts beneath him, and his own authority is related to his claim to descent from the Prophet Muhammed through Ali and Zaid. Education, which is in the hands of local clerics, is centered around religious tradition and is restricted to boys who gather for instruction at the mosques. Only a small segment of the urban males is literate, and when one considers that the large majority of the Yemenite people live in villages, this means a very small percentage of the total population. Apart from certain traditional agricultural accomplishments, such as irrigation, and certain artcrafts actively practiced only by Jews, whose products were widely appreciated by the Moslem Yemenites, material culture is characterized by a great simplicity verging almost on the primitive. That this, however, does not result from any lack of ability to cope with technical problems is manifested, for instance, by the existence of the multiple-storied buildings typical of Yemen and the Hadhramaut. The causes underlying the retarded development of material culture in Yemen must therefore be sought elsewhere.

As in all the other countries partaking of the traditional culture of the Middle East, cultural attention in Yemen, too, is focused on the transcendental aspects of life and the world: the religious outlook and attitude, typical of the Middle East as a whole, prevail in Yemen in a most intense form. The trust in Allah, so strangely coupled with the fear of demons, the unquestioning acceptance of the doctrine of predestination, the belief in the inevitability of predetermined events, and the certainty of punishment and reward in the Other World, all are conducive to a leisurely, unhurried and somewhat apathetic existence favored also by the tropical climate of the country.

Yemen has a social system characterized by greater rigidity than is usual for the Middle East. The highest social class consists of the Imam and his family; hereditary sheikhs and landowners make up the noble class; while the bulk of the population are free farmers. The lowest class within the fold of Islam is that of the workers. Outside the fold of Islam stand the lowest of the low, the *dhimmi*, or "protected" peoples, such as the Jews.

The Yemenite Jews have an old tradition according to which their ancestors first settled in the land of Yemen even before the destruction of the First Temple in Jerusalem (586 B. C. E.). When Ezra returned from Babylonia to Palestine, so the tradition runs, he sent letters to all the Jewish communities—and among them the Yemenites—asking them to return and share in the rebuilding of their ancestral land. But the Yemenite Jews refused, for they foresaw that the Second Temple also would be destroyed and that Israel would again be exiled; they preferred to stay in the happy land of Yemen. Thereupon Ezra put a curse upon them to the effect that they should always remain stricken with poverty.

The earliest historical data about the Jews of South Arabia stem from the centuries between the destruction of the Second Temple (70 C. E.) and the appearance of Muhammed (570-632). These centuries saw powerful Jewish warrior tribes in South Arabia, who jointly with their non-Jewish neighbors fought the Christian (Abyssinian and Byzantine) invaders and in the fifth and sixth centuries established an independent kingdom of their own. The Jews of Himyar (in South Arabia) maintained connections with Palestine as early as the third century, and in the first quarter of the sixth century the last Jewish king of Himyar, Yusuf-Dhu-Nawas, made use of Jewish priests (*Kohanim*) from Tiberias, Palestine, in his wars against the Abyssinians.

With the victory of Islam, the Jews of South Arabia became a subjugated and persecuted population, but remained nevertheless faithful to their religion and succeeded also in keeping alive their contact with other Jewish diasporas, especially those of Babylonia and Egypt. During the twelve centuries that ensued, occasional travelers and settlers from Yemen to Palestine, and emissaries from Palestine to Yemen, continued to break through the relative isolation of the Jews in that faraway corner of South Arabia.

2. The First Yemenite *Aliya*

It is most instructive and illuminating to follow the history of the Yemenite Jewish immigration to Palestine from the eighties of the last century to the beginning of the present one. The Yemenite immigration paralleled the waves of immigration which brought the Jews of Central and Eastern Europe to Palestine at the same time. What is even more remarkable, the difficulties the Yemenites encountered in Palestine seventy or sixty years ago were largely the same as those which beset the Jewish immigrants from Yemen and other Oriental countries today.

The first hundred Jewish families who set out from Yemen for

Palestine, in 1881, did so after rumors had spread in Yemen that Rothschild—whom they believed to be something equivalent to a king of the Jews—had bought large tracts of land in Jerusalem and was giving it away free to Yemenite Jews.

This is not the place to dwell upon the Sinbad-like adventures of the Jews who sailed from the ports of Yemen to the shores of Palestine. The first group arrived in Palestine in the summer of 1881, the second in the fall of the same year, thus beating the East European Bilu-immigrants to it by about one year. The first Yemenite immigrants were all from the city of San'a, the capital of Yemen, or its vicinity; and they all settled in Jerusalem.

The first experience which awaited them upon reaching the city of their dreams was one of bitter disappointment. No lands had been kept in readiness to be distributed among them by Rothschild, and as they had spent all their money to satisfy the often unreasonable demands of the Red Sea shippers, they arrived penniless and unable even to rent lodgings. Most of the Jewish settlement of Jerusalem was concentrated in those days within the narrow confines of the congested walled-in Old City, where most of the houses were owned by Arabs. The exorbitant rental demanded by the Arab landlords for a whole year in advance was paid by the Jews of Jerusalem with the help of their respective *Kolels*; but the Yemenite Jews, having no *Kolel* of their own to back them, were unable to pay even a reasonable rental. Thus, their trials began as soon as they arrived, and they had to be content with tents and booths for their temporary lodgings. When the dry summer season drew to an end, they were forced to flee before the rains, and many of them sought shelter in the caves and crevices of the Kidron Valley beneath the city walls of old Jerusalem. The first to help the Yemenite immigrants in their plight was Israel Dov Frumkin, editor of the Hebrew journal *Havatselet* in Jerusalem, and due to his efforts several offers of land for a housing project were made to the Yemenites. The offer they accepted was that of a wealthy Jew from Baghdad, who gave them land on the slopes of the Mount of Olives opposite the Well of Shiloah, the only fresh water well in Jerusalem. This site had the great advantage above others that here no cisterns had to be built, for the water of the Shiloah could be used by the inhabitants of houses situated nearby, thus considerably reducing the building costs. Various donors from Palestine, England and Germany contributed money for the building materials of stone and lime, while the Yemenites themselves supplied all the labor involved. In 1885 the first twelve houses were ready, each providing housing for six families. This Yemenite quarter in the village of Shiloah (or *Kafr*

Silwan, as it was called in Arabic) was the first foothold of the Yemenite Jews in Palestine, and it served as one of their most important centers for more than fifty years, until its abandonment in 1936 at the beginning of the Arab riots.

Nor was it easy for the Yemenite Jews to find employment in Jerusalem. Only a few of them were successful enough to make a living as silversmiths, which was the favorite and traditional specialization of the Jews in Yemen and an artcraft in which they possessed exceptional skill. Artisans of other trades and merchants had to take whatever jobs were available and whenever they were available, the men chiefly as building laborers in the new settlements which began to develop in those days outside the walls of the Old City, and the women (who had never worked for a living in Yemen) as servants in well-to-do Ashkenazi Jewish households. Some of the men were skillful enough to learn new trades, particularly those connected with the building activity, like stone-cutting, quarrying or plastering. Others, who were unable to adjust to the new situation, were forced to take up the age-old and accredited Oriental profession of begging.

The first wave of immigrants from Yemen, that which reached Palestine in 1881-82, brought to the country some 200 Jews; by 1885 they numbered 450. In 1890, the first Yemenite Jews settled in Jaffa where a considerable Russian-Jewish settlement had developed in the meantime. Here, the economic conditions were much better than in Jerusalem, and the Yemenites found employment both as artisans and as laborers without difficulty. However, both from Jerusalem and from Jaffa, the Yemenite Jews sent numerous letters to their countrymen in Yemen, in which the conditions in Palestine were depicted in the most roseate colors, so that those back home were encouraged to follow in the footsteps of the first pioneers. "By your life," writes one of the Yemenite immigrants from Jerusalem, "that my earnings of one single day in Erets Yisrael are equal to the earnings of a week abroad; and by your life that on no day do we go without drinks and raisins, not to mention the Saturdays and holidays, of which no mouth can tell enough. . . ."* Little wonder that letters such as these fanned the enthusiasm of the Yemenite Jews for emigration to Palestine, and that every year more and more of them arrived in the country.

However, just as after the establishment of the Jewish state the great immigration movement from the countries of the Middle East

* Cf. Abraham Yaari, "The Immigration of Yemenite Jews to Palestine" (Hebrew), in *Shvut Teman,* ed. Israel Yeshayahu and Aharon Zadoq, Tel Aviv, 1945, p. 28.

was caused jointly by the quasi-Messianic enthusiasm of the Jewish masses and the sudden deterioration of the socio-economic and political situation of the Jews in these countries, so in much the same fashion, at the turn of the century a deterioration in the position of the Jews in Yemen increased their desire to go to Palestine. In 1904, a year of heavy drought, the strife between the Imam Yahya al-Mansur and the Turkish overlords of Yemen caused thousands of Yemenite Jews to perish of hunger in beleaguered San'a. The victory of the Imam was crowned by the establishment of an independent Yemen. Although the Turks soon reconquered Central Yemen, which then remained in their hands together with the capital, San'a, until the first World War, the repercussions of the strife were keenly felt by the Yemenite Jews who were forcibly reminded of the uncertainty of their positions as a religious minority in a Moslem state. All the restrictions on the Yemenite Jews were renewed by order of the Imam, and the Jews who had had some respite during the Turkish rule over Yemen since 1872, found the situation very hard to bear. The result of all this was the second Yemenite *Aliya* which began in 1907.

3. The Second and Third Yemenite *Aliyot*

In contrast to the first *Aliya* which came from San'a and its vicinity in central Yemen, the second Yemenite wave of immigration was recruited mainly from northern Yemen, from the towns of Sa'da, Haidan and the villages around them, all more than a hundred miles from San'a. While most of the members of the first immigration were town dwellers, artisans and traders, inured to subservience to their Moslem neighbors, those who made up the bulk of this second Yemenite immigration were villagers, integral participants in the tribal structure of northern Yemen, used to the carrying of arms and able to stand up to any opponent. These immigrants were the first Yemenite Jews to settle in rural Palestine, in Rehovot and Rishon Lezion where they arrived, some 220 souls strong, in the fall of 1907. In the meantime, the number of the Yemenite Jews in Jerusalem continued to grow steadily until in 1908 it reached 2,500 in that city, while in Jaffa it reached 200.

This second Yemenite *Aliya* and the rapid adjustment of its members to agricultural work in Palestine made Dr. Arthur Ruppin aware of the possibilities of building up a Yemenite-Jewish agricultural labor force in Palestine to replace the Arab workers who were then commonly employed in the Jewish agricultural settlements. At that time Dr. Ruppin was head of the Palestine Office of the Zionist Organization in Jaffa. Here he felt was a human element as modest in its demands as the Arabs of Palestine, as able or at least as willing to carry out heavy physical labor under the blazing sun of Palestine, and yet Jewish, hence constituting no danger to the Zionist plans for development. Samuel Yavneeli, one of the first members of the Second (Russian) *Aliya*, was entrusted in 1911 with the delicate and difficult task of going to Yemen in the guise of a religious emissary to spread there the idea of immigration to Palestine. Yavneeli visited some forty places of Jewish settlement, towns and villages in southern and central Yemen, and his lectures and articles on the Jews of Yemen are one of the important sources of our knowledge of that faraway Jewish community at the beginning of the 20th century. In one of his lectures Yavneeli epitomized the argument he used *vis-à-vis* the Yemenite Jews: "I called upon them to bend to the yoke. Enough of your standing aside and taking no part in the upbuilding of Palestine. For hundreds of years you have been sitting here on this land, and have only received. You received the Talmud from there, and the books of Maimonides, the commentary of Joseph Qaro, the writings of Yitzhak Luria and his pupils. . . . Where are the stones which you have contributed to the building of the nation? Now you must send your strength to Palestine, the best of your sons. . . . He who takes part in the suffering of the community will have the merit to see its consolation. Go up to Palestine to take your share, go up to work, go up to watch!"[*]

The present-day efforts of Israel and the Jewish public bodies to organize the immigration by putting transportation facilities at the disposal of the immigrants were also anticipated by Yavneeli in connection with the Yemenite Jews. He obtained from the Austrian Lloyd Company a reduction on steamship tickets to less than half the usual price. What was even more important, he got money from the Palestine Office in Jaffa to cover part of the traveling expenses. The wave of immigration which was stirred into motion by Yavneeli's activities brought to Palestine in 1911 and 1912 some 1,500 Yemenite Jews who settled in the agricultural settlements of Judea, Samaria and the Galilee. This immigration can be designated as the Third *Aliya* of Yemenite Jews.

By the time World War I broke out, the Yemenite Jews of Palestine were a well established and integral part of the Jewish community, or New *Yishuv*, as yet quite small. The war, of course, interrupted the immigration from Yemen as well as from Europe; but those who had come before the outbreak of the war began to fulfill a very important function by showing the immigrants of the Second Russian *Aliya* an example how to take to the simplest and

[*] Cf. A. Yaari, *op. cit.*, p. 33.

often hardest work without showing visible signs of adjustment difficulties. As a matter of fact, the Yemenite immigrants did not experience the same difficulties which characterized the process of acclimatization of the European immigrants who came to Palestine at about the same time. They too had to undergo an often trying period of adjustment, but they were spared the hardships of changing professions from the typical East-European Jewish occupations to the unskilled labor required in Palestine. For them simple manual labor was not the despised occupation it was for the old generation of Jews in Eastern Europe; but neither was it the sacred and idealized thing the members of the Second Russian *Aliya* made of it. It was for them the most natural thing to do; the biblical pronouncement, "In the sweat of thy countenance shalt thou eat bread," was an everyday living reality for them.

In 1918, soon after General Allenby occupied Palestine, the Palestine Office took a census of the Jews in the country. The outstanding part played by Yemenite artisans and laborers becomes evident from the returns showing that in Jerusalem of 47 building laborers, 24; of 41 stone-cutters, 26; of 130 laborers, 63; and of 56 silversmiths, 28 were Yemenite Jews.

In similar proportion the Yemenite Jews participated also in the building trade in Jaffa (Tel Aviv), where they were found among the workers who built the "Herzliya" High School. The first well in Tel Aviv was dug entirely by Yemenite Jews, and, in the first strike in Tel Aviv, Yemenite laborers took part.

At first, when the Yemenite Jews arrived in "colonies" like Rishon Lezion, the Jewish colonists would not believe that these people with their small, narrow frames, thin limbs and finely chiseled features, could work as well as the much bigger and more powerful-looking Arab fellahin. But it was not long before it was evident that they were suitable for the work. Mr. Y. Even Moshe, one of those who had an active share in the settling of the Yemenites in the "colonies," wrote about them in 1910 as follows:

"This is not the place to explain the role the Yemenites can play in the solution of the labor problem. But one thing can be said: The experiment is successful. This is perhaps the most successful experiment of all we have tried to this day. The success of this experiment has had a very good effect on the mood of the workers: lately they were inclined to look darkly at their work; they saw lack of success in everything, and this caused bitterness and depression which threatened to destroy all our hopes. But since the Yemenites began to work, if not all, at least a part of them began to believe that Jews would conquer labor and that the attitude of the farmers [that is, the Jewish "colonists" who hired the agricultural laborers] to this problem would also undergo a change. And the attitude of the farmers did change. They expressed this clearly at their meeting in Rehovot. Several of those present cried, 'We must send somebody to Yemen for this purpose' . . ."[*]

Moshe Smilansky, well known author and leader of the Jewish farmers, wrote at about the same time:

"The Ashkenazi laborer, since he is a bachelor, can take his bag and go from colony to colony. The situation is different in the case of the Yemenite, who is tied to his family, so that whenever there is need for him the farmer can find him in the colony. And if, for instance, he proved a good watchman, the farmer can get him from year to year. Owing to the fact that the Yemenite lives with his family in the colony, the members of his family who are able to do some kind of work can also earn some additional money. And types of work which were previously done by strange hands (i.e. Arabs), are now being done by the Yemenites. The children of the Yemenites help their fathers from an early age in their work, and like any natural worker they get used to all kinds of work from childhood, and all the ways of labor are known to them already at the time when they begin to work as laborers. The value of such laborers should not be light in our eyes."[§]

In 1921, the Immigration Center of the General Federation of Jewish Labor in Palestine (the *Histadrut*) which was organized that year, entrusted the representative of the Yemenite Jews, Mr. A. Tabib, with the writing of an epistle to the Jews in Yemen containing a call for a renewal of their immigration to Palestine. In the same year the Imam Yahya renewed an old law which promulgated that all orphans would have to be converted to the Moslem faith and educated accordingly. Following the Arab riots in Palestine, Arab leaders sent representatives to the Arab countries, among them Yemen, to rally them to fight against the Jews. Under their influence the Imam Yahya ordered the confiscation of all the property of the Yemenite Jews who planned to emigrate to Palestine, and after the riots of 1929 he altogether forbade any emigration from his country. In spite of this, many Yemenite Jews set out from innermost Yemen, determined to face any danger to escape from the "House of Bondage." Leaving behind whatever possessions they

[*] *Hapoel Hatzair*, No. 3, 1910.
[§] Cf. *Hapoel Hatzair*, No. 12, 1910.

had, and trekking through two hundred miles of desert-like territory, walking at night and hiding during the day, they congregated in Aden where they waited for the immigration certificates to Palestine. It was now their turn to write letters to Palestine, letters of supplication for a speedy rescue. . . .

4. From the Fourth Yemenite *Aliya* to "Operation Magic Carpet"

The Fourth *Aliya* of the Yemenite Jews began in 1923. From 1923 to 1931, about 2,500 Yemenite Jews came to Palestine; the immigrants settled mostly in the cities and especially in Tel Aviv where most of them worked in the building trades. In the critical years of 1927-28, many of them were transferred to the settlements of Judea and Samaria, and in this manner the Yemenite quarters in these settlements grew considerably.

The Fifth Yemenite *Aliya* began simultaneously with the German *Aliya*, in 1933. In the three years 1933-36, over 4,500 Yemenite Jews immigrated into Palestine. The outbreak of the Arab riots in 1936, which caused a great decrease in the general Jewish immigration, had the same effect on that of the Yemenite Jews. In the first half of World War II, the Yemenite Jewish immigration petered out altogether. A new stream of Yemenite immigration started in 1943, and from that year until the establishment of the Jewish state another 4,500 Yemenite Jews reached Palestine. The total number of Jewish immigrants from Yemen to Palestine in the thirty years of the Mandatory period (1919-1948) was 15,838. This figure, however, includes only those who came "officially," that is, with immigration certificates issued by the British Mandatory government of Palestine. In addition to these, several thousand Yemenite Jews reached Palestine "illegally," and according to Mr. Zecharia Gluska, Yemenite member of the First Knesset and President of the Organization of Yemenite Jews in Israel, their number must be put at still another 15,000 for the thirty-year period of 1919-1948.[*]

The main port of exit for Yemenite Jews in recent years was the British Crown Colony of Aden. In October 1945, the British government there stopped the emigration of Yemenite Jews, and consequently about 4,000 of them remained stranded in Aden. Soon about half of these were placed in a camp called *Geula* (Redemption) which was established by the American Jewish Joint Distribution Committee. The stoppage of emigration from Aden to Palestine, however, did not put an end to the flow of Jewish refugees from

[*] Written communication of Mr. Zecharia Gluska, on August 3, 1950, in New York.

Yemen to Aden across the undefined desert frontier between the Kingdom of Yemen and the British Aden Protectorate. By September 1948, the number of refugees in the Geula Camp swelled to 5,500.

In May 1949, representatives of the Israeli Department of Immigration met with three of the rulers whose territories within the Aden Protectorate lay on the route between Yemen and the British Crown Colony of Aden. The purpose of the conferences, which were held with the knowledge and approval of the British authorities in Aden, was to persuade these rulers to permit the Jews fleeing from Yemen to pass through their respective lands. One of the sultans, in whose territory lay the airfield of Muqairis, a vital link in the long road which the Yemenite Jews must take to Israel, agreed to let the Jews pass through his domain, provided the neighboring sultan would do the like. Otherwise, he said, he had misgivings lest his neighbor use the leniency he showed toward the Jews to incite his subjects against him. The third sultan, the Sherif of Beihan, whose territory was within four days' walking distance from San'a, the capital of Yemen, stipulated that he would give his consent to the proposal that the Jews pass through his domain, if 2,000 Jews would stay behind in his land to thus enable him to fulfil the Koranic commandment to become a "defender of the Jews." When it was explained to him that for the Jews it was a great religious duty to go to Israel, he asked for a few sick and old Jews at least to remain behind.

In the meantime, conditions in Yemen were consolidated to such a degree that negotiations could be opened with the new Imam, Ahmad, son and successor of the old Imam Yahya who had been murdered in February 1948. Permission was finally secured for the Jews to leave Yemen. They had, it is true, to leave behind practically all their property and belongings—a stipulation reminiscent of recurrent events in Jewish history—but at least their persons were free to go.

Now a new transit camp had to be opened. This was again financed by the Joint Distribution Committee, and although at first planned only for 500, and then for 1,000 persons, the numbers of refugees arriving from Yemen surpassed all calculations, so that by September 1949, the camp contained 13,000 persons. The British authorities closed the Aden frontier several times. This caused additional suffering to the Yemenites who, once having left their homes, could neither return nor go straight to the transit camp, but were obliged to wander over roadless deserts, amidst hostile armed tribes, in the terrible heat of the merciless summer sun, until finally the frontier was again opened and they were let through to reach the camp. It has not been calculated, and probably never will be known how many lives were lost during the trek through the desert which took at times as long as six weeks. During 1949, a large new cemetery came into existence at Qataba, on the frontier of the Aden Protectorate.

In order to expedite the evacuation of the refugees from the camp, six big Skymaster planes were put into service and each of these carried about 130 Yemenite Jews to Israel on every single flight. This was the famous "Operation Magic Carpet" which has been described several times in news dispatches and reportage articles, and which brought to Israel over 40,000 Yemenite Jews within less than a year.

In the transit camp itself the arriving refugees were given as much care as possible under the terribly overcrowded conditions. A hospital was established, consisting of 12 pavilions with 30 beds each. Six doctors and sixteen nurses worked in the hospital, but their efforts were hampered by all sorts of unexpected difficulties. It often happened that even seriously sick persons objected to medical treatment, or even to being examined by a doctor, and physical force had to be applied. Even dangerously ill Yemenites, as soon as they recovered a little, stole out of the hospital, while others were helped by their relatives to get away, so that finally guards had to be placed around the hospital.[*] By March 1950, the great majority of Yemenite Jews was shipped to Israel, although according to Mr. Gluska there are ten thousand more of them who remained behind in Yemen.

Since no definite census figures are available, the present number of Yemenite Jews in Israel can only be estimated. In 1918, their number in Palestine was 4,234, or 7.6% of the total Jewish population of about 57,000. Their immigration after 1918 started only in 1923, and developed up to the end of February 1950, as shown in the table on page 194.

On March 1, 1950, the Yemenite Jews constituted over 10% of the total Jewish population of Israel, and about one-third of the combined total of all the Sephardi and Oriental Jewish communities in the country. Numerically, therefore, the Yemenite Jews were the most important non-Ashkenazi element in Israel until the Iraqi evacuation. We shall see below that theirs is also the most significant cultural contribution rendered by a non-Ashkenazi community to the nascent culture of new Israel.

[*] Cf. *Dapei Aliya*, edited by the Jewish Agency for Palestine (Hebrew), Marheshwan, 5710 (1950).

YEMENITE JEWISH IMMIGRANTS TO PALESTINE
AND ISRAEL FROM 1923 TO 1950*

Year	Immigrants	Year	Immigrants
1923	184	1936	708
1924	406	1937	322
1925	527	1938	322
1926	215	1939	182
1927	62	1940	70
1928	—	1941	—
1929	564	1942	236
1930	374	1943	2,419
1931	169	1944	1,788
1932	436	1945	1,024
1933	1,200	May 15,	
1934	1,907	1945-	
1935	1,339	March 1,	
		1950	43,982
		Total	58,436

* Sources: From 1923 to 1945: *Statistical Handbook of Jewish Palestine*, 1947, publ. by the Dept. of Statistics of the Jewish Agency for Palestine, Jerusalem, 1947. From 1945 to 1950: *Yemenite Jews in Israel* (Hebrew), Pamphlet published by the Organization of Yemenite Jews in Israel, April, 1950, Tel Aviv.

TOTAL NUMBER OF YEMENITE JEWS IN
ISRAEL ON MARCH 1, 1950

In Palestine in 1918	4,234
Official Immigration from 1923 to March 1, 1950	58,436
"Illegal" Immigration from 1919 to 1948	15,000
Natural Increase from 1918 to 1950*	35,000
Total	112,670

*

* The exact figure of the natural increase of the Yemenite Jews is unknown. The above figure (35,000) is a conservative estimate based on the known natural increase of all the Sephardi and Oriental Jewish communities together in Palestine from 1918 to 1939.

5. The Life of Jews in Yemen

The difficulties encountered by the Yemenite Jews in their new environment in Palestine were more or less the same seventy years ago as they are today. As far as security of life and property was concerned, the conditions in Palestine were, of course, incomparably better than in Yemen. Also there was the great emotional experience of homecoming to the country of their forefathers, to the Holy Land of their religion, to the birthplace of their sacred traditions. But the reality of everyday life in Palestine was many times harder than they could ever imagine. In Yemen, every head of a family was an independent master in his own right. In most cases he was an artisan who worked at home, beginning and ending his working day as he pleased. While working he could keep an eye on his children and could teach them his trade and, what was regarded as even more important, he could impart to them his knowledge of the Tora and of Jewish lore. He could also spend as much time as he wished in the synagogue, which was a room set aside for this purpose in the house of one of the more affluent members of the community. Here he prayed, met his friends, studied with them, brewed coffee, chewed the refreshing *Kat*-leaves, and in general spent his hours of leisure in a friendly and congenial atmosphere.

Houses were of varying sizes. The simplest and poorest kind consisted of a single room covered with a flat roof; the well-to-do variety boasted a two-story construction, the lower one serving as workshop and as shelter for the animals, while the upper one contained the living and sleeping quarters. In San'a, the capital, and other cities of central and southern Yemen, the most usual houses were of two or three stories; in north Yemen, especially in the townships of Sa'da and Haidan, the houses were of five or six stories, consisting of fifteen and twenty rooms. But all these houses of such diverse sizes and structures had one basic thing in common: each house served the needs of one single family, whether a small family consisting of parents and children only, or a large, extended family of several generations in the male line. "My home is my castle" was doubly true for the Jews of Yemen, since the value of the home was enhanced by the fact that outside it they encountered so often the painful manifestations of the *Galut*, the Diaspora, the exile. In his professional life the Jew had to come in touch daily with the Moslems of Yemen; he had to submit to humiliations and quietly suffer offenses. It was the law of the country that a Jew was forbidden to strike a Moslem, and even to raise his voice against a Moslem; a Jew had to rise before a Moslem who passed his way and to pay reverence to him. He was forbidden to discuss religious matters with a Moslem, was not allowed to ride on horseback, and was required to pay a head-tax called *Geziya*. Despite this, he had two refuges where he was lord and master, where he was deemed a man of high culture and the proud heir to a noble tradition: the synagogue and his home. While he was the sole provider for his home, his wife (polygyny has been on the wane for several decades) took care of all the housework, which included the daily grinding of the flour, the fetching of water and other tiring and monotonous tasks. Yet, although these chores took up the major part of their day, most of the women found time to do some profitable work, such as embroidering, weaving of girdles, making of earthenware pots, of brooms and the like. But the women never had to make use of their earnings in order to contribute to the household expenses; whatever they earned was theirs to keep, and for the most part they bought silver or golden jewelry with it. Only lately, a long time after the first Yemenite immigrants reached Palestine, did Yemenite Jewish women engage in household work in San'a and in a few other towns, in the houses of Turkish officials or as nurses in the women's department of the San'a hospital.

A certain separation of the sexes was customary among the Jews of Yemen, but it never reached the stage of complete segregation practiced by the urban Moslems. At home, in contrast to the Moslem Arab custom, husband and wife took their meals together, and this fact in itself gave women a much higher status in the family than was the case with the Moslem members of their sex. The Yemenite Jewish women were not veiled; they could visit each other; on Saturday afternoons and on the holidays especially, they would stroll in groups along the streets or sit around in the open. When the great events of the human life-cycle occurred, when a child was born, a couple married or someone died, the women of the village had their full share in the proceedings, whether they assembled separately or in the same room with the menfolk. They sang and danced and contributed their best to making the day memorable for the principals as well as for themselves. Though the girls received no formal education, were not taught how to read and write like the boys in their Tora school, they nevertheless acquired from their mothers not only the practical skills necessary for their lives as housewives and mothers, but also a considerable store of oral tradition, consisting of Jewish legends, stories, songs, proverbs, all in the colloquial Arabic language of Yemen. The magical element coloring the religion of the Yemenite Jews was more in evidence among the women than among the men, and this may have had something to do with the exclusion of women from the official and communal aspects of religion centering around the synagogue. The depth of their religious feeling nevertheless asserted itself and lent them an inner serenity and fortitude in the face of hardship and adversity.

In this manner the Yemenite Jews had lived a life practically unchanged for several hundreds of years in the country of their long exile. They were oppressed, constantly exposed to contempt which could at the slightest provocation flare into violence; they worked hard and long for their living within the limitations put upon them by their Moslem neighbors and overlords; but they found their compensations in their conviction that they were possessed of a spiritual nobility; and they learned to value those things which home and synagogue gave them and which filled them with a sense of modest but ineffable tranquillity.

6. Hardships in the Homeland

In Palestine all this was completely different. Instead of being their own masters, they were forced to do the bidding of others. They were regarded as unskilled laborers who must be prepared to work hard and to earn little. Witness even the words of Moshe Smilansky, quoted above, which were ostensibly appreciative in their intent (p. 190). In Yemen, it is true, they were a group apart from the Moslem majority, but they were filled with the consciousness of being the descendants of the blessed son of Abraham, while in their Arab neighbors they saw the children of the cast-out Ismael. How well they knew and felt that theirs was "the voice of Jacob" which they could lift up to their Creator and thus find protection and consolation from the "hands of Esau" which oppressed them. But once in Palestine, in the veritable land of their Father Abraham, they were treated by the other Jews as if they were an inferior tribe, lacking in education as well as in descent. Their life was hard. They had to hurry to work early in the morning, remain far away from home all day long, eat an unsatisfactory meal squatting in the field under a tree or in the narrow shade of an unfinished wall, run after new employment in the evening—and find that withal the piasters earned were not sufficient. Gone were the days when they could spend unhurried hours in the synagogue, teach their sons Tora and artisanship, take their leisurely meals in the soothing company of wife and children. And even the few hours of rest spent at home were not what a tired man's heart desires, for their quarters were in most cases inadequate holes, with several families cramped into every corner.

The inadequacy of a man's earnings soon forced also his wife to seek employment, and, as the only work to be found was domestic help, she too was lifted out of her home for the duration of the entire day leaving her smaller children in the care of the six and seven-year-olds. Another year or two, and the oldest girl, too, had to go to work, to serve in the house of some Ashkenazi *Gveret* (lady), while the boy was taken out of the Tora school and forced to fend for himself in the streets. The family was dispersed, paternal and maternal authority broken down, the home, once the proud, safe and sequestered castle of the family, turned into the occasional meeting-place for people who were becoming more and more estranged.

As early as 1920, the Council of Yemenite Laborers expressed their grievances in a resolution:

"The situation of hundreds of Yemenite families in the settlements, who immigrated to Palestine with devotion of soul and out of love for the country and desire to work its land and to take root in it, has become worse from year to year. The yoke of oppression was put on our necks, on our women and children, degrading our honor, suppressing our spirit and filling us with bitterness. The uncertainty and unemployment increased. The health of the immigrants has deteriorated. And the bad and oppressive conditions —no adequate housing, insufficient wages, no permanent work— with which we had to put up ever since we immigrated, have shown their effect: the generation which in the days of its immigration was in its best strength, has grown old and weak before its time, after ten years of work and suffering. The angel of death reaps his frightening harvest among our children who were born in this country, the number of our infants whom we buried in the ancestral soil has reached hundreds; the young generation which immigrated and grew up in this country has lost the pride of liberty and the power of resoluteness which beat in the hearts of the Yemenite Jews in their exile-birthplace. Our daughters and wives, whose necks never had to bear the yoke of earning a livelihood, have been compelled here, on account of impatience and great poverty, to leave their children and their houses and to go to the houses of the farmers. Our young generation has grown up without Tora and without education, and our numbers in all the settlements has diminished instead of growing. The *moshava*, in the shadow of which we wanted to live, has become for us a bitter disappointment."[*]

The desperate need for immediate income made it impossible for the great majority of the Yemenite immigrants to take up again in Palestine those trades which were their traditional occupations in Yemen. The Jews in the towns and villages of Yemen were practically the only artisans, and the overwhelming majority of the earners among the Yemenite Jews had been engaged in arts and crafts. The following list will give an idea of the great variety of trades engaged in by the Yemenite Jews:

Metal work: silversmith (this is the most important single craft of the Yemenite Jews), coiner, coppersmith, armorer.

[*] Resolutions of the Council of Yemenites, printed in the pamphlet *Ahdut Haavoda*, Siwan, 1920, quoted from *Shvut Teman*, p. 48.

Woodwork and related crafts: cabinet maker, sievemaker, wicker-worker.

Leatherwork: leatherworker, shoemaker, shoe-repairer, saddle-maker, furrier, tanner, flayer.

Clothing and related crafts: tailor, weaver, spinner, cushion-sewer, cotton-worker, dyer.

Earthenware, spices, etc.: potter, repairer of earthenware goods, pharmacist, millstone chamferer, charcoalburner, pulvermaker, soapmaker.

Food, etc.: miller, slaughterer, distiller, snuff maker.

Book production: copyist, bookbinder.

Building trades: building-laborer, stone cutter, carpenter, house-painter.

Services: cupper, barber, servant, manure collector, donkey driver, porter, cleaner of courtyards.

Commerce and finance: moneylender, clothes merchant, shop-keeper, peddler.

These occupations were in most cases transmitted from fathers to sons, and nothing would have been more natural than to continue at least in some of them after their immigration to Palestine. But to do so required a breathing space, for only rarely was it possible to find customers immediately for specialized products, most of which had been adapted to the special local tastes prevailing in Yemen. Only a few silversmiths were successful in the continuance of their old trade in Jerusalem, although incidentally their work had quite an influence on the development of Palestinian Jewish jewelry. For most of the Yemenite immigrants it was imperative to find work as soon as they arrived. This invariably meant engaging in unskilled labor, either in the building trade, in porterage or in street-cleaning in the towns, or as agricultural laborers to replace the Arabs in the "colonies." The same thing was true for the women, who were un-able to wait until they found customers for their beautiful colored embroidery for which they were famous among the Arab women of Yemen, and were forced to seek domestic employment which paid little and was regarded both by them and by their mistresses as a low-grade occupation.

7. The Yoke of Agriculture

For several generations there were practically no farmers among the Yemenite Jews. The Islamic law valid in Yemen made agricul-ture unlawful for non-Moslems; and, although the law was not everywhere consistently obeyed, Yomtob Semach who visited Yemen in 1910 states that he found only 20 Jewish families in the country whose earners worked in agriculture, while the total number of Yemenite Jews according to him was 35,000.* And even in the trades, most of them concentrated in those fields which do not require great physical exertion, but can be carried out in relative comfort, indoors, and which stressed, not muscular effort, but the highly developed skill and the accumulated knowledge of the rich lore of the artcraft. If we visualize this occupational background from which the great majority of the Yemenite Jewish immigrants to Palestine came, we will understand that like the *Halutzim* of the Second Russian *Aliya*, they too had to undergo a painful process of adjustment to the hard and exhausting labor in which they engaged in Palestine. But while for the Russian Jewish *Halutzim* it was their own free choice to "return to the soil" to rebuild their old-new homeland with the sweat of their brow, for the Yemenite Jews it was a matter of compulsion, of being forced by external circumstances into occupations unaccustomed and uncongenial to them. When viewed against this background, the undemurring readiness of the Yemenite Jews to "bend to the yoke" and thus to present an example to be followed by their Ashkenazi brethren, appears as an even more remarkable feat of human adaptability.

In spite of the complete lack of experience in agriculture, on the one hand, and the greater hold of tradition which makes it difficult for them to show initiative in new fields of activity, on the other, the output of the Yemenite agricultural settlements in Palestine did not fall short of that attained by Ashkenazi Jews, for instance, the German Jewish immigrants. This can be shown by a comparison of the condition and output of the four Yemenite Jewish smallholders' settlements (*moshavim*) which existed in Palestine in 1944, with the corresponding data of eleven German Jewish *moshavim*.

The *moshav* or Smallholders' Settlement, we will recall (cf. above, page 60), is a rural settlement form developed by the Second (Russian) *Aliya*. Most of the *moshavim* were established by the Zionist settling institutions and their beginnings go back to the years preceding World War I. The first *moshavim* were founded by middle-class immigrants mainly from Eastern Europe and were built mostly on lands of the Jewish National Fund with subsidies from the Keren Hayesod, the Palestine Foundation Fund. Several of the *moshavim* were established by organizations based on a common country of origin (such as Polish *moshavim*, Lithuanian *moshavim*, etc.), and their economic basis was citrus growing (in the Emek Hefer in the

* Cf. Yomtob Semach, *Une Mission de l'Alliance au Yemen*, Paris, n. d., pp. 85 and 108.

central Sharon, and elsewhere). Only those *moshavim* which were founded by East European immigrants, in the years of World War II, were based on mixed farming. By the end of 1946, there were 37 *moshavim* of East European Jews with a total population of some 14,000.

In particular, the *moshavim* of two immigrants' groups developed into rural settlements with special characteristics of their own. These were the *moshavim* of German Jewish immigrants and of Yemenite Jewish immigrants. Most of the German *moshavim* have organized into a separate body called "Organization of Communal Villages" (*Irgun Kefarim Shitufiyim*). Each one of these villages constitutes a closely knit socio-economic unit with a way of life which, apart from the actual farming work performed, is more typical of members of the professions and of the industrial and commercial class (which the majority of the settlers actually had been in Germany) than of farmers. The main branches of farming in these *moshavim* are vegetable gardening, fruit growing, and especially poultry raising—all specializations suited to the working capacity and the skills of middle-aged settlers from Germany. The settlements were mostly built with the resources of the settlers themselves, and only part of the investment required was allotted to them by the settling institutions, one of which, the Department for the Settlement of German Jews, was created especially for them by the Jewish Agency for Palestine. The first of these *moshavim*, Ramot Hashavim, south of Herzliya in the Sharon, was founded in 1933, soon after the onset of the German Jewish immigration. All the German Jewish *moshavim* were planned with care and with an eye to external appearance, and they make a pleasing impression due to the good architecture and the well-tended state of the farms themselves.*

The settlements of the Yemenite Jews were originally established with a view to serving as residential quarters only for the Yemenite laborers engaged in agriculture or other occupations in the larger *moshavot*. Only from the early thirties was the problem of independent agricultural occupation by the Yemenite settlers seriously considered, and it was only then that the Yemenite *moshavim*, as they exist to this day, were founded. In contrast to the German Jewish *moshavim*, these Yemenite *moshavim* have very few cooperative institutions for marketing, purchasing, credit, and so on. The rudimentary state of cooperation characteristic of these Yemenite Jewish *moshavim* seems to indicate the same lack of social preparedness for economic cooperation which has been shown to characterize

* One German Jewish *moshav*, Talmon, founded in 1937, was later abandoned by its settlers and, in 1945, occupied by Yemenite Jews.

the Palestinian Arabs.* These Yemenite settlements are thus reckoned as the *moshav* type of agricultural settlement, not because of their inner organizational likeness, but rather on account of such external considerations as their being situated on land owned by the Jewish National Fund and built with the financial help of the Keren Hayesod, which obliges the settlers to follow largely the rules laid down by these institutions for all the *moshavim*.

8. The Yemenite *Moshavim*

The first Yemenite *moshav* to be established was Mahane Yehuda, which was founded with the help of the Keren Hayesod, in 1912, in the Jaffa sub-district. In 1947, Mahane Yehuda comprised 590 dunams (c. 147 acres) of land and had 800 inhabitants.

Nearly twenty years elapsed before the second Yemenite *moshav* was founded. This was Kfar Marmorek, in the Ramle sub-district, established in 1931. This again is mainly a residential workers' quarter and borders the outskirts of the big agricultural settlement of Rehovot. Many of its people find work in the citrus-plantations as well as in other kinds of employment in Rehovot. In 1947, Kfar Marmorek had 750 dunams of land and 970 inhabitants. In 1932, Tirat Shalom was founded, situated between Rehovot and Nes Zionah; in 1947, it had 550 dunams and 329 inhabitants. In 1933, Elyashiv was founded south of Hadera; in 1947, it had 979 dunams of land and 345 inhabitants. All the four Yemenite *moshavim* are situated on the seashore and the land for them has been allocated by the Jewish National Fund at the average rate of 1.2 dunams per person (in 1947). In the German Jewish *moshavim* the average in 1947 was 2 dunams per person.

In order to compare the rates of output of the Yemenite Jewish *moshavim*, on the one hand, with those of the German Jewish settlements, we have to draw on figures and information dating from 1944. In that year, 2,250 Yemenite Jews lived in these four *moshavim*, and they had under cultivation a total area of 2,010 dunam (or about 500 acres), or 0.89 dunam of cultivated area per person. In the eleven German Jewish *moshavim*, there were 3,850 persons and 6,130 dunam (about 1,532 acres) were cultivated, or 1.59 dunam per person. The fact that the Yemenites cultivated per person only 56% of the area brought under cultivation by the German Jews was not caused by lack of additional land; the four Yemenite *moshavim* in that year had an additional 1,220 dunams at their disposal.

* Cf. Raphael Patai, *On Culture Contact and Its Working in Modern Palestine*, American Anthropological Association, Memoir No. 67, October 1947, pp. 39-42.

In their fruit plantations the Yemenite Jews concentrated heavily on citrus fruit: they had 530 dunams of citrus groves and only 60 dunams of other fruit-trees, like deciduous fruit-trees, vines, and the like. In the German *moshavim*, on the other hand, citrus trees played a secondary role compared with the more familiar fruit-trees of the Central European types: they had only 560 dunams of citrus groves as against 960 dunams of other fruit plantations. The Yemenites had 930 dunams of unirrigated crops, or 0.41 dunams per person; the Germans: 2,210 dunams, or 0.58 dunams per person. The Yemenites had 490 dunams of irrigated crops, or 0.22 dunams per person; the Germans, 2,400 dunams, or 0.62 dunams per person.

Even more interesting are the differences in the distribution of the land area among the various field and garden crops in the two types of *moshavim*. The Yemenites concentrated heavily on cereals, tuber and root crops, legumes and green forage; while the Germans had both relatively and absolutely more dry fodder, oil crops, and vegetables.

An additional significant difference between the Yemenites and the Germans was that the latter went much more heavily into dairy farming and especially into poultry raising. The Germans had about four times as many cattle per person as the Yemenites and about thirty-six times as much poultry. It is, however, most interesting that the productivity of the cows of the Yemenites was approximately the same as that of the cows in the German Jewish *moshavim*; that the egg-production of the poultry in the Yemenite *moshavim* lagged only a very little behind that of the German *moshavim*, and this despite the much greater inclination to the use of scientific and systematic methods shown by the German settlers in raising and feeding their cows and hens.

The only conclusion one can draw from this comparison is that in point of efficiency the German settlers had only a very slight edge over the Yemenites, and that the differences between the two groups with regard to kinds of crop planted by them must be related to culturally-conditioned predilection for certain foodstuffs. In another place (cf. above, page 139), it was pointed out that Oriental Jews consume more bread and legumes than Ashkenazi Jews, and this differential is reflected here in the fact that the Yemenite Jews planted ten times as many cereals and seven times as many legumes as the German Jews.

Since the independence of Israel, the Yemenite Jews, more than any other ethnic group among the immigrants, settled in rural agricultural settlements. Of all the immigrants to Israel up to the summer of 1951, less than 8% were Yemenite Jews. Yet these 8%

established nearly 25% of all the agricultural settlements founded in this period by new immigrants (57 out of 231). The principles of communality, and with them *kibbutz*-ideology, being foreign to the Yemenite Jews, their settlements were either workers' smallholders' settlements (23) or transit villages and work villages in all of which only limited cooperation was practiced. In the second half of 1951 and in 1952 several more of these rural settlements were set up and occupied by Yemenite Jews who thus will undoubtedly constitute one of the most important ethnic elements in the agricultural sector of Israel.

9. Politics and Religion

Although in 1950 the Yemenite Jews constituted about 10% of the total Jewish population of Israel, their political strength was far below this proportion. In January 1949, when the elections to the first Knesset were held, there were about 760,000 Jews in Israel, or, together with the non-Jewish minorities, about 870,000 persons. Of these, about 70,000, or 8 per cent, were Yemenite Jews. The independent party of the Yemenite Jews in Israel, however, received only 1% of the votes (4,399 votes), so that it obtained only one single seat in the Knesset. A substantial proportion of the Yemenite vote was drawn away by the party of the Sephardi and Oriental Jews by the United Religious Front and by the Mapai and Mapam parties. The party of the Sephardi and Oriental Jews—which incidentally obtained four seats in the Knesset—attracted Yemenite voters with the slogan of a united Sephardi-Oriental Jewish front; the United Religious Front could count on considerable Yemenite support due to the fact that the schools of the Yemenite Jews were (and are) affiliated with the religious school system of the Mizrahi Party; and the Labor parties exercised a hold over yet another large percentage of the Yemenite vote due to the membership of the Yemenite workers in the *Histadrut*, the General Federation of Jewish Labor in Israel, in which already in 1947 there were over 3,000 Yemenite members, constituting 2.4% of the total membership.

No substantial change occurred with regard to the fragmentation of the Yemenite votes at the elections to the second Knesset, on July 30, 1951. In spite of the fact that in the intervening 30 months over 40,000 Yemenites immigrated into Israel and that their percentage in the total Jewish population of the country increased substantially, the Yemenite party polled only 1.2% of the votes (7,965 votes), and was able thus to secure only the one single seat it held in the first Knesset.

As far back as 1923 an Organization of Yemenite Jews in Palestine was created which, ever since its inception, has fought for the rights of the Yemenite Jews both in Palestine and in Yemen and combated whatever discrimination against Yemenite Jews was brought to its attention. It was a paradoxical situation that, in its fight for the public benefit of the Yemenite Jews as a community, it had as often to oppose individual Yemenite Jews as Ashkenazi Jews or general Jewish organizations. With the increase in Yemenite Jewish immigration, the Jewish Agency for Palestine created a Section for Yemenite Immigrants manned by Yemenite officials belonging to the Mapai party. The main tasks of this Section were to care for the Yemenite immigrants in the immigration camps and to help their settlement in villages and residential quarters.

The work of this Section for Yemenite Immigrants caused dissatisfaction in the Organization of Yemenite Jews who argued that the Section did not really have the interests of the Yemenite Jews at heart, or at least was most ineffective in representing their interests. The Organization claimed that, whenever Yemenite Jews were settled with its help in mixed villages, they were discriminated against by being allotted those houses which were in the worst condition and were situated on the outskirts of the villages.

Much resentment was caused also over alleged discrimination against Yemenite Jewish workers. "The Yemenite worker was discriminated against and remains discriminated against to this day. In most of the general Labor Exchanges in the country, and especially in the *moshavot* (private villages) the Yemenite is automatically registered as a candidate for work with the hoe. All work yielding a better income, in industry and even in roadbuilding which is relatively easier, is given to others."*

In religious affairs the Yemenite Jews in Mandated Palestine were subordinated to the Sephardi section of the Chief Rabbinate of the country. Dissatisfied with this official arrangement, the Yemenite Jews waged a protracted fight for the recognition of the official status of Yemenite rabbis and ritual slaughterers (*shohetim*), feeling that the special religious needs of Yemenite settlements were being grossly neglected. The fight of the Yemenite Jews for the satisfaction of their religious needs in the fashion they desired became intensified after the establishment of the Jewish State. Their first important victory was scored when the Knesset passed a law making it mandatory for the local religious councils to include Yemenite representation if Yemenite Jews live within the territory under their jurisdiction. The Ministry of Religions fulfilled at least partly the

* Cf. *The Yemenite Jews in the State of Israel*, a pamphlet published in April 1950, by the Organization of Yemenite Jews in Israel, Tel Aviv.

demand of the Yemenite Jews to build synagogues and open ritual baths (*miqwaot*) and to share in the payment of salaries to Yemenite rabbis and *shohetim*. On the other hand, the negotiations of the Yemenite Jews with the Chief Rabbinate with a view to obtaining participation in the office of the Chief Rabbinate and the appointment of Yemenite rabbis to the Rabbinical Courts in the country, including the Rabbinical High Court, led to no positive result.

Closely connected with the problems of religion is the problem of education. The schools for Yemenite children are under the supervision of the Mizrahi school system, which is one of the four recognized educational trends in Israel. Although this situation has continued for many years, and although the Yemenites never contemplated the severing of the connections between them and the Mizrahi school system, this does not mean that they were always well satisfied with the ways in which the Mizrahi handled their education. As a matter of fact, there were unceasing negotiations between the Yemenites and the Mizrahi, in the course of which the possibilities for a fuller and more satisfactory educational regimen for the Yemenites were explored following the constant demands put forward by their representatives. Better buildings, more adequate furnishings, an educational plan better adapted to the needs of Yemenite children—these were some of the main points which caused friction between the Yemenites and the Mizrahi for many years. Today the demands of the Yemenites are concentrated around three main issues. The first is the inclusion of Yemenite teachers, who teach the Yemenite pronunciation of Hebrew and the Yemenite Jewish traditions, in the educational system and the award of the same status to them as to the teachers of other subjects; in this connection they also demand that the teaching of these subjects (Yemenite pronunciation and traditions) be included into the regular curriculum of Yemenite schools. The second demand is a representational one: the Mizrahi school system is asked to coopt representatives of Yemenite schools, since the Yemenite *Talmud Tora* schools constitute a considerable percentage in the total number of Mizrahi schools. The Yemenites wish representation on the central board of the Mizrahi school system as well as in the Educational Council of the Israeli Government. The third demand is that in every old or new Yemenite settlement a religious school be opened without delay.

In connection with the problem of education among the Yemenites, mention should be made, however briefly, of the struggle going on around the education of the new immigrants in the immigrants' reception camps in Israel. In the Israeli press, as well as in the sessions of the Knesset, the events which took place in the immigrants' camps as a consequence of the efforts made by the various political parties to obtain control of education within them, caused storms of indignation and embittered discussion.

10. Camp Problems

The outbreak caused by the appearance and subsequent detention of two orthodox Jewish agitators in the Ein Shemer camp on February 14, 1950, was an isolated occurrence. In general, the Yemenite immigrants were patient, quiet and contented, and for several months after their arrival in the reception camps in Israel they were still under the impression that something miraculous had happened to them. This feeling arose upon their arrival in the transit camp back in Aden. In spite of the crowded conditions in this camp, they felt that it was for them the beginning of redemption. The sufferings, and even the dangers of the trip from Yemen to Aden, they took with the usual uncomplaining endurance and detachment characteristic of Oriental peoples. Deep down lingered a feeling, rooted in the study of historical and cabalistic sources, about the inevitability of sufferings which must needs precede the Messianic redemption. Then came the amazing experience of the flight on the great planes to which the Yemenites reacted in typical fashion by quoting the biblical passage, "And I shall carry you on the wings of eagles . . ."

Their wonderment when the huge metal bird rose up into the air with a thundering voice was great. It was intensified when scarcely a few hours later the plane set them down again—and they found themselves in the Land of Israel, which they knew could only be reached from Yemen if one travelled for several months by caravan. Little wonder that in view of all these miraculous events, added to which were the food and the clothing they were presented with, the tents or barracks which were assigned to them in the immigrants' reception camps, their originally modest nature asserted itself. They neither asked for nor demanded anything, but received with gratitude whatever was given them.

Actually the situation of the immigrants was, and has remained, far from satisfactory. The great majority of them were housed in tents which were drenched from above and flooded from below during the heavy rains of the winter of 1949-50. The original plan called for a sojourn of a few weeks only in the immigrants' camps, after which each immigrant was to be sent to a permanent place of settlement. Actually, however, in view of the large number of immigrants, the rate of evacuation from the camps lagged constantly behind the rate at which the new immigrants were brought into Israel, and the period of sojourn in the camps was prolonged from three months to four months to six months to eight months. . . .

One of the main immigrants' reception camps was that of Rosh Ha'ayin, in which, at the height of its occupancy in 1950, there were some 15,000 Yemenite Jewish immigrants. They were all lodged in tents, fifteen of them in each tent. The few buildings in the camp were used to house the hospital and the clinics, the babies' homes, the kitchen and dining room and the school. When the immigrants arrived, many of them were very weak. Mortality was high, and as many as 20 deaths occurred daily. In this respect a definite improvement was noticeable very soon, mortality decreased and generally the strength of the people increased. Practically all the immigrants (98% to be exact) suffered from trachoma when they arrived at Rosh Ha'ayin. After a four months' sojourn in the camp, and constant medical treatment—often administered here too against the wishes of the patients—this percentage sank to 20%. The health of the children was also in very bad shape. Many adults as well as children suffered from venereal diseases which were transmitted in a great variety of ways. A circumciser (*mohel*), for instance, in the Aden camp, himself infected with syphilis, transmitted it to several infants whom he circumcised.

When the immigrants arrived, they were almost naked and barefoot. They were given clothing by the "Clothes for Winter" Drive. However, when they were given shoes, they hid them in their tents and did not want to wear them, so that finally the camp administration had to issue a warning to the effect that the shoes must be worn every day and that those who were found walking barefoot would be expelled from the camp. This warning had the desired effect, and the immigrant slowly got used to wearing shoes.

One of the great difficulties was that there was no work for the immigrants in the camp, and that they were not supposed to go to work outside the camp.* Nevertheless, many of them stealthily left every morning and went to nearby Petah Tikva, where they obtained a day's labor in return for a wage of some 40 to 50 piasters, which is about one-fourth or one-fifth of the regular wages of a day laborer. Yet they were happy even with this meager income and could, of course, not be expected to understand that by underbidding in the labor market they actually harmed the economy of the country which had received and supported them.

The school which was opened for the children of the immigrants,

---

* Only in August 1950 did the Jewish Agency reverse this policy, making it obligatory for the immigrants living in reception camps to work unless they wished to relinquish their rights to any of the Government's housing projects.

had 16 teachers and 1,100 pupils who attended classes in two shifts. Yet, even so, not all the children could be accommodated for lack of space. Many of them could be observed thronging outside the doors and windows of the classrooms, trying to listen to what went on inside, just as the great Jewish sage, Hillel, once did when he was a youngster thirsting for knowledge some two thousand years ago. Unfortunately, when the strong winter rains washed away the tents of many immigrants and they had to be housed in the school building, an end was put to the educational activities in the camp, for the time being at least.

The adult immigrants, too, demonstrated a strong desire to learn. It would seem that they understood well enough that their entire future depended upon their ability to master the language of the country and at least the rudiments of certain other elementary subjects.

Very few of the Yemenite Jewish immigrants are polygamous. Mr. Gluska puts their percentage at less than 3%. In the entire Rosh Ha'ayin camp there was only a single Yemenite Jew who had three wives. On the other hand, soon after their arrival in the camp, attempts were made by other Yemenite Jews, who were older inhabitants in the country, to contract marriages with the young daughters of the immigrants. Under the circumstances this amounted to actually buying a wife from her parents for whom even the modest amount paid by the bridegroom as bride-price meant a great deal of money. Instances where everything went smoothly were noticed only by the family and perhaps the immediate neighbors in the camp. The bride-price was paid to the father of the bride, the marriage celebrated by a Yemenite rabbi, and the bride quietly removed from the camp to her husband's house. It is therefore difficult to estimate the frequency of these marriages. Public notice was taken only of cases which ended in disagreement and in which outside help was called in. Such a case was that of a 40-year-old Yemenite who married a 12-year-old girl in the Rosh Ha'ayin camp, and soon after was forced to divorce her.*

11. Yemenite Cultural Influences

The Yemenite Jews are the best organized of all the Oriental Jewish communities in Israel. In addition to the Organization of Yemenite Jews in Israel (founded in 1923), there exists a Rabbinical Council of Yemenite Jews, an Organization of Yemenite Women, and two youth groups in Tel Aviv, called Organization of Yemenite

* Cf. Abraham, S., "In the Immigrants' Camp in Rosh Ha'ayin" (Hebrew), in *Haaretz*, Tel Aviv, January 27, 1950.

Youth and Organization of the Sons of Juda respectively. They have an American Committee for Relief of Yemenite Jews, which conducts independent fund-raising in the United States in defiance of the ban of the Jewish Agency on all such activities. They are the only Oriental Jewish community in Israel which was successful in the elections to both the first and the second Knesset, so that their independent party is represented by one member. They are the most articulate of all the Oriental Jewish communities. They are able to express their grievances, both orally and in writing, over actual or alleged discrimination against them on the part of the Government, the ruling political parties and other public institutions. There are in Israel about a hundred urban and rural settlements in which are found groups of Yemenite Jews of varying sizes; in the last three years alone 57, or almost one-fourth of all the new rural settlements were established by Yemenite Jews. In addition to all this, the Yemenite Jews differ most in physical type from the other Jewish communities—Ashkenazi, Sephardi or Oriental. They are sharply set apart by their dark, olive-colored complexion and by their small, frail stature, which make them easily recognizable as Yemenites even if by clothing, behavior and speech mannerisms they assimilate to the Ashkenazim, as the young people among them actually do in many cases. One can remain in Israel for a long time without becoming aware of the existence of such groups as the Turkish, Persian, Egyptian, or Syrian Jews; but the presence of the Yemenite Jews in the country is noticed within the first few hours of one's arrival.

The positive side of the picture is that no other non-Ashkenazi Jewish group has influenced the culture of new Israel to such a degree as the Yemenite Jews. Not that this cultural influence in itself were considerable or weighty; but when one gets down to an analysis of the cultural elements in modern Israeli culture which are neither Western in their origin nor the result of conscious effort on the part of Ashkenazi immigrants to revive the ancient Hebrew culture of the Jewish people, one will in almost every case find that they were contributed by the Yemenite Jews.

In accordance with the results of our analysis of Eastern and Western culture (cf. above, page 27 ff.) we shall not expect to find Yemenite influence in those traits which belong to the fields of technological and organizational development. True to the focal position occupied by religion and esthetics in Eastern culture in general, we shall look for possible Yemenite influence on the culture of new Israel in these fields. But even these fields will have to be narrowed down by the exclusion of religion, in which influence emanating from the Yemenites (or from any other Oriental Jewish community for that matter) is neutralized by an *a priori* negative attitude towards religion in general prevalent among the major part of the Ashkenazi Jews. Yemenite religiosity and Yemenite religious forms, however, seem to exert a certain influence on the other Oriental Jewish communities. Especially, the higher degree of learning in religious matters possessed by Yemenite Jews is a factor which plays a certain role in this connection. In Jerusalem, for instance, there are several non-Yemenite, Oriental Jewish synagogues in which the cantor (*hazzan*) is a Yemenite Jew; also, other religious functions are at times filled by Yemenite Jews in non-Yemenite, Oriental Jewish congregations. It would be interesting to study whether any comparable religious influence by the Yemenites upon the orthodox Ashkenazi groups can be shown to exist, or at least whether any cooperation in the religious field can be discovered between the two, apart from the cooperation between the Yemenite Jews and the Mizrahi Party with regard to the school system.

The influence of the culture of the Yemenite Jews on that of Israel as a whole in the field of esthetics is more palpable. In the first place, the artcraft of the Yemenite Jews has to be considered here. In Yemen, the Jews were the only silversmiths, there they developed a traditional style of their own, characterized by a very high degree of artistic refinement, of technical precision and of fineness in detail and elaboration. Especially outstanding in quality is their filigree work, executed in silver, more rarely in gold, and applied to such objects of female adornment as necklaces, earrings, armbands, fringes for headdress, and the like; or to male trappings such as dagger and sword hilts, gun butts and belts on which to hang these weapons; or to Jewish religious objects, like the containers of Tora scrolls.*

While the silversmiths were men only, artistic embroidering was an art form of both men and women. Other artcrafts of the Yemenite Jews were basketmaking, weaving and leatherwork.

After their immigration to Palestine, most of the Yemenite Jewish artisans were forced by circumstances to abandon their crafts and to engage in unskilled occupations (cf. above, page 186). Some of them, however, found work in the Bezalel School, founded by Boris Schatz in Jerusalem, and laid the foundations for the commercialized mixture of Oriental and Western styles known as "Bezalel work," which became typical of all products of this school for many years.

In 1924, the Federation of Hebrew Women in Jerusalem decided to encourage handicraft among the Oriental Jewish women of the Shim'on Hatzadik Quarter in Jerusalem. After an unsuccessful at-

* Cf. M. Narkis, *The Artcraft of Yemenite Jews* (Hebrew), Jerusalem, 1941.

tempt to teach them how to repair stockings and underwear, the women were given embroidery in the style which was traditional for them. Two rooms were rented in their quarter, one for those who worked and the second for their childen, who were in the meantime supervised in turn by several of the mothers. Most of the first women who began to work were from Iraq, but soon Yemenites from Kfar Hashiloah joined them, and their superior artcraft very soon became the earmark of *Shani*, as this undertaking was called. Both Yemenite men and women embroidered for *Shani*. The Federation soon found ways and means to awaken the interest of the public and thus was able to sell their products and provide satisfactory incomes for the workers. During the first few years after the establishment of *Shani* more than a hundred Yemenite men and women were employed. Their incomes enabled them to buy houses in Kfar Hashiloah and help their relatives in Yemen to emigrate to Palestine. After the 1936 riots, the Yemenites left Kfar Hashiloah and settled in the Nahlat Ahim Quarter.

Eventually *Shani* engaged silversmiths as well as a few weavers and leatherworkers. In Rehovot the residents of an entire Yemenite quarter were engaged in producing basketry. However, the crafts most outstanding in artistic quality remained embroidery and silverwork. Soon the problem arose of providing for greater variety in the patterns executed by the Yemenite craftsmen. The number of decorative patterns remembered by the individual workers was necessarily small, while the demand of the market was for new and unusual ones. A collection of Yemenite embroideries, silverwork, baskets, and all kinds of other objects made in Yemen was therefore initiated among the Yemenite Jews in Palestine. Based on these patterns, decorations were worked out for objects which the Yemenites had never before produced, like brooches, pendants, new types of ear-rings and other costume jewelry. In all these, however, only the outer form of the object was new, to which the original Yemenite style and decorative patterns were adapted.*

The end result of the activities of the Bezalel School and of *Shani* was that Yemenite handicraft became extremely popular in Palestine and has remained so in Israel to this day. A large number of souvenir shops, serving mainly tourists, carry Yemenite silver as well as other work, while a few shops of the Women's International Zionist Organization (WIZO) in the three main cities sell women's embroidered apparel, baskets, leather and silverwork, all made by Yemenites. The products of the Yemenite craftsmen have become widely known in Jewish circles outside Palestine under the collec-

* Cf. Hadassa Bat-Mordechai, "Shani," in *Shvut Teman*, 1945, pp. 96-99.

tive name of "Palestinian art." In Palestine itself it became fashionable among women, and especially those of the younger generation, to wear occasionally a blouse or a piece of silver costume jewelry made by Yemenites. Today, both in Israel and abroad, Yemenite artcraft is so intimately associated in the minds of the people with what is regarded as "original" Israeli artcraft that it always creates a surprise when it is pointed out that a certain art object is not "Israeli" actually but Yemenite.

With the great Yemenite immigration of 1949-50, a large number of highly skilled artisans came to Israel unspoiled by the commercialization which has affected so many of those who have worked in Palestine for several years. When these immigrant artisans are directed to unskilled labor, or are driven to it by immediate necessity, there is a great waste of human skill and cultural potential. The nascent culture of new Israel needs the contribution of these highly skilled and specialized Yemenite craftsmen, and constructive help to enable them to re-engage in their crafts after their arrival in Israel would, in the long run, pay a rich dividend in terms of cultural returns.

Another important contribution of the Yemenites lies in the field of music. While artcrafts—with the partial exception of embroidery and basketry—are a male occupation among the Yemenites, music is a female specialization in both its vocal and instrumental forms. Just as Yemenite artcraft is enormously appreciated in Israel, Yemenite music also, and especially folk-singing, has achieved great popularity. There is, however, an essential difference between the way in which these two—Yemenite crafts and Yemenite music—were accepted by the Jews of Israel as a whole. Although Yemenite crafts were popularized with the institutional help of Ashkenazi Jews and occasionally were even adapted to objects previously unknown to Yemenite Jews, they were nevertheless found to be enjoyable by the general Palestinian Jewish and Israeli public in their original, unadulterated form. The basic motives, the decorative details, the color scheme (in the case of embroidery or basketry), remained exactly the same as those which were executed by the Yemenite Jews in Yemen for many hundreds of years. The charm and appeal of these in their original form was such that they captivated Western imagination.

With Yemenite music the situation was and is different. Yemenite music, like all Oriental music is composed in scales very different from the Western tempered scale, the octave of which consists of twelve equal semitones. Oriental music, and consequently also the music of the Yemenite Jews, makes use of tone intervals smaller than a semitone. These microtones are quite indigestible for the Western ear educated exclusively on the tempered scale, and their strangeness is in most cases sufficient to drown out any perception of the melodious line. Even when the ear is able to discover the unfamiliar melodic tones, it tries involuntarily to assimilate the foreign impression to its own musical experience, so that the microtones become associated with the nearest half-tone of the tempered scale.

That Ashkenazi Jews found Yemenite music (as well as Oriental music in general) somewhat less strange than one would imagine after these remarks was due mainly to the familiarity of most Ashkenazi Jews with traditional Jewish synagogal music which is replete with intervals smaller than a semitone. Nevertheless, Yemenite music would never have attained its present popularity in Israel were it not for the Ashkenazi composers who, in their search for musical motives and material, hit on the Yemenite folk-tunes and converted a great number of them into songs made appealing to the Western ear by adapting them to the tempered scale and providing them with accordic piano accompaniments. It is only after these "arrangements" were made that the Yemenite Jewish folk-songs and other musical pieces became generally popular in Palestine. Once the foreign scale was eliminated and the main obstacle to its enjoyment by European ears was thus removed, the song in the new, Westernized form had to be given some exotic tinge in order to make it more attractive to the public than a simple European song would be. This exotic flavor was provided through having it sung by a Yemenite woman singer, preferably a young Oriental beauty, clothed in the heavy, floating garb of Yemenite women. The typical and specific Yemenite pronunciation of Hebrew was emphasized, the deep gutturals stressed, and the nasality of delivery accentuated. All this, underscored by allegedly Yemenite expressive gestures and facial movements, produced a performance uniting within itself the attractive features of a pleasant melody easy on the Occidental ear and the exotic by-play of mystical Arabia. For some reason which it would be difficult to analyze, the way in which these Yemenite singers performed proved so attractive to the general public that even non-Yemenite singers of a certain popular class consciously imitated them in order thus to increase their own success with an audience. The Yemenite singers, however, could not easily be surpassed. Several of their songs were popularized through phonographic records and were sung by all and sundry in the country.

In general, it can be stated that as far as popular music, and especially popular songs, are concerned, two dominant elements are distinguishable in modern Israel: the Europeanized Yemenite song discussed above, and the more sentimental kind of East European song which entered Israel via the Yiddish culture. These two account for the overwhelming majority of the songs popular in Israel; even the local composers often conform to either of these two patterns when writing in the popular vein.

Though these cultural contributions of the Yemenite Jews may in themselves seem meager, one must not lose sight of the fact that they are rendered by a Jewish tribe which for several hundreds of years has lived in relative isolation and serfdom in a faraway corner of the Arabian Peninsula. Historical data, as far as they exist, show that the culture of Yemen as a whole has declined considerably in the course of the last few centuries. Contrary, however, to what has happened in most of the other countries of the Middle East, the culture of the Yemenite Jews did not evidence a corresponding decline. This in itself is eloquent testimony to the tenacious vitality of Yemenite Jewish culture, which was virile enough to give rise at the beginning of the 20th century to a rationalistic reform movement counteracting the great influence of the Cabala on Yemenite Jewish religious life.* The days of the great Yemenite Hebrew poets have passed, but the folk-arts of the Yemenite Jews survive undiminished and can be rescued from the oblivion which threatens them by the impending assimilation of Yemenite Jews to the modern Western culture of Israel.

Thus an entire Jewish tribe has returned to the country of its origin after an absence of over two thousand years. It constitutes a numerically and culturally important element in Israel; but it suffers because of the culturally-conditioned differences between it and the dominant Ashkenazi majority in the country. The new Yemenite immigrants will have to undergo a painful process of adjustment to their new conditions. This process is fraught with many dangers. It is a narrow path flanked with numerous pitfalls. The State must see to it, not only for the benefit of the Yemenite Jews, but also on account of its own well-conceived self-interest, that they be led safely across the path and are helped to reach a high degree of socio-cultural integration with the rest of Israel, losing in the process as little as possible of the cultural and demographic values characteristic of them.

* Cf. Yehuda Ratzhabi, "The 'Dardaim,'" in *Edoth*, April, 1946, pp. 165-180 (Hebrew).

Chapter Eight

The Non-Jewish Minorities

1. Minorities in the Middle East

The concept of "minority," as used in the Western world by statesmen and politicians, and largely also by political and social scientists, reflects—as the conceptual basis of terms often does—their own experience with groups differing in certain respects from the majority populations of countries in Europe and America. A recent article, for example, in the U. S. Department of State *Bulletin* (of January 16, 1950), discussing the definition of the term "minority," states that this term refers "mainly to a particular kind of community, and especially to a national or similar community which differs from the predominant group in the state . . . It is safe to say that at least within the field of political science this term (is applied) almost always to communities of a national type. The members of such a minority feel that they constitute a national group, or subgroup, which is different from the predominant group. Members of purely religious minorities may feel, however, that they belong to the predominant national group."

Although this definition is applicable to most minorities in the Western world, it falls short as soon as the position outside the Euroamerican sphere is considered. In the Middle East, nationality until recently has played an insignificant role, though in the last two or three decades a definite nationalistic awakening could be discerned under the impact of Western civilization and Western ideas. Nevertheless, to this day the retention of original nationality is not as a rule conducive to the formation of minority groups, unless territorial isolation is added as a complementary factor (for example, the Kurds in the border-area between Turkey, Iran, Iraq and Syria). When a citizen, or a group of citizens, of one Middle Eastern country emigrates and settles in another Middle Eastern state, one of two things can happen: If the newcomers are of the same religion as the majority group of their new social environment, the differences between them will disappear very quickly and they will rapidly

216

become fully integrated members of the new country. If, however, the immigrants are of a different religious persuasion, they and their descendants for many generations will feel like strangers, like non-indigenous residents, in other words, as members of a minority group, and will be regarded as such by the predominant population. In brief, a minority group in the Middle East as a rule is a *religious minority*.

How disruptive the force of religion can be in Eastern countries has best been illustrated in recent years in India, where the religious difference alone between Hindus and Moslems was sufficient to tear them apart and to serve as the basis for the formation of two separate states. Where the religious minority is too weak, too small, or too scattered to establish for itself a sovereignty separate from that of the majority, it will survive as an unassimilable foreign element within the body of the majority. A fine example of this is that of the Copts in Egypt who remained faithful to their Christian religion through thirteen centuries of Moslem domination, and who do not intermarry or otherwise mingle with the Moslems in spite of the fact that they share their language, their customs (including circumcision), and practically their entire culture—apart from religion.

In Palestine, the British Mandatory Government adopted the practice of dividing the population according to religions for statistical purposes. In the last year of the Mandate (1947), it was estimated that, as against a great majority of Moslems numbering about 1,100,000, there were about 120,000 Christians in the country. The Christian community could be subdivided into Arab Christians and non-Arab Christians with the following church membership:

THE CHRISTIANS OF PALESTINE IN 1947 　✻

Church	Arab Christians Membership (persons) Minimum	Maximum	Church	Non-Arab Christians Membership (persons) Minimum	Maximum
Greek Orthodox	40,000	45,000	Armenian Orthodox	5,000	10,000
Latin	20,000	22,000	Armenian Catholic	800	800
Greek Catholic			European Catholic	5,000	6,000
or Melkite	18,000	21,000	Nestorians or Assyrians	1,000	1,200
Maronite	5,000	6,000	Assyrian Catholic		
Syrian Catholic	300	300	(Chaldean)	100	150
			Syrian Orthodox		
			(Jacobite)	1,000	1,200
			Coptic Orthodox and		
			Coptic Catholic	1,000	1,200
Protestant			Abyssinian	300	350
Churches	8,000	10,000	European Protestants	4,000	5,000
Total	**91,300**	**104,300**	**Total**	**18,200**	**25,900**

The total number of the Christians in Palestine in 1947 was therefore between 110,000 and 130,000.

2. The Christian Arab Communities

The *Greek Orthodox Church,* called in Arabic *Rum-Ortodoks* or simply *Ortodoks,* is the largest and most important Christian Church in Israel as well as in the entire Middle East.* In Mandatory Palestine, about 80% of the Greek Orthodox Arabs lived in towns, their majority in Jerusalem, Haifa and Jaffa; others in Bethlehem, Ramallah, Ramle, Gaza, etc. The remaining 20% were fellahin, agriculturists, living mostly in the villages around Jerusalem, Bethlehem, Ramallah, Nazareth and Acre. The Palestinian head of the church, the Patriarch of Jerusalem, has always been of Greek nationality, a member of the Greek Order of the Holy Sepulchre. He is equal in rank to the heads of the other Greek Orthodox Churches, the Syrian, Egyptian, Greek, Russian, etc., Patriarchs. The Patriarch of Jerusalem is assisted by a Council of Bishops who, as a rule, are likewise Greeks. The lower clergy, on the other hand, as well as the entire lay community, are Arabs. This situation has led to an old, almost traditional quarrel between the community and its religious leadership. The quarrel began in the middle of the 19th century, with the rise of nationalistic consciousness in the Orient, and it revolved around the control of the Church which the Arab community tried in vain to dislodge from the hands of the Greek high clergy. The Greek Orthodox community in Palestine had several secular committees, clubs, youth- and boy-scout groups and sport organizations, and it was very active both socially and politically. It took a prominent part in the Arab nationalistic movement in Palestine. Several Orthodox Arabs were among the political spokesmen for the Arabs in their struggle against Zionism.

Up to World War I, the Russians were very active and influential in the Greek Orthodox Church of Palestine. For Czarist Russia it was a matter of great political significance to gain as much influence as possible in the Orient through the Orthodox Church. On the eve of World War I, there were in Palestine and Syria—both under Turkish domination—over one hundred Russian educational institutions including a Russo-Arabic teachers' seminary in Nazareth. The Greek Orthodox Church received much financial aid from Russia, and acquired considerable landed property in Jerusalem and elsewhere in the country. With the Bolshevik revolution all contact was severed between Russia and the Orthodox Church in Palestine;

* With the exception of the Coptic Church which numbers some 1,200,000 members in Egypt.

but in 1944, following the change of attitude of the Soviet government towards religion, contact was restored. The Greek Orthodox Church has well established rights in the holy places, the Church of the Nativity in Bethlehem and the Church of the Holy Sepulchre in Jerusalem, which for many generations have been both the objects and the scenes of conflicts and even bloody strife among the various Christian churches in Palestine. Most of the Greek Orthodox Arabs who remained in Israel live in Nazareth and its environs.

The *Latin Church* in Palestine, which originated in the days of the crusades, is a part of the Catholic Church and subject to the direct supervision of the Catholic administrative apparatus. Its head, the Latin Patriarch of Jerusalem, is appointed by Rome and is a European, usually an Italian. He is subordinate to the Apostolic Nuncio who is an emissary of the Pope and whose domain comprises, in addition to Palestine, also Egypt and Eritrea. The Latin community in Palestine has always enjoyed the support of European Catholic countries, particularly Italy and France, and its members receive much financial help which is doled out to them in a manner resembling the *Halukka* system of the Jewish *Kolelim*.* The church itself is fairly rich and has many rights in the holy places. Of the more or less 20,000 Arab members of the Latin community more than half lived in Jerusalem until 1948; about 3,500 lived in Bethlehem; the rest in Jaffa, Haifa, Ramallah, Ramle, Nazareth and a few smaller towns and villages. While in the Greek Orthodox community the language of both everyday use and the ritual is Arabic, in the Latin community, though all its native Palestinian members are Arabs and speak Arabic, the language of the ritual is Latin. The quarrel within the Greek Orthodox Church was to a certain extent paralleled by a somewhat less embittered strife within the Latin Church between the Arab lay community and its European, mainly Franciscan, clergy. In the Arab nationalistic movement the Latin community participated to a lesser degree than the Orthodox. In this connection mention should be made of the circa 5,000 European Catholics who lived in Palestine, the great majority of whom were monks (Franciscans, Carmelites, Dominicans, Benedictines, etc.). The most important of these Orders is to this day that of the Franciscans, who are called the "Keepers of the Holy Places." Some of these monastic Orders are independent of the Latin Patriarchate of Jerusalem and are subject directly to the Pope.

In the 18th century part of the Greek Church "united" with Rome (hence the name "Uniate" Churches) and was in the 19th century recognized by the Turkish authorities as a separate Church under

* Cf. above, p. 81.

the name of *Greek Catholic* (in Arabic, *Rum-Katolik*) Church. In the entire Middle East the Greek Catholics are estimated to number about 150,000, all of whom speak Arabic. The language of their ritual is Arabic, with a very few remnants of Greek in it. Their spiritual head is the Greek Catholic Patriarch of the entire East whose official title is "Patriarch of Antiochia, Jerusalem and Alexandria" and who resides either in Egypt or in Syria. Subordinate to him is the head of the Palestinian Greek Catholics, called "Metropolitan (in Arabic, *Mitran*) of Acre and the Galilee," an Arab who used to reside in Haifa. Most of the members of this Church lived in Haifa, others in a few villages in Galilee, in Jerusalem, Bethlehem, Ramallah, etc. This Church possesses much entailed property (called *waqf*, like the Moslem charitable foundations) in Acre, Haifa and their vicinity; but being of recent formation, it was unable to acquire any rights in the holy places. Since both the higher and lower clergy of this Church are Arabs, the relationship between them and the lay community was characterized by harmony and close cooperation, the priests sometimes even taking the lead in Arab nationalistic affairs. Altogether, this community showed a fairly active participation in the political life of the Palestinian Arabs, with a special stress, however, on their own internal community affairs, social and cultural institutions, and the like.

The oldest of the so-called "Uniate" Churches of the East is that of the *Maronites* whose official union with Rome took place, in successive steps, from the 12th to the 18th centuries. They retained certain prerogatives, such as the autonomy of their Church administration and organization, the right to use their old language (old Syriac) in their ritual, to retain their old customs and, to some extent, even certain differences in doctrine. In everyday life the Maronites used the same old Syriac language up to the 18th century, when its place was taken by Arabic. Today only a few learned men among them can still speak Syriac. The center of the Maronites is in the Lebanon, where they number over 325,000 and are the largest single religious community. Their second largest group is that of the Maronite emigrants in America, where they number some 150,000. In Palestine, in 1947, they numbered circa 5-6,000, most of whom lived in Haifa, the rest in Jerusalem, Jaffa and three villages on the Lebanese border. In the Lebanon, the Maronites are very active in communal and political life and often find themselves in political opposition to Arab nationalistic or Pan-Arab movements. In Palestine, however, the Maronites took almost no part in Arab civic life. The Palestinian Maronites are subject to the religious authority of the Maronite "Patriarch of Antiochia" who resides in the Lebanon. They have considerable *waqf* property in Acre, Haifa and Jaffa. Being a "new" Church, they have no rights in the holy places.

The *Protestant* Churches in Palestine are the fruit of the activity of European missionaries since the beginning of the 19th century. Most of the Arab members of the Protestant Churches in Palestine were not converts from Islam, but recruited from the older Christian Churches in the country. Being new in Palestine, these Churches have no rights in the holy places, but are permitted to hold their services in the parts belonging to the Greek Orthodox Church. The Protestants are undoubtedly the most advanced in Westernization among the Christian Arabs of Palestine. Their religion is modern European in coloring, for they have had close social contacts with their European co-religionists residing in Palestine, such as the British and the German Protestants.

Of the 12-15,000 Protestants in Palestine in 1947, 5-6,000 were members of the Anglican Church, mostly British subjects who resided temporarily in Palestine while in the employ of the British Mandatory Government of the country. From Germany came about 2,000 Protestants of various denominations who lived in Jerusalem, Jaffa, Haifa and several agricultural settlements founded by them towards the end of the 19th century. For curiosity's sake it might be mentioned that the Protestants in Palestine (Arabs and non-Arabs) belonged to no less than 28 Churches or denominations, a list of which follows here in alphabetical order:

Anglican Church (including the Episcopal Church of Scotland and the Church of Wales), Armenian Protestant, Baptist, Bible Society, Christian Alliance, Christian Brethren, Christian Mason, Congregational, Dissenters, Dutch Reformed Church, English Protestants, German Evangelists (Evangelists, Protestant Evangelists), Jewish-Christians, Lutheran Church, Methodists (Primitive Methodists, United Methodists), Moravian, Nazarene, Nonconformists, Pentecostal, Plymouth Brethren, Presbyterian Church, Protestant, Protestant Friends (Quaker, Society of Friends), Sabbatarian, Salvationist, Templars, Wesleyan, Spiritualists.

The Protestant communities were the only ones in Palestine which had no religious courts of their own to deal with affairs of personal status, such as family matters, inheritance, and the like. Members of these communities brought their law-suits touching upon personal status before the civil courts established by the British authorities. All the other religious communities in Palestine, whether Christian, Moslem or Jewish, had their religious law-courts which were recognized both by them and by the British Government as the only authorized courts to deal with such affairs. Separate religious courts for each religious community were one of the factors which made for division in the Christian Churches among themselves, as well as between all the Christian Arabs, on the one hand, and the Moslem Arabs, on the other.

3. Between Christians and Moslems

Other factors separating the Christian and the Moslem Arabs, in addition to the all-pervasive importance of religion itself, were their different historical traditions, permeated with memories of wars, persecutions and massacres. In spite of the politically common cause against the Jews embraced by Moslem and Christian Arabs alike, there was between them a feeling of mutual distrust, contempt and even hatred, although this was but rarely given open expression. It was, however, a patent fact that the Christian Arabs looked down upon the Moslem Arabs, whom they regarded as uneducated, backward and inferior socially. On the other hand, however, being a relatively small minority in a predominantly Moslem Arab land, they found it politically expedient to side with them against the Jews, and in several cases they became the spokesmen for the Arab anti-Jewish nationalistic movement in Palestine. The relationship of the Christian Arabs to the Moslem Arabs was therefore characterized by a definite ambivalence of feeling, centered around two foci of consciousness: that of feeling individually superior and, at the same time, of knowing that they were collectively, that is, numerically, inferior to the Moslem Arabs.

The reverse was true among the Moslem Arabs. They despised the Christian Arabs as renegades who left the fold and embraced a foreign faith—an offense punishable, in independent Moslem states adhering to religious tradition, by the death penalty—though of course the conversion of most of the Christian Arabs took place several hundreds of years ago, while the ancestors of many of them have been Christians from pre-Islamic times down. At the same time, however, the Moslems had to recognize the cultural superiority of the Christian Arabs, their greater concentation in academic professions, their greater wealth, and their greater ability to assimilate Western cultural elements.

The feeling of cultural superiority, evinced by the Christian Arabs in relation to their Moslem co-nationals, was based on two factors: on the greater concentration of the Christian Arabs in cities and towns, and on their higher educational standards. The Christian Arabs of Palestine were a highly urbanized community, 80% of them having lived in cities and towns, and only 20% in villages, of whom again only three fourths were engaged in agriculture. Among the Moslem Arabs, on the other hand, the ratio was almost the reverse of this: over 70% of them lived in villages, 65% of these being agriculturists; and, while among the Christian Arabs there were relatively numerous merchants, artisans, industrialists, white-collar workers, office-employees, government employees and professional people, among the Moslems all these constituted only a very small percentage.

The higher educational standard of the Christian Arabs was especially marked among the women. Among the Moslem Arabs there was almost no education at all for girls, and between 95% to 97% of the Moslem women in Palestine were illiterate. As against this, the female illiteracy among the Christian Arabs was only 55%. The male illiteracy among the Moslems was 75%, among the Christian Arabs 30%. The Christian Arabs could send their children to schools for boys and girls set up and maintained by the numerous Christian missions. Due to the closer contact between them and European Christians in the country, they had a stronger drive towards advancement and Westernization, the first step towards which was to send their children to an educational institution.

The percentage of the children attending school among the school-age (6-14) population in the three religious communities in Palestine and in the neighboring Arab countries was as follows:

	per cent
Jews of Palestine (1944)	97
Christians of Palestine (1944)	89
Moslems of Palestine (1944)	25
Lebanon (1947)*	57.3
Egypt (1948)	28.5
Syria (1950)	37.0
Jordan (1948)	31.0
Iraq (1951)	20.8

* Over half of the Lebanon's population is Christian.

Better education and better socio-economic position tend reciprocally to reinforce and advance one another: among 80% of the Christian Arabs who lived in the cities and towns of Palestine, there was a considerable proportion of rich or at least well-to-do people; for people in a better economic position it is easier to educate their children, and for persons with a better education it is easier to achieve a higher economic and social status.

The contact between Christian Arabs and Europeans (British) in Palestine was facilitated by the absence of the seclusion of women among the former. A Christian Arab could invite to his home his

European friends with their wives—and especially members of the British officialdom who constituted a kind of tacitly recognized aristocracy in the good society of the country. He could receive and entertain them in the company of his own wife; or he and his wife could accept invitations to European homes. The leaders of Moslem society in Palestine were handicapped in all this, not so much because of a truly religious traditionalism, as on account of the political and social necessity to conform with the religious rules of Islam. The seclusion of women, prescribed for urban society by Moslem religious custom, was a very serious impediment in the social contact with the Europeans. The great difference in the position occupied by the women among Moslem and Christian Arabs, added its weight to the other factors separating the two communities. Intermarriage between Christian and Moslem Arabs was very rare, about as rare as was intermarriage between Moslems and Jews.

Important demographic differences could be observed between the Moslem and Christian Arabs in birth-rate, death-rate, rate of natural increase, and in life expectancy. In these, as in several other respects, the Christian Arabs took an intermediate position between Moslems and the Jews, with a tendency to approximate the latter. This can be shown in a brief table.

VITAL STATISTICS OF THE THREE RELIGIOUS
COMMUNITIES IN PALESTINE IN 1945.*

Community	Birth rate	Death rate	Natural Increase	Life expectancy Males	Females
Moslems	54.23	16.35	37.88	49.35	50.40
Christians	32.65	9.86	22.79	57.44	60.10
Jews	30.26	6.65	23.61	64.13	65.87

* Source: *Statistical Abstract of Palestine, 1944-1945.* Government Printer, Palestine. The rates of the category "Christians" are not quite conclusive for the Christian Arabs of Palestine, for this category includes also the non-Arab Christians.

A similar relationship exists between the three communities in the matter of infant mortality, which in 1931 was circa 186 per thousand of live births for the Moslems, 133 for the Christians and 81 for the Jews, and by 1945 was reduced to 94 among the Moslems, 71 among the Christians, and 36 among the Jews.

The Christian villagers of Palestine were in many respects very similar to the Moslem fellahin. Their mode of life, customs, clothing, were almost identical. Both groups evidenced a certain laxity in observing their respective Sabbaths: as the Moslem fellahin did not keep their Friday rest, so the Christian fellahin did not keep the Sunday rest. However, the Christian villagers in general had closer association with the townspeople than the Moslems. Many of them worked in the towns, in various offices and services, and less frequently as laborers. Many of the younger Christian fellahin preferred to dress in European clothes, in which they followed the example set by the urban Christian Arabs.

Both among the Christian and among the Moslem fellahin in Palestine—as among the agricultural populations in many other Middle Eastern countries—a definite trend was noticeable to migrate from the villages to the towns and to engage there in other than agricultural occupations, either temporarily or permanently. A main reason for this population movement can be seen in the under-privileged status of the fellahin and in the very low prestige the agricultural occupations carry in the eyes of the Middle Eastern peoples in general, including these of the fellahin themselves. A person leading the most precarious existence in the towns, living in slums, clad in rags and underfed, still feels superior to the fellah. The very word fellah is a sharp invective in the Arabic colloquial of the towns. A result of this migration from villages to towns in Palestine was that the Arab population of the towns, and especially of the three main cities, showed a much higher increase percentually, during the entire British Mandatory period, than that of the villages.

This movement from the villages to the cities and towns was much more pronounced among the Christian fellahin in Palestine than among the Moslems. The result of this differential, which was additional to the effect of the smaller natural increase character-istic of the Christian Arabs in general, was a gradual relative de-crease in the number of the Christian villagers in the country as a whole. In several villages and small towns, which a number of years before still had a Christian majority, this decrease was considerable enough to turn them into a minority by the time the Mandatory period drew to its close. (For example, Shafa Amr, Ma'lul, Yafa and Reina in the Nazareth district, today in Israel; and Bir Zeit and 'Abud in the Ramallah district, today under Jordanian administra-tion.)

In very general terms it can be stated that, of the Christian Arabs, the group which seems to be most similar to the Moslems in mode of life as well as in outlook is that of the Greek Orthodox; less pro-nounced is the similarity to the Moslems among the "Uniate" com-munities (Greek Catholics, Maronites, etc.) and the Latins; while the most progressive and most Westernized element are the Arab Protestants.

4. The Non-Arab Christians

Before turning to the non-Christian (Moslem and semi-Moslem) minorities and to the Moslem Arabs themselves, a few remarks seem in place about the non-Arab Christians in Palestine, a considerable part of whom is found today in Israel. Of these, the most important numerically is the *Armenian* community, organized in the Armenian Orthodox Church and numbering (1947), according to various estimates, 5-10,000 persons. Most of these lived in Jerusalem, Jaffa and Haifa. The majority of the Armenians had settled in Palestine only in the course of the 20th century as a result of the Turkish persecutions. They constituted in Palestine a definitely foreign community, continued to talk Armenian among themselves —though most of them have learned Arabic—and looked upon Palestine as a merely temporary place of residence. They kept close contact with Soviet Armenia which they regarded as their political, cultural and religious center. In 1947, many of them actually returned to Soviet Armenia. The head of the Armenian Church in Palestine is the Armenian Patriarch in Jerusalem whose superior is the Catholicos, the head of the Armenian-Gregorian Church residing in Soviet Armenia. The services of the Armenian Church are conducted in the Armenian language; the Church has property in the three main cities of Palestine and certain rights in the holy places. The Armenians were well integrated into the Arab economy of Palestine, and otherwise, too, had close connections with the Arabs. During the Arab riots of 1936-39, Armenians supplied the Arab terrorist gangs with skilled labor, manufacturing for them mines, bombs, and the like.

The *Syrian Orthodox Church*, also called Jacobite Church, is one of the oldest Christian Churches in the East. In Syria, Northern Iraq and in Palestine its members constitute the only Christian community which has preserved its own original language in daily use down to the present time. This is the so-called Neo-Aramaic language, which is spoken also by the Nestorian Christians and the Jews of Kurdistan,* and which is a modern dialect of the old classical Syriac used to this day in the ritual of the Syrian Orthodox Church. Most of the Palestinian Syrians, who number 1,000-1,200, are natives of Palestine, and speak also Arabic. The very fact, however, that they have kept alive their own language indicates their consciousness of being a separate community. The Syrian Bishop of Jerusalem, who is the head of this Church in Palestine, is subordinate

* Cf. E. Brauer, *The Jews of Kurdistan* (Hebrew), edited by R. Patai, Jerusalem, 1947.

to the Patriarch of Antioch who resides in Homs in Syria and has the title of "Mar Ignatius."

Neo-Aramaic is the language also of the 1,000-1,200 *Nestorians*, or Assyrians, in Palestine, a remnant of the once much more numerous Nestorian community of Northern Iraq which was almost exterminated in 1933. Their Patriarch, called "Mar Simon," now lives on the island of Cyprus.

A very old Christian Church is that of the *Copts*, the Christians of Egypt. In Palestine, where they number 1,000-1,200, they are mostly foreigners, though they speak Arabic, like their brethren in Egypt. The language of their ritual is Coptic.

The small *Abyssinian*, or Ethiopian, community in Palestine (300-350 members) consists mostly of priests, monks and nuns who live in Jerusalem or in a monastery near the Jordan. They have a church, a hostel and some other property in Jerusalem.

5. The Druzes

The semi-Moslem minorities were concentrated in the north of Palestine to an even greater extent than the Christian communities, while Moslem groups of foreign origin, in varying stages of assimilation to the Palestinian Moslem Arabs, were scattered all over the country. It is particularly in relation to these groups that the remarks concerning the nature of Middle Eastern minorities (cf. above, page 217) has a consistent validity. Arabic speaking groups, though differing from the rest of Moslem Arab Palestine only with regard to religion, have remained completely set apart from them and continued to constitute closed endogamous units; while, on the other hand, non-Arab Moslems who came to the country only two to three generations ago with a different mother-tongue, different nationality and tradition, became rapidly assimilated to the Moslem Arabs of Palestine.

A typical example of a Middle Eastern religious minority is that of the *Druzes* whose main concentrations are in Syria and the Lebanon. The foundation of their sect goes back to the 11th century, and their history is an almost uninterrupted chain of bloody wars fought against the Turks, against the Christians of the Lebanon, against their Moslem neighbors, and, last but by no means least, among themselves. Their fight for independence was directed especially against the Turks, and they succeeded in maintaining for hundreds of years a status of purely nominal subordination to the Turkish sovereignty. In the first half of the 17th century the Druzes ruled over the mountains of the Lebanon, down to the Beirut coast, as well as over all the north of Palestine, including Mount Carmel.

It was at that time that the Druzes founded their villages in Galilee and on Mt. Carmel. Towards the end of the 17th century the Druzes began to move eastward and to settle in the Hauran district of Syria which was very sparsely populated at the time. In 1840 and again in 1860, when the Druzes massacred the Christians of the Lebanon, European powers intervened, and as a consequence a Druze mass migration set in from the Lebanon to the Hauran which from then on became known as the *Jebel Druz*, or Mountain of Druzes.

Today the Druzes number about 180,000. Of these, about 75-80,000 live in the *Jebel Druz* in Syria and are ruled by the feudal family of el-Atrash. The second largest concentration of the Druzes is in the Lebanon, where their numbers are put at circa 70,000, and where the Arslan and Jumblat families compete for the overlordship. About 20,000 Druzes live in America and other lands of emigration, and 10-12,000 was their number in Palestine in 1947, all of whom lived in Galilee.

Before the Arab-Jewish war there were ten villages in the Acre district of Palestine which were inhabited by Druzes only or by a Druze majority amounting to 90%-100%. These were Jules, Yirka, Jat, Kesra, Yanuh, Beit Jan, Sajur, Ein el-Asad, Hurfeish and Daliyat el-Karmel. Two more villages ('Isafiya and Kafr Sumi'a) had an absolute Druze majority, and six additional villages (Shafa Amr, Kafr Yasif, Abu Snan, el-Buqei'a, er-Rama, Mugar) had a Druze minority and an Arab majority. With the changes which occurred during the Arab-Jewish war, the Druze minority in several of these villages became a majority. Thus in the fall of 1949 they constituted the majority in Daliyat el-Karmel (2,600 inhabitants), 'Isafiya (1,900), and el-Buqei'a (1,000). The total number of the Druzes in Israel in 1952 was put at 16,000, which is a considerable increase as against the 1947 figure. They have continued to live in their 18 villages.

All the Druzes speak Arabic, believe themselves to be of pure Arab descent, and the great majority of them in Israel are agriculturists, fellahin. In the customs of everyday life there is but little difference between them and the Arab fellahin, though their clothing is somewhat different. However, they keep apart from the Arabs everywhere and constitute a separate community sharply divided from the Arabs in the mixed Druze-Arab villages. Though intermarriages between Druzes and Arabs occur, there is a marked tendency to avoid such alliances. The tension, which characterized the relations of the Druzes with the Arabs for many centuries, resulted in a considerable social barrier between them. On the other hand, it is one of the tenets of Druze religion that its members are permitted to disguise themselves as Arabs when dealing with Arabs, if this can serve their advantage. At times political reasons prompted them to appear as Arabs, and in general in recent years there seems to have been a certain trend towards assimilation to the Arab environment.

This trend, however, could not prevent friction between the Druzes and the Arabs especially in the mixed villages in Palestine. During the 1936-39 riots, a number of Druzes joined the Arab terrorist gangs of Fauzi el-Kaukaji and Abu Dura. Later, however, the Arabs attacked the Druzes of Shafa Amr (where they constituted a minority of 18%). This was followed by numerous bloody incidents between the Druzes and the Arabs.

The Druzes, too, were caught in the age-old rivalry between the *Qais* and *Yaman* factions of the Arabs, which often caused fierce internal struggles among them. Most of the Druzes relate themselves to the *Qais*, or northern faction, but several noble leading families of the Lebanese Druzes hold that they are of the *Beni Qahtan* tribe, that is, of *Yamani*, or South Arabian descent.

The Turkish government did not recognize the Druzes as a distinct community. During the British occupation of Palestine, however, the Palestinian Druzes enjoyed the status of a separate group, headed by a Sheikh as their own religious leader. This Sheikh—who was from the Tarif family of the village of Jules—was their authority also in civil law as far as cases between Druzes and Druzes were concerned. The religious charitable foundations (*waqf*) of the Druzes, however, were administered under the British Mandatory regime by the Moslem *waqf*-committee.

Relatively little is known of Druze religious teaching and practice due to the secrecy in which their religious affairs are shrouded. Even among the Druzes themselves only those who are admitted to the inner circle of the *'Uqqal*, or Knowers, are initiated into the secrets of the Druze religion. The others, the *Juhhal*, or Ignorants, remain in the dark about their own faith. All the Druzes, however, call themselves *Muwahhadin*, or Those Who Declare the Oneness of God.

The Druze religious tenets include the belief that God was incarnated several times in human form, the last time in the body of the Sultan el-Hakim (996-1021). They believe in the transmigration of the soul. In contrast to the Moslem place of worship which is called *Masjid*, or Place of Prostration, the Druze place of worship is called *Khalwe*, Place of Seclusion.

The Druzes do not practice polygyny; their women go unveiled, have equal rights and duties with the men in all religious matters, can take part in the religious services and can even be admitted to the class of the 'Uqqal. In brief, the status of women among the Druzes is much higher than among the Moslem Arabs, although the Druze women, too, generally avoid meeting strange men.[*]

The extent of animosity felt by the Druzes towards the Arabs became evident when, soon after the independence of Israel, the number of Druzes in the country was found to have increased instead of decreasing during the upheavals, in the course of which the majority of the Moslem Arabs fled from Israel as well as from the rest of Palestine. As early as the summer of 1948, the Druzes in Israel offered their services to the new State. In September of the same year, they were formed into a unit in the Israeli army which was joined also by several volunteers who came from Syria. They actively participated in the fighting against Fauzi el-Kaukaji in Galilee, with whom they had an old account to settle dating back to the Arab riots of 1936-39 when much Druze blood was shed by Kaukaji's gangs.

In August 1949, as a consequence of a clash between Druzes and bedouin Arabs in the minorities' camp near Haifa, in the course of which a Druze tribesman, a Jewish officer and two bedouin were killed, the Israeli authorities felt obliged to confiscate all the fire-arms in the two Druze villages of 'Isafiya and Daliyat el-Karmel.[§] In the same month a certain consolidation of the status of the Israeli Druzes took place when they formed a Council of Representatives of their villages.

The Druzes in Israel wish to be treated as a minority group distinct from the Moslem Arabs; accordingly, the status of a separate religious community was granted to the Druzes, in August 1949, by the Israeli Ministry of Religious Affairs.

6. Splinter Minorities

Second in importance among the semi-Moslem minorities in Palestine were the *Metualis*, or Mutawalis, who numbered in 1947 circa 4,000. The origins of this group are hidden in the mists of the past. They themselves have a tradition to the effect that they are the descendants of the first Arab conquerors of Palestine, but, like many other myths of origins which serve to enhance the prestige of populations, it cannot be credited with historical accuracy.

[*] Cf. Philip K. Hitti, *The Origin of the Druze People and Religion*, New York, 1928; N. Bouron, *Les Druzes, Histoire du Liban et de la Montagne Hauranaise*, Paris, 1930.

[§] Cf. *Davar*, Tel Aviv, August 7, 1949.

Scientific opinion concerning their descent is divided: some hold that they are the offspring of Persians who were transplanted from their home in the 7th century by the Caliph Muawiya; others believe that they are the progeny of Kurds who moved westward in the 12th century under Saladin; yet others seek their ancestry in the south, in Yemen, and hold them to be of mixed foreign descent. Historical sources mention them for the first time as late as the 18th century.

The main concentration of the Metualis is found in the south of the Lebanon, where they number some 200,000. Their settlements in Palestine were along the Lebanese border and consisted of several villages all of which were destroyed or evacuated in the course of the Arab-Jewish war.

Just as the origin of the group is unknown, the origin and the meaning of the name Metuali is also uncertain. The most likely derivation is from the Arabic verb *wly* which means "to be a devoted friend," and thus the name would mean "Those Who Are Devoted," that is, to Ali ibn Abu Talib. In contrast to the Druzes whose religion is definitely non-Islamic, the Metualis are Shi'ites, that is, they have not seceded from the fold and constitute merely a separate sect within the community of the True Believers. However, their sectarianism was strong enough to erect a great barrier between them and the rest of the Palestinian Moslems, who are Sunnites.* In the past the Metualis held themselves so strictly aloof from the other Moslems that they declined even to eat at one table with strangers. Recently, however, these observances have tended to decline and disappear. The younger generation especially allows itself considerable freedom in ritual matters. The rule of endogamy is still in force, so that the religious community of the Metualis constitutes also a definitely delimited ethnic group. The Metualis differ from the other Moslem Arabs in Palestine also in their special Arabic dialect, and in certain details of their clothing habits.

The 1,000-2,000 *Turcomans* in Israel are the remnants of Turcic tribes or armies which passed through Palestine and conquered it several times in the course of the last fifteen hundred years. But it is unknown when and how the small Turcoman tribe in Israel came to the country, and to which of the numerous Turcic tribes it is most closely related. Until recently the Palestinian Turcomans were nomadic herdsmen who engaged in some agriculture (like most of the bedouin of Palestine). They were, however, quite advanced in their process of sedentarization and began turning their camps into permanent villages, although most of them still continued to

* Sunnites and Shi'ites are the two great divisions of Islam.

live in tents. Their settlements as well as their wandering territory were mainly situated around the southern part of Mt. Carmel. Here, along the Haifa-Jenin highway, was their main concentration, the purely Turcoman village of Ein el-Mansi and some three more villages in which they constituted minority groups. Their seasonal wanderings used to extend deep into the Valley of Yezreel (the Emek), but since the Jews brought the Emek under cultivation, they had to restrict their movements. Until lately the Turcomans in Palestine still spoke their own Turcic dialect which was given up only in recent decades for Arabic. A similar acculturative process took place also with regard to their clothing, their customs and their way of life in general. The Turcomans took an active part in the nationalistic activities of their Arab neighbors; in the 1936-39 riots they energetically helped the Arabs, and Yusuf Hamdan, second-in-command of Abu Dura's gang, was a Turcoman from Umm el-Fahm. In 1950 only a few Turcoman families were left in Umm el-Fahm (total Arab population on December 31, 1949: 4,861).

The *Circassians* are a Shi'ite Moslem tribe from the Caucasus of whom about 10,000 settled in Transjordan and less than 1,000 in Palestine. In 1864, when Russia conquered Daghestan (in the Caucasus), many of the Moslems living in the territory preferred to emigrate rather than live under Christian rule. Among these were the Circassians who were received with open arms by Turkey and assigned places of settlement in Transjordan, in the neighborhood of Amman, and in the Gaulan, near el-Quneitra (east of the Hule Lake). Here they served as defenders of the sparsely populated villages against the attacks of the bedouin. They constitute today an important part of the population of Jordan in spite of the fact that numerically they are a very small minority. Many of them serve in the armed forces of the country.

The Turkish government also helped some of the Circassians to settle in western Palestine, in three villages, two of which are in Galilee. The third was in Samaria, but was soon given up by them on account of the malaria which wrought havoc in their ranks. Their two villages, which are today in Israel, are Kafr Kama and Rehania, and the number of Circassians inhabiting them was put in the summer of 1949 at 1,200, of whom, however, only 806 were left by Dec. 31, 1949.

Almost all of the Circassians in Israel are agriculturists, though some entered the army, the police or the frontier force of the British Mandatory government of Palestine. Their agriculture is based on better methods of cultivation than those generally practiced by the Moslem Arab fellahin. They are active, hard working and industrious. Their villages are built in a more modern style than those of the Moslem Arabs. Most of them can read and write. Lately a strong tendency became noticeable among them to assimilate to the Arabs in such matters as language (they had previously spoken their own language) and way of life (for instance, a decrease of cleanliness in their villages). Also intermarriage with the Arabs began, although for the time being only between Circassian men and Arab women— as is usual between a superior and an inferior population group. At the same time, a tendency toward assimilation to European customs was also evident among them. The younger people, for instance, exchanged their old national costume for European-style clothing. The Circassians took no active part in the Arab national-istic movement, an attitude which they evinced also in Syria where they remained loyal to the French during the Syrian-French struggles of 1945. In Palestine they have shown sympathy for the Jewish settlement movement from its very beginnings. After the establish-ment of Israel, many Circassians volunteered to join the Israeli army and participated in the Negev campaign.

The *Moghrebites* of Palestine came from Moghreb, the Arab "West," that is, the North African territories of Tunisia, Algeria and especially Morocco. In their migration to Palestine two phases can be distinguished. The first of these was the result of the pilgrimage from North Africa to the holy cities of Islam, Mecca and Medina, which passed through Palestine for many generations. Many of the pilgrims visited Jerusalem, either on the way to Arabia or on the way home, and settled in this city, the holiest one in Islam after Mecca and Medina. A special hostel for Moghrebite pilgrims was opened as early as 1303 in Jerusalem, near the Wailing Wall of the Jews, and around this hostel a Moghrebite quarter (*Hārat el-Maghāribe*) soon grew up. One encounters the name el-Moghrebi in many parts of Palestine, which seems to point to Moghrebite settlers also out-side Jerusalem.

The second phase of Moghrebite immigration to Palestine has not a religious but a political origin. In 1856, the Emir Abd el-Qader, who had revolted against the French in Algeria, was given political refuge together with large numbers of his followers by the Turkish government in Damascus. From Damascus these scattered in several villages in Syria and in Galilee. In Palestine they numbered in 1947 between 1,500 to 2,000, concentrated mainly in two areas: in Upper Galilee around the Hule Lake, and in Lower Galilee around Lake Tiberias. These succeeded in preserving something of their old traditions, including the Berber language which, however, was superseded among the majority by Arabic. In general, the Moghrebites constitute a backward group even in relation to the Moslem-Arab fellahin. Their villages are neglected, their architecture poor, their clothing mostly dilapidated, their agriculture primitive. Socially and culturally their status is low. They are regarded by their neighbors as lazy, and there is a tendency among the Palestinian Arabs not to intermarry with them. This relationship of the Palestinian Arabs to the Moghrebites is especially noteworthy in view of the very similar attitude displayed by many among the Jews of Israel towards the present Moghrebite Jewish immigration. (Cf. pages 294 ff.)

The remaining small minority groups can be dealt with in a sentence or two. There were in Palestine (in Haifa and Acre) some 300 *Bahais*, Persian followers of a sect which split off from Shi'ite Islam. About 100 of these returned to Haifa in the summer of 1949. A few *Ahmadiyyas*, followers of a heretical Shi'ite sect, continue to live in the village of Al-Kababir on Mt. Carmel and publish a religious monthly called *Al-Bushra*, "The Message." In addition to these, there were in Palestine a number of groups who were the descendents of immigrants once constituting separate communities, but who in the course of time have almost completely assimilated to the Moslem Arab majority of the country. These are the Egyptians, the Sudanese, the Negroes, the Ghawarna, the Kurds, the Syrians, the Lebanese, the Persians, the Afghans and the Gypsies. These minority groups, each in itself of no great consequence, accounted together for the mosaic-like appearance of the non-Jewish population of Mandatory Palestine. As the overwhelming majority of all these groups lived in Galilee, which today is part of the State of Israel, those of them who did not abandon their homes during the critical months of fighting automatically became citizens of Israel.

Special mention must be made here of two quasi-Jewish groups, the Samaritans and the Karaites. The Samaritans have lived, since the days of the Second Temple, in Nablus (Sichem). During the last fifty years their numbers have slowly dwindled and it began to look as though they were doomed to extinction. After the establishment of the Jewish State, however, they began to infiltrate into Israel, and today (spring, 1952) they constitute a community of 60 persons in Jaffa-Tel Aviv.

The Karaites, stemming mainly from Egypt, have arrived in Israel after the establishment of the State. There are now about 200 families in Israel, half of whom live in a workers settlement which they founded and called Matzliah, after a 10th century Karaite author. The rest are dispersed in various places throughout the country.

The eventual absorption of these two groups into the Jewish com- ✳
munity can be foreseen.

7. The Bedouin

The Moslem Arabs of Israel are either bedouin, nomadic herdsmen, or fellahin, settled agriculturists, or townspeople. The life-
form of the bedouin is wandering within their traditional tribal
territory, mostly in the Negev, and leading a precarious existence
on the subsistence level. Notwithstanding their poverty in material
goods, the bedouin are possessed of a great pride coupled with a
deep contempt for sedentary people, especially for the fellahin. "The
Bedu is the king of the world, the Fellah is the ass of the world,"
says one of their proverbs. In 1947 the bedouin in Palestine numbered about 50,000; their number today in Israel is estimated at
17,000.

The Israeli bedouin are not real nomads like the great camel-
herding tribes of Saudi-Arabia, Transjordan, Syria and Iraq, whose
tribal territory stretches across political boundaries and who roam
with their rich camel herds over hundreds of miles of desert and
steppe. The bedouin of the Negev are semi-nomads; their livestock
consists mostly of sheep and goats; and they are tied to fixed camp-
ing-places for a considerable part of the year, wandering during the
rest of the year within a much smaller tribal territory, nearer to the
settled and cultivated land. Tribal structure and other traditions of
the proud full-nomads are declining. Together with tribal disintegration goes a trend toward sedentarization, that is, a settling down
permanently within the tribal territory, on a stretch of land capable
of being cultivated and of yielding some crop. This trend makes it
imperative to divide the land, which previously was held in common
by the whole tribe, into individual holdings to be owned either by
a family or a private person. The division of the land occurs usually
in the form of "occupation," this means that a family occupies a
piece of land *de facto*, cultivates it all the year round, and thus
becomes its sole owner also *de jure*. Usually the sheikhs, the tribal
chieftains, who are the most powerful members of the tribe, succeed
in occupying considerable tracts of relatively good land and become
in time feudal lords and big landowners. Other strong members of
the tribe also prevail when it comes to dividing the tribal lands
and occupying tracts, so that the weaker and poorer tribesmen
remain altogether left out and inevitably become tenants. In this
manner the social classes which are characteristic of the Arab
village develop at the very moment when the semi-nomadic tribe
become a settled community.

According to the last census of Palestine (1931), there were 66,337 Moslems in the country who were classified as "nomads," that is bedouin, but of these the occupation of 54,834 was given as "Ordinary Cultivation," and only 5,850 were described as "Herdsmen, Shepherds, Goatsmen etc." (The rest were engaged in "Insufficiently Described Occupations.") In other words, of the so-called nomadic population of Palestine less than 9% were actually bedouin characterized by reliance on animal husbandry as their sole or main source of livelihood, while the rest were half-settled tribes whose sole or main occupation was ordinary cultivation. Almost all the nomads who subsisted on animal husbandry lived in the Negev (5,113 to be exact, or 10.7% of the total bedouin population of the Negev), the rest (42,868, or 89.3% of the total) having given also here ordinary cultivation as the basis of their livelihood.

While these figures show the extent of sedentarization among the bedouin in Palestine-Israel, the tribes in question constitute a tradition-bound and primitive population even in comparison with their fellah neighbors. Literacy is almost non-existent among them: in 1931, of the 48,000 nomads of the Negev only 52 males and one single female claimed to be literate. The proportion of polygamous marriages is relatively high, 125 married women having been found in 1931 to every 100 married men. Their life expectancy is considerably lower than that of the settled Moslem population of the country.

The trend toward sedentarization—a phenomenon not confined to the bedouin within the borders of Israel—is motivated by several circumstances. In the case of the true bedouin, whose entire economy was based on the camel, a general impoverishment set in when the camel as a means of transportation was gradually replaced by the railways and motor vehicles, causing a sharp drop in the price of camels. The half-bedouin were affected adversely by the growth of agriculture which constantly diminished the extent of pastures in the vicinity of the sown land, depriving them precisely of the best grazing lands, while the remaining lands were of inferior quality and unable to sustain the flocks. Other sources of income for the bedouin, like the raiding of villages on the outskirts, and the *khuwwa*, or protection-money, paid them by the fellahin and travelers passing through their territory, have also dried up with the establishment of regular armies, frontier and police forces by the central governments of the Middle Eastern states in general and by the British Mandatory Government in Palestine in particular. To all this must be added the effect of constant contact with the villagers, enabling the nomads to get better acquainted with settled life, which began to appear to them, contrary to the traditional stereotype, as safer and richer—at least in material benefits—than their own precarious existence.

These internal incentives, experienced by the bedouin themselves, have become reinforced by the conscious political line taken by practically all the Arab politicians and social leaders. These spokesmen believed that it was the duty of the government to promote the sedentarization of the bedouin and thus to turn the roaming, evasive and irresponsible fleetfooted tribes into sedentary and sedate taxpayers. In the British Mandatory Government of Palestine, it is true, arguments were voiced at times against the sedentarization of the nomads, but this was done not for any reasons of political or economic expediency but on account of the romantic admiration some British colonial officials harbored for the bedouin, the proud and picturesque Arab of the Desert.

The bedouin tribes of Israel, most of whom live in the Negev, will in the very near future be faced with a choice between the only two possible alternatives: either to settle down completely and to engage in agriculture, thus vacating a considerable part of their tribal wandering territories for the settlement of others; or to leave the country and continue in their nomadic life in one or more of the neighboring states. The plans of the Jewish State for the Negev call for settling there a large part of the immigrants. As more of the Negev is brought under cultivation, less will remain for the nomads, so that they will have to give up extensive nomadic pasturalism even as a subsidiary occupation. *

8. The Fellahin

Of the 1,100,000 Moslem Arabs in Palestine in 1947, about 800,000, or 72.7%, lived in villages and pursued agriculture as their sole or main occupation. At the end of the Mandatory period there were about 900 Arab villages in Palestine, varying in size from those which consisted of a few dozen houses only to large ones with several thousand inhabitants. Most of the villagers were agriculturists, that is, fellahin, although in the larger villages there were a number of artisans, craftsmen, watchmen, teachers, etc. The agriculture of the fellahin has changed but little in several hundreds of years. Most usual is the so-called two-field method, which consists of one field used for winter crops, such as wheat and barley, and another field used for summer-crops, such as *durra* (a kind of maize), sesame and melons. Sometimes the land is divided into three fields, the third one being left fallow so that a piece of land gets a rest every third year; this is very essential in view of the fact that practically no fertilizers are used, the dung of the few cows being carefully collected, dried and used as fuel. In the mountain regions, more olive, fig and other fruit trees are found. Only very small plots are irrigated and used for vegetable growing where conditions are favorable; otherwise the fellah relies on the rain of the short winter months. The plough with the pointed tip, which is the main implement used, has scarcely changed its shape in the last four thousand years. Most of the produce of his field and animals is eaten by the fellah and his family, while only a small part of it is sold to obtain a little cash needed for things he cannot produce at home, such as sugar, rice, coffee. This great shortage of cash results in indebtedness to usurers who are often the same landowners on whose lands many of them work as tenants. Fellahin who work the land they own are more often than not in debt and have little hope of ever being able to repay.

In spite of the traditional reluctance of the fellahin to adopt innovations and improvements, the effects of the nearby modern Jewish agricultural settlements were markedly felt in the Arab villages. The observation made by the British journalist and author, Ernest Main, as far back as 1936, may be quoted in this connection:

"The Arab villages in Palestine have clearly benefited from the Jewish example. Those Arab villages with no Jewish settlements near them are like villages anywhere else in the Arab countries. The average Arab village possesses a single well with a "public" water-carrier, who draws water from the well with a petrol tin fastened to a long rope. The houses are of clay with no windows; the roofs are of reeds or straw covered with clay. In the case of two-storeyed houses the ground-floor is for the domestic animals. The working animals in such a village are the skin-and-bone oxen, small lean cows or donkeys. Ploughing is done by small wooden ploughs drawn by two oxen, or an ox and an ass, or an ass and a camel. These ploughs merely scratch the surface of the soil. Only grain of a poor quality is grown; fig and olive trees are planted sporadically and indifferently tended. In the middle of the village is an old-established dung-hill. The children run about naked and dirty. The women grind their corn on mill-stones and make their bread in primitive ovens.

"The Arab villages near the Jewish settlements present a different picture. The houses are better, stone in many cases having taken the place of mud, and there are usually separate compounds for the village livestock. Such villages usually have access to bus services to the nearby town; the villagers are learning from their

Jewish neighbors about irrigation and better methods of agriculture."*

A very important factor in the life of the villagers is the contact between them and the towns. It is due to this contact that the towns —and through them certain second-hand forms of Western culture traits—have a considerable influence on the villages, or at least on those not too far away. This influence is characterized by a reversed ratio to the distance between the town and the villages. Villages far away from towns are conservative, backward, and remain practically untouched by Western cultural elements; while those near towns are affected by this proximity both to their advantage and disadvantage.

First of all, certain economic benefits accrue to the village from the closeness of the town. It is easier for the people of such a village to sell their produce; they can themselves take care of its transportation and save on expenses. Also the value of their land is higher. Many villagers find supplementary work in the town during the dead season in agriculture, and can thus augment their meager earnings. Others settle altogether in the towns§ and let a brother or some other relative take care of their lands against a certain payment. Economic advantages, in their turn, enable them to make improvements in the buildings, following styles observed in the towns, so that such a village makes a cleaner, more prosperous impression.

The people of such villages are more inclined—and also financially more able to afford—to build a school and to send their children to it for several years. Some of the children are even sent to the school in the nearby town. The villagers themselves acquire the habit of spending much of their leisure time in the town, sitting around in the cafes, listening to the litigations in the law-court, learning the ways of the townsfolk, getting infected with their interest in local and national politics, and the like. Men who frequent the towns, or who spend some time working in the towns and then return home, acquire increased prestige which makes them important personages in their village. They are approached for advice, their opinion is heeded, and they have a good chance of becoming *mukhtars*, or headmen, if such a post should become vacant in the village. In villages thus affected by the influence of the town one of the enterprising fellahin may open a cafe in which the men could sit up late at night, drinking thick black coffee, smoking the gurgling *narjile*, or water-pipe, and playing the checker-like game of *shash-*

* Cf. Ernest Main, *Palestine at the Crossroads*, London, 1937, pp. 218-9.
§ Cf. above, p. 225.

bash. An inevitable concomitant of these developments is that the traditional patriarchal way of life declines and is replaced by the less restrained ways of the town, that juvenile delinquency increases, and that the village has to contend with several other critical phenomena resulting from a too rapid cultural change.

9. The Townspeople

Towns have been a characteristic feature of the lands of the Middle East for the last five thousand years at least. In Palestine no clear distinction could be made between a large village and a small town as far as the occupational structure of the inhabitants was concerned. Architecturally, the older towns were distinguished from the villages by the wall which surrounded them and turned them into fortified places of refuge for the inhabitants of the nearby open and unprotected villages. The numerous "kings" whom the Hebrew tribes fought and conquered three thousand years ago in Canaan, resided in such fortified towns and ruled over them and their "daughter"-villages. Later, when larger tracts of the country were brought under centralized rule, these towns became the district centers and seats of district governors.

The Arab town is first and foremost a place of exchange, a market and a *suq,* or bazaar, where both the bedouin and the fellahin come to sell the products of their economy and to buy the things produced by the townspeople and needed by them. The *suq,* with its narrow streets mostly covered by vaulted roofs or by matting or awning, with its small shops arranged according to trades in separate alleys, with its cafés and with its throngs of passers-by in pursuance of their business or loitering aimlessly, is the nerve-center of the Arab town as far as commercial, financial, social and political activities are concerned; it is the hub where news is gathered and from where it is again disseminated with astonishing rapidity. Around the bazaars are the offices of the few doctors and lawyers of which an Arab town can boast, and not far from it are the mosque (*masjid*) and the school. Farther away are the residential sections, the older and poorer ones usually within the narrow confines of the city walls, the newer and richer in the more spacious sections built outside the old city.

The division of labor characteristic of Western towns is not found in the same pronounced form in the towns of the Middle East. Here a much greater interchangeability is found among the occupations of the laborer, the artisan or industrial worker, the merchant and the professional man; they flow into each other almost imperceptibly. A considerable portion of the inhabitants of the smaller towns in

Palestine were (and are) whole-time or at least part-time agriculturists, and many of these are also merchants who deal in agricultural products. The artisans are in most cases also merchants who sell the articles they manufacture, often supplementing them with the products of others. Among the commodities sold by the shopkeepers is often the much needed one of money; in other words, the merchants are often also moneylenders.

In general, the Arab townspeople can be divided into three social classes, an upper or ruling class, a middle class, and a lower class. The classes themselves are, however, composite units, which shade imperceptibly into one another.

The lower class, comprising small artisans, shopkeepers, pedlars, day-laborers, porters, fishermen and various types of unemployed, constitutes the great majority of the town populations. Most of these are as illiterate as the fellahin and take no part in the social, political or cultural life of the town. The living standard of these people is incredibly low; they pay next to nothing for their lodgings, eat the traditional cheap food, mainly *pita* (the Arab flat bread) and olives, and have practically no expenses for their clothing which is scarcely better than rags. Consequently, the relatively higher wages obtaining in Palestine, and especially in the mixed Arab-Jewish cities, were more than sufficient for their needs and in many cases they preferred to work only a few days a week and spend the rest of their time in the Arab counterpart of the Italian *dolce far niente.*

Some 70% of the Arabs in Jaffa and some 50% in Jerusalem actually * lived in slum-like quarters or sub-standard lodgings. In many cases, however, this was not due solely to economic conditions: it was caused by a lack of understanding and appreciation of better living conditions, a heritage of the situation in the villages. Housing habits developed in the villages, if transplanted into the much more congested urban quarters of the poor, create a situation many times inferior to any village in point of sanitation and hygiene. The proverbial Oriental indifference, often bordering on apathy, coupled with a lack of initiative on the part of the municipal authorities, contributed to the perpetuation and even aggravation of this situation from year to year. The attraction of city-life for the fellahin, which resulted in a constant stream of migrants from the village to the town, could therefore not be attributed to better living conditions available in the urban areas, but rather to such factors as the wish to get away from the hard work of the fellah, the desire to acquire something of the prestige enjoyed by every townsman (in the eyes of the fellahin) and the determination to enjoy at least the hope of easy money-making and participate in the pleasures and entertainments of city life.

The slums in the Arab towns were not only the breeding ground for many diseases, they were also the hotbeds of crime and vice. To take Jaffa as a typical example: this city was characterized by great economic difficulties affecting the major part of its population. This was increasingly felt during World War II, which brought about a virtual paralysis of its port and of many occupations dependent on it. It suffered from a dearth of suitable housing to cope with the immigration from other parts of the country and from abroad, with a consequent increase of the slum areas, and the population density in general. It manifested all the cancerous outgrowths of Levantine port-cities: smuggling, prostitution, gambling and *hashish*-smoking. It lacked adequate social and educational services, while at the same time it was directly exposed to the presence on its very borders of the big and modern Jewish city of Tel Aviv, the proximity of which added considerably to the mental unrest of many in the lower age-brackets.

A few words will suffice concerning the relatively small middle class and the very influential but very thin upper class. The middle class of Arab towns consists of small merchants, small houseowners, owners of workshops, the lower officials as well as professional people and the intelligentsia which does not belong to the upper class. There is a strong tendency observable in the middle class to mingle with the upper class, to follow its lead in many respects and to become like it. While the political leadership is, so to say, reserved for members of the upper class, the actual work in the parties, the organizational and propagandistic activities, are all carried out by members of the middle class. The social mobility characteristic of Arab society as a whole, is especially pronounced between the upper and the middle classes. Persons (or families) belonging to the middle class, if successful in making money and becoming influential, rise into the upper class, and vice versa.

The upper class consists, as a rule, of a few great families whose members occupy key positions in the economic, professional and other occupational fields in the country. These families are the leaders of social and political life and are amply represented in the municipal councils of the towns, among founders and directors of companies, in governmental and other offices and committees, at the bar and on the bench, at public meetings and the like. In Mandatory Palestine they were among the recipients of honors from the Government on occasions such as the King's birthday, among the heads of political parties, clubs, associations, newspaper owners, and the like.

It was this small but extremely wealthy and influential class which represented Arab Palestine in practically every manifestation of social, civic, economic and political life. The opinions expressed in the Arab press as being representative of all the Arabs of Palestine were actually merely those of this class. It was common knowledge that their interests were often diametrically opposed to those of the fellahin who constituted three-quarters of the Arab population of Palestine but were illiterate, inarticulate and unable to voice any opinion. Whenever the viewpoint of the Arabs of Palestine had to be presented to a committee of inquiry, British or international, the spokesmen for this group appeared in the name of a population which did not delegate them.

10. The Story of Abu Gosh

It was only extremely rarely that individuals or groups not belonging to this ruling upper city class had the courage to form a dissident opinion in weighty political matters and were able to give expression to it. An exceptional case of this kind was that of Abu Gosh, a sizable village some ten miles west of Jerusalem, on the Tel Aviv highway. According to local legend, the village was founded some three hundred years ago by Isa Abu Gosh, whose four sons became the ancestors of the four *hamulas* (clans) of the village. During the entire history of new Palestine Abu Gosh was friendly to its Jewish neighbors. Its people never succumbed to the anti-Jewish agitation of the Mufti of Jerusalem. They mustered enough independence of spirit and courage to pursue a course of action of their own with regard to both their internal affairs and their relationship with the Jews. When the communal settlement of Kiryat Anavim was founded in their vicinity in 1920, the best neighborly relations were established between the Arab village and the Jewish *kibbutz*. During the Arab rioting of 1929, when Kiryat Anavim was isolated and surrounded by inimical Arab villages, it was due to the influence of Abu Gosh that the *kibbutz* was not attacked. The people of Abu Gosh even offered to send their women and children to Kiryat Anavim as a guarantee for the safety of the *kibbutz*. Moreover, they made public their opposition to the political line taken by the Mufti of Jerusalem and other members of his influential family, and when the first Arab delegation, headed by Musa Kazem el-Husseini, was in London, they sent a telegram to the British authorities announcing that these delegates did not represent the Arab people.

Again, during the riots of 1936-39, the village of Abu Gosh actively helped the British forces to track down the terrorist gangs in its neighborhood. During the war of liberation, in 1948, they rendered all assistance they could to the Jewish army. A convoy which was attacked a few miles below Abu Gosh, in the gorge of Bab el-Wad, was given asylum in the village. It happened several times that the Jewish wounded were treated and damaged cars were repaired by the people of Abu Gosh. In the most critical days of the war, when it seemed that the Jewish cause was lost, the Arabs of Abu Gosh remained consistently on the side of the Jews. During the decisive battle of the Kastel—a hill dominating the Tel Aviv-Jerusalem road not far from Abu Gosh—the commander of the Arab forces, Abd el-Qader el-Husseini, sojourned in the village; but in spite of his personal appeal to the people, they refused to be drawn into the fighting.

The Jews for their part did what they could to make the lot of the villagers easier during the months of the fighting. They helped them with much-needed food supplies and other assistance; they took care to cause as little damage as possible to the village, and intimated that the villagers were welcome to stay in their village. Nevertheless, when the people of Abu Gosh saw that the neighboring Jewish settlements evacuated their non-combatant residents, they concluded that serious and large-scale fighting was expected in the neighborhood, and a considerable part of the population left the village and sought safety behind the Arab lines. However, the two competing leaders of the village, Mahmud Rashid Abu Gosh and Yusuf Abu Gosh, stayed behind. There was keen rivalry between Mahmud Rashid and his kinsman Yusuf, caused by differences over inheritance and land holdings and a competition in influence and leadership in the village; the resulting feud had been part of the village's life for many years.

Both of these men served the Jewish cause, each in his own way. Mahmud Rashid Abu Gosh had been for many years the leading spirit in the village, and his influence had grown from year to year. He had actively helped the Jewish institutions to purchase lands from the Arabs in the neighborhood of Abu Gosh, and had close connections with the *Hagana*, the Jewish underground defense army. During the war he helped the Jews to obtain arms and other supplies.

Yusuf Abu Gosh, together with a number of young men from the village, joined the Irgun and the Stern Group (Jewish underground right-wing terrorist groups) and participated in their attacks on the British. It was he who helped Geula Cohen, Yemenite member of these groups, who was captured by the British, to escape from the hospital where she was being kept in detention pending her recovery from wounds suffered during an attack. Several months before the outbreak of the war of liberation, Yusuf Abu Gosh himself was captured by the British and spent the critical months of the war in prison.

After the end of the hostilities, those who left the village began to return. They achieved this not by applying officially to the Israeli authorities for entrance permits, but by infiltration which was for them both simpler and quicker. The Israeli authorities took the position that infiltration could not be tolerated, whoever the infiltree might be, and from time to time those who could not show papers were rounded up in the village—as was done periodically in other frontier areas—and shipped across the border. Among the people who were thus deported were the wife and children of Yusuf Abu Gosh. This caused a storm of protest, not only from the people of Abu Gosh but also from those Jews who were familiar with the antecedents of the village and with the role played by the Abu Gosh family and especially by Yusuf Abu Gosh himself. Attention was thus focused on the village, and it was felt that the Israeli authorities had not yet done all they should have done to restore the normal flow of life in it. Yusuf Abu Gosh himself disappeared. It was suspected that he had been spirited away by his friends from the Fighters for the Freedom of Israel (popularly known as the Stern Group) in order to cause embarrassment to the Israeli authorities. His rival, Mahmud Rashid Abu Gosh, was appointed *mukhtar* (headman) of the village and began to practice a sort of benevolent autocracy in matters of employment, food distribution and the like. At the same time a certain improvement became noticeable in the economic situation of the village; the marketing of its agricultural products was taken over by *Tnuva*, the great food-marketing organization of the *Histadrut*; several villagers got employment from the Israeli Custodian of Absentees' Property and in public works such as road building.

In the 1951-52 school-year, 200 children were registered in the elementary school (kindergarten and four grades). Of these about 160 attended regularly; the remaining forty, often busy on the farms of their parents, came to school on and off. The studies included Arabic, arithmetic, agriculture and religion. From the fourth grade Hebrew was taught as a foreign language by two Jewish teachers (a man and a woman), both new immigrants from Iraq.[*]

[*] Cf. Naphtali Ushpiz, "The True Story of Abu Gosh," *Davar*, Tel Aviv, Sept. 2, 1949; Shmuel Bazaq, "Abu Gosh," in *Hatzofeh* (Hebrew Daily), Tel Aviv, Jan. 3, 1952.

The story of Abu Gosh is a good example to demonstrate that even in the case of an Arab village which had shown undaunted sympathy for the Jews for nearly three decades, the process of incorporation and absorption into the Jewish State is accompanied by many difficulties both for the village and for the State.

11. Westernization and Readjustment

But to return to the Arab towns in Palestine in general: there was apparent a marked correlation between their degree of social advancement and the penetration of Westernization: the higher the social class the more advanced the processes of Westernization. The lower class was almost untouched by Western influences; its mode of life, outlook, mentality and attitudes were largely the same as those of the fellahin. They knew, of course, a lot more than the fellahin did about Western technical advancements; they saw daily many machines, gadgets, utensils and other elements belonging to the realm of technological development and could observe the behavior of people who came from the Western world. But in all this they remained passive spectators, and in the rarest cases only were they able to break through the invisible wall which separated them from the Westerners, Jews or Britishers.

In the middle class the situation was different. Members of this class to some extent assimilated outwardly to Western ways; they dressed—at least in the streets and at work—in European clothes; they tried to acquire European mannerisms in their behavior; many of them spoke a smattering of English, and their ideal was quite manifestly to be like a European—an ambition which was spurred on by the example set by the upper class which was considerably more advanced in this process of Europeanization than they themselves. At home, however, the old customs and traditions still persisted; the social unit living together in one house was still the old extended family consisting of parents, unmarried daughters, unmarried and married sons and the wives and children of the latter. The women, either by turns or jointly, cooked in one common kitchen for the entire family, feeding them the traditional Arab dishes; the furnishing of the house remained largely the old Oriental one; the women remained secluded and enjoyed uncontrolled fertility; and the men, when returning home from work, would doff the European suit and don the more comfortable Oriental garb.

The upper class was most advanced in Westernization. Many of this group, especially of the younger generation, were educated in foreign institutions and spoke a European tongue (English or French) as fluently as their own; home and clothing were Westernized, food habits less so; the seclusion of women began to lose its stringency and social contact with Europeans (Englishmen) was sought after. Also in entertainment and ways of spending one's leisure, members of this class assimilated to the West; books and magazines were read either in originals imported from Europe and America, or at least in their Egyptian Arabic imitations. In all classes, the tendency to assimilate to European ways was reinforced by the Arab films, mostly made in Egypt, in which the action usually revolved around heroes and heroines belonging to the high Arab society of Egypt, who dressed, acted, behaved and lived like Europeans.

Of the circa 1,200,000 non-Jewish inhabitants of Palestine in 1947, about 700,000 resided in those parts of the country which were later included within the borders of the Jewish State. The majority of these fled in fear, the causes and circumstances of which have been adequately described more than once by observers. What the exact number of the non-Jews was who remained in Israel during the crucial months of the fight for independence following the establishment of the Jewish State on May 14, 1948, is a matter of guess-work. As soon, however, as the fighting subsided, their number began rapidly to increase through officially authorized re-entry, on the one hand, and infiltration, on the other—an indication of the confidence they felt in the administrative control of the new Jewish State. In November 1948, they numbered some 69,000; a year later, about 170,000; and in November 1951, about 180,000.

It is not yet possible to obtain exact figures of the ethnic and religious compositions of the non-Jewish minorities in Israel today. The Israeli Ministry of Religious Affairs estimated that on January 1, 1949, there were about 14,000 Druzes, 31,000 Christians and 62,000 Moslems in Israel, of the latter about 12,000 having been nomadic bedouin with a traditionally established tribal territory in the Negev. In 1952 there were 120,000 Sunni Moslems, 40,000 Christians, 16,000 Druzes, and 5,000 others in Israel.   *

In the very first year of its existence the Government of Israel began its efforts for the betterment of the social and hygienic conditions among the non-Jewish inhabitants of the country. In the course of one year, medical treatment was organized for the bedouin in the Beer Sheba area, and separate Arab units were established in the Israeli army. In Haifa, courses were opened for social workers (men and women) among the minorities; in Nazareth, classes were set up for Jewish and Arab teachers, with an initial enrollment of 52 Jews teaching Arabic in Jewish schools, and 72 Arabs teaching Hebrew in Arab schools. By the fall of 1949, some 15 Catholic schools in Jerusalem, Jaffa, Ramle, Haifa and Nazareth had introduced Hebrew into their curriculum, some of the teachers being priests and nuns, others Jews. The state has not made the teaching of Hebrew obligatory, so that this was a purely voluntary gesture on the part of the Catholic school authorities in Israel.

With the consolidation of conditions, several Christian churches resumed their regular activities. By the summer of 1949, the following Christian Churches had their official representation in Israel: the Abyssinian Church, the Anglican Church, the Arab Episcopal Church, the Armenian Church (headed by the Archimandrite in Jaffa), the Baptist Congregation, the Church of Scotland, the Coptic Church, the Greek Catholic Church (headed by Archbishop Hakim at Haifa, formerly a sharp opponent of Zionism and the Jews), the Greek Orthodox Church (headed by four Archimandrites in Jaffa, Haifa, Nazareth and Tiberias), the Latin Church, the Lutheran Congregation, the Maronite Church, and the Russian Orthodox Church (with its Archimandrite in Jerusalem).* Several Christian schools, convents, monasteries and hospices were re-opened, as well as Moslem places of worship.

The non-Jewish religious courts were also reactivated. Shari'a courts of the Moslem religious authorities have functioned since 1949 in Acre, Nazareth, Jaffa and Taiyiba. Greek Orthodox religious courts have resumed jurisdiction over their flock in Jaffa, Ramle, Haifa and Nazareth. Greek Catholic (Melkite) religious courts function in Haifa and Nazareth, while the Roman Catholics (Latins) have a religious court in Nazareth.

12. Nazareth in Israel

The life of an Arab town like Nazareth (which, incidentally, is the largest non-Jewish town in Israel with about 20,000 inhabitants of whom some 12,000 are Christians and 8,000 Moslems) displayed in the summer of 1951 a curious blend of the old and the new. In family relationships and to a lesser extent also in the relationship between employers and employes, the old Oriental patriarchal patterns seemed to have retained much of their vigor. On the other hand, the intrusion of modern features was strongly felt. Wages earned by Arab laborers became equalized with those of Jews and a similar adjustment was made with regard to working hours and other conditions. The prices of manufactured goods however, as well as of agricultural products, were regulated by general Israeli ceilings, so that while the income of the wage-earners showed a

* Cf. *Christian News from Israel*, No. 1, August 1949. Edited by the Department for Christian Communities in the Ministry for Religious Affairs, Jerusalem.

considerable rise over that of pre-Israel days, the profits of employers were curtailed, much to their dissatisfaction. In this manner the wide gulf separating the Arab effendi, on the one hand, from the fellah and the day-laborer, on the other, was perceptibly narrowed.

A major part of the Nazareth labor force, who were mainly skilled mechanics, found employment in industrial enterprises in Haifa, which meant that their employers were almost exclusively Jewish. Many of the workers who found jobs in Nazareth itself were also in the employ of Jews, for example, those who worked on public works programs, policemen, teachers, bus-drivers, and the like. This circumstance, namely, that a considerable proportion of the wage-earners worked for the State or for public or private Jewish employers, helped to break down the initial resistance shown by Arab employers to any wage increase. The few die-hards had to give in when their workers resorted to strikes.

Another significant innovation was the successful establishment of cooperatives. During the Mandatory period the British Government attempted several times to induce the Arabs of Palestine to set up agricultural or industrial cooperatives, but its efforts remained largely fruitless.* Under Israeli administration, however, the impact of the Jewish example was more potent, and one of its results can be seen in the successful establishment and maintenance of industrial cooperatives by the Arabs in Nazareth and elsewhere. A co-operative carpentry with twenty members was set up in Nazareth with the help of a £.I. 3,000-loan from the *Histadrut's* Workers' Bank. (The loan has been repaid.) Two cooperatives for the production of burnt lime had 10 members each. Seven Christian Arab women were organized into a shirt and dressmaking cooperative. In addition, a cooperative bank was organized in Nazareth.

In the long run, the change observable in the field of education will prove even more significant. Under the British Mandate regime full elementary education was the privilege of only a few among the Arab children; today, it is an obligation for all, established by law. Every Arab village, whether large or small, has an elementary school; in the larger villages with a full curriculum of eight grades, in the smaller ones with fewer classes but with an annual addition of one successive grade. In the 1948-49 school year there were 73 schools for non-Jews, with 11,129 pupils (of whom 7,417 were in 46 government schools taught by 170 teachers). In 1949-1950 there were 76 such government schools with 350 teachers and 15,600 pupils; in 1950-1951—103 government schools with 708 teachers

* Cf. R. Patai, *On Culture Contact and Its Working in Modern Palestine*, Am. Anthr. Ass., Memoir, No. 67, Oct. 1947, pp. 39-42.

and 27,000 pupils, and 35 non-governmental schools with about 4,500 pupils.* A more rapid expansion of Arab education is hampered by the lack of teachers, which has forced the Ministry of Education to resort to such a stopgap measure as organizing quick courses for their training; and by the lack of buildings. In 1950-51, 75% of all the Arab and Druze children of school-age actually attended school (31,500 out of 42,500), which is a much higher percentage than achieved by any Arab country.

The Government of Israel has recognized the non-Jewish population elements in the country as minority groups, and as such has accorded them the right to use their own languages, to practice their own religions, and to have their own separate schools. In all Arab elementary schools the first foreign language taught is Hebrew (by specially appointed Jewish teachers), and in this manner the foundation is being laid for the future possession of a common language for the Israeli Arabs and the Jews. But these arrangements have not satisfied the minority groups in all cases. Many of them demand, or would prefer if it were technically possible, that their children attend mixed Jewish-Arab schools; they want their children to learn Hebrew much more thoroughly than can be afforded in an all-Arab school with only a few hours weekly devoted to Hebrew; they wish them to speak Hebrew like the Jewish children; to receive a full Israeli education; to be given the same opportunities to learn and advance and to fill positions in the new State.§

An important medium of modernization, the presence of which is increasingly felt in the entire township of Nazareth, is its Government Secondary Boys School, at present the only Arab secondary school in Israel. The foundations for this school were laid by the British Mandatory Government and it has considerably expanded since the State of Israel took it over. In 1950-51, 500 pupils were enrolled in it. All the 15 teachers of the school were Christian Arabs. The headmaster, Mr. Raif Ahmed Zu'bi, was a Moslem Arab, a member of the widely ramified and influential Zu'bi family, which boasts 300 male members in Nazareth, one of whom, Sayf ed-Din Zu'bi, is a member of the Knesset (reelected to the second Knesset on

* The figures for 1948-49 are taken from the *Statistical Bulletin of Israel*, vol. I, No. 4, p. 300; the 1949-50 and 50-51 figures are based on oral information supplied by Mr. Shelomo Anfia, head of the Cultural Division of the Israel Labor League in Haifa (in an interview on August 2, 1951), to whom the author is indebted for much valuable information on the *Histadrut's* work among the Arabs. Cf. also the *Jewish Agency's Digest*, IV, 13, Dec. 28, 1951, p. 432, and *Zionist Newsletter*, IV, 6, Dec. 25, 1951, p. 8.

§ Cf. Itzhak Ben-Zevi, "Problems of the Majority in Israel," in *Davar*, Nov. 25, 1949.

July 30, 1951). The school had seven grades in 1950-51, for pupils from 11 to 17 years of age, thus corresponding to the four upper grades of an elementary school and the first three grades of a four-year secondary school. It was expected, Headmaster Zuʿbi explained, that in 1951-52, with the addition of the last (fourth) secondary grade, the structure of the school would be complete, and its graduates admitted to Israeli matriculation. This would entitle them to continue their studies at the Hebrew University or at the Technical College in Haifa. Also, it was anticipated that in 1951-52 the first crop of graduates from Israel's Arab elementary schools would flock to Nazareth, although those seeking admission were not as numerous as they could be, because many parents wanted their children to learn trades rather than the general secondary-school subjects taught in the Nazareth school. The expanding student body would create new problems. The out-of-town pupils would have to find lodgings for themselves with private families in Nazareth, while the school planned to put up a number of barracks to accommodate their classrooms.

In the days of the British Mandate, the Arab motion-picture houses in Palestine were amply provided with Arab films coming mostly from Egyptian studios. Now, due to the economic blockade and boycott imposed on Israel by the Arab states, the Israeli Arabs are unable to obtain films from Egypt and have to feature English-speaking films (mostly Hollywood products) with added Arab subtitles. These films add their own to the Westernizing processes of the Israeli Arabs.

The assimilation to Western ways is expressed also in the adoption of European clothing. In the more outlying Arab villages one can still see the old traditional Arab robes and headdresses worn by men, and the beautiful embroidered long dresses worn by women. In a town like Nazareth, however, the European jacket or shirt for men and the calico-print dress for women is becoming more prevalent.

The results of the efforts made by the Government in the field of social welfare also have begun to appear. The trainees are Arab social workers (in Haifa and elsewhere), youths and girls of about 17 years of age, coming mostly from families of workers and officials. (Children of wealthy families are not attracted to this vocation.) After finishing their course, the graduates become employees of the Ministry of Social Welfare and are sent to Arab towns and villages to work.

Public health is one of the gravest problems of Middle Eastern society everywhere. Among the Palestinian Arabs a slight beginning was made in public health services by the British Mandatory Government, and these have been rapidly improved and expanded since the establishment of Israel. The Government has set up clinics for the Arabs in the towns and the larger rural centers, and has started the organization of ambulatory clinics for the benefit of the more distant villages. The government hopsitals are, of course, open to Arabs as to Jews for more serious cases.

The Arab workers, in addition, have the benefit of the *Histadrut's* Sick Fund (*Kuppat Holim*). In Nazareth itself more than 1,000 Arab workers are members of the Sick Fund, which has opened a clinic for them staffed with two doctors and a nurse. About 100 cases of TB were found in Nazareth, and those who have to be hospitalized are laid up in the special Tuberculosis Hospital organized by a number of doctors in Nazareth and housed in the building of the former German orphanage belonging to the Schneller Foundation (the so-called "Syrisches Waisenhaus," the main institution of which was in Jerusalem).

The modern institutions established by the Jewish authorities for the Arabs in Israel brought about either directly or indirectly important social changes. The schools, three-fourths of which are coeducational, have made a definite breach in the ancient wall of segregation which confined Moslem women, more stringently in the towns than in the villages. If the parents object to their daughter being sent to a coeducational school, no punitive measure is resorted to, but persuasion and the example of others usually have the desired effect. In Arab society the education of girls has always been greatly neglected. In Israel, as a result of the greater number of female over male children in the Arab population, there are actually more girls than boys in the first two grades of elementary schools. Another unheard-of development has taken place in Israel among the Arabs with regard to women teachers: for the first time in Moslem history, women teachers continue with their work even after marriage.

In connection with the establishment of schools in the Arab villages, educational committees have been appointed by the Ministry of Education. The task of these committees, whose members are chosen from among the more advanced villagers, is to supervise the general functioning of the school by helping the teachers with their problems, and by overcoming the reluctance of recalcitrant parents so that one hundred percent attendance is achieved.

As far as the general affairs of the villages are concerned, for the time being these are in most cases conducted, as they were in Mandatory days, by a *mukhtar* (village headman). Appointment to the office used to be an elastic combination of Government choice, election by popular approval if not actual vote, and hereditary family privilege. By 1951, however, good beginnings were being made by the government in setting up local councils in each village to conduct affairs more democratically. The initial reaction to this innovation was usually objection on economic grounds. The villagers fear that the functioning of a local council will mean the introduction of taxation for local purposes and needs; and while they can easily imagine what tax-paying means, they cannot, as a rule, visualize the public benefits which would ultimately accrue to them. A few villages, however, have shown surprising civic maturity in readily accepting the innovation and in going ahead with it enthusiastically. These local councils will undoubtedly prove an important factor in the development of the Arab villages from the economic (agricultural) and social viewpoints.

Similarly, a wide variety of responses is shown by the Arabs to yet another great tenet of democracy, which they have encountered for the first time under Israeli rule. In the days of the British Mandatory regime, as a consequence of the unbroken continuation of semi-medieval feudalism, the Arabs of Palestine remained in what amounted to political serfdom. Entire villages, or *hamulas*, owed political allegiance to one or the other of the "great" families, based in most cases on economic dependence, and the question of an independent formulation of political opinion could not arise. When the British set forth rules in the Municipal Corporations Ordinance, stating that municipal councils would have to be elected once in so many years (generally every 5 years), or when the Arab leaders felt that, in order to strengthen their positions vis-a-vis the British Mandatory power, they would do well to transform the old family alliances into formally constituted political parties with votes, elections and statutes—the economic, familial or social dependencies of the "great" families voted *en bloc*, according to instructions received, for candidates of their own patron-family. Accordingly, the force of habit was so strong that even at the second Knesset elections in Israel in 1951, several Arab villages as a whole asked through their spokesmen from the nearest Jewish authoritative source—in many cases the police officer—for instructions as to which party to support with their votes.

Now, in Israel, the Arabs, used to tight political reins, suddenly find themselves faced with the great democratic principle of freedom of opinion, speech and expression. Concretely, they find that they are allowed to speak up against the Government, to express dissatisfaction freely, and to demand what they believe is their due.

Those who can read and write find in Arab periodical publications or pamphlets that these criticisms and demands can be put down in writing and freely circulated. Inevitably, some confusion ensues. Unprepared as they are for this sudden change in the order of things, some of the Arabs can not help seeing in this freedom a sign of weakness on the part of the Government of Israel. What strong Government would tolerate such a state of affairs, they reason. Israel must be weak, must be afraid of the Arabs, not to try to suppress such open manifestation of opposition. Some of the writers, misinterpreting their newly-won democratic freedom of expression, actually confuse opposition to the Government with hatred of the State itself, and their articles at times come dangerously near disloyalty and treason.

The majority of the Arabs, however, are undoubtedly beginning to appreciate what the democratic principle of freedom of expression actually means. They begin truly to utilize the right to speak up, to criticize, to complain and demand; to explore the right to organize, to seek out or change party affiliation; to enjoy the right to be treated as equals by the Jews, and even more so by the Arab effendis.

Some of the Arabs made use of these rights to support the communist party in Israel, which polled 3.9% of the votes at the elections to the second Knesset on July 30, 1951. In Nazareth, however, which is the biggest Arab urban center and whence presumably a major part of the Arab communist votes came, the communist party as a whole was not taken seriously. The communist vote, it was generally held, came from people who for one reason or another were dissatisfied with the Government of Israel, or with the major political parties, and who in protest voted for the communists. Confirmed communists, who·understood communistic ideas and ideals, were extremely few; in the whole of Nazareth they were believed to number not more than half a dozen individuals. All the rest just tagged along. Even some "capitalists" and employers who nursed private grievances sought the remedy for them in the communist party. An energetic campaign of explanation and enlightenment could, without too much difficulty, reduce the communist party to a fragment of its present numerical strength and secure the rest for the Mapai. As it was, the Israel Labor League, which is an organization for Arab workers set up by and affiliated with the *Histadrut*, the General Federation of Jewish Labor in Israel,* had about 1,300

* In the whole of Israel, the Israel Labor League numbered in 1951 circa 12,000 Arab members in 35 local chapters, making it by far the largest Arab labor organization.

members in 1951 in Nazareth, and another 1,500 members organized in 8 branches in the Arab villages of the neighborhood. Each branch of the League elects its leadership and representation, so that the functioning of the League itself is a day-to-day demonstration of democracy in action. The Congress of Laborers, affiliated with the left-wing Mapam party, had about 800 members in Nazareth, while a third labor union with about 400 members, mostly Catholic (Latin) Arabs, recently agreed to join the Israel Labor League. One tangible result of the activities of all these Labor unions was the trebling of the wages earned by Arab laborers since the days of the Mandate.

13. Integration

With regard to material benefits, economic level, social, educational and health conditions, the Arabs of Israel have thus experienced a vast improvement, of which they are certainly fully conscious. The improvements are most markedly felt by the laboring classes, whose general standard of living has risen high above anything known to them under the British Mandatory regime and still higher when compared with conditions in the neighboring Arab countries. Most of the members of the small effendi-class of landowners, contractors, planters, owners of factories and business enterprises have found their place within the new economic structure of Israel. They derive their full share of the general prosperity which characterizes the business and industrial sector in Israel. If they feel the pressure of controlled prices and high wages, the shortage of raw materials, the limited amount of imports, the pinch of high taxes, they know that all this has to be borne equally by Arabs and Jews in the country. The very thin stratum of intellectuals and academicians, such as doctors, lawyers, teachers, journalists, as well as office workers, is undoubtedly facing a steadily improving situation, and many of them experience great new stimuli in working in close collaboration with Jews, or in the employment of the State or other Jewish institutions. In fact, the only open and concrete complaint that could be heard among the Arabs of Israel in 1951 was directed against the restrictions imposed upon the return to Israel of those Arabs whose families had stayed behind in Israel during the Arab-Jewish war and with whom their families would have liked to be re-united.

Factors making for dissatisfaction with the changed situation, even if not discussed overtly, have also to be taken into consideration. Whether they admit it or not, the Arabs, and especially the Moslem Arabs who constitute the largest minority in Israel, feel that their political status has seriously deteriorated. The Moslem Arabs who remained in Israel had been, prior to the war, an integral part of a great Palestinian Moslem Arab body politic embracing more than a million people, which developed organically in the course of many centuries and which was the only political organization they ever knew. Under the impact of the Israeli-Arab war, this political organization disappeared and its political institutions disintegrated, so that the Arabs remaining in Israel found themselves, not only shrunk to one-tenth of their numerical strength, but also completely without institutions, organization and leadership. While actually the Arabs of Palestine enjoyed very little self-determination in Mandatory days due to the feudal organization of their society, they at least retained the illusion of it. Now, in Israel, in spite of the objective increase in self-determination, there is a feeling of dependence on the non-Arab majority.

It is within this frame of reference that the sources of Arab political dissatisfaction in Israel must be viewed. Herein lies the fundamental reason for the doubts felt in Israel in the face of Arab declarations of Israeli patriotism and demands for complete freedom of movement and civic equality. Already in the very first months of Israel's independence, when the country was still at war with the invading Arab armies, and when the remaining local Arabs were placed in virtual isolation by a strictly enforced curfew, their representatives and spokesmen asked for the lifting of these restrictions, arguing that the Arabs were as reliable as the Jews as citizens of the State of Israel. Those Arabs, they said, who opposed the Jewish State, had fled the country and had placed themselves under the protection of the enemy; but those who chose to stay behind showed by this very act where their true sympathies lay, and therefore ought to be accepted by the State as full and equal citizens. Several minority groups, and especially those who had been minorities also in the days of the Mandate, such as the Druzes and Circassians, followed words with action and joined the fighting forces of Israel. Some of the contingents formed by the minorities actually participated in the fighting.

The majority of the Israeli Moslem Arabs, however, chose not to become involved in the Arab-Jewish fights. On the Jewish side there was never any pressure exercised on them to take up arms against their own brethren; and they themselves tried hard to escape the demands of the Arab armies and guerillas for active help or financial support. Many of the moderately-minded Arabs, who during the fighting remained in what is today Israeli territory, were repeatedly threatened from the Arab side. Quite a number of them, especially those of some prominence or wealth, had to go into hiding. A typical example is that of an Arab contractor and tobacco grower in Nazareth, who in the days of the Mandate used to have excellent business connections with the Jews and was therefore known as a person friendly to the Jews.* During the months of the war this man disappeared so completely that not even his relatives knew where he was, or whether he was alive or dead. Soon after the cessation of the hostilities, he re-emerged from underground and quickly resumed and even expanded his business, going into partnership with the Solel Boneh, the giant contracting corporation of the *Histadrut*. (He boasted jokingly that his partnership with the Solel Boneh is the only one in the whole country in which he, the private partner, owned more than half the shares, and the *Histadrut* contractor less than the half, whereas in every other partnership the Solel Boneh had at least 51%.) At the same time he established business connections also with a number of private Jewish ("General Zionists," as he said) manufacturers. In reply to a question as to the stand the Arabs would take in case of the renewal of hostilities, he summarized concisely the point of view officially adopted by the great majority of the Israeli Arabs by quoting an old Arab proverb: "The believer will not be bitten twice by a snake from the same hole." "We have been bitten hard," he added by way of explanation, "by the snake of the war. We will not be bitten by the same snake again. If the Arabs of the neighboring countries should attack Israel, we certainly will not help them. But in all frankness I must tell you that neither will we take up arms against other Arabs."

In the first few months after the war, the Jews took statements such as these with a grain of salt. There was much scepticism and suspicion towards every non-Jew in the country. The distrust was directed first of all against the Moslem Arabs. The Christian Arabs were regarded similarly because it was known that large numbers of them had identified themselves with the Moslems and had taken active and often leading roles in the anti-Jewish movement. Inevitably the members of the Jewish army, who were the only people having direct contact and experience with the Arab enemy during the months of the war, felt suspicious of everyone. Curfew regulations were imposed, to restrict the movements of the Arabs in the country until such time as identity cards could be issued to them, and were strictly enforced; borders were closely watched and guarded, and the Arab villages carefully searched. However, when military operations ceased, freedom of movement was restored to the citizenry and to all residents of Israel, Arab and Jew alike.

* As told to the author in August 1951.

Nevertheless, the law of general military service which applies to every Jewish citizen or immigrant, has not been extended to members of the non-Jewish minorities.

One of the problems which continued to trouble the Government of Israel was that of the infiltration of Arabs through its disproportionately long frontiers. The only effective measure which could be taken against this was the evacuation of Arab villages on the frontier, the transfer of the inhabitants to other villages farther inland, and their replacement with Jewish settlers. This was done several times and often evoked the spirited protests of the Arab evacuees or their spokesmen. When the Maronite Christian Arab village of Bir'im, on the Lebanese border, was evacuated and its fellahin transferred to Gush Halav, at a distance of less than three miles, the protests voiced found sympathetic ears among Jews who had some influence on public opinion in Israel. Since the fall of 1949 a special Israeli frontier force guards the borders of the Jewish State.

In principle, the minority groups in Mandatory Palestine could have followed either of three possible lines of political attitude with respect to the struggle between the Jews and the Arabs: they could have remained neutral, in the sense of not identifying themselves with either the Jewish or the Arab side; or they could have made common cause with the Jews on the basis of the mutual interests of different minorities vis-a-vis an intolerant and aggressive majority. They chose neither of these two alternatives. They unhesitatingly embraced the third course, that of siding with the Moslem Arab majority and turning fiercely against the Jews.

This attitude was taken by the Palestinian minorities not after a conscious and thoughtful evaluation of the pros and cons of each of the three courses mentioned, but following the precedent of many centuries of experience which had taught them that a religious minority in Palestine (or in the entire Middle East for that matter) has but one chance of securing its survival, and that is by ingratiating itself with the ruling majority. The ruling majority did not always actually hold the political reins of the country, but might be powerful through the sheer weight of its numbers. In Palestine the Moslem Arab community constituted such a majority. Consequently, the minorities felt that only one road lay open to them, that of the closest and most complete cooperation with the Moslem Arab majority in all those political and communal affairs in which they were embroiled. Thus it came about that, in spite of centuries of mutual hatred and continued smoldering enmity, which was never wholly allowed to emerge to the surface, the Christian Arabs linked their destiny with the Moslems in complete solidarity and identification in opposition to the Jews.

With the establishment of the State of Israel, the situation for most of the minorities in Israel underwent a most unexpected and radical change. In place of the Moslem Arabs, it was now the Jews who were the ruling majority in the new country, ruling this time in the fullest sense of the word. Now the same old historical experience, which had dictated the behavior patterns of the minorities in Palestine in the strife between the Jews and the Arabs, clearly pointed the way also in the new situation: the majority group must be ingratiated. If the ruling majority has changed overnight, this required a certain readjustment which in itself was possibly unpleasant, but a readjustment which could be made, and in fact was made, in conformity with the age-old and oft-proven principle. Apart from the fact that for many centuries in Palestine the Christian Arabs had been used to the minority status which they continued to maintain in Israel, their situation in the new State was easier than that of the Moslems on account of yet another circumstance: they retained at least their religious organization, that is, their churches and their religious leadership in the persons of their bishops, patriarchs and clergy.

As to the Moslem Arabs, although immediately after the conclusion of the Arab-Jewish war they emerged as a disorganized and leaderless community, reduced from a majority to a minority position, they too soon found that it was to their well-conceived advantage to cooperate with the new Jewish State. Today, the Moslem Arabs as well as the other non-Jewish minorities are firmly tied to Israel by overwhelming economic interests; they own property; they make an adequate living, and, incidentally, earn a considerably higher income than people of the same status in any Arab country; and having lived first for many years in the neighborhood of Jews, and recently for a couple of years under Jewish rule, they have seen that, as far as security of life and property is concerned, there is no reason for complaint. They have remained unrestricted in their freedom of religion and also have recently begun to enjoy certain benefits in the fields of sanitation, medical care, social welfare and education; they have received, in addition, the right of representation exercised through universal suffrage and direct and proportionate elections— all marked improvements over their position under the British Mandatory rule and above the status enjoyed by the people in Arab states. All these factors suffice to develop in the non-Jewish minority groups in Israel a consciousness of common interests between them and the State of Israel. And a consciousness of common interests is one of the main component elements in the common factor which determines the quality of the processes of culture contact and change.

At the same time, there is present a feeling of uncertainty among the non-Jewish minorities. They feel that they have to demonstrate their identification with the State of Israel in order to strengthen their positions. They must show that they are both able and willing to go wholeheartedly along the path chosen by the country, different though it be from their old accustomed ways of life. As a member of the Arab intelligentsia in Israel put it in a private conversation, "The Arabs will be even more patriotic than the Jews themselves; firstly, because every minority always endeavors to prove in a most demonstrative manner its self-identification with the aspirations of the majority; and secondly, because the Arabs in Israel will enjoy better conditions than those in the Arab countries and will thus have a justified cause to love their fatherland."*

In order to asseverate their loyalty to Israel, the non-Jewish minorities show themselves amenable to changes injected into their lives by the State of Israel. The law raising the minimum age of marriage for girls to 17, opposed bitterly though unsuccessfully by Sephardi and Oriental Jewish representatives in the *Knesset*, was welcomed in public statements by the Arabs in Israel, although it made unlawful marriage practices as prevalent among them as among the Sephardi and Oriental Jews. While the Yemenite Jews fought for separate educational facilities for their children in order to preserve their specific community-traditions, the Arabs in Israel announced their wish to have their children educated together with Jewish children and taught to speak Hebrew like any Jewish child. These examples, which could be multiplied, show, not that the non-Jewish minorities in Israel are less tradition-bound than the Sephardi and Oriental Jews, but that they are more willing to abandon their traditional ways for the definite advantages they see in rapid assimilation to the mores of modern Israeli society. The basic feeling of uncertainty, therefore, is turned into yet another positive factor making for rapprochement between the non-Jewish minorities and the modern Israeli socio-cultural scene. Together with the consciousness of common interests, it becomes a constituent element in the common factor facilitating the processes of culture change.

A third factor which enables the non-Jewish minorities to adjust in a relatively frictionless manner to the new cultural demands put to them by the new situation in which they find themselves in Israel is their undisturbed continuity of residence. The majority of the non-

* Cf. *Hapoel Hatzair* (Hebrew weekly), Tel Aviv, Sept. 20, 1949.

Jewish population groups in Israel have remained where they had lived before the establishment of the Jewish State. Where the population fled, as from the towns of Jaffa and Haifa, the situation, of course, underwent decisive changes. But even here, the few Arab residents who chose to stay remained largely in the same quarters, streets and houses which they had inhabited previously. As far as the villages are concerned, those which were not abandoned remained in much the same condition in which they were before the outbreak of the hostilities, with the exception of a few in border areas which had to be evacuated as a precaution against infiltration. The significance of the continuity of residence for socio-cultural continuity can hardly be overestimated, especially in the case of conservative, tradition-bound Oriental peoples. As long as a Middle Eastern village population remains working the soil on which it was reared, it will continue to live in much the same manner as did its forefathers, whatever changes occur outside the village and whoever happens to be the overlord to whom it pays its taxes. Against this socio-cultural and local continuity the changes introduced into the lives of the people, unless too drastic, sudden and incisive, are like pebbles thrown into the smooth waters of a pond: they sink easily into the depths and the ripples they caused subside quickly.

A fourth and last factor working both for and against cultural fusion must also be taken into consideration. This is religion, the great separating force among Middle Eastern peoples. Due to the fact that the non-Jewish minorities differ from the Jews in religious persuasion there can never be the complete amalgamation in Israel between them in the sense that might be expected to happen ultimately between the Ashkenazi and the Sephardi-Oriental divisions of the Jewish population. In the traditional structure of Middle Eastern culture, difference in religion is sufficient to make for a complete separation between population groups. Religion being an all-pervasive force which extends its influence into all phases and spheres of life, it is the chief socio-cultural determinant.* The continued adherence of each group to its own religion is taken for granted by both the State of Israel and the members of the minority groups themselves. On the other hand, this circumstance makes it considerably easier for the non-Jewish minorities to adopt new cultural traits or institutions introduced by the State of Israel. Since its focal concern, religion, remains intact, the group feels that its social continuity is not being infringed upon by new cultural traits or institutions. Their adoption appears advantageous and at the same time merely of secondary significance. What the minority groups do not

* Cf. above, pp. 39 ff.

foresee, because as yet they have never experienced such processes of cultural change, is that the adoption of Western cultural elements in the economic, social and technological fields will very likely bring about a change in their attitude towards religion; or more correctly, will gradually remove the major phases of life from the influence of religion, until finally religion will find itself confined to those narrowly delimited spheres which it was able to retain in modern Western civilization.

Unaware of this probable outcome, the non-Jewish minorities in Israel have embarked wholeheartedly upon what they feel to be a partial assimilation to the dominant population group. They feel that this is a feasible and even logical solution to the problem of preserving as much as possible of their identity as a separate minority-group, and at the same time achieving identification of the group with the dominant population of the country. It is their endeavor to retain their separate character and status as a religious group and to assimilate to Jewish Israel in all other respects.

In the light of the history of the minorities in Palestine and in the Middle East as a whole, it would seem that in general their desire to become full and equal members of the new Jewish State, and their assertions to the effect that they already are true and faithful Israelis, are sincere and genuine. The religious fatalism—which in the Middle East is by no means confined to the Moslems—works in the direction of a complete and unquestioning acceptance of any major *fait accompli*. However, a far-reaching, positive and constructive policy will have to be worked out and put into effect in order to create a relationship between the minorities and the Jewish majority which will enable the former to find, not only material compensations for their lack of political self-determination, but also spiritual and intellectual ones. In other words, they must be made partners not only on the material level, in the higher standard of living which sets off Israel from the Arab countries. They must partake also in the esthetic-intellectual fields of cultural development peculiar to the Jewish State.

A step in this direction is represented by the educational effort which involves the opening of schools in every Arab village and the teaching of Hebrew. The acquisition of Hebrew as a second medium of communication in itself will enable the members of the minority groups to participate more fully in the economic, political, social and cultural life of Israel. The proximity of the Jews as well as legislation will produce their inevitable effect on the position of the women, especially among the Moslem Arabs. The technical facilities which will be increasingly put at the disposal of the villages inhabited by minorities—in the same measure as they serve the Jewish villages—will within a relatively short period bring about basic changes in the modus vivendi of the Israeli fellahin, who will become more and more like the Israeli farmers and less and less like the fellahin of neighboring countries. Changes of similar magnitude will occur in the non-Jewish town-population. The sooner the Israeli minorities advance on this road to modernization and Westernization, the less the likelihood that they will prefer to return to live under Arab rule. As an Arab leader expressed it in Nazareth in the summer of 1951: "If a plebiscite were held in Israel among the Arabs, most of them would express their wish to stay in Israel. We have already gotten used to a democratic way of life. If a liberal Arab went from Israel to any Arab country, he would think it his right to speak up and to oppose things which are wrong, and he would find himself in jail. In the past, our fears were closed in in our hearts, now we can freely express our thoughts."

Among the young town-Arabs the trend towards assimilation to the Jews is especially pronounced even today. They work together with Jews, or at least earn wages equal to those of the Jews, and they wish to spend their money as the Jews do. They want to dress like the Jews, to go to the movies, to sit in the cafes, to take part in the social and political life, and even to read books like the Jews. It is a safe prediction that in the near future we shall witness a rapid assimilatory process of urban Arabs to the general, Western culture of Israel.

The State of Israel is thus heading for a long-time partnership with sizable minority groups in its midst, all of whom have one basic thing in common: they all are Oriental peoples saturated with the traditional culture of the Middle East, of which also the Oriental Jews are heirs. Numerically, the two together have already become the majority in Israel; culturally, their presence has precipitated a crisis in the country. The problem of integrating the non-Jewish minorities, on the one hand, and the Oriental Jews, on the other, into the structure and dynamics of the modern state that Israel is today, are at once similar and different; similar—because in the case of both the main task is to graft upon the common Middle Eastern cultural stock the shoots brought along from the West; and different—because the non-Jewish minorities are separated from the rest of Israel, while the Oriental Jews are tied to it, by the powerful bonds of religion. In both cases the tasks ahead are of such magnitude and intricacy that only a considerable easing up of pressure on the political and economic fronts holds out any hope for their successful fulfillment.

Chapter Nine
The Religious Issue

For a full comprehension of the basic problems underlying the religious issue in Israel, reference must be made once more to the fundamental differences between the role of religion in Eastern and Western culture.* For just as in other aspects of culture, so also in the sphere of religion the behavior of the Jewish groups in the lands of the Diaspora closely approximated that of their non-Jewish neighbors. The general attitude towards religion differs greatly in the East and in the West, and differences of about the same magnitude are evinced also among the Jews hailing from these two worlds and meeting in Israel.

1. Jewish Religious Attitudes in the Middle East

In the lands of the Middle East the Jews were in many respects a close replica of the Moslem majority. In physical type they approximated the Moslems; they were natives to the countries for as long a time as the Moslems, and in several cases even preceded them; they spoke the same language, either exclusively or as a second medium in addition to their own tongue; their standard of living was the same, unless forcibly kept low by prohibitory regulations imposed upon them; their clothing, too, differed from that of the Moslems only to the degree to which they were forced by them to abstain from wearing the same garb, or, to a lesser extent, as a result of their own religious traditions. Occupational structure was very similar, the differences again being caused mainly by restrictions imposed upon them from the outside. Outlook on life, philosophy and basic attitudes, too, would have been almost identical were it not for the fact that an oppressed minority can in this respect never exactly duplicate the oppressing majority.

In addition to all this, even the attitude towards religion was

* Cf. pp. 39 ff.

largely the same among Jews and Moslems—religion playing in both groups the same comprehensive role, having the same manifold functions, and occupying the same central, focal and ruling position. Only in concrete content of religious doctrine, tradition and ritual did Moslem and Jew differ. But this difference was decisive enough to keep the two groups completely apart, to make intermarriage between them unthinkable, to cause them mutually to distrust and despise each other, and to induce the Moslem majority to oppress and occasionally actively to persecute the Jewish minority. Thus, it was more than once forcefully driven home to the Jews that their status of minority hinged solely upon the one circumstance that their religion was different from that of the majority. But religion being the force it was in Middle Eastern culture, the adherence to a different religion meant total separation. The Jews of the Middle East have been, ever since the days of Ahasuerus and Esther, "a people scattered yet separate among the nations . . . their religious laws differing from those of every people . . ." (Esth. 3, 8)

In the eyes of the Moslems they were stubborn unbelievers who refused to accept the True Faith. Those who did accept, under the threat of death or expulsion, or who became renegades on their own account, were received with open arms. With the removal of the religious barrier they soon became a part of the Moslem majority.

What the Oriental Jews therefore expected to experience in Israel was total integration and complete fusion with the other Jewish inhabitants of the country and, at the same time, the possibility of retaining as much as they wished of their own traditions. The only effective barrier between population groups known to them—the religious barrier—would not exist in Israel. They would all be Jews there, all brethren in one faith, and would, therefore, in the words of the traditional prayer, "all constitute one community." Most of them knew, of course, that there they would meet Jews differing from them in language and custom, but they believed and expected these differences to be of subordinate importance in relation to the great cementing and unifying power of the same religion.

They soon found, however, that the dominant Ashkenazi element which confronted them in Israel was strange to them not only with regard to most aspects of material culture, but also in its negative or indifferent attitude towards religion. This was a most baffling situation, for irreligious Jews were about as alien to them as religious Moslems had been. Religion thus again set apart the Oriental Jews in Israel just as it did in the countries of their origin.

It was to be expected that in this situation a wholesale transference of ingroup-outgroup stereotypes would occur in the attitude of the

Oriental Jews towards their new social environment in Israel. And this is what actually happened. The old feeling of hidden superiority in the face of a manifestly more powerful and more prosperous group, which kept them apart and aloof in all countries of the Middle East, re-emerged in Israel and had the same effect of erecting a barrier between them and the Ashkenazi Jews. But while in the countries of the Middle East this attitude of the Jews towards the Moslems had a definite survival value, in Israel its manifestation towards other Jews was harmful, and even dangerous, because it created a rift between two sections of the young nation which desperately needed harmony, understanding and inner peace.

2. Western Jewish Religion

In the Western world, especially since the Emancipation, the development of Jewish religiosity took a very different form. The cultural imperative of assimilation made for a progressive restriction of religious life, until the hold of religion became considerably loosened. Christianity, the ruling religion in the West, has become relegated to a corner of existence and detached from the central interests and pursuits in life. The same process was manifest also among an increasing majority of Western (Ashkenazi) Jews.

If Ashkenazi Jews already in their European home-countries were caught in the general drift away from religion, this trend became even more pronounced among those who immigrated into Palestine-Israel. Many of those who were not extremely orthodox and most firmly rooted in their religion became, soon after their immigration, religiously indifferent. Among the early pioneers, there was a consciously fostered reaction against the atmosphere of the parental home, and this included a complete break with religion. In the case of the later immigrants, the mere fact that immigration suddenly cut them off from contact with the home community, resulted in a feeling that they now could live a freer, less restrained life as far as religious observance was concerned the burden of which they felt they had originally carried only for the sake of their parents. The terrible experiences of the Nazi charnel-house added their share to the obliteration of religious feelings and forms. Finally, many found, upon taking root in the ancient land of the Bible, that the religious minutiae developed in the Diaspora could be discarded in Israel. However, they soon also found themselves in the position of having tossed out the baby with the bath.

The religious indifference of the great majority of the Ashkenazi Jews in Israel accounts for two otherwise puzzling phenomena in the socio-cultural life of the country. Firstly, it explains the absence of synagogues and congregations other than orthodox. Western Jews, and especially Americans, have become used to the existence of a considerable proportion—if not the majority—of their ranks organized into non-orthodox congregations; conservative, liberal, or reform synagogues. Almost nothing of all this exists in Israel. All the synagogues and all the rabbis, with one or two exceptions, are orthodox. The entire rabbinical organization of the country, with its rabbinical courts, offices, burial societies, is strictly and exclusively orthodox. Only the indifference evidenced by the great majority of Ashkenazi Jews in every religious matter can account for this situation. Most of them do not feel the need, as they did in Europe or America, for religious forms adjusted to the requirements of a modern society. They feel that their Jewishness can and is fully expressed in their daily life, in their being Jews in Israel as the French are French in France.

The same religious indifference accounts for the seemingly paradoxical fact that, the numerical weakness of the religious element notwithstanding, its influence on the political life and in the administrative fields is yet so considerable. Were there in the country a liberal religious element ready to fight for liberal religious principles and practices, it could unquestionably counteract the influence of the orthodox religious groups. But such an element does not ✳ exist. In every public body, from the government and the parliament down to the smallest local and temporary committee, one finds the line of demarcation drawn between a religiously indifferent majority and a minority group of orthodox religious spokesmen. But this minority is militant, demanding and vociferous, ready to fight to the bitter end when it comes to carrying a motion or drafting a law which has religious significance. The non-religious majority, on the other hand, is indifferent, neutral, almost apathetic in religious matters and is therefore inclined to let the religious few have their will, unless some weighty consideration enters into the picture. Thus it has come about that in many cases the religious party or the religious viewpoint has won the day, so that the casual observer gains the impression that a kind of ecclesiastical rule is developing in Israel, while in reality such a possibility is quite remote.

3. Orthodoxy in Israel

One would expect cultural affinity alone to be sufficient to knit together the religious and non-religious elements in the Ashkenazi division of Israel. But so powerful is the religious fervor of the orthodox Ashkenazi Jews that they feel a closer kinship with the religious Sephardi and Oriental Jews in spite of the great cultural gulf separating them. Thus the Sephardi and Oriental Jews found unexpected allies and champions of their cause in the politically more articulate religious Ashkenazi Jews and the political parties formed by them.

While for the average non-religious Ashkenazi Jew religion is a minor or negligible factor, for the orthodox Ashkenazi Jews Judaism has remained the same total way of life it is for the majority of the Oriental Jews. To them the Law (the Torah) is as all-pervasive, all-embracing, and all-permeating as to the most tradition-bound Middle Eastern people. This attitude was forcibly illustrated by the statements of the orthodox Minister of Social Welfare, Rabbi Itzhak Meir Levin, made in opposition to the proposed Israel constitution:

> "Our Torah is a Torah of life which directs and regulates the life of the individual from the day of his birth to his last day. It (the Torah) is not confined to the field of thought; it penetrates into all fields of life . . . It also fixes the way for regulating the relations between man and man, between individual and society, between one people and another . . . The *Shulhan Arukh* contains the array of laws which regulate all fields of life . . . It is the endeavor of religious Jewry that only the laws of the Torah should be the determinants in all fields of the State's life . . ."*

The religious Ashkenazi minority which constitutes the modern Israeli version of the *Ecclesia Militans*, found the way early in the history of the Jewish settlement of Palestine to turn religion into a political weapon, and, after the establishment of the State, to make religion a pivotal issue on the Israeli political scene. Within the religious sector itself, however, minute variations in religious observance, together with differences in social outlook, served as a fragmentizing force and gave rise to several distinct religio-political formations, all of which would appear to a liberal Western observer as extremely orthodox. They are, in ascending order of religious orthodoxy: The *Hashomer Hadati* (Religious Watchman), a quasi-Marxian offshoot of the Mizrahi party; the *Hapoel Hamizrahi* (Mizrahi Worker), a left-wing party of religious socialists which grew out of the Mizrahi party and is today much stronger than its parent body; the *Mizrahi Party*, the orthodox wing of the Zionist movement, organized in Wilna in 1902; the *Poale Agudat Yisrael* (Workers of Israel's Union), a labor organization of the *Agudat Yisrael* party which in itself is the party of the extremely orthodox who for a long

---

* Speech in the Knesset on Adar 3, 5710. On September 23, 1952, Rabbi Levin resigned his cabinet post because of his disagreement with the government on the recruitment of girls into the army.

time have opposed Zionism as a heretical movement and joined forces with it only in 1947 in connection with the United Nations' deliberations on the future of Palestine; and finally the *Neture Qarta* (Guardians of the City), a small and fanatical group in Jerusalem, members of which are recruited exclusively from the ranks of the Old *Yishuv*, and which to this very day opposes Zionism, has not been reconciled to the existence of the Jewish State and holds itself aloof from the civic life of the country.

Prior to the elections for the first Knesset (parliament) of Israel, all these parties, with the exception of the *Neture Qarta*, joined forces and formed the United Religious Front. In the elections which took place on January 25, 1949, the United Religious Front obtained 16 out of 120 seats in the Knesset.

On the eve of the elections to the second Knesset, which took place on July 30, 1951, the United Religious Front broke up and each of the four main constituent parties ran independently. The sum total was a slight percentual decrease in the valid votes obtained: 12.5% as compared with 13.8% thirty months previously. Consequently, the religious parties lost one seat and their voting strength was fragmentized. The 15 remaining seats were divided as follows: 8 to the Hapoel Hamizrahi, 3 to the Agudat Yisrael, and 2 each to the Poale Agudat Yisrael and the Mizrahi Party.

The 12-13% vote for the religious parties in two parliamentary elections thirty months apart is significant as an indication of the permanent relative strength of the religious element in Israel. The expectation of the religious parties of being able to attract a high proportion of the religious Oriental Jewish immigrants did not materialize—the influence of the Mapai party in the immigrants' reception camps and in the transit and work villages proved too strong. But they succeeded in holding their own in face of a quasi-messianic appeal which Ben-Gurion's figure evoked in the immigrants camps, and they continue to look forward to a fusion of all religious elements in the country under the spiritual guidance of the rabbinate and the political leadership of the Ashkenazi political parties. 　*

4. Political Religion

Having coalesced into political formations long before the establishment of the State, the religious wing has taken an active part in all the governments since the birth of Israel. Moreover, repeated political exigencies made the religious parties the major partners helping Mapai to form coalition governments three times in the course of three years. Once inside the government, the religious parties fought for issues dear to them in much the same manner as the other parties, which at one time or other formed parts of the coalition (notably the Progressive Party and the Sephardim). When wishing to press a point, they quoted the Bible and the Talmud just as the Mapam quoted Marx, or the Communists Lenin—and, in general, with as much effect.

There are some basic agreements among the major parties represented in the Knesset concerning vital political issues. In addition to these, however, each party has one favorite plank in its platform which is exclusively its own. In the case of the religious parties this additional plank is their insistence on religion as the foundation of the State and its institutions.

Up to the Emancipation and the Enlightenment, Jewish religion was of the all-pervasive Oriental type in the Ashkenazi world as well as among the Oriental Jews. Consequently, much of what by modern non-religious Jews is held to constitute the cultural, historical and national heritage of the Jewish people was originally a part of religion and is to this day regarded as such by the orthodox. Certain minimal demands of the religious groups are thus automatically satisfied without making the non-religious majority feel that it allows the orthodox to dominate its life. The Sabbath, the major Jewish holidays, the Jewish calendar, the study of the Bible, circumcision, and the like—all these are, for the religious, basic precepts of Judaism, while for the secularly minded they are integral parts of the Jewish cultural-historical tradition without which the new national life in Israel would be colorless and poor in content. In this sense, the religious issue in Israel is, therefore, not a question of mutually exclusive alternatives, but of how much of this Jewish spiritual heritage to infuse into the developing cultural climate of the country.

Interference with the private lives of individuals is inevitable in a complex modern society in which it is often difficult to strike a satisfactory balance between the exercise of personal freedom and the limitations imposed by membership in an organized community. In the democratic world it is a basic tenet that the individual must surrender much of his personal freedom to the will of the majority. In thoroughly democratic Israel the majority of the voters gave the mandate to the government to impose on the population numerous stringent measures demanding heavy sacrifices of individual freedom. The very heavy taxation; the tightest rationing of food, clothing and other consumer's goods a country ever had in peace time; a strict control of wages, prices and profits; thirty months of general compulsory military service; severe restriction of foreign travel and imports; the prohibition of the possession of foreign exchange—

these are a few of the more serious limitations the citizenship empowered its elected representatives to introduce.

At the same time, the politically mature population accords full right to every group to fight for its convictions. There is an extreme tolerance of attempts to obtain majority backing, as long as legal and democratic procedures are employed. Within the framework of a multi-party system this means the necessity of concluding political *quid pro quo* deals in both the legislative and the executive arms of the government as well as on lower levels.

In such a political setup the relatively more frequent successes of the religious parties in carrying their points become understandable. Issues such as socialism versus private enterprise evoke bitter parliamentary struggles, for each party has firm convictions about them. The results of such clashes give, therefore, a true picture of the relative strength of the parties involved. When, however, it comes to religious issues, only the religious parties feel strongly on the subject, while the non-religious parties are in most instances too indifferent to put up any opposition. Only when the matter on the floor has serious social implications, do the non-religious make use of their majority position to override the religious point of view. The Marriage Law (1950) and the Women's Equal Rights Bill (1951) were the first major breaches in the wall of religious jurisdiction, replacing outmoded traditional approaches by modern legal principles. These will undoubtedly be followed by further legislative measures which will ultimately remove all affairs of personal status from the realm of religious jurisdiction. For the time being, concessions are being made to the religious demands on such issues as kosher meat imports, a ritual commissariat for all the enlisted men and women, and special emphasis on the Sabbath rest, since in these, it is felt, only religious principles are involved without any serious social or political implication.

It is further characteristic of the position of the protagonists of religion that they have never as yet attempted to have traditional Jewish ritual injunctions incorporated into the civil or penal laws of the State. A consequence of this is the absence of direct interference in the name of religion with the private lives of individuals. The Sabbath, it is true, is the official day of rest, but whether the private citizen keeps it in the traditional religious sense or not is up to him. The state-controlled imports bring only kosher meat into the country,* but nobody checks whether the individual citizen obtains non-kosher meat from abroad (in the form of food-packages from Amer-

* As late as July, 1951, 400 rabbis felt the need of protesting against the import of non-kosher meat. Cf. *The Jewish Agency's Digest*, Sept. 28, 1951.

ica), or whether he keeps a kosher kitchen at home. Institutionally, some Jewish religious traits were thus unofficially adopted by the authorities as rules of conduct; however, a Jew can, if he wishes, live as un-orthodox a life in Israel as in Paris or New York. As a matter of fact, large segments of the population, both in the towns and in the rural areas, live a life in which Jewish religious ritual as such simply does not exist. In most of the *kibbutzim*, for instance, contact with religion in its traditional form is confined to two occasions: circumcision and marriage. Other rites of a religious origin are drawn upon as a mere source of folklore and changed freely to suit the new actualities. Passover is observed with a gathering around the *seder*-table—from which bread is by no means absent—to recite the recent deliverances from Europe and the Arab attacks, rather than the three-thousand-year-old story of the Exodus; at Pentecost (*Shavuot*) the offering up to the Jewish National Fund of schoolchildren's pennies collected throughout the year takes the place of the Feast of the Torah, in a sweeping modernization of the original Feast of the Firstfruits. The American Jewish emphasis on *Bar-Mitzvah* would be regarded as ridiculous religious formalism by the great majority of Ashkenazi Israeli parents and youths who rarely if ever see the inside of a synagogue.

5. "Church"-less Judaism

The unpopularity of religion and the limited role religious law plays in the life of the average individual are, to be sure, not due to a liberal attitude on the part of the religious parties. If these could have their way, they would clamp a tight religious rule over the country. But then, if any of the other political parties could have their way, they too would re-model the country in the shape of their ideals. Fortunately, the several parties balance one another, and the religious forces too have only their political strength to rely upon.

One of the reasons why the religious groups in Israel can act only through their political formations is inherent in the extremely loose and informal organizational structure of Jewish religion itself. The basic factor which in this connection is often overlooked by authors who warn against the "dangers of theocracy" and proclaim the need for "separation of Church and State" in Israel,* is that *Judaism has no Church*. There is no such thing as a Jewish Church-organization. The Jews have no priestly hierarchy and no ordained priesthood. A rabbi is simply a man versed in Jewish religious tradition, in recent times preferably but not inevitably, a graduate of a *yeshiva* or a rab-

* Cf. e.g. Paul Blanshard's article in the *Nation* of May 27, 1950, or William Zuckerman's in *Harper's Magazine* of November, 1950.

binical seminary. No rabbi is subordinate to any other rabbi in matters of religious import. The rabbis of the biggest congregation with
a palatial synagogue, and of the smallest group meeting in a private
home or a hired room, are equal in "rank," because there exists no
such thing as a rabbinical rank. Authority and prestige depend on
such individual factors as learning and personality. There is no central or district authority in Judaism which could give instructions to
individual rabbis, move them from one congregation to another, promote them or hold them responsible. The relationship between the
rabbi and his congregation is regulated by private and direct agreement. The rabbi can accept or decline an invitation to another congregation according to his own inclination. The conduct of services,
the ways and forms of religious practice, and even the interpretation of religious doctrine and belief, are rarely exactly identical in
two synagogues; they depend on the consensus of opinion among
the members of each congregation separately. The members will, of
course, be guided by the persuasive powers of their rabbi who, in
his turn, will find directives in traditional religious literature, which,
however, is subject to his own interpretation. Any group of Jews—
and this holds true for Israel as well as for the rest of the world
where Jews live—can join together and decide to form a congregation; they can meet at someone's home, or hire a room, or build a
synagogue and hold services there whenever they desire. Any one
of the members can volunteer to read the prayers and the Bible, or
to preach sermons and fulfil all sorts of other religious functions of a
non-technical nature; or they can employ any Jew they wish to fulfil
these functions or part of them.

As a consequence of this lack of formalized religious organization,
Judaism did not develop schisms and sects, only a wide range of
trends, all of which, however, are institutionally unseparated variants
of the one Jewish religion. The range of variants includes many
shadings of religious observance and doctrine, sometimes concep-
tualized, sometimes merely incidental, from the most scrupulously
orthodox to the most modern liberal or reform variety. Congregations occupying similar positions within this wide range of possible
variants found it to their mutual advantage to form voluntary associations. It is in this manner that, in the United States, for example,
the associations of orthodox, conservative and reform Jewish congregations came into being, and that the practice developed for each
of these congregation-types to employ rabbis who are graduates of
the orthodox, conservative and reform rabbinical schools respectively.

In Israel, the entire rabbinical organization is a heritage from the

British Mandatory regime which in its turn inherited it from the Ottoman *millet*-system. Under this system, while Moslems, Jews and Christians alike were subject to the civil and criminal law of the country, in matters affecting personal status the traditional religious laws of each community were recognized as valid. This meant, roughly, that in Turkish and British days the religious courts of each community had jurisdiction over such matters as marriage, divorce, alimony, maintenance of children, validation of will or testament, and guardianship. The Jewish rabbinical organization in Mandatory Palestine, therefore, derived its organizational framework (with the two Chief Rabbis, one Ashkenazi and one Sephardi, at its head) and its authority from the British Government of the country. Its powers were limited to matters ceded to it by the civil legislature, that is, to religio-juridical affairs. It had no power to intervene in matters of purely religious (i.e., non-juridical) observance.

Israel took over this entire system and left the rabbinate with as much or as little power as it had had. Therefore, if religious groups in Israel today wish to act, they can do so only through their influence on governmental and other political or civic organizations. It lies, however, in the nature of these organizations that there are relatively few points of contact between them and the religious aspects of life. One of the few such points of contact is the control of the municipalities over the public services, utilities and conveyances. With regard to electricity, water supply and telephone service, no attempt has ever been made by any organized religious party to obtain the suspension of their operation during the Sabbath and the holidays, or, at any rate, no such move was ever publicly discussed. As to the public conveyances, a certain customary law developed during the years of the British Mandatory regime. In places where it was deemed dispensable, the Jewish-operated public autobuses were halted from Friday night to Saturday night. Where distances were too great, as, for example, from Hadar Hakarmel to Mount Carmel in Haifa, they continued undisturbed through the Sabbath. After the attainment of independence, the *status quo* was retained in this respect. In the summer of 1952 permission was granted to buses to be run in Haifa on the Sabbath to take people from the town to the bathing beaches.* Since in Mandate days there were Arab-operated buses as well as a Government-operated train service connecting the major towns of the country, the stoppage of the Jewish interurban buses on Saturdays did not cause any special inconvenience. Here, too, the *status quo* has remained in effect for the time being, although the new situation in which taxis are the only public vehicles

* Cf. *Zionist Newsletter*, Jerusalem, August 5, 1952, Vol. IV, No. 21, p. 10.

operating on Saturdays and holidays definitely calls for reforms in ✳ this aspect of public transportation.

The provisional retention of the *status quo* is responsible for several other phenomena which are pointed out by those who accuse Israel of being a virtual theocracy. To this category belongs the much publicized fact that in Israel a Jew can be married only by a member of the rabbinate and that, consequently, marriage in Israel today between a Jew and a non-Jew is impossible. The peculiar political constellation in which the Government can maintain its majority position only with the help of the religious parties, is undoubtedly responsible for the postponement of parliamentary attempts to rectify this situation. However, the fact that the Knesset has begun to tackle the civil regulation of marriage (cf. above) indicates that this problem will not have to wait long for legislative attention.

In this connection it has been asserted that in Israel only orthodox rabbis are recognized and that only orthodox rabbis can function at a marriage ceremony or even at an ordinary Sabbath service. The foregoing discourse makes it unnecessary to refute this argument *in toto*. As to the marriage ceremony, according to Jewish law as laid down in the religious codes, no rabbi at all has to be present. What is needed is the presence of two witnesses in front of whom the bridegroom puts a ring on the finger of the bride and pronounces the traditional Hebrew formula: "Behold, thou art betrothed unto me with this ring according to the laws of Moses and Israel." This is an incontestably valid Jewish marriage ceremony. Therefore, to say, that "Jewish children born of a marriage not performed by an orthodox rabbi in Israel are regarded as illegitimate and subjected to the rigors and discriminations with which pre-medievalism regarded illegitimacy" is just as much nonsense as to complain that in Israel even reform congregations "must conduct their services in accordance with the Orthodox pattern."✳

6. Religious Tutelage

What the religious aspect of the present cultural crisis in Israel really means can be fully evaluated only when approached from quite a different angle. The religious issue can become a stumbling block for Israel, not because there is no complete separation of "Church" and State, nor because there is any imminent danger of Israel's becoming a theocracy, but because of a possible religio-

---

✳ Cf. William Zuckerman, "Church and State in Israel," *Harper's Magazine*, November 1950, p. 77.

political fusion between the orthodox European Jews and the orthodox Oriental Jews.

The statement that there is a danger in such a fusion does not imply a criticism, and certainly not a deprecation of Jewish religiosity, nor a denial of its rightful place in the socio-political configuration of Israel's new society. As a matter of fact, politics and religion were inseparable during all those phases of Hebrew and Jewish history the locale of which was Palestine. Today, within the general democratic structure of the new State, religious parties have at least as much justification as the right wing, center, left and radical left-wing parties. Regarded in the perspective of the history of the Jewish people, one feels that something would be wanting if there were no religious parties in Israel today.

Jewish religion has always been characterized by an extraordinary flexibility and adaptability. Under the impact of the Emancipation and Enlightenment, and among those who did not forsake religion altogether, it transformed itself from a total way of life to a great spiritual factor with a more or less precisely circumscribed domain of its own within the context of modern life. But this transformation took place only in the West, within the orbit of Euroamerican culture, where it was probably the chief process of Jewish self-adaptation to the changing pattern of the social environment. In the Middle East, no commensurate development or transformation has taken place. Religion there, both Moslem and Jewish, has remained in the "total-way-of-life" stage. As such, religion is equivalent to tradition; it is a powerful determinant in the mental disposition which harks back to the past for both precept and precedence, and is thus a static factor making for unchanging continuance of the past.

The orthodox Ashkenazi Jews occupy an intermediary position between modern Western and tradition-bound Oriental Jews. They have retained much more of the "total-way-of-life" aspect of Judaism than their non-religious brethren, but at the same time they have absorbed enough of the European mental climate to make them familiar with the idea and the manifestations of progress especially in the technical fields.*

In Israel, orthodox Ashkenazi Jews have, for the first time in their experience, a chance actively to participate in the formulation of a Jewish way of life within the framework of an independent Jewish

---

* Chief Rabbi Herzog of Israel, for instance, recommends the use of a mechanical appliance for milking cows to be set off by a pre-set clock, to avoid desecrating the Sabbath. Cf. *The Religion of Israel and the State of Israel* (an anthology, in Hebrew), New York, 1951, p. 17. To Yemenite Jews such a device would be utterly strange and repulsive.

State. Their endeavor under these circumstances is to find what they regard as a happy combination of traditional Judaism and modern technical and social attainments. As the Chief Rabbi of Israel, Rabbi Itzhak Halevi Herzog, expressed it in a somewhat abstract phrasing: "The Jewish State—within the frame of the Torah and considering sufficiently the actual situation—will of necessity be neither fully theocratic nor fully democratic in the modern sense . . . but theocratic-democratic; the separation between religion and state is absolutely forbidden . . ."*

The orthodox Jew in Israel will fight for the retention of tradition whenever religious questions arise, but his Western cultural background has predisposed him to join the forces of advancement, change and improvement in the spheres of other cultural attainments. The religious Oriental Jew, on the other hand, is totally tradition-bound, for religion encompasses his entire life. He cannot conceive of any change, in any sphere of life, as being good and desirable, since religion is unchangeable and all his life is spent under its aegis. Whenever the Oriental Jew adapts himself to even the slightest change in any aspect of life, the totality of his religious tradition is being impinged upon. Oriental Jewish religiosity is thus a powerful immobilizing and retarding factor.

Yet this essential difference notwithstanding, in their outer, formal aspects, Ashkenazi orthodoxy and Oriental religiosity are so similar as to appear almost identical. Apart from some minor differences to which reference has been made earlier (page 15), the life of the religious Jews, whether Western or Eastern, is regulated by the same code of religious laws. The prayers, too, are practically identical and differ from one community to another merely in their melody.

This external similarity is sensed by both sides as a very strong bond, a unifying tie, a platform of common interests so powerful that the sub-surface differences in cultural attitudes pass unnoticed. The claim of the orthodox wing to the control of education in immigrants' reception camps and among the Oriental Jews in general is based on this community of interests: the Oriental Jews want their children to enjoy a religious education, and this exactly is the field in which the orthodox wing has specialized. Should orthodox Ashkenazi Jewry succeed in winning the support of the Oriental Jews through a control of their education, this would result in an enormous increase in the ranks of the politically-organized religious sector. The 1951-52 figures of the distribution of the school population among the four officially recognized trends indicate that definite

* *Yabne, Academic-Religious Anthology* (Hebrew), Jerusalem-Tel Aviv, Nissan, 5709 (April 1949).

gains have already been made by the orthodox in this respect. In that school year no less than 25.1% of the total school population was enrolled in the schools expressing the two religious trends (the Mizrahi and the Agudat Yisrael), which is about double the percentage of those adults who in the two Knesset elections voted for the religious parties. Since the children of today will be the voters of tomorrow, the religious groups will, if this trend continues have a good chance of becoming the majority in the country within a short time. Such a religious coalition would be composed of a European orthodox minority and an Oriental Jewish majority with a rapidly increasing percentage of Orientals. The attitudes of the Oriental majority would inevitably impress themselves upon the European orthodox minority, and thus imperceptibly the surface similarity in matters of religious observance would lead to a deeper identification in outlook and mentality.

Should this come about, the fears of the pessimistic observers and forecasters concerning the possibility of Israel's becoming but another Levantine state, "a State of Jews by religion, Moslem by custom and thought, an autonomous province of Arabia,"[*] would prove to be well founded. Under the spiritual tutelage of the European orthodox sector, the Oriental Jews would not be channeled toward that transition from an essentially religious Middle Eastern outlook to an essentially secular Western outlook which is a *conditio sine qua non* of further pioneering progress. The European orthodox Jews could not achieve this transformation, for although they themselves have come a long way in absorbing secular Western cultural elements, they are not consciously aware of the decisive difference between their own, somewhat Westernized attitude towards religion and the typically Middle Eastern religious outlook of the Oriental Jews. Moreover, Ashkenazi orthodoxy is ideally oriented toward the same religious totalitarianism which is the Oriental heritage of Judaism. In their endeavor to preserve religion intact, the orthodox Ashkenazi Jews unintentionally encourage the perpetuation of an Oriental state of mind among their Oriental Jewish protégés, while they themselves run the serious risk of succumbing to the same mental atmosphere.

The fight for the future party-allegiance of the Oriental Jewish immigrants appears thus to be more than a mere struggle for political power. The issue is, to state it in extreme terms, whether Israel will in another generation harbor a culturally divided population, consisting of a majority which will be Oriental not merely in religious outlook but also in cultural attitudes, and of a Western Jewish minor-

[*] Cf. Kenneth W. Bilby, *New Star in the Near East*, New York, 1950, p. 427.

ity faced with the prospect of submersion demographically as well as culturally. This is what must be expected to happen should the "battle for the immigrants" be won by the orthodox wing. The alter- ✳ native, represented by the victory of the Labor groups and the swelling of their ranks by the masses of immigrants, is also fraught with many dangers which will be examined in the next chapter.

Chapter Ten
The Cultural Crisis

The foregoing chapters sketched the origin of the ethnic composition of modern Israel, traced the main characteristics of its population elements, and analyzed—against the background of Western and Eastern cultures in general—the main phases of the new Jewish State's nascent culture. Certain disharmonies marring the otherwise encouraging overall picture of significant achievement in the immigrational, economic, social and cultural fields, have also been noted.

Cognizance has also been taken earlier of the fact that the various Jewish communities or ethnic groups differ from one another in several objectively measurable respects. It has been found that especially where these differences are pronounced—as between the Ashkenazi (European or Western) Jews, who constitute one of the main divisions of the Jewish people, and the Oriental (Middle Eastern) Jews, who form another such division—they have often occasioned tension and even friction. Yet never in the history of Mandatory Palestine did this tension or friction reach the intensity of a crisis. The equilibrium was held and the proper perspective preserved because of the fact that continuous struggle had to be carried on against British restrictions and Arab political opposition, with the need which arose repeatedly of resorting to armed self-defense. There was also the equally imperative necessity for contending with the increasingly severe restrictive measures of the British Mandatory Government. During the War of Liberation, in the face of the gravest threat to the existence of the entire Jewish population, all its sectors united to offer joint resistance. Since the end of the war, with the arrival of large number of immigrants who had no part in the great experience it provided, the culturally-conditioned differences between the Western and Eastern sectors of the Jewish population of Israel have been increasingly felt and have rapidly assumed a critical character. ". . . Cultural differences tend to produce crises and to separate [men] into conflicting groups as if they were members of different species."* This generalization is borne out by the situation which has developed within less than a year after the cessation of hostilities in Israel. At that time the immigration in general was in full swing and in it the share of the Sephardi and Oriental Jews was rapidly increasing towards an absolute majority. This had the immediate effect of increasing the interaction between people of two widely differing cultures to an extraordinarily high frequency. Now, for the first time in the history of modern Palestine-Israel there arose a contact situation affecting practically everybody. The differences between the two types of people, virtually separated them into conflicting groups, "as if they were members of different species," which developed all the manifestations of acute cultural crisis.

1. Social Change and Cultural Change

Both the European and the Oriental immigrants have to undergo an incisive and mostly painful process of adjustment upon their arrival in Israel.. In the case of the immigrants coming from Europe, however, the change required to make a successful adjustment is merely *social*; in the case of the Oriental immigrant it is *cultural* as well. The European immigrant is faced with necessity of learning a new language, Hebrew. He also must learn a new trade in order to be able to make a living, and in most cases a trade which by the old European scale of values is of a lower type than the one in which he or his father before him engaged. In his business dealings he has to adjust to a special type of economy which is essentially a combination of socialistic and capitalistic practices. However, while the precise form the way of life takes in Israel is new to him, he is familiar with each of its elements from his European background, and thus he soon recognizes Israeli culture as merely a new mutation of several of the factors which formed his old social and technological environment in Europe.

Difficult as it is to weather the stress of this *social change* required from the immigrant from Europe, the strain under which the Oriental Jewish immigrant labors until he accomplishes the *cultural change* demanded of him is greater still. He too has to undergo social changes which frequently are even farther-reaching than in the case of his European fellow immigrant. But in addition he has to find his place in a culture many of whose main features were completely unknown to him before his arrival in Israel. For a group of

* D. Bidney, "The Concept of Cultural Crisis," in *American Anthropologist*, Oct.-Dec., 1946, p. 537.

immigrants like the Moroccan and Iraqi Jews, and even more so for the Yemenite Jews, to adjust to Israeli life means to enter, and to learn to participate in, a culture different from the one in which they were brought up and in which they had learned to move. The cultural change to the stresses of which they become exposed as soon as they land in Israel, extend into practically all aspects of life. They have to familiarize themselves with a new technology; circumstances often force them to abandon their old accustomed forms of social organization, such as the extended family and the religious community, and to pattern their social life after the dominant European model. Highly prized old cultural specializations such as arts and crafts, folk music, religious vocations and the like, suddenly become valueless. Cherished personality traits such as religious faith, contentment and detachment, become discolored when viewed in the new Israeli frame of reference, and appear instead as superstition, indolence and apathy.

The road the immigrant has to travel in Israel is thus by no means an easy one. Nor is it easy for the young State to absorb economically, socially and culturally an immigrant mass which is more numerous than the older inhabitants who themselves consist of an immigrant majority of but slightly older standing. Nevertheless, there are signs that the venture is succeeding. Certain economic and technological improvements in the circumstances of the immigrants are already visible. The reception camps have been emptied; housing conditions in the Work Villages, Transit Villages and other settlements hastily constructed for the absorption of immigrants are being improved. With the increase of acreage under cultivation and the regulation of food imports, the nutritional situation too shows promise of betterment. The schools, attendance in which is compulsory for eight years, and the army in which every person has to serve upon reaching his eighteenth year, are potent factors in the cultural absorption of the younger element among the immigrants and in welding them together into one people. The social and health services and recreational facilities of the widely ramified institutional network of the *Histadrut* are available to every member, and for the last few years over two thirds of Israel's wage earners have been members. The increasing participation of the immigrants in these and other institutions, whether compulsory like the schools and the army, or voluntary like the *Histadrut*, has created a growing community of interests and a feeling of belonging together which is the basis of national unity.

Changes of a social and cultural nature, not unlike those which are expected in Israel today from the Oriental Jews, have been demanded from their countrymen by such reformers as Kemal Ataturk in Turkey and Riza Shah Pehlevi in Iran. The concrete details of the "reforms" varied from place to place and from time to time, but essentially they all concerned such fundamentals as mechanization, education, sanitation and a reduction of the influence of religion, or rather, of religious functionaries. The reaction of the people to the changes imposed upon them was also essentially the same in every place; a definite correlation could be discerned between the extent, suddenness and incisiveness of the change decreed by the rulers, and the extent, intensity and stubbornness of the resistance on the part of the population: the greater the first, the greater the second, and vice versa. This correlation in itself indicates the desirability of *gradual change*, if friction and crisis are to be avoided.

The *a priori* attitude of the Oriental Jews to the Western cultural traits which they encounter in Israel, and which they are expected to absorb, is to a high degree analogous to the attitude displayed by other Oriental peoples to the cultural traits introduced by their governments as innovations or reforms. The traditional cultural heritage constituting the base line upon which the effect of the reforms is directed is, in the case of both the Oriental Jews and the other Oriental peoples, the common substratum of Middle Eastern culture to which some attention has been devoted earlier in this book.* The newly introduced elements are taken in each case from the rich Western storehouse of cultural traits and institutions deemed desirable. The base line of culture change is therefore the traditional culture of the Middle East, and its direction is towards Westernization among the Oriental Jews in Israel, among the people of Turkey and Iran, as well as in any other Middle Eastern state with a "progressive" government. All over the area we have thus peoples with basically similar cultures being led by extraneous forces other than their own free choice, in basically analogous directions.

In addition to the base line and the direction of the culture change, the quality and extent of the common interests and intentions of the initiators of the change, on the one hand, and of its subjects, on the other, exert a decisive influence in any acculturative situation. Were it not for the primary role played by this common factor, one would expect a largely identical attitude on the part of the Oriental Jews and of the non-Jewish minorities towards the demands of acculturation which confront both groups in present-day Israel. The common factor, however, differs with regard to both groups, and with it differ the attitudes displayed by them.

The acculturative situation in which the Oriental Jewish immi-

* Cf. above, chapter 2.

grants find themselves after their arrival in Israel is profoundly different from that of the non-Jewish minorities. For one thing, the economic and general material situation of the newly arrived Oriental Jews is worse, not better, in Israel than it was in their old home countries. In the home countries, though the majority of the Jews suffered poverty, slum-housing and disease, these drawbacks were endured as accustomed elements of life, unchanged for many generations, much as one accepts the rigors of an intemperate climate. Upon their arrival in Israel, the Oriental Jews are faced with inferior housing conditions in the tents and barracks of the reception camps; they find themselves penniless and subsisting on charity as did beggars in their home communities; the jobs available are poorly paid and only rarely of the kind to which they are used from previous experience. Lack of satisfaction of these basic needs could scarcely be made up for by medical care, social work and educational facilities put at their disposal. The value of these is recognized as a rule only after a certain predisposition has been created for them, which in itself is scarcely a negligible educational task. Any change in the economic and material conditions, therefore, evokes the emotions of the poor man when he becomes completely destitute, or of the owner of a hovel when he becomes altogether homeless: it creates dissatisfaction with the present, coupled with a nostalgia for the past.

In contrast to the feeling of uncertainty which made the non-Jewish minorities in Israel amenable to cultural change in the direction of the dominant group, the Oriental Jews come to Israel with a feeling of homecoming, of returning to the country which is as much theirs as any other Jewish group's, whether coming from the East or from the West, simultaneously or several years or decades previously. The question of Zionist activity and organizational effort aside, in their consciousness the Land of Israel is their fatherland to which they return of right and not by sufferance. Their loyalty to Israel, its cause and its aims, was sufficiently expressed, they opine, when they chose to come to Israel, and they feel nothing like the urge of the non-Jewish minorities to demonstrate their identification with the dominant element in the country by subordinating their own folkways to those deemed desirable by the Ashkenazim. Hence, instead of acquiescing in legislation which aims at Westernizing certain aspects of life in Israel, they fight against it, vociferously and unrestrainedly, for in their eyes the passing of such laws means the imposition of the mores of one part of the Jewish population of Israel upon the whole country. That is why, instead of welcoming common schooling for their children and those of the Ashkenazim, the most numerous Oriental Jewish community insists on separate schools for their own children. They know that common schooling means the elimination of their traditions from the lives of their own children.

The Oriental Jewish immigrants as well as all the other immigrants are at a great disadvantage compared with the non-Jewish minorities in Israel because their continuity of residence has been disturbed. The mere fact of migration from one place to another is a serious upheaval in locational continuity which can have far-reaching repercussions even when the conditions found in the new place of residence are favorable. If they are unfavorable, they almost inevitably cause a serious disruption in the socio-cultural life of the immigrant individuals, families and larger groups. This is a phenomenon well known in the history of colonization where entire tribes or populations were transplanted from one place to another, with the result that "societies were broken up, their unity was destroyed, their traditions swamped, their customary law obliterated."[*]

Inevitably, the locational arrangements awaiting the Oriental Jewish immigrants in Israel have to be regarded by them as inadequate on several counts. First of all objectively, in terms of square feet of housing placed at the disposal of the immigrants in the reception and transit camps, in the transit and work villages, or in the abandoned Arab houses in villages or towns, the reality in Israel falls far short of what they had left behind them, unsatisfactory as the conditions had been even there. Then there is the difference in the nature of the social environment: in the old places of residence it was in most cases the ghetto, the *mellah* or *hara*, situated, it is true, amidst a hostile or at least unfriendly environment, but containing within its walls only one group of people, closely knit together by common history, language, upbringing, customs, mores, outlook and attitudes—in brief, by a common culture. In Israel, they find themselves in an unknown, unaccustomed environment, strange and alien, encroaching upon them even within their crowded quarters. It is an environment of Jews, to be sure, but of Jews who are in many ways more foreign to them than were the non-Jewish neighbors in their old places of residence. In some cases they are settled in places where they are cut off from daily contact with others from their own home-community, which makes them feel lost and forlorn. The customs, habits, mannerisms, behavior and personality traits which are the only ones they possess and which have gone unquestioned and unnoticed even in Israel among people of their own kind, become a stumbling-block for them in the contacts to which they are exposed

[*] Cf. René Maunier, *The Sociology of the Colonies*, London, 1949, vol. II, p. 481.

without any previous preparation, and which involve close day-to-day interaction with people different from them by cultural conditioning. Thus the change of locale in their case often is equivalent to a complete disruption of life-sequence, and a critical break in socio-cultural continuity.

2. Mutual Reactions

The Ashkenazi Jews, who share the Western concept of a minority, consider the Oriental Jewish immigrants in general—or the older Oriental Jewish inhabitants of the country, for that matter—a group differing from themselves in all respects which count and which decisively set off one population group from another. Here are Jewish "tribes," or communities, who lack in everything they themselves were taught to value from childhood; people who differ from them in behavior and manners, in physical appearance and clothing, in mentality and outlook, in abilities and inclinations, and who—worst of all—are ignorant even of the existence of that entire culture which gave meaning to their own lives and strivings both before and after their immigration into Palestine. The Oriental Jews, they feel, differ from them profoundly even in the motivation of their *Aliya* to Israel: discarding the common impetus given to many in both groups by the deterioration of the political and socio-economic situation in their respective home countries—a circumstance which all of them equally tend to minimize even in their own recollections, since it was anyway only a negative motivation—there remained on the positive side two distinctly different incentives. Among the Ashkenazi Jews this is the politico-nationalistic endeavor, first to achieve the Jewish State and then to participate in its consolidation, development and life in general, with all that this means for people reared in the ideas and ideals of the Western world. For the Oriental Jews the positive impetus for immigration to Palestine and later to Israel was a religiously motivated one: it was the religio-romantic idea of the fulfillment of ancient prophecies concerning the return to Zion, the redemption of the remnant and the Messianic ingathering of the exiles. The activistic outlook of the Western world, in its manifestation among the Ashkenazi Jews, rejected the passive expectation of divine intervention and substituted political and organizational action. The Oriental division of Jewry remained true to its old contemplative traditions. Although individually several Jews from the Middle Eastern lands made the great decision to emigrate to Palestine, they showed little initiative collectively and refrained from "hastening the end" (as the Cabalistic phrase goes), but continued to put their trust in Divine Providence. It was therefore only thanks to the efforts of the Western Jews as well as a few Oriental Jews who have lived long enough in Palestine to become sufficiently Westernized, that the large-scale immigration of Oriental Jews to Israel was organized. But even when this came about, it did not mean that it occasioned any conscious politico-nationalistic awakening among the Oriental Jews either in their old countries or in Israel. They continued to interpret the great events of their times in terms of their religious experience, and their homecoming assumed a religious character not unlike that of the first Return-to-Zion movement in Babylonia some two and a half millennia ago. The religio-nationalistic attitude of the Oriental Jews thus remained something very different from the politico-nationalistic activity of the Ashkenazi Jews.

The Ashkenazic Jews consequently cannot help seeing in the Oriental Jews, whom they first encountered in Palestine-Israel, a minority group of the kind that was known to them from their old home environment. They equally cannot help showing towards them the same attitudes which were the customary ones in Central and Eastern Europe towards a national minority: an attitude composed of a mixture of condescension, distrust and a wish to keep their distance.

It has been mentioned that the first disappointment which awaits the Oriental Jews upon their arrival in Israel is in the field of material commodities. Very soon thereafter, a second reason for discontent becomes apparent: the realization that instead of a rapid and complete social fusion with the rest of the Jewish population of the country, they are denied the chance of participating within a short period as equal partners in the Israeli scene; that they are treated as a separate group, in fact, in a manner reminiscent of the treatment they received in the old countries at the hands of their Moslem neighbors. But there is a decisive difference between the two experiences: back there they were in the *Galuth*, the Diaspora; it was, therefore, only to be expected that they would be treated like inferiors by the Sons of Ishmael. In the course of the long centuries of exile in Moslem lands, efficiently working defense-mechanisms were developed both communally and individually by the Jews: the effects of social, economic and political oppression were counteracted by cultural and psychological attitudes; the actual insults and injuries to which they were exposed were neutralized by the subjective conviction of moral and intellectual superiority derived from the incontestible fact of being descendants of the rightful son and heir of Abraham and possessors of the true and only religion revealed by God to His chosen people.

In Israel, vis-à-vis other Jews, the Oriental Jews can muster no such effective defense. When they encounter here an attitude not unlike the one they experienced in the countries just left behind, they cannot set against it any of those psychological bulwarks which helped them to weather emotionally their long Moslem *Galuth*. They cannot comfort themselves with a feeling of intellectual, moral and spiritual superiority, a belief in being the sons of Abraham and followers of the only true religion. After all, this is possessed or claimed also by the other Jews in Israel, who, in addition, wield the secular power, are the numerical majority and obviously the dominant element in the country. For lack of effective defense mechanisms the realization of this situation could have created only one reaction, the one it actually did create: jealousy, resentment and bitterness at times mounting to undisguised hatred, levelled against those who are brothers by blood and tradition but behave towards them as did the evil rich brother towards his poor brother in the famous story of the Arabian Nights.

The ethnic composition of the *Yishuv* in pre-independence Palestine has to be held responsible for an additional factor which makes the present cultural crisis in Israel more acute. This factor is the almost complete absence of Zionist educational activity in the countries of the Middle East during the entire Mandate period. Since the first three waves of immigration came from Eastern Europe, the leaders of these groups occupied the responsible positions in Jewish Palestine and decisively influenced Zionist political, propagandistic and educational policies. People coming from Eastern Europe were, understandably, interested primarily in fostering the Zionist movement in the countries of Eastern Europe. Thus it came about that it was Eastern Europe which became the center of Zionist educational and propagandistic activities, emanating to a constantly increasing extent from Palestine itself. Hundreds of emissaries, teachers, educators, organizers were sent from Palestine to Eastern Europe where they initiated and organized a great pioneering movement. The fruits of their efforts were seen in the constant stream of immigrants who came to Palestine after sufficient practical and ideological preparation, and who had little difficulty (relatively speaking) in making satisfactory adjustments in the country. When World War II ended in Europe, hundreds of teachers, youth-leaders, social workers and organizers were sent from Palestine to the refugee and displaced persons camps in Germany, Austria and Italy. Although the atmosphere and the objective conditions were much less favorable here than they had been in the pre-war home-communities, still the educational and social work carried out resulted in preparing to some degree the inmates of the camps who finally succeeded in reaching Palestine-Israel.

Only with the achievement of statehood was it realized that the Zionist movement, in its great concentration on East-European (and later also Central-European) Jews, had neglected other great Jewish communities. For example, it neglected American Jewry. It has been repeatedly pointed out recently that the number of emissaries sent to America was very small and inadequate; as a consequence, the American *Aliya*, which could have provided Israel with a rich flow of most essential, highly trained and excellent immigrant-ma- ✳ terial, sent only trickles and dribbles.

But if American Jewry was simply neglected, Oriental Jewry was completely overlooked. During the Mandate period there were neither enough nor sufficiently influential Oriental Jews in the Zionist leadership in Palestine to call attention to their demands. To the Ashkenazi Zionist and *Yishuv* leadership the situation of the Oriental Jews, while not an altogether unknown quantity, appeared to be of no special urgency. Consequently, the Zionist movement as such practically disregarded the existence of the Oriental Jewish communities in Asia and Africa, and of the Sephardic communities in the Balkans, Turkey and elsewhere. No emissaries were sent to them, no Zionist educational and organizational work was initiated, and with the exception of a few representatives of the Labor movement who worked in Iraq and in North Africa, no ties were established between the *Yishuv* and the Oriental Jewish communities.

It cannot be denied that in this respect the Zionist movement ignored the Sephardi and Oriental Jews. But it need not assume the entire blame for the situation which has prevailed until recently. Equally responsible were the local Jews themselves, who by dint of their traditional cultural background lacked the organizational ability and initiative necessary for the creation of a Zionist movement from within, as was accomplished elsewhere in several instances. Also responsible to a great extent were the few rich Jews who were found in every Oriental Jewish community, who wielded considerable influence, and who in nearly every instance used this influence to keep their community from any Zionist activity which they feared—not without cause—could easily be used by the Moslems as an excuse for oppressive measures against the Jews, or even for violent outbreaks.

The sum total of all these factors was that the Oriental Jews in general had little if any inkling of what was going on in Palestine. Many of them had first-hand direct contact with Palestinian Jews for the first time during World War II when Palestinian Jewish soldiers or civilian employees in the service of the war effort appeared in North Africa and in Syria, in Iraq and Iran. The ideals of pioneering, of self-labor, of the return to the soil, of service to the people and to the country, all important focal concerns in the life of modern Jewish Palestine, have in most cases not reached them even in the form of hearsay and were practically nowhere methodically explained to them. Neither did practical training exist, the preparedness for which must, in any case, be first created by a theoretical introduction to Zionist ideology. Consequently, Oriental Jewish youth had no such opportunities of preparing itself for life in Israel as were given to youths in Europe (and to some extent also in America) in the training-farms established by various Zionist bodies.

If we take these circumstances into account, it will become clear that in addition to the initial cultural differences, the Oriental Jewish immigrants stand as strangers in the modern socio-cultural scene of Israel because of the differentials in specific preparation for life in the new Jewish state. On the negative side, this lack of specific educational preparation for a full participation in the life-forms of modern Israel manifests itself in an unpreparedness to take a full share in the pioneering effort required from the new immigrants, the actual meaning of which is merely toil and sweat, privation and hardship when it is divested of its ideological contents and values. On the positive side, this lack of preparation manifests itself in a wish to forego in Israel as little as possible of the few material comforts which were theirs in their home countries, and, in a more general way, to establish for themselves life-forms resembling as closely as possible those left behind in the various countries of the Middle East.

Pitted against the general trends prevailing in modern Israel, and against the conviction that the newly received elements must conform to norms laid down by the East and Central European pioneers who came before them and who made the country what it is today, the efforts of the Oriental Jewish immigrants to preserve their cultural continuity cause friction, clashes and disturbing incidents in which cultural crises are typically demonstrated.

One of the more painful of these is re-emigration, a phenomenon not unknown in the history of modern Palestine, although its reasons in the past were usually economic only. Since the independence of Israel, re-emigration of Oriental Jews has occurred in relatively large numbers, reaching, according to some sources, several thousands.*

✳ The causes of re-emigration are usually couched in vague phrases

* Cf. e.g., K. Shabtai, in *Davar*, Tel Aviv, March 3, 1950. The total number of re-emigrants from May 15, 1948 to Nov. 1, 1952, was circa 28,000, according to Y. Raphael, head of the Immigration Department of the Jewish Agency in Jerusalem, cf. *The Jewish Agency's Digest*, Nov. 21, 1952, p. 131. This corresponds to 4% of the total immigration during the same period. It is significant that during this period only about 2,700 veteran citizens left Israel.

like "dissatisfaction with conditions" and often simply "it was better at home"; but upon closer scrutiny they can be broken down into several categories, such as inability to find employment or adequate lodgings, and so forth. Beneath the immediate economic reasons, however, there is the conviction that the setbacks suffered are not caused by the general economic difficulties of the country which affect everybody indiscriminately, but by discrimination practiced against Oriental Jews specifically. As the spokesmen of a group of 150 Jewish immigrants from India put it when demanding to be sent back to India: "In Beer Sheba we were told that we should eat only black bread as we were black, and the white bread was only for white Jews."* Returning to their old home countries such re-emigrants have much to tell those who stayed behind about the difficulties they encountered in Israel simply because they belonged to an unwanted community, thus causing many who had already decided to go to Israel to change their minds and remain at home.

Not all, however, who wish to return to their place of origin can do so. Although their transportation to Israel is paid for by the Jewish public institutions, the immigrants have to undertake certain financial obligations the fulfilment of which can be demanded from them if they want to leave the country. For the time being, only persons in possession of an official exit permit can leave the country, ✷ and to obtain this is not always easy. Consequently, a considerable proportion of those who want to leave the country must stay behind. These in their embitterment cause as much tension in Israel as those who leave and harm the country by spreading "an evil report of the land."

3. Discrimination

As to the actual presence or absence of discrimination against the Oriental Jews, all those who give serious consideration to the matter admit that discrimination does exist.

According to the head of the Department for the Jews of the Middle East of the Jewish Agency for Palestine in Jerusalem§ (Y. Zerubavel), discrimination "begins not when the immigrants arrive in the camps and have no suitable social workers to take care of them; it is expressed in the very fact that Oriental Jewry is aban-

* Cf. The New York *Times*, Nov. 22 and 23, 1951. In March 1952, this group was given permission to return to India and a few months later they again wished to be allowed to re-emigrate to Israel. Cf. *The Jewish Agency's Digest,* ✷ Nov. 21, 1952, pp. 131-2.

§ This Department functioned for three years. On Sept. 17, 1951, the Executive of the Jewish Agency decided to close it and to transfer its functions to other Departments of the Agency.

doned and left to itself, and that we content ourselves with sending to them a few solitary emissaries without budgets and without the possibility of wide activity."*

The editor of the "Middle East Miscellany," the official Hebrew organ of the Department for the Jews of the Middle East of the Jewish Agency for Palestine, is somewhat more outspoken in describing the attitude of the *Yishuv* towards the Oriental Jewish immigrants:

"The mass immigration from the Orient, perhaps with the exception of that of the Yemenites, causes a reaction of amazement and some confusion in the *Yishuv*; and at times this reaction takes on the form of attack. As usual with all reaction to an unaccustomed element, it takes no account of facts and truths. Together with a feeling of discomfort in the face of something foreign and new, there is a possibly unconscious impetus toward self-protection, a will to safeguard undiminished all the privileged positions. It is a fact, whatever its causes, that the reins of civic and intellectual leadership in the *Yishuv* and in the country are in the hands of those who came from the West. In the professions, medicine, white-collar jobs, public leadership and various kinds of management, which prevalent views hold preferable to other occupations, the part of the Oriental communities is scarcely recognizable, or is altogether negligible. This situation is wrong even if its origin was due to purely objective circumstances, and even if all the office-holders were most suitable and talented, which, however, as is well known, is not the case.

"It is only natural that reaction should come in the form of complaints over discrimination, in which the rebelliousness finds an outlet. Discrimination exists in every country of immigration, due to the presence of an old population well entrenched in its positions, and a new element which lacks standing. From this viewpoint there is discrimination even on the part of the older Oriental Jewish *Yishuv*, many of whom have firmly established positions, towards the Oriental Jewish newcomers. There is also a type of discrimination, one of considerable extent, the basis of which is objective, which originates in the greater ability of some to find a place for themselves, and their greater vitality in the struggle for existence. Then there is discrimination which is based on a certain attitude towards Oriental immigrants, an attitude of

* Cf. Zerubavel, "Turning Point in Zionist Work," in *Yalqut haMizrah haTikhon*, Jerusalem, Jan.-Feb., 1950, p. 5. Cf. also S. S., "In the Camps Today," *ib.*, March-April, 1950, pp. 54-55, etc.

the superior to his inferiors, caused by a lack of confidence in their
ability, and justifying the existing situation by referring to the
meagerness of their needs and the lowness of their level of subsistence. And discrimination begets more discrimination in the
actual position of the communities and in the complex of relationships and connections with the authorities and the office-holders.
Towards one community at least this discrimination is enveloped
in an attitude of wholesale contempt which goes so far that some
of the members of the community in question try to escape from
it by camouflage. . . ."*

These utterances, however significant they are in themselves,
merely reflect the understanding attitude of those whose task it has
become to attend to the problems of the Oriental Jewish immigrants.
Yet another statement of this type adjudges this negative attitude
towards the Oriental Jewish immigrants as merely a sharply pronounced special case revealing the general dislike displayed by the
older inhabitants of the country towards all newcomers:

"I do not go so far as to say that the *Yishuv* as a whole lacks
good will towards them [the Oriental Jewish immigrants], but it
is an undeniable fact that there exists a lack of ability to understand them and a lack of interest, and in many cases also a more
or less sharp opposition . . . Since May 15, 1948, 350,000 persons
immigrated into Israel, and it is no wonder that many of the social
workers who dealt with the reception of immigrants, their housing
and all the other activities which are connected with their absorption, were not of the first grade. This is admitted by everybody
without argument. It is also pointed out that no workers of Mediterranean extraction were found to care for the immigrants who
came from the countries of the Middle East. To this day, most of
the administrative, social and other workers do not understand
the mentality of the Oriental immigrants—do not understand
them at all . . .

"What is the sum total of the complaints of the Oriental Jews
and to what extent can they be met? Their main complaint is that
they are the victims of discrimination, intentional or unintentional,
on the part of the rest of the population, and, what is worse, on
the part of their public representatives. They argue that other
immigrants enjoy privileges, are helped more, reach a solution of
their problems more easily and quickly, and are absorbed into the
country. They argue that those who have been commissioned to

* M. Zelcer, "The Oriental Jew in Our Days," in *Yalqut haMizrah haTikhon,*
Jerusalem, Jan.-Feb., 1950, p. 14 ff.

take care of them neglect them and do not understand them, or that in the immigrants' camps the performance of all sorts of tasks is entrusted to people who are unable to do justice to them.

"The immigrants complain bitterly that no effort is being made to enable the unskilled among them, who are the majority, to learn a trade. They have no experience or knowledge of the fields where there are possibilities of absorption, and no efficient guidance is given to them . . . The investigation of their affairs is not speeded up. One cannot enumerate or describe all their complaints and the cases which show the hardships of life in the camps, but many of them are justified and it would be proper that the responsible people should investigate them more thoroughly than they have done hitherto.

"A man of European origin who fulfils an important task in a national institution, and follows closely the problem of the Oriental immigrants, admitted frankly that discrimination does exist. Its source is, first of all, a feeling of hate on the part of the established population towards the immigrants in general. This feeling is weaker towards those who came from Europe, the remnants of the great massacre. The older inhabitants have a sort of guilt-feeling towards the last witnesses of the death of their families; this is not the case with regard to the Oriental immigrants . . ."*

4. The Moroccan "Peril"

The attitude of the general public, repeatedly referred to in these statements, is more rarely put into writing. One of its most outspoken public expressions was that of a reporter of the Hebrew daily, *Haaretz*, who spent one month in studying the situation in the immigrants' camps. He does not mince words when criticizing the Ashkenazi immigrants who came from European displaced persons' camps or who reached Israel via Shanghai, after a prolonged sojourn in China. However, he castigates the North African immigrants ruthlessly. Of them he has the following to say:

"A serious and threatening question is posed by the immigration from North Africa. This is the immigration of a race the like of which we have not yet known in this country. It would seem that certain differences exist between the immigrants from Tripolitania, Morocco, Tunisia and Algeria, but I cannot say that I was able to discern the quality of these differences, if they exist at all . . . (By the way, none of these immigrants will be happy to

* S. S., "In the Camps Today," *ib.*, March-April, 1950, pp. 54-55.

admit that he is an African—'Je suis Français!'—they all are French, they all are from Paris, and nearly all of them were captains in the *Maquis*.)

"Here is a people whose primitiveness reaches the highest peak. Their educational level borders on absolute ignorance. Still more serious is their inability to absorb anything intellectual . . . They are completely ruled by primitive and wild passions. How many obstacles have to be overcome in educating the Africans, for instance, to stand in line for food in the dining room and not to cause a general disturbance. When one Bulgarian Jew argued with them about standing in line, an African immediately pulled out a knife and cut off his nose. It happened several times that they attacked the official of the Jewish Agency and beat him up. The workers in the camps do their jobs in constant danger of such attacks.

"In the living quarters of the Africans in the camps you will find dirt, card-games for money, drunkenness and fornication. Many of them suffer from serious eye, skin and venereal diseases; not to mention immorality and stealing. Nothing is safe in the face of this asocial element, and no lock can keep them out from anywhere.

"These life-forms are brought along by the Africans to their places of settlement, and small wonder that the general crime wave in the country is on the increase. In several parts of Jerusalem it is again unsafe for a girl, and even for a young man, to go out alone in the street after dark. And this was the situation even before the young Africans were demobilized from the army. By the way, these soldiers promised us more than once: 'When we finish the war with the Arabs, we will go out to fight the Ashkenazim!' In one camp they 'planned a revolt' which included robbing the arms of the guards and murdering all the local officials of the Jewish Agency. Often, when the police appears on the scene, there are fights.

"But above all these there is a basic fact, no less serious, namely, the lack of all the prerequisites for adjustment to the life of the country, and first of all—*chronic laziness and hatred of work*. All of them, almost without exception, lack any skill, and are, of course, penniless. All of them will tell you that in Africa they were 'merchants'; the true meaning of which is that they were small hawkers. And all of them want to settle 'in the town.'

"What, therefore, can be done with them? How to 'absorb' them? . . .

". . . Has it been considered what will happen to this country if this will be its population? And to them will be added one day the immigration of the Jews from the Arab countries! What will be the face of the State of Israel and its level with such a population?

"Certainly, all these Jews have the right to immigrate, no less than others. And they have to be brought here and absorbed, but if this is not done in accordance with the limits of capacity and distributed over periods of time—they will 'absorb' us and not we them. The special tragedy of this absorption is, in contrast to the low-grade human material from Europe, that there is no hope even with regard to their children; to raise their general level out of the depths of their ethnic existence—this is a matter of generations! (Perhaps one should not wonder that Mr. Begin and *Heruth* [The Freedom Party] demand that all these hundreds of thousands be brought in immediately, for they know that boorish, primitive and poverty-stricken masses are the best material for them, and only such an immigration is likely to raise them to power.) . . ."*

This description of the North African Jews partakes of all the characteristics of racial or ethnic stereotypes which emerge everywhere where two or more ethnic groups live together in close physical proximity. The picture painted is based on a superficial and short-range observation of a few individuals in a peculiar and unusual situation of stress. The character-traits are deducted in an unwarranted manner from a few disconnected chance happenings, observed but incompletely understood, and are put together to build a composite picture of the deplorable individuality of all North African Jews. In addition, complete ignorance is shown of those fundamentals of psychology and anthropology which are by now practically commonplace and with which some familiarity is indispensable even for a non-scientific and amateurish description of the "character" of a population-group. Statements such as "inability to absorb anything intellectual," "completely ruled by primitive and wild passions," "even with regard to their children there is no hope," reveal clearly that the writer, in complete disregard of long-established scientific fact, believes character-traits to be genetically transmitted and therefore incapable of rapid modulations.

It would not have been necessary to quote this example of journalistic superficiality, were it not for two factors which raise it somewhat out of the ephemeral frame of newspaper reportage. The first

* Arye Gelblum, "The Truth About the Human Material," in *Haaretz* (Hebrew daily), Tel Aviv, April 22, 1949.

of these is that the opinions and the underlying attitudes it expresses are largely shared by a considerable portion of the Ashkenazi division of the Jewish population of Israel; and that the fact that there exists "racial" discrimination against the Oriental Jews, and especially against the North African immigrants, which has reached at times the intensity of "racial hatred," is admitted by many who are bold enough to speak up against it.* Secondly, even those who sympathize with the North African immigrants, and who are fully conscious of the social injustice being done them, share in most cases the misconceptions concerning the "racial" basis of mental and cultural traits. This turns the Gelblum article, from an isolated and insignificant outburst, into a critical symptom expressing the prevalent approach to the insufficiently understood and improperly evaluated ethnic and socio-cultural heterogeneity, irrespective of the question of positive or negative judgment.

One of the staunchest defenders of the Oriental Jews, for instance, goes so far as to compare the attitude of Gelblum to that of Otto Ollendorf, the Nazi henchman who, when asked at his trial in Nuremberg why he exterminated Jewish children as well as adults, answered: "Jewish children become in the course of time Jewish adults." At the same time, however, this protagonist of the Moroccan Jews has this to say about them:

"This is exactly the 'race' we need. We suffer from an overdose of intelligence, of brain-workers and of brain-work. The psychological background of Zionism—and especially of Labor Zionism—was the will to flee from the exaggerated ballast of intellectual worrying to simple, natural, better life. We need, like air to breathe, sizable 'injections' of naturalness, simplicity, ignorance, coarseness. These simpletons, these childish Jews, with their simple-mindedness and their [natural] intelligence . . . are a life-elixir against our over-intellectual worrisomeness which is the source of many of our troubles, among them—our stubbornness and obstinacy in party life . . ."§

These examples could be multiplied at will. The main trends of the attitudes towards the Oriental Jews, however, can be seen clearly enough already. The public attitude to the Oriental Jews ranges from full sympathy and readiness to go all out to help them in their adaptive processes, on the one end of the scale, to scornful derision and an overt wish to prevent their influx into the country, on

* Cf. e.g. Efraim Friedman, "On the Immigration from North Africa—A Reply to Mr. Gelblum," *Haaretz*, May 8, 1949.
§ K. Shabtai, in *Davar* (Hebrew daily), Tel Aviv, March 3, 1950.

the other. The official attitude, as expressed, not in statements and pronouncements, but in parliamentary acts and in actual deeds by the Government of Israel and its departments and affiliated institutions and agencies, is to help them come into the country even at the greatest financial and economic sacrifices, and thereafter to pay them somewhat less attention, to give them somewhat less help, and to show towards them somewhat less patient understanding than is the case vis-à-vis the Ashkenazi immigrants. The all-out effort to bring them to Israel does not stem purely from brotherly love, and the second-grade treatment is not accorded to them merely because of a lack of sufficient brotherly love. They are brought to Israel because the country's leaders are ready to sacrifice the present well-being of the entire population for the sake of long-range benefits; in other words, because the country still needs people, because the more numerous its population the greater the chances that its currently hostile neighbors will abstain from a "second round." These considerations must be regarded as the main motivation for the financial and organizational efforts to transport thousands and tens of thousands of immigrants from Yemen, North Africa, Turkey, the Balkans, and most recently Iraq, while keeping the country's doors unconditionally open for every Jew who wishes to immigrate and is able to come on his own. But just as this all-out effort cannot be ascribed solely to the wish to save as many as possible of the Oriental Jewish communities from a precarious existence, the relative indifference of which they complain immediately after their arrival in Israel must be ascribed to reasons other than, or at least additional to, the undeniable presence of a greater ethnic barrier between them and the predominant Ashkenazi element. The reports say that the majority of the Oriental Jews lived in slums in their home communities—consequently second and third-rate housing will still be adequate for them; they have no skills needed in a Western-type mechanized and specialized civilization—let them therefore fill the ranks of unskilled labor for which there is always much need—thus the reasoning goes. To this same category of reasoning must be counted the omnipresent recommendation of the cure-all patent-medicine: rapid and complete assimilation to the Western folkways and mores established in Israel by the Ashkenazi Jews.

5. The Fate of Oriental Culture in Israel

The cultural crisis in the grip of which the Oriental Jewish immigrant finds himself in Israel can be fully understood only when viewed against the background of the traditional culture which was his up to his immigration. In an earlier chapter we recognized five crucial complexes of traditional Oriental culture which were focal concerns in the life of the Oriental Jewish communities as much as they were in that of their non-Jewish neighbors.* A brief analysis of the impact of the modern Israeli scene on these focal culture complexes seems therefore to be called for in order to isolate some of the more important stresses within the total mechanism of culture change to which the Oriental Jewish immigrants are exposed in Israel.

Oriental culture has been found to be characterized by a greater permeation of the *esthetic* element in everyday life than is the case in Western culture. The majority of the Oriental Jewish immigrants has to pursue a life in Israel in which the traditional esthetic component is completely or at least largely lacking. In most cases they were unable to bring along any of those esthetically highly valued objects in which their traditional artistic sense expressed itself. Artistically decorated furnishings and clothing, household and other articles, were in most cases sold, or had to be left behind. Jewelry, if brought along, soon had to be sold when money was lacking for basic needs. Only the vocal arts remain, the love and practice of poetry and music, but even these shrivel for lack of congenial atmosphere and on account of exhausting physical labor and a social environment in which a group from one single home-community can only rarely preserve its privacy. The artistic elements in modern Israeli life remain unknown or unattainable for them, and life drained of the accustomed and cherished esthetic component appears bleak, cold and impoverished.

With regard to *religion*, the Oriental Jewish immigrants find themselves in great confusion in Israel. In their home communities religion was the solid and broad foundation of every activity, of every phase and aspect of life. Upon their arrival in Israel they find that most of the leaders of the State are irreligious, are in fact also the heads of strong political parties which are either directly opposed or at least indifferent to religion. They also learn soon enough that the majority of the people of Israel are not religious and that to be religious in the orthodox sense is often a disadvantage. They see that the laws of the Sabbath-rest are openly disregarded in the streets of the towns of Israel, that vehicular traffic continues unhampered, and long before they are in a position to understand the differences between observing the Sabbath in a small Yemenite or North African ghetto and in a big all-Jewish city like Tel Aviv,

* Cf. p. 55.

they cannot help comparing the two and feeling compelled to reject what they see and find in Israel.

The educational issue, the efforts of the religious party, on the one hand, and the Labor party, on the other, to gain the upper hand in the educational institutions organized for the new immigrants, adds to the confusion. The existence of a religious group among the Ashkenazim of Israel is acknowledged with satisfaction, but at the same time it has to be recognized that the Labor trend is more powerful, has more to offer, and can, in general, help more effectively.

The outcome of the religious confusion is a division of the Oriental Jewish immigrant groups along the lines of a religious cleavage. Those who continue to cling to their old religious precepts and ideas feel forced to reject many things they encounter in Israel in addition to the non-religious attitude, because of their conviction that they must avoid associating with non-religious people in Israel as they did in their home communities. On the other hand, those who are attracted by the new and free atmosphere in Israel, who become persuaded that they can discard their religious traditions, find themselves separated from their old community-group and even from their own families; their lives soon become denuded of a second important focal concern long before new values and interests can fill the void.

The *"broader outlook on human existence,"* which in the original cultural configuration of the Oriental Jewish communities is closely tied up with the religious attitude, does not fare any better than religion itself. The more obvious and immediately apprehensible manifestations of the broader outlook on human existence are rejected by the predominant Western element in Israel. The Oriental type of religious faith, we must repeat, appears to the unsympathetic Westerner as mere superstition, Oriental contentment as indolence, and Oriental detachment as apathy and dullness. Such traits as a lack of inclination to all-out effort and exertion for the sole purpose of deriving the greatest possible material benefit for oneself, for one's group, or for both, are unhesitatingly stamped as "chronic laziness" or "Oriental lethargy." They are found to be painful and unpermissible deviations from precepts fundamental to the pioneering effort required for the upbuilding of Israel. It occurs to no one that they can be ultimately the outcome of certain basic and in themselves completely justified philosophies, as well as the results of habits acquired from childhood on in the specific socio-cultural environment. The philosophical basis of such typically Oriental attitudes remains hidden from and even unsuspected by the Westerner, the more so as only in the rarest cases are the Oriental Jews them-

selves conscious of it to a degree which would enable them to formulate it in terms meaningful for people brought up in Western
civilization.

The rejection by modern Israel of the Oriental Jewish outlook on
human existence is therefore the result of no conscious process. The
tension between the two groups came into being on the level of
manifestation and not on that of basic principle. But whether conscious or not, here is an important focal concern of Oriental Jewry
which profoundly influences their traditional attitudes and which in
Israel meets with misunderstanding, rejection and pressure towards
its elimination.

We found that traditional Oriental culture is characterized—as
far as social structure is concerned—by the primary importance of
the *extended family* as the basic economic and social unit, and by
the subordination of the individual to the extended family. In the
countries of the Middle East the extended family has played as
important a role in the lives of the Jewish communities as it did in
those of the non-Jewish population groups.

All over the Middle East the extended family has for the last two
or three decades been caught in a process of slow and gradual disintegration as a result of the persistent and general modernization
or Westernization of the entire area.* In addition to this general
trend, however, the breakup of the Jewish extended families was
greatly speeded up, first, by the desire of some of the members to
go to Palestine, and, most recently, by the actual emigration to Israel
of considerable parts of practically every family. The immigrants
who arrived in Israel came either individually or with their small
immediate families only. Though they were prepared both in principle and in practice to detach themselves from the protective and
accustomed environment of the large extended family and to undertake the long trip to Israel, they were completely unqualified to
countenance not only a new, different and wider general social
environment, but also a new immediate situation in which they
found themselves either literally alone or in a home-atmosphere
which did not in the least resemble what they were used to in the
old countries.

With regard to the earlier Oriental Jewish immigrants, the situation was similar but not quite so acute. They were in many cases
able to establish in Palestine common residence for an entire extended family. Thus they succeeded in transplanting a considerable
part of the home-atmosphere to the new environment and in creat-

* Cf. René Maunier, *The Sociology of the Colonies*, London, 1949, vol. II,
p. 586 ff.

ing a new "home base" in which they found a firm foothold amidst a maelstrom of new and confusing impressions. The joint household of the large extended family was the fortress, a refuge which lent the individual a sense of security and made adjustment to the new environment easier, smoother and less critical for him.

Nevertheless, many of the older immigrants from the countries of the Middle East were unable to integrate into such an extended family in Palestine; while the Oriental Jewish immigrants who have come to Israel since its independence are practically all in this situation.* The overwhelming majority of the Oriental Jews in Israel today are thus forced to live in a social setting which is for them unaccustomed and therefore unsatisfactory. The changeover from the old to the new situation is both sudden and overwhelming. Everything around them is completely different: they find themselves in a new country, in a new social environment, in a new economic organization, and engaged in new occupations. But over and above all this, there is the most baffling circumstance that even the *home* is different—in its physical-external aspects as well as with regard to the size, structure and function of the family inhabiting it. The old extended family has disappeared; the man, the breadwinner, has now to face the outer world as a single individual without the strengthening and heartening influences of a large family-group of which he was an organic part. If he is married, the pressure of the new economic conditions forces his wife, too, to leave home for the major part of the day to seek work in the employ of strangers. All this means a simultaneous internal and external change, causing disturbance, crisis and, at times, tragedy.

No correspondingly abrupt, drastic or shattering changes have occurred in the social continuity of the Ashkenazi Jewish immigrants. It is true that those who reached the shores of Palestine with the earlier immigration waves, broke to a considerable extent with family, traditions, customary occupations and many other aspects of the diaspora-life left behind. However, whenever they did so, it was done after a conscious process of ideological clarification which culminated in the final determination to seek a new life-form in the

* The only potential exception is, for the time being, that of the Yemenite and Iraqi Jews. Since practically all these were transported to Israel, theoretically at least they should have been able to reconstitute their extended families in Israel more or less completely. In practice, of course, the re-establishment of the extended families depends not only on the presence of all the members of these families in Israel, but also on the settlement plans carried out by the Israeli authorities. A detailed study of the fate of the old Yemenite extended families after their arrival in Israel and their settlement in the country would be valuable practically and significant scientifically.

old-new home of the Jewish people. It was this conscious and deliberate inner resolve, ripening without any immediate external compulsion, that motivated their departure for Palestine and became the core of the pioneering mood. This volunteer spirit which implied a readiness to face changes and hardships and privations, was a chief characteristic of those early *Aliyot*, sharply distinguishing them from the recent mass-immigrations of Oriental Jews.

No such differentiating trait exists, of course, between the recent Oriental Jewish and the recent Ashkenazi immigrants. Both of these groups continue to come to Israel partly because their original position has become untenable, and partly because they are motivated by a rather vague idealism concretized in the wish to live in the State of Israel, where a Jew can feel as much at home as a Frenchman is in France. From Europe this immigration began with the ascension of Hitler; in the Middle East it started with the independence of the Jewish State. Common to the majority of the immigrants from both areas has been the unpreparedness to face changes and to put up with hardships; both want to resume in Israel a life as similar as possible to the one left behind in pre-war Europe and in the Middle East respectively. Therefore both are dissatisfied when they encounter the harsh and trying realities of life in Israel. Among both, there are those who feel that they are unable to endure the demands of the new country, and who try, and at times even succeed, in leaving Israel.

But there is at least one decisive difference between the two groups. The hardships, privations and sufferings experienced by the Ashkenazi Jews are for the most part of a purely material nature. They suffer from unemployment, lack of housing, lack of adequate food and clothing, and the like. Their experiences in the Europe of the last decade hardened them against such vicissitudes. They also believe, together with the rest of the population of Israel, that these difficulties are only transitory and that within a relatively short time a general amelioration will be attained in the whole country in which they will share equally with the older inhabitants. In non-material respects, satisfactions are found already now. They find themselves in a society which, by and large, is constituted and organized like the one which they still remember from the "good old days" of pre-World War II Europe. One very significant factor here is the possibility of continuing or resuming family-life in practically the same form in which they knew it from the old countries. As soon as the Ashkenazi immigrant has a roof over his head and four walls around himself, his wife and children, he possesses the same "home-base" from which he, and his father before him, operated in Europe.

Whatever the vicissitudes outside, he faces them from the same "operational base" from which he used to face the hostile world before the great catastrophe swept everything away. For him, the adjustment to the new conditions in Israel may still be very difficult to take, but it will rarely result in a *crisis*, since in this one fundamental point at least continuity has been preserved.

The last basic feature we distinguished in the traditional configuration of Oriental culture was the *composition of the larger social units as being not of individuals but of extended families.* This meant that the individual had an ascribed status depending on that of the family to which he belonged. He did not have to *achieve* his status, or at least not if he was content with the one accruing to him in his capacity as a scion of a certain family. Only if he was ambitious, and wanted to achieve a status higher than the one traditionally belonging to his family, did he have to labor for it. Such cases were relatively few, however.

Yet, at the same time, this also meant that the majority of the Oriental individuals in their traditional social setting were unable to achieve any status at all. They have never been educated with this end in view. All they can do expertly is to occupy the positions for which they were predestined by birth, descent and membership in a certain extended family. The inheritance in the male line of certain traditional occupations, like trades and handicrafts, is a corollary of this situation. Another is the valuation of pure and noble descent, prevalent especially among the nomadic peoples, but easily discernible also among the settled villagers and the townsfolk.

The transition from a society in which the ascribed family-status is all that counts in social prestige to a society in which each individual has to fight for his own achieved status is a very difficult and laborious process. The individual feels lost without the actual presence of a numerous family surrounding him, and doubly lost when he finds himself in a social setting in which ascribed family status is not regarded in principle, while in practice his actual family and its status are quite unknown. The average individual of the Oriental Jewish communities was used to moving around in his society, to participating in the social life of his wider social environment, in his capacity as a member of a certain family. He did not belong to many associations besides the primary and "natural" one of his own extended family, but if he did, he joined them together with his family. In Israel, the Oriental Jewish immigrant is approached by several voluntary associations with a bid for his membership: political parties, labor organizations, and other groups vie for his individual participation, and impress him with the desirability of joining up. The necessity for making a choice among several alternatives is even more baffling and confusing for him since in the old country he had never experienced such a situation at all.

The sum total of the foregoing examination leads to the conclusion that, under the impact of the modern Israeli socio-cultural scene, none of the five crucial complexes of traditional Oriental culture, which were focal concerns in the lives of the Oriental Jewish communities, can stand up. The suddenness of the air-transport from Yemen or Iraq to Israel within a few short hours is matched by the abruptness of the change from the old, accustomed, traditional environment to an entirely new socio-cultural situation. The European Jewish immigrants can retain certain important socio-cultural traits in almost undisturbed continuity. The Oriental Jewish immigrants, on the other hand, are forced into the retort of *total cultural change*. The Europeans in Israel experience socio-economic difficulties; the Orientals—a cultural crisis.

Chapter Eleven
Challenge and Outlook

1. Numerical Increase and Cultural Influence

It is now time to turn to the developments which can be expected to take place in Israel in the future, and especially to those which can be brought about by purposefully channeling the socio-cultural drifts already discernible at the present time. Before doing this, however, it will be well to recapitulate some of the insights gained from the examination of the current situation in the new Jewish State.

We found, to summarize very briefly, that a keen sense of community of fate pervades Israel and manifests itself in the determination of its leadership to shoulder the responsibility for the Jewish communities wherever they may be. The existence of a Jewish State means the existence of a country to which every Jew can come as of right. This principle was re-endorsed by the popular vote of the 1951 elections to the Knesset, and embodied in the Law of Immigration. As recently as September 30, 1951, Prime Minister David Ben-Gurion reaffirmed, in his New Year's Day message, that, regardless of the sacrifices, "the gates of Israel will remain open to all Jews."*

In addition to the humanitarian imperative, the military and political interests of the State also demand the continuance of the sacrifices for the sake of unabating mass immigration: the greater the population the greater the manpower of Israel, and the greater its manpower the greater its security in the face of external threats.

The material aspects of the sacrifices this policy demands from the population of Israel can be summarized in a few words: very tight rationing of food, clothing and all other consumer goods; unsatisfactory and often sub-standard conditions of housing, affecting especially the newcomers; strict economic controls, including an almost brutal restriction of the import of scarce consumer goods; high prices, inadequate services and a great many minor discomforts

* *The New York Times*, October 1, 1951, dispatch from Tel Aviv.

which can make life unpleasant. These sacrifices are heavy, but are borne in the knowledge that they are temporary and that as soon as the gigantic task of the "Ingathering of the Exiles" is completed— in two or three years—a definite easing-up will set in on the ✻ economic front.

No such comfort of relief in sight exists on the socio-cultural front. The population of Israel in 1952 was found to be composed of two numerically more or less equal elements: Jews of European (Ashkenazi) extraction, dominating in the economic, political, social and cultural spheres; and Middle Eastern peoples—both Jewish and non-Jewish—constituting what is felt by many Western Jews to be a backward, retarded, lagging element. Upon closer scrutiny, it was discerned that the differences between these two main groupings in Israel are but the specific, concrete expressions of the wider and more general disparity between two great developments of human culture: the culture of the modern West and the culture of the tradition-bound Middle East.

Given the ethnic composition of its population, the cultural crisis which threatens to undermine the socio-cultural foundations of the newborn State was found to originate in the unchanneled and overly rapid processes of culture contact literally sweeping the Oriental population elements off their feet, and in the repercussions created in the Western half of the population by the presence in ever increasing numbers of culturally alien groups in their midst. A major aspect of the cultural crisis finds its expression in the religious crisis, potentially present within the Western Jewish division itself due to cleavages along religious lines. Now this religious cleavage is brought to the fore and becomes acutest reality due to the presence of great masses of newly immigrated religious Oriental Jews who are energetically wooed by both the conservative religious parties and the socialist non-religious parties for the obvious purpose of securing the support of voters.

A more thorough examination of the demographic differences which set off the Ashkenazi and the Oriental Jews from each other showed that, due to natural increase alone, the Oriental Jews would soon become the majority in Israel; and a survey of the immigration currents, with the sharp increase of the Oriental Jewish percentage since the establishment of the State, indicated that also a continuance of the immigration with its present ethnic composition would in itself suffice to turn the Oriental Jews into a majority. What the combined effect of the high rates of natural increase, characteristic of the Oriental Jews, and their high percentage among the immigrants will be is self-evident.

308

Culturally, this situation means that while today the predominant element which determines standards in Israel is still the Ashkenazi division, the maintenance of this position will become more and more difficult in view of the increasing numerical preponderance of the Oriental Jews. And this again means that the problem of the cultural future of Israel appears to assume the character of a race between two processes: the increase of the Oriental population elements in Israel, on the one hand, and the progress of Westernization, on the other. Should it prove possible to Westernize the Oriental Jews sufficiently before they become the majority, the cultural future of Israel will continue to rest on the Western foundations laid down by the European Jewish pioneers. Should, however, the Westernizing process prove unable to keep up with the numerical increase of the non-European population, Oriental mentality, attitudes and outlook may become predominant and turn the whole of

✳ Israel into an Oriental or a quasi-Oriental country.

As to the correlation between numerical proportion and cultural give-and-take, it has been pointed out elsewhere that, "if the differences between two contacting cultures are not too pronounced, then, other things being equal, the culture of the greater community will exert a greater influence on that of the smaller community than vice versa."✳ Applied to Israel this means that the Ashkenazi Jewish division stands the best chance of assimilating to itself the non-European elements in the country only as long as it is numerically stronger than they.

2. The Acculturative Demand

It is the realization of this position which prompts the Israeli leadership in general to seek the solution of the present cultural crisis in an effective and total, but primarily rapid assimilation of the Sephardi-Oriental Jewish groups to Ashkenazi-Western standards.

The head of the Jewish Agency's Department for Middle Eastern Jews wrote as recently as September 1951:

"There are among us those who protest against the increase of the Sephardim (and) the Oriental immigrants in the country . . . lest they become too numerous and overwhelm the cultural values and endow us and our children with a Levantine culture." [The remedy is of course assimilation:] "The mass immigration streaming now from backward and primitive countries to the Land of

✳ Cf. Raphael Patai, *On Culture Contact and Its Working in Modern Palestine*, p. 21. Memoir No. 67 of the American Anthropological Association, October, 1947.

Israel is apt to inundate with its flow all our achievements. It is necessary, therefore, to toil in order to impart to those who now come to us, the experience and the will of the first-comers . . ."*

In order not to offend the sensibilities of the Oriental communities, the demand for their cultural assimilation is usually couched in cautious terms, ostensibly referring only to the general necessity of eradicating the jarring differences between the various ethnic elements of the Jewish population of Israel.** This is the avowed policy also of the Department for Middle Eastern Jews of the Jewish Agency, a recent statement in whose official publication reads as follows:

> "The special problem which came into being in Jewry as a consequence of its dispersion in the diaspora and the ingathering of the exiles in Israel—the problem of ethnic isolationism—inhibits the national, cultural, social and economic development of the State and the people. One must not rely on the 'natural' trend towards the merging of the diasporas and the elimination of the inter-community barriers in Israel; it is necessary to accelerate the process by means of coordinated and planned political and public action."§

Mr. Berl Locker, veteran political leader, writes: "Let the child be called by its name. There are prejudices between one community and another . . . And the main problem is how to overcome the existing prejudices against the Oriental Jews among the Ashkenazim, both in Israel and abroad, and how to quicken the process of integration of the new immigrants into the existing *Yishuv* and merge them with the Ashkenazi Jews.¶

Although these statements, and many more which could with ease be culled from the current Israeli press and literature, all speak merely of a homogeneous or uniform Israeli culture which is expected to emerge after the eventual elimination of the present cultural diversity, actually one is left in no doubt as to the quality of this future Israeli culture which is invariably envisaged as differ-

---

* Cf. J. Zerubavel, "The Central Problem," in *Yalqut haMizrah haTikhon* (Hebrew), Publ. by the Dept. for Middle Eastern Jews of the Jewish Agency, Jerusalem, Aug.-Sept. 1951, p. 2.

** Cf. e.g., the speech of the Prime Minister, Mr. David Ben-Gurion, in the Knesset, as published in the *Divre haKnesset* of March 8, 1949, p. 56.

§ A. N., "Outlines of the Solution of the 'Problem of the Communities,'" *Yalqut haMizrah haTikhon*, Aug.-Sept. 1951, p. 29.

¶ Berl Locker, "One People," *Zion, Incorporating the New Judaea*, Jerusalem, August, 1951, p. 19.

ing but little from the present-day culture of the Ashkenazi division of the Jewish population of Israel.

The same note was sounded even in pre-State days, when a *Histadrut* leader of the Yemenite Jews wrote:

"The flood of immigration and the intensification of building activity in the last fifty years already has had the effect of obliterating differences and breaking down barriers to a considerable extent. Especially great is the power of the Hebrew language which imparts to the people not only a common colloquial medium but also uniform concepts of life and thought. But we have still much to do in order to obliterate differences and to break down barriers."*

Political and institutional leadership is followed by social workers whose specially assigned task is to attend to the needs of the new immigrants. These officials who came in close daily contact with Oriental Jewish immigrant groups understand soon enough to what extent they are confronted by a population element significantly different from "us." Their assigned duty, however, is to minister to the social needs of the Oriental immigrants. By doing so, they endeavor to make their charges accept Western standards of social welfare, of material amenities and the like, thus ultimately facilitating their assimilation to the Western socio-cultural forms made dominant in modern Israel by Ashkenazi Jews.

Public opinion, as reflected in newspaper reports or articles, and as far as it does not reject the Oriental Jews altogether,§ evinces the same approach to the solution of the problem of the Oriental Jews in Israel.

A columnist of the biggest daily paper in Israel, himself most sympathetic to the Oriental Jews and a spirited champion of their rights, states: "Nobody denies that they are good-hearted, that they have a love for the land of Israel and the people of Israel; but there is something childish in their entire being. They take offense easily, they hate easily, and get reconciled easily." And he reports that the opinion has been expressed by several people that the Oriental Jews "are formless material, a sort of soft dough which one can knead into anything one wants; they are good-hearted children who await the hand which will form them."¶

Another writer views the differences between the Ashkenazi Jews

* Israel Yeshayahu, "The Oriental Jews in the Yishuv and in the Histadrut" (Hebrew), in *haHistadrut, Meassef*, Tel Aviv, 1946, pp. 245-6.

§ Cf. above, pp. 296-7.

¶ K. Shabtai, *Davar* (Hebrew daily), Tel Aviv, March 3, 1950.

and the Oriental Jews in the wider context of the differences between Orient and Occident. After expounding his view of the backwardness of the Oriental peoples in general, he says:

"What must therefore be the task of the 'Ingathering of the
Exiles?' Not only to bring them [the Oriental Jews] to the soil of
Israel, but also to restore to them their first exalted value. The
same thing holds good with regard to all parts of the people who
were dispersed—to their misfortune, by the hand of fate—among
low-grade (*yarud*) peoples. And every Jew who is not seized by
fear of the possibility, whether it is imaginary or not, that we will
not be able to prevail and to purify our [Oriental] brethren from
the dross of Orientalism which attached itself to them against
their will, will be held accountable for this before the guardian
spirit of the nation . . . There is reason for the most serious anxi-
ety . . . how to cleanse and to purify these brethren, how to lift
them up to the Western level of the existing *Yishuv* . . ."*

3. The Implications of Culture Contact

Practically the same premises underly the approach of the few
students of society in Israel who have taken up the investigation of
the adjustment of the immigrants, and especially those from the
Middle East.§ That the goal must be the eventual assimilation of the
Oriental groups to an Ashkenazi cultural prototype seems to be
taken for granted. Some researchers have gone so far in their acceptance of the official point of view that they start out their investi-
gations with the—scientifically unwarranted—assumption that the
Oriental Jewish communities are incapable of continued existence
in Israel. Therefore, they contend, the central problem is how to
make their self-liquidating process easier and how to substitute for
"their present segregated residential existence, which is empty of
any real social content," a participation in the general social life of
the country with a possible retention of "certain elements" of their
original community-life.

Attention is also given to the processes of change observable
among the Oriental Jewish immigrants after their arrival in Israel,
without any attempt, however, at correlating these changes with the
total configuration of the traditional culture upon which the impact

* M. A., "On the Oriental Quality," *Davar* (Hebrew daily), Tel Aviv, September 29, 1950.

§ Several independent research projects have been initiated in the last three
years in Israel and are still in progress (1952), all concentrating on the study
of the adjustment of immigrants. There is apparently no coordination among
these projects.

of the change takes place. But without such a correlation, no basic understanding of the problems specific to the Oriental Jewish immigrants is possible. What is arrived at is, at best, an analysis of the difficulties encountered by all immigrant groups, whether coming from the East or from the West. The study of a contact-situation involving population-groups of different cultural backgrounds is doomed to failure if it concentrates exclusively on social differentials observable in the locale of the contact. Such a study cannot succeed if its working hypotheses are formulated without full cognizance of the underlying basic differences in cultural equipment which decisively influence the mutual attitudes and reactions of population-groups.

In order to grasp fully the problems of *culture-contact* present in such a case, as distinct from *social contact* which takes place between different sectors of one and the same cultural group, the sociological approach must be supplemented by the anthropological approach. This latter views contacts between population-groups hailing from different cultural backgrounds in the full light of these cultural backgrounds themselves. It aims at fulfilling the fundamental prerequisite of thorough acquaintance with the total structure and functioning of each culture whose carriers are involved in the contact processes. Lacking such acquaintance with the cultural background of the Oriental Jewish immigrant groups, the students of adjustment difficulties in Israel are almost as remote as the political and social leaders, the social workers, the journalists and the average Ashkenazi Israeli citizen, from envisaging the desirability, for both the immigrant groups themselves and Israel as a whole, of preserving as much as possible of the socio-cultural identity of the Oriental Jews. The simple truth, that the manifestations of the specific cultural content brought along by the Oriental Jews to Israel are *not symptoms of deficiency* of which the group must be cured as quickly and as completely as possible, has, it would seem, not yet dawned on anybody, or at least has not yet been voiced or given serious consideration.

As against this Western ethnocentric attitude, it must be stated most emphatically that the specific culture of the Oriental Jewish communities is as much a valid variety of human cultures as is that of the Russian Jews, the Polish Jews, the German Jews, or any other Jewish or non-Jewish human group. It is paradoxical, and more than that, it is unforgivable, to declare the principle of open door to any Jew, to undertake heavy economic sacrifices for the transportation of 377,000* Oriental and Sephardi Jews into Israel, and then,

* From the beginning of 1948 to the end of 1951.

after their arrival in the country, to say to them, in effect, "We want your physical presence, but we do not want your personality; we admit your body, but we exclude your soul." Yet this is what even the most "understanding" attitude towards the Oriental Jewish immigrants in Israel amounts to. Wherever the Oriental Jew goes in Israel, he meets with this constantly reiterated demand: "You must become like us!" The efforts aiming at the absorption of the Oriental Jewish immigrant and at facilitating his "integration," even the studies made of him and his ways in the new homeland, all have the one ultimate goal: to make him like "us," to assimilate him to one's own favorite European-Jewish prototype, either of the class-conscious socialist worker, the nationalistic enthusiast, the individualist middle-class-man, or the conservative religionist.

4. Stereotypes of East and West

In order to reach a fuller understanding of the problems involved in the Israeli contact situation, it will also be necessary to consider other processes of culture-contact and change in which the cultures concerned are similar to the cultures possessed by the Ashkenazi and the Oriental Jews respectively. The basic premise here, of course, is that where the cultures involved and the contact-situations developing are similar, the range of possible processes of change also will be similar; hence a familiarity with processes of contact and change in which the *dramatis personae* are, on the one hand, Europeans and, on the other, Middle Eastern peoples, is indispensable for a correct evaluation from a wider perspective of the probable, possible and desirable outcomes of the Israeli cultural crisis. When thus placed against the wider background of European-Middle Eastern culture-contacts, the phenomena encountered in Israel will be divested of their apparent and startling uniqueness, will be recognized as merely new variants of a certain type of situation which has occurred in the past elsewhere and has been grappled with at times with a measure of success.

The first thing one can learn from a conspectus of the Israeli and other Middle East-European contact-situations is the inevitable outcropping of *mutually derogatory stereotypes*. Stereotypes developed in other Middle Eastern countries can, as a matter of fact, serve as useful background information for the proper evaluation of the attitudes of the European Jews towards Oriental Jews, and vice versa, and can throw light on the judgments passed by the two divisions on each other. René Maunier, who made an intensive study of this problem, found that the European reproaches the "native" for his instability, emotionalism, impulsiveness, unreliability and incompetence. The natives, on the other hand, charge the Europeans with an exercise of authority and a mania for regimenting and regulating; with simplicity, that is absence of ostentation; with punctuality which appears to them monotonous and tyrannical; with irreligiousness; with indecency on account of the Europeans' close-fitting clothing which lack modesty, their social intercourse with women, their dances and games and the like—all of which are taken as marks of ill-breeding.* In introducing this discussion, Maunier says: "In spite of having already entered into close relationship, native and European nevertheless misjudge and despise each other, because they misapprehend each other."

Missapprehension and its resultant misjudgment and contempt frequently characterize also the mutual stereotypes of European and Middle Eastern Jews, notwithstanding the fact that these two groups have much more in common than the Europeans and the natives of whom Maunier speaks. It seems to be a general human psychological trait to misunderstand and dislike those who are different. In Israel, the stereotype of the Oriental Jew (and especially of the Moroccan and North African Jew), as seen through the eyes of the average European Jew, is composed of all the features contained in the stereotype of the "native" as analyzed by Maunier. In addition to instability, emotionalism, impulsiveness, unreliability and incompetence, he is also accused of habitual lying and cheating, laziness, boastfulness, inclination to violence, uncontrolled temper, superstitiousness, childishness, lack of cleanliness, and in general "primitivity" and "lack of culture."§

The reverse stereotype, that formed by the Oriental Jews with regard to the Ashkenazim, also parallels to a remarkable degree the opinions found among the "natives" concerning the "whites." "They exercise authority and rule us," is one of the frequent complaints on the lips of Oriental Jews; or, "they are obsessed with punctuality, with efficiency, with being delivered the goods at the promised hour," and the like. They also appear to be irreligious, impious and godless, and therefore bad and evil. To these can be added the more specific and often reiterated complaint of discrimination practiced by the Ashkenazi Jews against the Orientals, which is the manifestation of the Oriental Jews' conviction that the Ashkenazim regard
✳ them as inferior, second-rate, lowgrade.¶

Wherever such negatively weighted stereotypes develop between

* Cf. René Maunier, *Sociology of the Colonies*, London, 1949. I, 82-85.

§ These expressions are culled from various Hebrew newspaper articles on the Oriental Jews.

¶ Sources the same as in the previous note.

two population-groups, they inevitably create opposition and tension and can easily precipitate a crisis. That in the colonies under "white" domination things rarely came to a head, and the mutual dislike or distrust did not as a rule reach the point of a critical outbreak, can be explained by the balance of power obtaining in colonial areas. There was in most cases a definite cleavage between "white" and "native," between ruler and ruled, between the few who controlled and the many who were powerless and disorganized. The objective situation—which in itself, to be sure, was created by the "whites" —was such as to develop unfailingly a "native mentality" among the "natives," and a mentality of "white supremacy" among the "whites." Leadership, decisiveness and managerial ability were expected from the "whites" by the natives as well as by themselves; while submissiveness, docility, obedience and subservience were traits which were part of the "nature" of the "natives," again according to both "white" and "native." In spite of mutual distrust and dislike, these ingrained doctrines neatly complemented each other and—as long as the controls worked—made for relatively smooth sailing with the "natives" working the oars and the "whites" beating the rhythm.*

In Israel no such mentality exists on either side. Being a modern democratic country, one of its fundamental doctrines is that all its residents have the same rights and duties, and are either actually or at least potentially equal in every human respect. In principle, therefore, no discrimination can exist against any section of the population, Jewish or non-Jewish. At the same time, however, there is the concomitant principle (and conviction) that the *potential* equality of Oriental Jews with Ashkenazi Jews has to be turned as speedily as possible into *actual* equality—by reshaping them after the pattern of the latter. There exists, therefore, a definite contradiction in terms of the avowed principles of relationship to the Oriental Jews: in principle they are equal to us, yet, again in principle, they have to be re-formed to be like us—which, of course, implies that the principle of equality is null and void. The principle of equality is also contravened by the feelings and attitudes of a large part of the Ashkenazi division of the Jewish population of Israel, expressed in actual behavior and leaving no doubt whatsoever as to the presumed inferiority of the Oriental Jews. The presence of the large Oriental Jewish population in Israel and the inevitable close contact between it and the Ashkenazi division thus create *conflicts* within

---

* These observations are no longer valid where the parties involved are European and Mediterranean (or Middle Eastern) peoples. Cf. the recent developments especially in the French territories of North Africa.

the Ashkenazi sector itself: a conflict of competing parties, a conflict of groups and individuals who have reached different understandings of the problem, and, last but not least, a conflict of conscience.

Complete equality and brotherhood with the other Jewish groups was the expectation of the Oriental Jews who came to Israel. Whatever "colonial" mentality they had acquired in the countries of the Middle East in their relationship to the members of the European dominant class (in North Africa especially) and towards the oppressing Moslems (in all the Middle East generally), their attitude to Jews was (and is) completely different. What this attitude and expectation were, and how the disappointments they experienced in Israel affected them, has been analyzed in some detail in an earlier connection.* Here it should be emphasized that, in addition to the inner conflict caused by this situation within the Oriental Jewish division itself, the mutually incongruous actual interrelationships between the Ashkenazi and the Oriental sectors of the population have created a situation many times more difficult and hazardous than the one usually accompanying "white" and "native" symbiosis. In the latter well-defined reciprocal rights and duties have generally been worked out, with mutually complementing stereotypes and with a social stratification acquiesced in by practically everybody and therefore regarded as relatively stable and well-balanced.§ In Israel on the other hand, the objectively existing and also keenly apprehended differences between the Ashkenazim and the Oriental Jews have resulted in tension and conflict, because there has been no mutual agreement, and certainly no forcibly imposed solution, with regard to the innumerable problems arising out of these differences. The Ashkenazi leadership of the country voices and reiterates the principles of equality, thus confirming and supporting the Oriental Jewish immigrants in their original belief and expectation. At the same time many—too many, in fact—of the Jewish immigrants encounter actual discrimination, slights and offensive attitudes, which they are convinced they do not have to take from other Jews, just as they were convinced they had to take them from Moslems or other dominating foreigners. The end result of all this is that the *opposition* —which is one of the well-known phenomena of the socio-cultural life in every country where two or more different population-groups live together—has on occasions become extraordinarily sharp in Israel.

* Cf. above, pp. 287-8.
§ Cf. above, p. 315.

5. The "Colonial" Attitude

The Ashkenazi Jews in Israel actually exhibit the same general attitude towards the Oriental Jews which was characteristic of the more enlightened Europeans in their relationship to the so-called "colonial" natives from the time they first met overseas peoples of different cultures and racial stocks. Scarcely had the New World been discovered when Pope Alexander VI addressed a Bull to Ferdinand and Isabel of Castile (in 1493) proclaiming that the conquest of the "remote and unknown islands and firm lands" must have as its aims the teaching of the Catholic faith, Christian religion and morals. A century later, the noted French essayist Montaigne, discarding the religious motivation, affirmed that the conqueror's duty was "gently to reclaim and polish the natives. . ."* Ever since then it has been a fundamental urge among well-meaning white colonizers to re-create, re-form and re-shape in their own image the natives whom they conquered or over whom they otherwise gained control or influence. One of the latest phrasings of this attitude was that of Kipling who spoke of "the white man's burden."

In Israel there is of course no such dichotomy in the population as that between "conquerors" and "conquered." Yet the Ashkenazi sector in Israel unmistakably shows the attitude of people brought up in Western civilization towards groups and individuals possessing a culture other than their own. Theirs is the pronounced ethnocentrism of the West, the conviction that only Western culture (or, more correctly, that particular brand of Western culture which happens to be one's own) is good, valid and therefore desirable; and the concomitant urge to impose it on every group or individual of a different cultural background. The basic motivation of this urge is undoubtedly altruistic; it is a matter of willingness to help, to share, to teach, to educate and to remedy—but it overlooks, because it is unaware of, the dangers of disintegration, demoralization and other dissolution generally termed "deculturation," accompanying every speedy process of culture-change.

Mutual distrust and misunderstanding can easily lead to the eruption of physical violence, especially in the case of certain Oriental Jewish communities who in their old homelands were used to the idea and practice of defending their rights by the use of actual or implied force. On a small scale it has already occurred several times in Israel that Oriental Jewish immigrants tried to rectify real or imagined wrongs by a threat of force or by actually resorting to violence.

* Montaigne, *Essais*, 1580, Book III, ch. 6.

Another highly undesirable possible outcome of the socio-cultural situation in Israel is the perpetuation of the ethnic isolation leading ultimately to the emergence of two distinct and separate sectors in the country, not unlike the Jewish and the Arab populations in the latter days of Mandatory Palestine. Admittedly, a certain amount of isolation along ethnic lines is inevitable in the conditions prevailing at present in Israel. It has been shown above* that spatial segregation of European and Oriental-Sephardi Jewish communities was the rule also during the days of the Mandate. This trend which led in the past to a high degree of residential separation (on a preferential basis and conditioned mainly by economic, social, sanitary and similar considerations), has been greatly reinforced after the establishment of the State and the onset of the mass immigration. The shortage in housing, which already characterized Israel on the very day of its birth, was a heritage of World War II conditions when building activity was drastically curtailed. The new immigrants, therefore, could under no circumstances be housed in the midst of the old population. They had to be accommodated either in abandoned Arab towns and villages, or in completely new housing projects set up for them on the outskirts of existing urban settlements or in more detached localities in rural areas. As a consequence of this, after four years of mass immigration, Israel in 1952 was found to be divided, as far as settlement is concerned, into two distinct sectors: a sector of the older inhabitants with only a sprinkling of newcomers in their midst, and a second sector of new immigrants with practically no older inhabitants living among them. Again, within the sector of new immigrants there is a secondary isolation according to countries of origin and communities, though this is not so pronounced as the overall residential segregation between "oldtimers" and newcomers. Nevertheless, in the majority of cases there is a clearcut separation of Oriental and European groups, either in the form of separate rural settlements, or in separate urban housing projects. Moreover, in the relatively few cases when newcomers succeed in settling down in older quarters in the cities, the Oriental Jews go to those quarters which are inhabited by people of their own community, while the same tendency is observable among the European Jewish immigrants. The result of this is an augmentation of the number of residents in the segregated quarters, with an increase of density and with it a worsening of the slum conditions ✱ especially in the areas inhabited by Oriental Jews.

A second aspect of ethnic isolation is also merely a continuation and intensification of trends which existed in the Mandatory

* Cf. above, pp. 92-7.

period. We have dealt at some length with the occupational structure of the European and the Oriental Jewish communities, and have seen that significant differences existed between the two. In most general terms, it was found that the European Jews concentrated in the "higher" occupational brackets, including skilled labor, while the Oriental Jews tended to occupy "lower" rungs, and especially unskilled labor.* This occupational dichotomy, too, has become more pronounced with the mass immigration since the establishment of the State. Although most of the European Jewish immigrants, too, had to be satisfied with less remunerative and less specialized jobs to start with, in most cases skills possessed or rapidly acquired soon enabled them to obtain better jobs and better conditions. The great majority of the Oriental Jewish immigrants, on the other hand, were unskilled when they came and have remained in the same low-paid and low-status jobs which were given them after their arrival. A poignant illustration of this difference in occupational achievement between Oriental and European Jewish immigrants was seen in the case of Beit Dagon discussed earlier in this book.§ Unskilled labor opportunities in public works (such as road-building, tree-planting, stoning of fields, removing of ruined buildings, etc.) are provided for new immigrants especially in the labor and transit villages, and those who, for lack of a better choice, engage in these low-paid, temporary and undesirable occupations are for the most part Oriental Jewish immigrants.

We also saw that the Oriental Jewish immigrants engaged in agriculture to a much greater extent than their percentual proportion in relation to other immigrant groups would warrant.¶ It can therefore be expected that, if this trend continues, the share of Oriental Jews in agriculture will be greater than their percentage in the total population. In a country where agricultural pioneering has been a vocation carrying the highest prestige, it would be perilous to allow agriculture to sink to the low status it possesses in the Moslem countries of the Middle East, which could result if it is allowed to become the domain of untrained and uneducated Oriental Jews. As several speakers put it at the Zionist Congress in the summer of 1951, there exists an acute danger of the emergence of two peoples in Israel if the distribution of functions prevailing today should continue for many more years, if the task of "conquering the wastelands" should continue to be placed only on the shoulders of "our brothers the Yemenites" and other Oriental Jews, who would thus become the

* Cf. above, 90-2.
§ Cf. above, 123-7.
¶ Cf. above, p. 92, and the table on p. 93.

modern counterparts of the biblical "hewers of wood and drawers of water," while "safe" Jewry, that is the established *Yishuv*, should
✱ continue to regard itself as exempt from taking part in this work.✱

The differences in occupational structure between the two main divisions of the population of Israel derive, as has been pointed out,§ from their respective cultural backgrounds. For this reason, nothing can be done at present to prevent a crystallization of these differences into general patterns in direct ratio to the influx of immigrants for whom work must be provided immediately. This entails the inevitable allocation to each group or individual of such occupations for which they are equipped and into which they can be absorbed. Great efforts will be needed, however, to prevent the perpetuation of this situation. For ultimately it might lead to the retention by the European Jews of an occupational structure not unlike the one which characterized their communities in pre-World War II Europe, with the menial, unskilled and agricultural labors, as well as the low-status services, relegated to Oriental Jews.

Continued residential and occupational segmentation would inevitably lead to a perpetuation of cultural inequalities between the European and the Oriental Jewish divisions of Israel. The European Jews would reside in the better quarters and in the better houses; they would enjoy better incomes and would be able to give their children a better education. They would thus come to form a cultural elite, with all the characteristics such a sector has everywhere in the world, including small numbers and aggravated by a pseudo-racial separatism. The Oriental Jews, on the other hand, would occupy the slums in the cities; they would become the "backward" rural population; they would have small and inadequate incomes; they would be unable to educate their children beyond a certain compulsory minimum; and thus they would come to form an urban and rural proletariat, underprivileged, dissatisfied, embittered, inimical,
✱ and a constant menace to the elite.

6. The Danger of Levantinism

The opposite of ethnic isolation also has its dangers and pitfalls. Undirected and uncontrolled fusion between the European and Oriental elements in Israel can lead to a general Levantinization of the country. By dictionary definition the term Levantine means a "native or inhabitant of the Levant, specifically, in the Near East, one descended from European settlers who speaks the language of

✱ Cf. *The Jewish Agency's Digest*, August 24, 1951, p. 1904, and August 31, 1951, p. 1941.
§ Cf. above, p. 92.

the natives, follows their customs, etc."* In the socio-cultural context this would mean an adoption by the European Jews of the ways, customs and mores of the Oriental Jews. It would mean a loss of the social and cultural attainments brought into the country by the European pioneers of the great and creative *Aliyot*. In the extreme case, it would mean the creation of a huge Jewish ghetto amidst the Moslem states of the Middle East.

There is, however, another, reverse kind of Levantinism with which anyone who spends even the shortest time in a Middle Eastern city cannot fail to become familiar. This is the Levantinism exhibited by natives of the Levant, or the Middle East in general, who speak the language of Europeans and follow their customs. The characteristic feature of this type of Levantine is, first of all, a liberally exhibited contempt for his own discarded native culture, including the language. The typical Levantine will prefer the company of Europeans, and in their presence he will miss no opportunity to show that he personally has become emancipated from the language, the customs and the traditions of his more old-fashioned compatriots. Arabic to him is a barbarous and primitive tongue, not suited for expressing refined, that is, European, ideas. The traditional garb of the natives is ridiculous and unsuitable for a "gentleman." The houses in the native quarters of his city are filthy, unfit to be inhabited by him. The traditional items of furniture, including the masterpieces of Damascene inlay, are "tasteless, childish things." Native art simply does not exist for him, nor does native literature or poetry. He has completely dissociated himself from the culture of the country in which he lives and from the people with whom he feels no kinship.

Why does he go to such lengths to abnegate his own culture? Because he feels irresistibly attracted to Europeans and to what they stand for. Whatever they possess, use, do or say, he feels compelled to imitate. In his endeavor to imitate them, he sheds all that has been his, that distinguished him from them. And in place of the discarded culture, he tries to adopt the culture of his European idols. He succeeds in aping the external and superficial manifestations of Western culture exhibited in certain limited fields of overt behavior by the few Europeans with whom he happens to be acquainted. In most cases, however, the very fact that Western culture has a rich ideational content, endowing its carriers with a specific set of attitudes, endeavors and value-judgments, remains unknown to the Levantine. His efforts, consequently, become concentrated on imitating as perfectly as possible the surface traits of

* Webster's *New International Dictionary*, s. v. Levantine.

Western existence which can easily be copied. The result is an individual who has become culturally rootless, who consciously negates the culture into which he was born and whose equally conscious efforts to acquire European culture never allow him to penetrate its outermost shell. He is characterized by an undue emphasis on appearances, on the acquisition of the material equipment and external trappings of Western culture, and at the same time by an inability to grasp this culture's non-material essentials.

The danger of this kind of Levantinism has existed in the Palestine of the Mandate among both Oriental Jews and Arabs. But due to the small number of the former and the relatively scanty mutual contact, it never assumed the proportions of a serious social problem. In Israel, however, the problem becomes increasingly serious with the growth of the Oriental Jewish sector. The all-too-rapid assimilation to a Western cultural prototype demanded of the Oriental Jews, and consciously promoted by officials, social workers and all those with whom the immigrants have their first contacts, creates a climate highly favorable to the growth of Levantinism. Rapid assimilation inevitably means the adoption of external, easily assimilable traits. The negative attitude, encountered among the Ashkenazi Jews with regard to the evaluation of the overt manifestations of the traditional Oriental cultures brought along by the immigrants, carries sufficient prestige to be contagious. In short order it is likely to create a similar attitude among the Oriental Jews themselves towards their own culture, including the conscious discarding of religious observance and other traditional customs preserved in the parental home and in the community group. The younger people especially among the immigrants are easily swayed. The figure of the Ashkenazi friend, foreman, official, employer, trainer, or social worker, rapidly assumes in their minds the character of an ideal image which, however, consists solely of external and superficial features. Accordingly, attempts will be made to imitate him in externals only: his dress, his mode of speech, his smoking, his ways of seeking entertainment, his disregard for religious precept, the material objects he possesses and uses—these are the things observed and readily emulated. Of the mental equipment, the inner values which are acquired by a person brought up in Western civilization, little if any notice is taken. This imitation of the externals of European behavior smacks strongly of Levantinism. Its tragedy is that it involves the repudiation of the solid core as well as the forms of a self-contained rich and age-old culture without acquiring in its stead anything but the outermost shell of a new civilization.

The danger of the Levantinization of the Oriental Jews in Israel would be much more acute than it actually is had the *Yishuv* not laid the foundation from the very beginning of the Mandate period for a number of important social and cultural institutions which today function as instruments of a very different and quite positive kind of Westernization.

7. Instruments of Westernization: The Knesset

Several important institutions have been developed by the *Yishuv* since the early days of Mandatory Palestine primarily in order to serve the economic, political, social and cultural advancement of the Jewish population as a whole, but incidentally becoming powerful instruments for the socio-cultural assimilation of its non-European elements. As has been pointed out earlier,* these institutions were created by European Jews and, since their purpose was to serve the *Yishuv* as a whole, Oriental and Sephardi Jews were successively drawn into them and elected or appointed to responsible positions in their administration. Sometimes they received appointments even on the policy-making level, although never in proportion to the full numerical strength of the Sephardi and Oriental Jewish divisions.

The most important political institution of Israel today is the *Knesset*, the Israeli parliament. Its forerunner was the *Assefat haNivharim*, the Elected Assembly, which was recognized in 1927 by the British Mandatory Government of Palestine as the official representation of the country's Jewish population. The first elections to the *Assefat haNivharim*, which took place in 1920 when the percentage of the Sephardi and Oriental Jews in the *Yishuv* was approximately 40%, gave 74 (or 23.5%) seats out of 314 to representatives of the Sephardi, Yemenite, Bokharan, Georgian and other Oriental Jewish party-groupings. In the second Elected Assembly (1925), the percentage of Sephardi and Oriental representation sank to 18.5% (41 out of 221 seats); and in the Third (1931), when the total percentage of Sephardi and Oriental Jews in the *Yishuv* was 29%, their representation constituted 25.3% (18 seats out of a total of 71.)§ In the first Knesset (elected January 25, 1949) 7 (or 5.8%) out of a total of 120 seats were occupied by Sephardi and Oriental Jewish representatives, including those who were elected on general lists, such as that of the Mapai party. In the second Knesset (elected July 30, 1951), again 7 (or 5.8%) of the same total of 120 were Sephardi and Oriental Jewish members, in spite of the fact that in the meantime the proportion of the Sephardi and Oriental Jewish

* Cf. above, ch. VI, Western Foundations.

§ Cf. Moshe Attias, *Knesset Yisrael beEretz Yisrael* (Hebrew), Jerusalem, 1944, pp. 21, 29, 35.

elements in the country had increased to about 36%. Compared with the weakness of the Sephardi and Oriental Jewish representation in the legislative body of Israel, the non-Jewish minorities attained a relatively fuller representation: in the first Knesset there were 3, and in the second 8, Arab and other non-Jewish (Druze) members, ✻ for a population which constituted 17% in 1949 and 12% in 1951.

Irrespective of the proportion of parliamentary representation, however, the fact remains that the Oriental Jews *are* represented in the highest legislative body of Israel; the laws passed by that body are enacted with the cooperation of the Sephardi and Oriental Jewish representatives, even if this cooperation is expressed—as it often is—in negative votes and other legal means of opposition. In this manner the Knesset, and its predecessor the Elected Assembly, became a significant *legal Westernizing factor* in the Palestine of the Mandate and in Israel. The very fact that the *Yishuv* had a supreme and central representation which was elected with the participation of the great majority of all the three divisions of the Jewish people in Palestine, meant close cooperation in several important fields, with the health, social, educational and cultural services extending to all sectors of the population.

An interesting example of legislation which will ultimately result in a definite assimilation of the Oriental communities to Western standards was the marriage law, which was passed by the Knesset over the stiff resistance of a combined Sephardi, Oriental Jewish and religious opposition. Following the initiative of Miss Ada Maimon (of the Mapai party), Minister of Justice Pinhas Rosen submitted to the Knesset, on January 24, 1950, a bill the essence of which was to make marriage unlawful for girls who had not yet completed their seventeenth year. The ensuing debate in the plenary session of the Knesset was most instructive owing to the light it shed on the relative degree of loyalty of certain Knesset members to the political party which they represented, on the one hand, and to the community-group to which they belonged, on the other. Supporters of the law, like Miss Maimon (Mapai), Nahum Nir-Rafaelkes (Mapam), and Benzion Dinaburg (Mapai), argued that it would prevent the enslavement of women and put an end to the "selling" of daughters by their fathers for £.I.100 or £.I.50 at the early age of 12 or 13 years to husbands old enough to be their fathers or even grandfathers. Those who opposed the bill, like Joseph Burg and Zerah Wahrhaftig (Religious Front), Abraham Elmaleh (Sephardim), Abraham Tabib (Mapai), emphasized the necessity of taking the traditions and customs of each community into consideration and not forcing upon the Oriental Jewish communities and upon the Arabs in Israel a law which is contrary to their old traditions. Especially interesting in this connection was the argument of Mr. Abraham Tabib, a member of the Mapai party, himself a Yemenite Jew and a husband to two wives, who, instead of following the party line and supporting the bill introduced by another Mapai member, sided with his Yemenite and Oriental brethren in voicing his sharpest opposition. After explaining that the defects found by the doctors in the health of the Yemenite and Oriental Jewish women are not caused by their early marriages but are due to their exertions in bringing up their children and the poverty from which they suffer, Mr. Tabib stated categorically: "My opinion is that any new law which puts a time limit on marriage beyond the age of physical maturity is against the law of nature and the laws of the Torah and of Judaism . . ."*

However, these and similar protests were of no avail. The Ashkenazi majority of the Knesset, with the exception of a few representatives of the United Religious Front, arrayed itself solidly behind the initiators of the marriage bill, which was thus easily written into law in June 1950, equally mandatory for all the citizens of the new State. Here was a clear case of the "unification" of divergent usages by legal measures, which in practice, however, meant an elimination of the Oriental version in favor of the European.

It is easy to imagine what would have happened had this question been left in abeyance until such time in the future when the Knesset was composed of a majority of Oriental Jewish and a minority of Ashkenazi representatives. The bill would have been defeated, unless, of course, the Sephardi and Oriental Jewish members would have become in the meantime so thoroughly Westernized in their thinking that they, too, would have regarded child-marriage as a backward and harmful custom. This example, by the way, illustrates in concrete form what was meant at the beginning of this chapter by the reference to a race between the increase of the Oriental element in the population of Israel and its Westernization.§

Another legal measure enacted by the Knesset, and resulting in a Westernization of traditional Middle Eastern family life, was the abolition of polygyny, the marriage between one man and several women.

Among the Hebrews in biblical times polygyny was permitted and practiced. In later times it was retained by the Oriental Jews only, who lived among polygynous Moslem peoples. The Sephardi Jews, who lived among both Moslems and Christians, abandoned

* *Divre haKnesset*, January 30, 1950.

§ Cf. above, p. 308.

polygyny in practice, but retained the principle of its legality. And, finally, the Ashkenazi Jews, who lived for hundreds of years among monogamous Christian peoples only, gave it up in practice and forbade it legally. Their acceptance of the ordinance of Gershom ben Yehuda (960-1040) of Mayence, the greatest rabbinical authority of his times in the Ashkenazi Jewish world, amounted to a ban on polygyny.

Under the British Mandatory regime in Palestine each religious community, whether Moslem, Jewish or Christian, was allowed to follow its own religious code and practice in matters affecting personal status.* Under the provisions of a special clause in the Penal Law of 1936 of the British Mandatory Government of Palestine, "bigamy" was permissible for members of those religious communities whose religious laws countenanced plural marriages. This made polygyny lawful for Oriental Jews and Moslems.

In July 1951, the Knesset adopted the "Women's Equal Rights Bill," which grants equality to women before the law. Clause 8A in the bill invalidates all discriminatory provisions embodied in other laws and imposes the prohibition of "bigamy" upon members of all the religious communities in the State of Israel.§ This new law does not invalidate existing plural marriages, but makes it unlawful to contract "bigamy" from the day on which it came into force.

It was a remarkable fact that, while a year earlier, the Marriage Law encountered sharp opposition on the part of the Sephardi and Oriental Jewish representatives in the Knesset, this was not the case with regard to the clause in the Women's Equal Rights Bill. A partial explanation of this absence of opposition may be found in the fact that with regard to polygyny the Sephardi and the Oriental Jews were divided between themselves, while early (child) marriages were practiced by both divisions to an almost equal extent. Moreover, the Chief Rabbinate had already taken a definite stand against polygyny a long time before the problem came up in the Knesset. According to the statutes of the *Knesset Yisrael* (the official name of the Jewish Community Organization in Mandatory Palestine), the Council of the Chief Rabbinate, invested with the highest religious authority in the *Yishuv*, consisted of one Sephardi and one Ashkenazi Chief Rabbi, and of three Sephardi and three Ashkenazi members (all rabbis). This structure of the Chief Rabbinate was retained after the foundation of the State. Thus, while the Ashkenazi

* Cf. p. 274.

§ Cf. *Reshumot, Hatza'ot Hoq* (Official publication of the Knesset), No. 75, May 9, 1951, p. 192.

half of the Chief Rabbinate represents only the Ashkenazi division of the *Yishuv*, the Sephardi sector represents both the Sephardi and the Oriental Jewish divisions.

This mode of representation in the Chief Rabbinate, ultimately going back to the ritualistic dichotomy of the Ashkenazi and the Sephardi-Oriental Jews which antedates the *Shulhan Arukh*,* was responsible for the unanimous opposition on the part of the highest rabbinical body in Israel to the continuation of the practice of polygyny in certain Oriental Jewish communities (like the Yemenites), which in turn may have exerted a restraining influence on the Sephardi and Oriental Jewish representatives in the Knesset. In this manner the full law of equal rights for women was passed without any discussion on the question of polygyny, and a bill was enacted which will become another factor in equalizing Eastern and Western family life, or rather re-casting Middle Eastern marriage into forms developed by Western Jewry.

8. Instruments of Westernization: The Schools and the Army

Another legally enacted measure of Westernization is the law of universal compulsory and free elementary education which was adopted in 1949. The education law makes it incumbent upon every child, male or female, Jewish or non-Jewish, to attend elementary schools for nine full years, from the age of 5 to 13** and up to the age of 18 if he has not yet completed his elementary education. The statistics compiled by the Ministry of Education and Culture show that two years after the passage of this law, that is at the end of the school-year 1951-52, practically all the Jewish children of school-age (about 300,000) were actually attending school. This was the situation notwithstanding the unabated influx of immigrants, which made necessary a very rapid expansion of the educational facilities. Also among the non-Jewish minorities the goal of total school-attendance is being rapidly approached. By the end of the 1950-51 school year out of a total Arab and other non-Jewish school-age population numbering about 42,500, more than 31,500 (or 75%) were actually attending school,§ making the Israeli Arab community the most advanced today in the matter of schooling.¶

---

* Cf. above, p. 15.
** One year in kindergarten and eight years in elementary school: cf. *Reshumot, Sefer haHuqim*, Sept. 18, 1949.
§ Cf. E. Rieger, "The Education Scene in Israel," *Zionist Newsletter*, vol. IV, no. 6, Jerusalem, Dec. 25, 1951, pp. 4 ff.
¶ Cf. above, pp. 249-50.

Little need be said with regard to the Westernizing effect of school attendance on the boys and girls of the Oriental Jewish communities. The curriculum of the school itself is, of course, adapted to Western standards (with certain modifications to account for a special Israeli-Hebrew flavor in subject matter, such as a study of the Bible, of Jewish history, literature, etc.). Whatever else the school teaches in addition to subject matter—cleanliness, orderliness, neatness in clothing, politeness and good behavior, cooperation, participation in group work, and so on—is also in conformity with modern Western norms and pedagogical ideas. The school thus is a powerful Westernizing agent even in the event the pupils are all from one and the same Oriental Jewish community or from several Oriental communities. Where part of the student body is Oriental and part Ashkenazi, there is the added factor of the close contact and friendship with Ashkenazi children, which as a rule proves to be a very strong stimulus for imitation and hence assimilation and Westernization. The traditional home environment, of course, counteracts to a not inconsiderable extent the influence of the school; nevertheless, a child who goes through several years of schooling in an Israeli school, whatever his ethnic background, turns out in the great majority of cases to be a strong approximation of a modal Israeli personality.*

The task performed by the schools among the immigrant children and youths to the age of 18 is paralleled by the army among those who at the time of their arrival in Israel are too old to go to school. Every young man and woman in Israel, upon reaching 18 years of age, has to enlist in the armed forces of Israel. The period of service is two years for men§ and one year for women. The law of general military service adopted in 1949 is equally binding for the Jewish and the non-Jewish permanent residents of Israel, but at present the policy of the State is not to enforce conscription among the minorities. If Arabs, or Druzes, or members of the other minority groups in Israel wish to volunteer, they are accepted, but as long as no peace treaty is signed with the neighboring Arab countries, the conscription law is not applied to them, for obvious reasons.

* In the above statement the emphasis is on the Westernizing influence of the schools in general among the Oriental Jewish youth. At the same time, one cannot overlook that the division of the school system into four trends tends to perpetuate the existing fragmentation of the population along party lines. In the 1951-52 school year, 37.3% of the total school population of Israel attended Labor schools; 32.7% General schools; 18.5% Mizrahi schools; 6.6% Agudat Yisrael schools; and 4.9% schools belonging to none of the four trends. Cf. *Zionist Newsletter*, Jerusalem, Dec. 25, 1951.

§ On August 26, 1952, this was raised to 30 months.

With regard to the Jewish population, including the Jewish immigrants, however, the situation is different. Not only are all the citizens of military age obliged to serve, but any person of military age (men up to 29 and women up to 26) who comes as an immigrant into the country is also drafted into the army within a very short period after his arrival. For the Oriental Jewish youths of both sexes the army thus becomes the framework within which they first meet European Jews under equal circumstances, get closely acquainted with them, form friendships with them and learn their ways.

The educational results achieved by the army are extremely valuable. The young people when taken into the army are completely Oriental in their habits and attitudes; they are strangers to the land; they cannot speak Hebrew; they have no idea of the meaning of time; they do not know how to use European tableware and object to eating European food; and they have never seen a toothbrush. All this they are taught together with their training in arms, discipline, order and punctuality. In their mixed units, they live in one barrack with Ashkenazi youths and meet frequently army girls from different communities. The frequency of intermarriage between Oriental and Ashkenazi Jews is several times higher in the army than in civilian life.*

Of the 30-month military service, only six months are devoted ✻ to training; the remainder of the time, though spent in the army, is utilized for purposes economically useful to the country. For, in addition to training young people for armed service, the Israeli army is a powerful national labor force deployed according to need and especially in the event of sudden emergencies. When the approaching rainy season threatened to inundate the tents and barracks of several immigrants' reception camps and transit villages in the severe winters of 1950-51 and 1951-52, units of the army were detached to dig drains and channels and to strengthen the tents against the expected winter storms or to help those hit by the inclement weather. When the agricultural settlements found themselves in need of working-hands in order to gather in a harvest or to perform some other urgent and important work, army units were sent to help out. In this manner, during their two years in the army, the recruits are sent all over the country from Metulla to Elath; acquire a first-hand knowledge of the various regions and sectors of the *Yishuv*; and by the time they are discharged, are no longer

---

* Oral information imparted in the Haqirya offices of the army, in July 1951, by a high officer who wished to withhold his name.

new immigrants but Israelis solidly entrenched within the Jewish State. The army thus is a powerful instrument of acculturation.

9. Instruments of Westernization: The *Histadrut*

The most important single institutional factor in the acculturation of adult Oriental Jews in Israel has been and is to this day the *Histadrut*, the general Federation of Jewish Labor in Israel. The numerical aspects of the absorption of Oriental Jewish wage-earners and their families have been dealt with in an earlier chapter.* The gradual growth of the Oriental Jewish membership in the *Histadrut* in the period from which relevant figures are available (1939-1947), shows that the acculturative processes—of which the joining of the *Histadrut* is certainly most telling evidence—are progressing slowly but steadily in the Oriental Jewish communities. During the eight years in question, there was only a very meager immigration of Oriental and Sephardi Jews to Palestine; therefore, almost all such Jews who joined the *Histadrut* in this period must have lived in Palestine prior to 1939, and, in most cases, must have been residents of the country for quite a number of years. A simple but basic lesson can be learned from this observation, a lesson which is in fact so simple as to sound almost like a truism, but which is nevertheless only too often overlooked: *the acculturative processes should not, and in fact cannot with impunity, be hastened.* Given enough time, the assimilative effect of the enticements of the modern Western socio-cultural environment will make itself felt, and will create among the Oriental Jews an increasing wish to enjoy the benefits and the advantages inherent in participation in its institutional aspects, until the wish grows strong enough to overcome the innate shirking of unaccustomed duties and limitations.

The increase of the Sephardi and Oriental Jewish element in the *Histadrut* did not, of course, come about without special efforts made by the *Histadrut* leadership. A Department for Oriental Jews was organized within the Executive Committee (the highest governing body) of the *Histadrut*; it is headed and staffed by Oriental Jewish officials. Affiliated with this Department are two committees, one for the affairs of the Yemenite Jews (18 members), the largest single Oriental Jewish group in the *Histadrut* (as well as in Israel as a whole up to the Iraqi *Aliya*); and one for the affairs of the other Oriental Jewish communities (36 members).

The Department and the Committees serve in an advisory capacity for the Oriental Jews and their public workers in all phases

* Cf. above, p. 161.

of their life within the framework of the *Histadrut*. They train them for active participation in the workers' movement and help them to develop their ability of self-expression and their feeling of self-assurance as an integral part of the working class in the country. On the other hand, the Department and its Committees represent the Oriental Jewish communities within the *Histadrut*, and it is their task to make practical recommendations to the Histadrut as to ways and methods of activity among the Oriental Jews. The existence of the Department for Oriental Jews, and its activities carried out by Oriental Jewish officials, greatly facilitate the absorption of Oriental Jewish wage-earners into the framework of the *Histadrut*.

The *Histadrut*, through its Department for Oriental Jews, endeavored to establish *Histadrut* nuclei in the residential quarters of the Oriental Jews. The penetration of the *Histadrut* into the Oriental Jewish communities was almost invariably opposed by the latter's traditional leadership who feared the consequent decline of their own influence over the community. It was also difficult to find the required personnel to carry out the organizing campaign in the Oriental communities. The problem of the personnel was especially acute because of the traditional isolationism of each community and the sharp dividing lines existing, not only between those who originated in two neighboring countries, but also between those who came from two neighboring districts or towns within the same country.

All these difficulties notwithstanding, the recruiting work of the *Histadrut* among the Oriental Jewish communities was crowned with success. The *Histadrut* has become perhaps the most significant single factor making for a breakdown of the barriers in the Oriental Jewish communities among themselves, as well as for a gradual disappearance of the dividing line between the Oriental Jewish division as a whole and the Ashkenazi division.

The *Histadrut* has also initiated a special effort with a view to acquainting the Oriental Jews with the cultural achievements of the West. It has set up, in the residential quarters of the Oriental Jews, schools for the working youth, day and evening classes for Hebrew and for vocational training, youth and children's clubs, organizations of working mothers, and general clubs. By 1948, over 200 scholarships were awarded to Oriental Jewish youths of both sexes to enable them to undergo and complete vocational training. The great significance of all these efforts towards transforming considerable parts of the tradition-bound Oriental Jewish communities into more active, working and productive population-groups, and

the great leveling, equalizing and integrating effects which participation in the largest socio-economic institution has on them,
cannot be overestimated.*

No less importance must be attached to the organization of
gar'inim, that is nuclei—small groups of young people who prepare for settling in agricultural settlements. By 1948 eighteen such
gar'inim with Oriental Jewish membership were established, several
of which have already set up their communal settlements in various
parts of the country.§

The activities of the *Histadrut* among the Oriental Jews are too
many-sided to be described or even listed here. The fact that the
number of Oriental Jews in the *Histadrut* is greater than in any
other public body in Israel seems to indicate that, both in objective
enticements represented by these activities and in ways and means
to make the benefits of *Histadrut* membership understood and appreciated by the Oriental Jews, the *Histadrut* was able to offer more
than other organizations.

The basic purpose of the *Histadrut* in devoting special attention
to the Oriental Jews is twofold: first, to make the workers and wage-
earners among the Oriental Jewish communities acquainted with
the *Histadrut* and its work, to attract them into its ranks and thereby
place them on a level with the Ashkenazi worker; second, to
strengthen in this manner the *Histadrut* itself. Once within the
Histadrut, the Oriental Jews reap the benefits of the social and
educational efforts which it expends on all sectors of its membership.
As a result of specially channeled activities on their behalf, there is
an increasing bond of common interest between Oriental Jewish
members and the rest of the *Histadrut*, which eventually culminates
in greater unification of the working element of the Jewish population, irrespective of communities and countries of origin. Unification,
of course, once against means adaptation of the Oriental Jews to the
Western standards established by the *Histadrut*.

10. Cultural Synthesis

The growth and successful functioning of such major institutions
as the Knesset, the school system, the army and the *Histadrut* are
the chief factors which hold out definite hope that Israel will, after
all, be successful in meeting the great challenge of creating one
people out of the many ethnic and cultural elements making up its
present-day population. These institutions encompass among them

* Cf. *Hahistadrut, Meassef* (Hebrew), ed. Z. Rosenstein, Tel Aviv, 1946, pp.
249-251.

§ Cf. *Hahistadrut Bishnot 1945/1948*, Tel Aviv, 1949, pp. 141-143.

practically the entire population of the country. Their effect, together with that of other institutions of minor dimensions, is a gradual but definite homogenization, a levelling off of the cultural differences looming large on the traditional horizon of each community.

It is true, of course, that the conscious efforts made by these institutions all lie in one direction. They all aim at the cultural absorption of the non-European groups into the mesh of Western cultural structures, without ever envisaging any changes in the dominant Western cultural contents themselves in the direction or under the influence of the Middle Eastern cultural attainments. Yet, as should be sufficiently clear from the analysis contained in this book, it is due precisely to this circumstance that the acculturative efforts of Israel are threatened with failure. It is on account of the total rejection of the traditional culture of the Oriental population-elements in Israel, either explicitly in overt attitudes, or implicitly in the demand for total cultural assimilation, that the cultural crisis continues unabated, that the cleavage between the two halves of the population persists, and that the otherwise constructive institutional efforts fail to come to full fruition.

The palliatives such as are at present resorted to with a view to eliminating occasionally the cruder outcroppings of tensions and clashes must and will remain ineffective. Remedial measures will have to be applied to the root of the trouble. What is needed, to put it summarily, is a basic change in the current ethnocentric cultural attitude characteristic of the European Jewish leadership of Israel. It must be recognized, first of all, that a culture which is different from the Western (Euro-American) is not necessarily inferior to it; that, as a matter of fact, it is impossible to find objective and unbiased criteria by which two different cultures can be compared; that every comparison of necessity means the evaluation of an alien culture by standards of one's own.

Secondly, it will be necessary to understand that cultural complexes are traditionally-evolved responses of society to certain human needs, and that the same human need can and usually does give rise to different responses in different cultures. A change in the natural or social environment can make it necessary to introduce commensurate changes in the traditional cultural response to a given need, or can create new needs to which the culture has not evolved traditional responses. Specific and concrete differences in cultures must be viewed, therefore, in terms of both the total traditional background and the whole of the new cultural context.

Yet another requisite will be the clear apprehension that the inability of the traditional responses of a culture to meet newly arisen needs does not by any means signify deficiency in the culture as a whole. Even if a whole aspect is found wanting in a culture, as traditional Middle Eastern culture undoubtedly is wanting in technology, sanitation and the like, this does not afford the slightest justification for a wholesale condemnation and rejection of the culture in its totality. It has been shown above* that traditional Middle Eastern culture contains a number of complexes which are lacking in Western civilization and the adoption of which into Israeli culture would undoubtedly serve to enrich and invigorate it.

The principle, therefore, to be substituted for the currently dominant ideology with regard to the cultural future of Israel must be *cultural synthesis instead of cultural absorption;* an ingathering of cultural contributions from each ethnic element in the country, instead of the assimilation of all to the Western culture of Ashkenazi Jewry.

The first prerequisite to this end is the recognition of several focal concerns, that is, intensively developed complexes, in the traditional culture of the Oriental Jews and the non-Jewish minorities in Israel. These foci can be valuable for the culture of Israel as a whole and, therefore, must not be eradicated, but retained, preserved, fostered and in some cases even revived and revitalized. Some of these focal concerns, for example, the esthetic achievements of the Oriental Jews in folk-music and the decorative arts, their well-functioning extended family-organization, their deep and all-pervasive religiousness, and the balance between material and spiritual values, have been examined in the foregoing pages. Others will undoubtedly be discovered when the total culture of the Oriental communities is made the subject of thoroughgoing studies.

The idea that the cultures of the East and the West can and should mutually enrich and complement each other is neither new nor revolutionary. Soon after contact was established between certain European nations and overseas populations, and the cultural differences between Europe and the non-European world were realized, the desirability of interchange aiming at an ultimate synthesis was voiced and advocated. Père Enfantin, pupil and successor of Saint-Simon, preached the brotherhood of East and West well over a hundred years ago and emphasized that, while the Orient would have much to receive from the Occident, the West also would have much to gain from the East especially in strength and in faith.§

* Cf. Chapter Two.

§ Cf. Enfantin, *Correspondence politique,* Paris, 1849; quoted after R. Maunier, *Sociology of the Colonies,* London, 1950, p. 334.

In our own day Julian Huxley has repeatedly spoken of the necessity for enriching Western culture with the attainments of other cultures which contain valuable features lacking in the Western cultural configuration.[*]

More systematically and more comprehensively than others, F. S. C. Northrop probed the problem in his significant inquiry, *The Meeting of East and West.*[**] He found that the fundamental problem of merging the East with the West with safe and positive results involves the task of relating the esthetic and the emotionally immediate religious values, to which the East has primarily devoted its attention, to the scientific, doctrinal and pragmatic values upon which the West has concentrated. He expressed the hope that such a merging would occur, and that, when it did occur, it would result in "genuine additions to and enrichment (aesthetically, scientifically, economically, and religiously) of the traditionally incomplete cultures of the two civilizations." He believes that "it should eventually be possible to achieve a society for mankind generally in which the higher standard of living of the most scientifically advanced and theoretically guided Western nations is combined with the compassion, the universal sensitivity to the beautiful, and the abiding equanimity and calm joy of the spirit which characterizes the sages and many of the humblest people of the Orient."[§] As an example of a culture which attempts to achieve a combination of locally prevalent elements with others derived from modern Western civilization, he offers an analysis of the culture of the Mexicans who "have introduced also the more universal and secular education with its power, through scientific technology and medicine, to lessen disease and lighten the physical labor of men. Of the intrinsic human value as well as the practical utility of these things they are not unmindful . . . But they do not want to see these good things, modeled in part upon the United States, come at the price of destroying their own indigenous, traditional values and of taking all the sparkle and individuality of emotions and the sentiments out of their hearts and their faces."[¶]

[*] Cf. Julian Huxley, "Population and Human Destiny," in *Harper's Magazine,* New York, Sept. 1950, p. 45.

[**] Cf. F. S. C. Northrop, *The Meeting of East and West, An Inquiry Concerning World Understanding,* New York, 1947.

[§] Northrop, *op. cit.,* pp. 376, 496. Cf. also pp. 375, 436.

[¶] Northrop, *op. cit.,* p. 7. It is a most encouraging development that very recently leading Israeli statesmen have become acutely aware of this problem. After the completion of my manuscript a transcript of the address of Israeli Foreign Minister Moshe Sharett to the U. N. General Assembly in Paris on November 15, 1951, became available to me, and from it I wish to quote the following passage significant in this connection: "The issue between the Occi-

What for the rest of the world remains an ideal desideratum—the meeting of East and West—has today already become an actual reality in Israel, though for the time being only in the physical sense. But with the presence side by side, within the narrow confines of the small country, of two population elements, one the convinced exponent of modern Western culture, and the other the faithful carrier of traditional Eastern culture, the stage is set for the enactment of the great drama, the cultural interpenetration, merging, fusion, and finally synthesis of East and West. The numbers involved, several hundreds of thousands on each side, are considerable, and the developing action will be watched eagerly and even anxiously by all mankind.

For Israel is today the only place in the world where the carriers of both cultures have the possibility of meeting on an equal footing, and where, therefore, the successful resolution of the cultural crisis arising out of this meeting has at least an even chance. In other regions of culture-contact—of which there are several even on the margins between the West and the Middle East—the balance of contact suffers either from the numerical smallness of the European element and the exceptional position it occupies, or from the theoretically proclaimed and legally validated inferiority of the "natives" and all they stand for. In all these places, therefore, one cannot expect cultural synthesis, but only cultural domination, or, at best, cultural absorption.

In Israel, as indicated above, the theoretical basis for the meeting of the Western and the Eastern population-elements is complete equality. In practice, though inequality undeniably exists, it is only partial and relative. The cultural crisis, which is a powerful and dangerous factor making for the separation of the population into conflicting groups,§ is counteracted and mitigated to some extent by the unifying efforts of the great Israeli institutions, as well as by the

---

dent and the Orient is not merely one of temporary adjustment of the most pressing conflicts. What should be sought is a broad current of positive cultural integration. Mutual respect for the great human values crystallized in the tradition of both worlds is the basis for a relationship of trust and solidarity leading to the organic unity of the future. In this it is up to the Occident to go more than half way. In bringing to the Asian continent its own modern civilization, it has so far been hardly aware of the latter's ancient cultures. Yet it may be that in them is hidden that spiritual strength which alone can ennoble and purify technological progress and save man from becoming the slave of matter. Much as the Orient can benefit from Western science, the Occident can enrich its spiritual treasury by drawing upon the wisdom of the East." Quoted from *The Jewish Agency's Digest*, Nov. 30, 1951, pp. 261-62.

§ Cf. David Bidney, "The Concept of Cultural Crisis," in *American Anthropologist*, Oct.-Dec. 1946, p. 537.

great common, and therefore consolidating, experiences of being at home, of being among the rebuilders of the ancient homeland, and of witnessing and participating in the growth and development of the new State.

The cultural crisis itself, in its actual and precise form, is specific and different from the cultural crises experienced by other peoples in contact with Euro-American civilization: it is the conflict between the carriers of two cultures neither of which is ready to concede the superiority of the other, at least in theory. In practice, however, the Euro-American culture of the Ashkenazi Jews gains the upper hand —which is a very different thing from the theoretically acknowledged and practically acquiesced-in supremacy of Western culture in other areas of culture-contact. From this viewpoint, the present crisis itself can be viewed as the first phase in the process of amalgamation which is to lead eventually to the cultural synthesis between East and West. For the mutual reaction, about equal in intensity on both sides, to the presence of a culturally alien element, indicates that neither side is prepared to submit, and that the end-result of the process is not likely to be the total submergence of one culture in the other.   *

Significant as the experiment is for the world as a whole, for Israel itself its importance is greater. Israel may at the present juncture not be vitally interested in the question of whether the new cultures it is about to develop will be valuable in global relations, or become a blueprint for mankind—a "light of the nations," as the old prophetic imagery has it. Having had for two thousand years a "mission" without a home, Israel may well be satisfied for the next millennium with having a home and no mission. But as far as its own future and fortunes are concerned, the present cultural crisis poses for Israel a most fateful choice, the most serious challenge since it became an independent nation, compared to which its economic and material problems must seem insignificant and transitory. Whether the austerity will become lighter or more severe, whether it will persist for one or ten years; whether the present pace of immigration can be maintained or its flow forced to slow down; whether the country will achieve economic stability in five or ten years—all these are, to be sure, weighty questions which will affect the lives of individual and nation alike in the next few years. Nevertheless, they are questions merely of the hour, however protracted that hour may be.

The problem of the cultural synthesis represents a challenge to Israel unmatched and unequalled in its gravity. As Israel knows only too well from the pages of its own long and tortuous history, the survival of a people depends not merely on its technological equipment, nor on its standard of living, nor even on its armed might, but also, and perhaps even primarily, on a combination of such imponderable factors as the spirit which pervades it, the cohesion which characterizes it, the determination it possesses and the values it cherishes. A new culture evolving out of a happy synthesis of all that is found valuable in every surviving bough of Israel's ancient tree is far more likely to inspire and to sustain the new nation than a mere facsimile of a generalized Euro-American cultural prototype.

A culturally vital Israel can play a role in world relations quite out of proportion to its small size and limited economic capacity. Its influence on world development will flow through two direct and one indirect channel.

First, it will directly affect the lives of Jews all over the world. It can be foreseen that, apart from a few numerically small Jewish groups in Western Europe and the countries of the British Commonwealth, the Jewish people in another one or two generations will consist of only two main fractions: the Jews of Israel and of America. The initial enthusiasm for the Jewish State which revitalized the Jewish consciousness of American Jewry in the first few years of the new State's existence, will by then long have subsided. Assimilationist tendencies—which seem to become inevitable whenever a Jewish group lives in the midst of a population culturally of high standing and liberal in its attitudes—will by then undoubtedly have made deep inroads into the body of American Jewry. In this situation the cultural and spiritual influences emanating from Israel will become the main factor in preventing the total engulfment of American Jewry within the magnetic field of the great Western civilization.

Secondly, Israel's success in merging and amalgamating the cultures of the East and the West will serve as a powerful, direct stimulus for the countries of the Middle East in whose midst it is located geographically. Although at the time of this writing—four years after Israel gained its independence—the Arab States have not yet become reconciled to its existence, there are signs indicating that presently they may follow the example set by the non-Arab states of the Middle East in establishing regular relationships with Israel. Already today, with the borders between Israel and its neighbors still closed, Israel's influence is felt in the Arab world as a challenging force which is stimulating the attitude "if you can do it, we can too!" A rapprochement between Israel and its neighbors will enable them to study at close range the ways and methods adopted by Israel in fusing Oriental and Occidental cultural traits, and in creating a new and vital culture. The newly developed West-Eastern culture of Israel can serve as a prototype for other peoples of the Middle East, and can thus become an important factor in channeling the general processes of Westernization taking place in the area, away from the pitfalls of deculturation and towards a profitable incorporation of Western elements into their ancient cultures.

Thirdly and indirectly, the results achieved by Israel in creating one people out of a large number of ethnic elements separated at present culturally and ideologically, will hold forth a great hope for the world. Though the Israel experiment in global relation is merely a pilot-plant project, its success will nevertheless indicate that it can be reproduced on a magnified scale. Israel is thus again hurled back into a position which it has occupied before in the course of its history: the position of serving the whole of mankind by fulfilling its own destiny.

This then is the challenge of Israel. It calls for great vision and careful planning. During the first four years of Israel's statehood much of its planning and vision went into the immediate and threatening problems of the economic, political and technological fields. These problems are not yet solved, but they are being brought gradually under control. It is now imperative for Israel to apply itself to the long-range, and therefore graver, problems looming on the cultural horizon.

As a first step into this intricate realm, certain basic reorientations will be necessary. To the clarification of this, much of the present volume was devoted. Popular but scientifically untenable ideas concerning "racial" characteristics of ethnic groups will have to be discarded, and the scientifically well-established theorems of the cultural conditioning of each generation anew will have to be accepted as a basis for any approach to the solution of the present cultural crisis. It will also have to be realized that each culture has complete validity for its own carriers, and that the forcible imposition of wholesale acculturative measures can therefore not be justified. The understanding will also have to be reached that a rapid, and hence of necessity superficial, acculturation is in most cases merely a deculturation, the effects of which may be highly undesirable and even dangerous.

After these and similar fundamentals have been realized, Israel will be prepared in principle to take up the challenge. It will be able to substitute—via appropriate procedures and with the help of qualified personnel—the Western types of responses to generally existing human needs in cases where the traditional Oriental responses obviously fall short—as in the fields of medicine, education, sanitation, social welfare, technology. At the same time, it will carefully refrain from belittling the traditional culture of any community as a whole, so as to avoid creating offense, ill will, bitterness and resentment.

On the other hand, the cultures of all the Jewish and non-Jewish communities in Israel will be studied with a view to isolating those complexes which can prove valuable for the total culture of the country, and in this manner the spontaneously commenced and haphazardly on-going processes of cultural contact, imitation and change will consciously be advanced in the desired direction of fruitful cultural synthesis. Israel thus will become the scene of a great challenge successfully met, a new cultural development significant in global relations, the prime locale of the meeting between East and West, and the stage for future developments of unfathomed cultural dimensions.

Supplementary Notes

p. 22. *Number of Jews in the World.* Following the years of the Nazi holocaust the number of Jews in the world increased as shown in the following table.

NUMBER OF JEWS IN THE FIVE CONTINENTS, 1947–67

	1947	1957	1967
Europe (including Asiatic USSR and Turkey)	3,920,100	3,466,350	4,054,000
America	5,754,500	6,066,730	6,822,000
Asia (excluding USSR and Turkey)	917,500	1,855,244	2,477,000*
Africa	639,500	585,750	200,000
Australia and New Zealand	35,000	61,500	74,500
Total	11,266,600	12,035,574	13,627,500

* Including 2,383,554 in Israel.

Source: *American Jewish Year Book*, 1947–48, 1958, 1968.

p. 24. *The Question of Jewish Race.* A more detailed discussion of the diversity in physical type evinced by the Jewish communities scattered over the world and of its bearing on the question of the Jewish race can be found in Raphael Patai, "The Jewish Race Problem," in Karl Saller (ed.), *Rassengeschichte der Menschheit,* R. Oldenbourg Verlag, Munich and Vienna, forthcoming.

p. 26. *Population of Jerusalem.* By 1968 the population of Israel, including East Jerusalem, reached 2,733,900, of whom 2,383,600 were Jews and 390,300 non-Jews (mostly Arabs).

p. 28. See also R. Patai, *Golden River to Golden Road: Society, Culture and Change in the Middle East,* Philadelphia: University of Pennsylvania Press, 1969 (3rd ed.), pp. 13–38: "The Middle East as a Culture Continent."

p. 31. Cf. op. cit., pp. 39–72: "Some Problems of the Middle Eastern Culture Continent."

p. 46. *Westernization of the Middle East.* The Middle Eastern cultural pattern, described above on pages 32–46, has undergone considerable modification in the 17 years that have elapsed since those pages were written. The percentage of people who in 1969 were still carriers of the traditional cultural pattern had decreased all over the Middle East, while the percentage of those who were caught up in the processes of Westernization had increased. In the Arab world, Westernization, meaning modernization, urbanization and industrialization in general, and the successive replacement of traditional Middle Eastern by modern Western culture complexes in particular, had been making headway especially in those countries that border upon Israel: Lebanon in the first place, followed in decreasing order by Egypt, Jordan and Syria. The changes in the direction of adopting the Western responses to cultural and social needs were apparent in each of the areas in which the desirability of such a development is emphasized on pages 46–50. Technological processes, medicine, education —these are the fields in which the Middle East has most readily followed in the footsteps of the West. That these processes were accompanied by a breakdown of the traditional Middle Eastern patriarchal family and of all the other traditional social relationships in the past largely patterned after the family, can be most clearly seen in such a recent phenomenon as the wave of student unrest that by 1969 has reached even such a quasi-totalitarian country as the United Arab Republic (Egypt).

p. 57. *Petah Tikva.* By 1968 Petah Tikva numbered 73,500 inhabitants.

p. 59. *Literature on the Kibbutzim.* Since 1952 numerous studies were published on the Israel *kibbutz*, including Melford E. Spiro's two books *Kibbutz: Venture in Utopia*, Cambridge, Harvard University Press, 1956, and *Children of the Kibbutz*, Cambridge, Harvard University Press, 1958; H. Darin-Drabkin, *The Other Society*, New York, 1962; A. I. Rabin, *Growing Up in the Kibbutz*, New York, 1965; Peter B. Neubauer, *Children in Collectives: Child-Rearing Aims and Practices in the Kibbutz*, Springfield, Ill., 1965; Alan Arian, *Ideological Change in Israel*, Cleveland, 1968; Bruno Bettelheim, *The Children of the Dream*, New York, 1969.

p. 60. *Literature on the Moshavim.* Recent studies on the *moshav* include Axel Weingrod, *Reluctant Pioneers: Village Development in Israel*, Ithaca, Cornell University Press, 1966; Dorothy Willner, *Nation-Building and Community in Israel*, Princeton University Press, 1969.

p. 70. *The Number of Middle Eastern Jews.* Of the estimated 750,000 Jews who lived in Middle Eastern countries outside Israel in 1952, 324,275 actually immigrated to Israel in the years 1953 to 1967. In 1967 only about 223,000 Jews were left in all Middle Eastern countries outside Israel, of them 80,000 in Iran, 50,000 in Morocco, 44,500 in Turkey, 10,000 in Tunisia, and the remaining 39,000 in Lebanon, Syria, Algeria, Egypt, Iraq, Afghanistan and Libya. Thus the reservoir of Middle Eastern Jewish immigrants to Israel was rapidly nearing depletion. In the same period of 1953 to 1967, some 250,000 Middle Eastern Jews migrated to countries other than Israel.

p. 72. *Growth of Moshavin and Kibbutzim.* Both the *ma'abarot* and the *k'fare 'avoda* disappeared within a few years after the cessation of the 1948–52 mass immigration. Their inhabitants were absorbed into old and new towns and old and new *moshavim*. As a result, as well as because of other factors that made the *moshav*-type of settlement more attractive to newcomers than the *kibbutz* or other type of villages, the increase in the number and size of *moshavim* continued at a rapid pace after 1952. By 1968 there were no less than 367 *moshavim* in Israel (including *moshavim shitufiyim*) with a total population of 126,583, while the number of *kibbutzim* in the same year was only 233, with a population of 72,052. Of the *moshavin*, 283 were established after the independence of Israel, and the population of those new *moshavim* in 1968 was 97,757. Of the *kibbutzim*, 98 were established after the independence of Israel, and their population in 1968 was 21,572. Roughly speaking, therefore, the *moshavim* absorbed about 4½ times as many newcomers as did the *kibbutzim*. In 1968, 5.3% of the Jewish population of Israel lived in *moshavim*, and 3.5% in *kibbutzim*.

P. 73. *Kibbutz Organizations*. In 1968 the *kibbutzim* were organized in the following countrywide federations:

Organization	Number	Population
HaKibbutz HaArtzi Shel HaShomer HaTza'ir	76	28,781
Ihud HaK'vutzot V'haKibbutzim	76	19,523
HaKibbutz HaM'uhad	58	17,275
HaPo'el HaMizrahi	11	3,662
Ha'Oved HaTziyoni	5	1,422
Po'ale Agudat Israel	2	590
No affiliation	5	799
Total	233	72,052

P. 74. *Immigration*. The immigration picture from May 15, 1948, to December 31, 1966, is shown in the table, p. 346 (top).

P. 75. *Ethnic Composition of Israel*. The prediction that the numbers of Sephardi and Oriental Jews "are bound to show additional increase in the next few years due to continued immigration from the Middle East" (p. 74) has come true both absolutely and relatively. This is shown in the following table:

ETHNIC COMPOSITION OF THE JEWISH POPULATION OF ISRAEL FROM 1961 TO 1967

(Dec. 31) Year	Total	Per cent	Ashkenazi Jews	Per cent	Sephardi & Oriental Jews	Per cent
1961	1,981,702	100	1,078,721	53.43	902,981	45.56
1962	2,068,882	100	1,094,845	52.91	974,037	47.08
1963	2,155,551	100	1,114,101	51.68	1,041,450	48.32
1964	2,239,177	100	1,148,332	51.28	1,090,845	48.71
1965	2,299,078	100	1,166,719	50.74	1,132,359	49.25
1966	2,344,877	100	1,177,978	50.23	1,166,899	49.76
1967	2,383,554	100	1,182,414	49.60	1,201,140	50.39

The above table contains my estimates based on data published in the Statistical Abstract of Israel, 1968. However, the Central Bureau of Statistics

JEWISH IMMIGRATION TO ISRAEL FROM MAY 15, 1948, TO DECEMBER 31, 1966, BY CONTINENT OF ORIGIN

Year	Total No.	From Europe & America	Per cent*	From Asia & Africa	Per cent*	Not known
1948	101,819	77,032	85.6	12,931	14.4	11,856
1949	239,076	123,097	52.7	110,780	47.3	5,199
1950	169,405	84,638	50.4	83,296	49.6	1,471
1951	173,901	50,204	28.9	123,449	71.1	248
1952	23,375	6,647	28.4	16,725	71.6	3
1953	10,347	2,574	24.9	7,760	75.1	13
1954	17,471	1,966	11.3	15,493	88.7	12
1955	36,303	2,562	7.1	33,736	92.9	5
1956	54,925	7,305	13.3	47,617	86.7	3
1957	69,733	39,763	57.5	29,361	42.5	609
1958	25,919	14,428	55.7	11,490	44.3	1
1959	22,987	15,348	66.8	7,635	33.2	4
1960	23,487	16,684	71.0	6,801	29.0	2
1961	46,571	24,564	52.7	22,004	47.3	3
1962	59,473	12,793	21.5	46,677	78.5	3
1963	62,086	19,028	30.7	43,054	69.3	4
1964	52,193	30,362	58.2	21,831	41.8	—
1965	28,501	15,025	52.7	13,476	47.3	—
1966	13,451	7,537	56.0	5,914	44.0	—

*The percentage of the Euro-American and Afro-Asian immigrants is calculated, as was done on p. 74, on the basis of the sum total of only those immigrants whose country of birth was known.

of the Government of Israel groups the population of the country as well as the immigrants according to continent and country of origin. These categories coincide roughly with our division of the Jewish population of Israel into Ashkenazi and Oriental Jews. However, the Jews born in Europe and America include the Sephardim of the Balkans (including Istanbul), while the Sephardim of Asiatic Turkey are included in the Asian and African category, which also includes the Ashkenazi Jews of South Africa. The third category, "Persons or their fathers born in Israel," is, of course, a composite of Ashkenazi, Sephardi and Oriental Jews. The categories of the Central Bureau of Statistics result in the following figures:

JEWISH POPULATION OF ISRAEL BY CONTINENT OF BIRTH

Year	Total Number	%	Europe & America Number	%	Asia & Africa Number	%	Israel Number	%
					Persons or their fathers born in			
1961	1,981,702	100	1,023,364	51.64	847,623	42.77	110,715	5.58
1967	2,283,554	100	1,101,190	48.22	1,119,915	46.98	162,449	7.11

P. 77. Compared to the 1949–51 period, the occupational structure of the 1961–67 immigrants showed a marked increase in the "industry, construction and unskilled labor" category, and in the "public administration and professions" category, balanced by a decrease in the other categories. This is shown in the following table.

PRIOR OCCUPATIONAL STRUCTURE OF NEW IMMIGRANTS (1961–1967)

	Number	%
Agriculture and primary production	811	0.148
Industry, construction and unskilled labor	32,023	53.28
Transport and communications	2,038	3.42
Commerce	6,399	10.76
Public administration and professions	7,500	12.61
Domestic, personal service and clerical work	10,668	17.94
Total gainfully occupied	59,439	100.00
Total number of immigrants	134,017	
Percentage gainfully occupied in total		44.35

Calculated on the basis of data in the *Statistical Abstract of Israel 1968*.

P. 79. Note 1. *Israel's Native and Foreign-Born Population*. The Israeli-born contingent in each Jewish community gradually increased and the foreign-born correspondingly decreased after 1952, due to the fact that in these years the natural increase was greater than the immigration. The following table shows this shift from 1951 to 1967, and the projected percentage in 1985.

ISRAEL-BORN AND FOREIGN-BORN IN THE JEWISH POPULATION OF ISRAEL, IN PERCENTAGES

Year	Total	Israel-Born	Foreign-Born Total	Asia & Africa	Europe & America
1951	100	25.5	74.5	27.6	46.9
1954	100	31.4	68.6	26.9	41.7
1957	100	33.9	66.1	29.0	37.1
1960	100	37.4	62.6	27.6	35.0
1964	100	39.4	60.6	28.7	31.9
1967	100	42.8	57.2	27.5	29.7
1985	100	62.88	37.12	18.76	18.36

P. 79. Note 2. *Demographic Ethnic Studies*. Since 1952 the Israeli Central Bureau of Statistics, under the capable leadership of its director, Prof. R. Bachi, has accumulated and published a very large and very valuable amount of statistical information on Israel, without which many of these supplementary notes would not have been possible. However, the complaint that the demography of the individual ethnic groups has not been sufficiently studied is almost as valid in 1969 as it was in 1952.

P. 84. *Demographic Rates.* From 1952 to 1967 the rates of birth, death, infant mortality and natural increase in the Jewish population of Israel showed the following development:

Year	Birth Rate	Death Rate	Infant Mortality	Natural Increase
1952	31.6	6.8	38.7	24.7
1953	30.2	6.3	35.7	23.9
1954	27.4	6.4	34.1	20.9
1955	27.2	5.8	32.4	21.5
1956	26.7	6.3	35.6	20.4
1957	26.0	6.2	33.4	19.9
1958	24.1	5.6	30.7	18.4
1959	24.3	5.8	27.7	18.5
1960	23.9	5.5	27.2	18.4
1961	22.5	5.7	24.3	16.8
1962	21.8	5.9	27.5	15.9
1963	22.0	6.0	22.5	15.9
1964	22.4	6.2	24.0	16.1
1965	22.6	6.4	22.7	16.2
1966	22.4	6.3	21.7	16.1
1967	21.5	6.6*	20.8	14.9

* Excluding war casualties.

Source: *Statistical Abstract of Israel 1968*, p. 54.

It is interesting to note that from 1963 on, the Jewish infant mortality rate in Israel was consistently lower than that of the United States (1963: 25.2), and continued to decrease to 20.8 by 1967, while in the United States it showed a much more moderate decrease (1966: 23.7). This was quite a remarkable achievement in Israel considering the fact that as recently as in 1949 it was as high as 51.71, due to the mass influx of Jewish immigrants from the Middle East. The spectacular reduction of infant mortality among the latter within less than two decades after their arrival in Israel is yet another index of the rapid Westernization of the Oriental Jews in Israel in the realms of technology and medicine. It would be most instructive to compare this development with the situation in the Arab and other Middle Eastern countries from which these immigrants hail, but regrettably, no information is available.

As to the consistently decreasing rates of natural increase of the Jewish population of Israel, the explanation lies in these considerations: since the death rate has been kept at a constant low of about 6, the low and decreasing natural increase is due only to the low and decreasing birthrate. The birthrate among the Ashkenazi communities was low in 1938–40 and remained about the same through the subsequent 30 years. The birthrate of the Sephardi and Oriental Jews (or, more precisely, the number of children born annually per 1,000 mothers who themselves were born in Asia and Africa), decreased gradually from 1949 to 1966 (see next note). Since these Asian and African mothers gave birth, even in 1966, to three-and-one-half times as many children as the European and American mothers (30,651 as against 9,105), it is evident that the decreasing general birthrate of the Jewish population is a result, primarily and mainly, of the diminishing birthrate among the Asian and African Jewish mothers.

These general observations, based on a study of the demographic rates published by the Central Bureau of Statistics of Israel, received independent confirmation by an investigation of prime importance conducted by R. Bachi and J. Matras on the basis of a 1959/60 survey of maternity cases in Israel. Their findings show that "past practice of contraception" was reported by 64% of the women born in Europe and America, 61% of the women born in Israel and 25% of the women born in Asia and Africa. They also found that among women born in Israel and in Europe-America, socio-economic differentiations in fertility patterns were, by and large, absent; but that among women born in Asia and Africa, family planning was characterized by "very notable differentiation and steep gradients": the higher their socio-economic status, the longer their residence in Israel, the higher their education, etc.—the more frequent the practice of birth control and the smaller the actual number of their children. On this basis Matras concludes that "it may be anticipated that ... the fertility of women born in Asia and Africa will be reduced quite substantially in the near future" (Judah Matras, *Social Change in Israel*, Chicago, 1965, p. 185).

The significance of this phenomenon from the point of view of the acculturation of the Asian and African Jewish immigrants to the dominant Western culture of Israel is that these Oriental Jewish communities are evidently moving toward Westernization even in the most intimate and most value-laden aspects of their lives. Although their birthrate was in 1966 still about twice as high as that of the Ashkenazi Jewish communities in Israel, it was at the same time only about half as high as that of the Arab women in neighboring countries. In other words, they had moved away considerably from the base line of extremely high fertility that they had shared with the Arab women of their old home countries.

p. 85. *Fertility and Contraception.* Following the establishment of Israel, the Central Bureau of Statistics has published information concerning the gross reproduction rate of Jewish mothers (i.e., the average number of female children born to a woman throughout her lifetime) by continent of their birth. The figures show that in 1949–52 the gross reproduction rates of Jewish mothers born in Europe and America fluctuated between 1.59 and 1.48; from 1953 to 1959 it declined from 1.39 to 1.13; and from 1960 to 1966 it fluctuated between 1.20 and 1.13. A gross reproduction rate of 1.13 corresponds to a net reproduction rate of just over 1, i.e., it is barely enough to maintain the population without change.

In the same period (1949 to 1966) the gross reproduction rate of Jewish mothers born in Asia and Africa varied from a maximum of 3.06 to a minimum of 2.17. A trend towards a slight decrease was noticeable from 1959 when it was 2.56 to 1966 when it ebbed to 2.17. Nevertheless, even this last figure points to a doubling of population within one generation (Central Bureau of Statistics, *Statistical Abstract of Israel 1968*). In other words, the "Oriental" Jewish contingent in Israel was still rapidly increasing in the late 1960s, while the "Ashkenazi" barely managed to hold its own.

It is of interest to compare the above rate of reproduction of Jewish women of various communities with those of Arab women. In 1966 the gross rate of reproduction among Israeli Arab women and the women of other minorities was 4, indicating an almost fourfold population increase within one generation. Also, after the Six Day War of 1967 Israeli statisticians found that in the territories that came under Israeli control the average number of children per woman aged 45 to 49 was 8.7 which roughly corresponds to a gross rate of reproduction of 4.

P. 86. Note 1. The actual increase of the Sephardi and Oriental Jewish communities in both absolute numbers and percentages from 1952 to 1968 can be seen in the table contained above in note to p. 75.

P. 86. Note 2. The further reductions achieved in infant mortality from 1952 to 1967 can be seen in the table contained above in note to p. 84.

P. 87. Note 1. The prediction that Israel would become "a country with a growing majority of Oriental population" had become true by the 1960s as can be seen from the table contained above in note to p. 75.

P. 87. Note 2. *Size of Family*. The difference between Ashkenazim and Oriental Jews with regard to size of family has been maintained down to 1967, as shown in the table below.

Number of Persons in Family	Head of Family Born in	
	Europe and America	Asia and Africa
1	13.9%	7.7%
2	29.0	13.1
3	21.7	13.1
4	23.9	17.2
5	8.4	15.1
6	2.2	11.2
7+	0.9	22.6
Total	100.0	100.0

Source: *Statistical Abstract of Israel 1968*.

Although on the basis of these data it is not possible to calculate the average size of family (because the total number of persons in families having 7 or more members is not given), a rough idea as to the marked differences in family size between the two groups nevertheless can be obtained. Thus, e.g., while only 11.5 per cent of the European and American families had three or more children, the corresponding percentage among the Asian and African families was 48.9 percent, or more than four times as high.

P. 88. *The 0–19 Age Group.* The percentage of those aged 0–19 in the various Jewish communities in Palestine in 1946 can be compared to the corresponding percentages in 1967:

	Born in Europe and America or Father Born in Europe and America		Born in Asia and Africa or Father Born in Asia and Africa	
Total	Absolute No. 1,101,190	Percentage 100	Absolute No. 1,119,915	Percentage 100
Aged 0–4	53,329	4.84	146,383	13.07
5–9	64,708	5.87	143,781	12.83
10–14	85,247	7.74	144,228	12.87
15–19	114,824	10.43	126,171	11.26
Aged 0–19	318,108	28.88	560,563	50.03

Source: *Statistical Abstract of Israel 1968.*

The table shows that, in 1967, of all the Israeli Jews who were born in Europe and America or whose fathers were born in Europe and America 28.89 per cent were aged 0–19, while among all Israeli Jews who were born in Asia and Africa or whose fathers were born in Asia and Africa the corresponding percentage was 50.05 per cent. Of the entire young generation of Israel (997,150 aged 0–19), 31.90 per cent were of European and American extraction, 56.22 per cent of Asian and African extraction, and 11.88 per cent were third-generation Israeli. Assuming that of the third generation Israelis one half were of Euro-American and the other half of Afro-Asian extraction, we find that, in 1967, 37.84 per cent of all Israeli Jewish youth aged 0–19 were either born in Europe or America or were of European or American extraction, and 62.16 per cent were either born in Asia or Africa or were of African or Asian extraction.

P. 90. Note 1. *Demographic Projection.* The projection that "Israel will very soon have a majority of Sephardi and Oriental Jews," i.e., a majority, within its Jewish population, of Jews of Sephardi and Oriental extraction, came true in the year 1967, as shown in the table contained above in note to p. 75.

As to the future demographic developments that could be anticipated in 1969, the picture is as follows: in 1967, of all Jewish youths up to 20 years of age 37.84 per cent were of European or American extraction and 62.16 per cent of African or Asian extraction (see preceding note). Since the fertility of the Africans and Asians is considerably higher than that of the Europeans and Americans, it can be expected that in another generation (say, around 2003) the *total* Jewish population of Israel (barring immigration) will be composed of a group of African and Asian descent that will constitute a significantly higher percentage of the total than 62.16, while those of European and American descent will constitute a correspondingly smaller percentage than 37.84.

This projection is borne out by calculations made by the Central Bureau of Statistics of the Government of Israel. The Bureau published in 1968 a *Projection of the Population of Israel up to 1985* (Special Series No. 242, Jerusalem, 1968). According to this projection, every 10,000 Jewish immigrants born in Asia and Africa were expected to increase in 17½ years, i.e., by 1985, to 16,514, and every 10,000 immigrants born in Europe and America to 10,420. The Bureau also calculated that (assuming an annual immigration of 10,000 Jews from Europe and America and of 5,000 Jews from Asia and Africa, as well as a certain annual emigration), the total number of Jews in Israel by 1985 will be 3,263,700. On the basis of these data and of our own estimate of the size of the Euro-American and Afro-Asian contingents in 1967 (see above note to p. 75) we can project that in 1985 there will be in Israel about two million Jews (or 62 per cent) of African or Asian extraction, and about 1,232,000 (or 38 per cent) Jews of European or American extraction. Assuming that a similar demographic development continues for the subsequent 17½ years, we can project (although more tentatively) that in the year 2,003 there will be in Israel about 3,300,000 Jews of African or Asian, and 1,284,000 Jews of European or American extraction. In percentages, in that period the African-Asian contingent will constitute some 72 per cent, and the European-American 28 per cent, of the total Jewish population of Israel.

P. 90. Note 2. *Immigrants' Occupations.* The differential distribution of Jewish immigrants from Europe and America on the one hand, and from Asia and Africa, on the other, among the various occupations in Israel in 1967 is indicated in the following table.

Occupation	Immigrants from Europe & America	Immigrants from Asia & Africa
Professional, scientific, technical and related workers	19.27	7.30
Administrative, executive, managerial and clerical workers	19.66	11.40
Traders, agents and salesmen	11.10	9.33
Farmers, fishermen and related workers	6.80	11.13
Workers in transport and communications	4.27	5.84
Construction workers, quarrymen and miners	4.97	8.97
Services, sports and recreation workers	11.36	18.33
Craftsmen, production process and related workers	22.57	27.70
Total	100.00	100.00

Source: *Statistical Abstract of Israel 1968.*

Compared with the table on p. 90, these data indicate a considerable shift in the occupational structure of the Oriental Jews (immigrants from Asia and Africa) towards that of the Ashkenazi Jews (immigrants from Europe and America). In 1939, for instance, the Sephardi and Oriental Jews had only 14 persons in the professions as compared to 100 Ashkenazim; in 1967 their number increased to 7.30 as compared to 19.27, or 37.9 to 100. In 1939 there were 263 Sephardi and Oriental Jews in public works, transport and porterage as against 100 Ashkenazim; in 1967 their number decreased to 137.8 to 100. This development is yet another index of the Westernization of the immigrants from Asia and Africa, that is to say, their assimiliation to the Ashkenazi occupational pattern in Israel which is one of the constituent complexes of the Western Israeli cultural configuration.

A related question of considerable importance is this: to what extent do sons follow the occupations of the fathers, or, conversely, to what extent are they able to switch to other (and, presumably, more skilled and better paying) occupations? A rather complex table assembled by Judah Matras gives the answers (as of 1955), some of which are surprising indeed. Among sons of "unskilled" fathers born in Europe and America, only 18.82 per cent remained in unskilled occupations, while 60.52 per cent moved up into skilled or semi-skilled occupations, and only 7.01 per cent became agriculturists. Among sons of "unskilled" fathers born in Asia and Africa, 48.47 per cent remained "unskilled," 39.29 per cent became skilled or semi-skilled workers, and only 6.12 per cent went into agriculture. The greatest occupational mobility was shown by sons of unskilled fathers born in Israel: of their sons only 11.28 per cent remained unskilled, while 62.41 per cent became skilled or semi-skilled, and no less than 18.05 per cent moved into farms. The latter figure seems to indicate that the old pioneer ideal of the "conquest of the soil" was still much more meaningful for sons of *sabras* than for sons of immigrants. Even more surprising is the fact that in the "highest" occupational group, that of professional, technical and managerial workers, 39.09 per cent of the sons of *sabras*, 37.40 per cent of the sons of immigrants from Europe and America, but only 12.36 per cent of the sons of immigrants from Asia and Africa entered the same occupational group. By and large, however, it becomes clear that there is a considerable upward mobility in the occupational structure of African-Asian immigrants and their sons, although not quite as great a mobility as in the European-American sector (cf. Judah Matras, *Social Change in Israel,* op. cit., pp. 160–66).

p. 93. *The Population of Jerusalem.* The number of the Jewish inhabitants of Jerusalem at the beginning of 1967 (i.e., prior to the Six Day War) was 195,000. In 1968 the number of Jews of Jerusalem (of whom a certain number had settled in the Old City following the unification of Jerusalem) was 200,443. The total number of the population of East Jerusalem in September, 1967, was 65,857, of whom 53,834 were Moslems, 10,970 Christians, and 1,053 others or unknown. Thus the total population of united Jerusalem was 266,300.

p. 97. *Residential Segregation.* The 1961 census of Israel showed that the tendency to residential segregation evinced in Jerusalem in 1939 (see above, table on p. 95) was maintained ten years after the cessation of the mass immigration. For example, it was found that sub-quarter 13 (for census purposes the city was in 1961 divided into four quarters each of which was further subdivided into several sub-quarters) had an Afro-Asian-born population of 3,880 and a Euro-American of 1,040. Sub-quarter 15 had 5,215 Afro-Asians and 1,585 Euro-Americans, sub-quarter 16 had 440 Afro-Asians and 4,400 Euro-Americans.

P. 103. *Inter-Division Marriages.* The table on p. 99 shows that in Jerusalem, in 1939, 1.5 per cent of all the married Ashkenazi men had taken non-Ashkenazi brides; 10.9 per cent of all the married Sephardi men had taken non-Sephardi brides; and 7.6 per cent of all the married Oriental Jewish men had taken non-Oriental Jewish brides. As to the brides, 1.5 per cent of all married Ashkenazi women were married to non-Ashkenazi husbands; 20.1 per cent of all married Sephardi women were married to non-Sephardi husbands; and 3.2 per cent of all married Oriental Jewish women were married to non-Oriental Jewish husbands. All in all, 4.5 per cent of the existing marriages were between husbands and wives who did not belong to the same one of the three major divisions of the Jewish people.

Since that time the percentage of out-division marriages continuously increased. The following table shows the development from 1955 to 1965.

GROOM FROM EUROPE AND AMERICA

Year	Bride from Europe and America		Bride from Asia and Africa	
	Number	Per Cent	Number	Per Cent
1955	6,466	86.59	1,001	13.40
1958	6,372	83.32	1,275	16.67
1959	6,245	82.45	1,329	17.54
1960	6,214	81.93	1,370	18.06
1961	5,915	82.28	1,273	17.71
1962	6,065	81.95	1,335	18.04
1963	6,296	81.55	1,424	18.44
1964	6,873	83.38	1,369	16.61
1965	7,329	84.54	1,340	15.45

GROOM FROM ASIA AND AFRICA

Year	Bride from Asia and Africa		Bride from Europe and America	
	Number	Per Cent	Number	Per Cent
1955	5,301	90.12	581	9.87
1958	6,314	90.04	698	9.95
1959	6,190	90.19	673	9.66
1960	6,104	89.40	723	10.59
1961	6,076	88.66	777	11.22
1962	6,477	88.33	855	11.66
1963	7,268	87.46	1,042	12.53
1964	7,754	86.44	1,216	13.55
1965	8,002	84.88	1,425	15.11

Based on *Statistical Abstract of Israel 1968*, p. 63.

Analysis of the table shows that, at least since 1958, there was no clear-cut trend with regard to the percentage of out-division marriages entered into by Ashkenazi grooms (i.e., those born in Europe and America). The percentage reached a maximum of 18.44 per cent in 1963, then diminished to 15.45 by 1965. Even so the percentage of out-division marriages of Ashkenazi grooms in 1955–65 was at least ten times as high as their percentage in Jerusalem up to 1939. In other words, the readiness of Ashkenazi men to take non-Ashkenazi wives increased at least tenfold in the intervening years. This can be explained as due to two major factors: (1) the increasing socio-cultural attainments of the girls of Afro-Asian extraction which made them more eligible in the eyes of the Euro-American young men; and (2) the change in the prevailing atmosphere which made out-division marriage socially more acceptable in the eyes of the young man of Euro-American extraction.

As to the grooms of Afro-Asian extraction, the trend is very clear: there was a gradual but steady increase in the percentage of those who married Euro-American girls. Up to 1939 (in Jerusalem) this percentage was 7.6; in 1955 (in all Israel), 9.87; by 1965 it had reached 15.11. That is to say, the increase in the percentage of Afro-Asian young men who were able and willing to marry Euro-American girls was matched by a corresponding increase in the percentage of those Euro-American girls who were willing to marry Afro-Asian men. This clearly indicates a gradual and steady process of approximation of Ashkenazi socio-cultural standards by Oriental Jewish young men.

The gradual equalization of the out-division marriage percentages in both directions is an eloquent testimony, coming as it does on top of the overall long-range increase, to the levelling off of the cultural differences between the two divisions and the gradual elimination of the socio-cultural barriers that in the past had made of them two predominantly endogamous groups.

Regrettably, no breakdown of the inter-division marriages as to the communities of the brides and grooms is available. Therefore it is not possible to check whether the prediction made on p. 103 concerning the probable merger of the "upper-class" Sephardim into Ashkenazi division, and the fusion of the "lower-class" Sephardim with the Oriental Jewish division is or is not being borne out by the trends of inter-division marriage in 1955–65. However, the increasing percentage of intermarriages does indicate that the two numerically largest sectors of the *Yishuv*, those of Afro-Asian and those of Euro-American extraction, are merging to a greater extent and more rapidly than could be foreseen in 1952. This, in turn, means that the entire issue of intercommunity differences and tensions may become resolved within another two generations by the mere fact of interbreeding. It can now be foreseen that the greater the socio-cultural assimilation of the Afro-Asians to the Euro-Americans, the faster will be the growth of the intermarriage rates between them.

p. 105. *Juvenile Delinquency.* This eightfold rate of juvenile delinquency among Afro-Asian Jewish youth as compared to Euro-American, declined by the 1960s. In 1966, of every 1,000 Jewish juveniles (boys aged 9–16 and girls aged 9–18) born in Europe and America, 3.1 were convicted of a juvenile offense. The corresponding figure for those born in Israel was 7.9; for those born in Asia, 9.6; and for those born in Africa, 22.9. While the rate for those born in Africa was thus 7.39 times higher than that for Euro-Americans, the combined rate for the Afro-Asians was only 5.24 times as high as that of the Euro-Americans (calculated on the basis of data in the *Statistical Abstract of Israel 1968*).

P. 110. In 1966, of all Jewish juvenile offenders 3,980 (or 88.7%) were boys, and 503 (or 11.3%) were girls. Among Arab juvenile offenders in the same year 731 (or 85.3%) were boys, and 126 (or 14.7%) girls. (Source: *Statistical Abstract of Israel 1968*, p. 577.)

P. 113. Note 1. The incidence of juvenile delinquency in Israel from 1948 to 1968 is shown in the table below.

CONVICTED JUVENILE OFFENDERS IN ISRAEL, 1960–66

Year	Number	Rate per 1,000 Juveniles
1960	3,988	10.0
1961	3,973	9.3
1964	5,139	10.3
1965	5,330	10.5
1966	5,340	10.3

Source: *Statistical Abstract of Israel 1968*.

P. 113. Note 2. *Criminality*. The general criminality of the Jews in Israel from 1951 to 1965 is shown in the table below.

CONVICTED ADULT OFFENDERS IN ISRAEL, 1951–66
(EXCLUDING AFFRAY AND MINOR ASSAULTS)

Year	Number	Rate per 1,000 Population
1951	8,320	8.9
1955	12,443	10.8
1960	14,102	11.2
1963	14,565	10.5
1966	16,168	10.3

Source: *Statistical Abstract of Israel 1968*.

P. 121. *Clothing*. By the 1960s the exotic appearance of the Iraqi and other Oriental Jewish immigrants was a thing of the past. The clothes they had brought with them in 1950–51 had been worn out and replaced by the less colorful but more practical khaki pants and shirts (to which short jackets are added in the cold winter months) worn by most Israelis. Thus yet another traditional Oriental cultural trait, that of the apparel, has disappeared.

P. 122. *Rural Industries*. The prediction that the industrial-rural settlement, whose economy is based on both agriculture and industry, will become a new development in Israel has come true. By the 1960s there were in Israel many rural settlements of the *moshav* as well as the *kibbutz* type which had sizeable industrial plants, and *kibbutz* industry had taken a recognized and economically significant place in the factors of the Israeli gross national product. By 1969 the number of industrial enterprises established and functioning in *kibbutzim* could be estimated at well over a hundred, and included food (canning), metal, wood (furniture), plastics, etc., industries, accounting for almost half of the total value of *kibbutz* production.

p. 123. *Tarshiha.* The pessimistic prediction concerning the ability of the Rumanian families to adapt to conditions in the emerging *moshav*-type settlement of Tarshiha was borne out by subsequent developments. The settlement continued to exist, its name was changed to *Me'ona 'Ironit*, and it became affiliated with the *Moshav* Movement (*T'nu'at HaMoshavim*). However, by 1961, when a population census of all Israel was taken, only 38 persons born in Rumania remained in the *moshav*. The place of those who had left had been taken by 235 North African (Moroccan, Algerian and Tunisian) immigrants. Four years earlier (in 1957) an urban settlement was established near *Me'ona 'Ironit*, called *Ma'alot Tarshiha*, into which the *moshav* was subsequently incorporated and which in 1968 had a population of 4,650. This figure included a strong contingent of North Africans, as well as 1,520 Arabs.

p. 127. *Beit Dagan.* Following the initial period of settlement (1948–51), the population of Beit Dagan (the name was changed so as to give it a Hebrew, instead of a Philistine, form) continued to increase for several years. The increase, however, was due not to immigration, but to natural increase. The 1961 census of Israel showed that Beit Dagan had a total population of 2,928, of whom 1,843 were foreign-born. Most of the latter (1,439) had immigrated between 1948 and 1951.

The major ethnic groups in 1961 were the Yemenites (775 immigrants), the North Africans (375), the Poles and Russians (184), the Bulgarians and Greeks (146), the Rumanians (117), the Egyptians and Libyans (82), and the Turkish and Iranians (64). Also a few Iraqi, German, Austrian, Hungarian, Czechoslovak and other families lived in Beit Dagan (a total of 100 immigrants). After 1961 the population of Beit Dagan gradually decreased. In 1963 it was 2,820, in 1966 it was 2,750, and in 1968 it was 2,680. Since at least half of Beit Dagan's population belonged to high fertility groups (Yemenites, North Africans, etc.), the decrease in subsequent years indicates, not a lack of natural increase, but a movement out of the town by those who hoped to make a better living elsewhere, and primarily in the nearby big city of Tel Aviv.

p. 129. *Slums.* In spite of considerable improvements in the housing situation (see next note), it was still true in 1969 that whatever slum or near-slum quarters had remained in Israel were inhabited mostly by Oriental Jews.

pp. 131, 136, 147, 241 AND 318. *Housing Standards.* While the acquisition of electrical and other appliances requires a considerable outlay, nevertheless many Israelis of Asian and African extraction can afford it once they rise above a minimal income level (cf. below, note to p. 146). The upgrading of housing, on the other hand, is a much more costly, time-consuming and difficult task. In the years following the mass immigration period of 1948–52, both the government of Israel and private interests have applied themselves energetically to the construction of dwellings, thereby gradually alleviating the acute housing shortage. In the eight years 1960–67, no less than 277,000 dwelling units were completed, comprising a total of 23,433,000 square meters of residential-living floor space. During the same eight years immigration into Israel was moderate, resulting, together with the natural increase, in an increase of the population from 2,150,400 in 1960 to 2,780,500 in 1967. The intensive building activity of 1960–67 therefore greatly improved the housing situation in the country. In the three years of 1964–66 alone no less than 113,550 dwellings were built, of them 55,480 by private builders and 58,070 by the government. The great majority of the dwellings (some two-thirds) consisted of three rooms plus kitchen (*Statistical Abstract of Israel 1968; United Nations Statistical Yearbook 1967*, New York, 1968).

As a result of this intensive building activity the temporary housing facilities hastily set up in 1948–52 to accommodate the sudden influx of mass immigration had almost completely disappeared by 1967. However, the inequality in housing between European-American (i.e. Ashkenazi) Jews and Asian-African (i.e. Oriental) Jews persisted, and was especially pronounced between the new immigrants of the two ethnic groups (see table below).

PERCENTAGES OF JEWISH FAMILIES BY NUMBER OF PERSONS PER ROOM AND BY HEAD OF FAMILY'S CONTINENT OF BIRTH, 1967

No. of Persons per Room	Born in Asia & Africa New Immigrants	Veterans	Born in Europe & America New Immigrants	Veterans
Total	100	100	100	100
Less than 1.00	6.1	8.0	15.8	27.0
1.00 – 1.99	38.1	45.8	64.3	58.6
2.00 – 2.99	31.5	31.7	17.0	12.8
3.00 – 3.99	14.2	9.8	1.6	1.2
4.00 and over	10.1	4.7	1.3	0.4

Source: *Statistical Abstract of Israel 1968.*

As the table shows, of all veteran Israelis born in Europe and America only 1.6 per cent had substandard housing, i.e., one room for three or more persons. The corresponding percentage among new immigrants born in Europe and America was 2.9; among veteran Israelis born in Asia and Africa, 14.5; and among new immigrants born in Asia and Africa, 24.3. The luxury of two persons or fewer per room was enjoyed by 85.6 per cent of the veterans born in Europe and America, and by 80.1 per cent of the new immigrants born in Europe and America; but by only 53.8 per cent of the veterans born in Asia and Africa, and 44.2 per cent of the new immigrants born in Asia and Africa.

Yet, and this is a point that one must not lose sight of even while deploring these ethnic inequalities, the dwellings of the Oriental Jewish immigrants in Israel were, even before the building spurt of 1964–66, considerably better in every respect than the dwellings they had left behind in their home countries. Since no statistical information is available on their dwellings in Iraq, Morocco,

Yemen, etc., if we wish to get any idea as to those housing conditions we must adduce data from those countries in general and from the comparable dwellings of urban Arabs, e.g., in East Jerusalem, where a survey was carried out by experts of the Israeli Bureau of Statistics soon after the Six Day War of 1967. A comparison of whatever data are available yields the significant result that the housing conditions of Asian and African Jewish families in Israel are markedly better than those of urban Arab families in Arab countries and in East Jerusalem, with respect to such indices as toilet and bath facilities, and the availability of electricity, piped water inside or outside the dwelling (see table below). Thus, even though no equality has been reached as yet between Ashkenazi and Oriental Jewish families with regard to housing standards, the housing of the Oriental Jews in Israel represented by 1967 considerable improvements over their living conditions in their old home countries. And, needless to say, these improvements constituted in every case a shift in the direction of Western standards.

HOUSING STANDARDS IN ISRAEL, ARAB JERUSALEM, JORDAN
AND IRAQ IN PERCENTAGES OF ALL DWELLINGS

Facility	Israel 1963	Arab Jerusalem 1967	Jordan 1961	Iraq 1956
Toilet	94.9	93.3	55.4	—
Flush-type toilet	80.9	—	9.7	33.6
Bath	87.5	26.6	8.7	10.3
Electricity	89.8	70.1	17.0	17.1
Piped water inside dwelling	89.5	40.6	21.3	—
Piped water inside or outside dwelling	93.2	—	36.2	20.8

Source: *United Nations Statistical Yearbook 1967*, New York 1968; *Statistical Abstract of Israel 1968*.

P. 135. *School Attendance of Boys and Girls*. The differential between the school attendance of boys and girls that was noted among the Oriental Jews of Jerusalem in 1944–45, has long disappeared in all Israel. This is graphically illustrated, e.g., by the following figures: in 1965, the total number of pupils enrolled in elementary and high schools was 558,289. Of these, 272,975 (or 48.89 per cent) were girls, and 285,314 (or 51.10 per cent) were boys. The fact that the number of boy pupils was higher than that of girls by 12,339 is due to the differential between the boys' and girls' school enrollment among the Arabs of Israel whose statistics are included in the figures.

P. 136. See note to p. 131.

P. 138. See note to p. 131.

PP. 139, 148–49. *Food Consumption*. In this area, too, constant improvement could be observed once the mass immigration of 1948–52 subsided. Food rationing was abolished, the black market in food disappeared, and nutrients became available in increasing quantities and varieties. While no recent information on the food consumption of the various segments of the population is available, it is clear that the increases in the average net food supply for the country as a whole signifies improvement in both the Ashkenazi minority and the Oriental majority of the Jewish population of the country. The table (p. 361) shows the changes from 1950/51 to 1966/67, with data from Iran and Iraq added for comparison and for the purpose of showing the type of food intake that the Oriental Jews, prior to their immigration into Israel, shared with the other peoples of the Middle East.

P. 141. *School Attendance in the Middle East and in Israel.* Among the veteran settlers who had come to Israel prior to 1948 from Asia and Africa, 21.8 per cent of the males and 53.2 per cent of the females never attended any school. Among those Afro-Asians who immigrated after 1948, 22.5 per cent of the males and 57.8 per cent of the females had not attended school (cf. Matras, *Social Change in Israel,* op. cit., p. 75). If one adds to the above percentages those who had not completed primary education and who, therefore, were functionally almost illiterate, one gets 61.6 per cent for male Afro-Asian old-timers, 76.6 per cent for female Afro-Asian old-timers, 72.0 for male Afro-Asian new immigrants, and 84.0 per cent for female Afro-Asian new immigrants (ibid.).

As against this background it becomes even more remarkable that by 1965 practically the entire school-age population in Israel actually attended schools, and that a rapidly increasing percentage of youths aged 14–17 born in Asia and Africa received post-primary education as well (see below, note to p. 206). This meant that whatever illiteracy still remained among the immigrants from the Middle Eastern countries was confined to the older generation.

As to the Middle Eastern countries, the percentage of those attending school among the school-age population has increased and is continuing to do so, although at greatly varying rates. Thus in Egypt (United Arab Republic), where in 1937 only 23.4 per cent of the male, and 6.1 per cent of the female, population aged 10 years and over was literate, by 1965 no less than 64.73 per cent of the boys, and 44.36 per cent of the girls aged 6 to 13 were enrolled in schools, which, of course, is indicative of a marked decrease in illiteracy. In some Arab countries, notably Saudi Arabia, Yemen and Southern Yemen, education, and especially that of girls, still lagged far behind (calculation based on data contained in *United Nations Statistical Yearbook 1967,* New York, 1968. Cf. R. Patai, *Golden River to Golden Road,* op. cit., p. 491).

P. 142. *"Sabra" — Hebrew.* See Raphael Patai, "The Phonology of 'Sabra' — Hebrew," *Jewish Quarterly Review,* July, 1953, pp. 51–54.

P. 146. *Appliances.* The scarcity of commodities emphasized on this page has disappeared from Israel by the 1960s. Consumer goods have become available in sufficient quantities and adequate qualities to satisfy the demands of all sectors of the population, whether of Afro-Asian or Euro-American extraction, whether belonging to a low-, middle- or high-income group. Even air conditioning, of which in 1952 only "a few of the most modern office buildings in Tel

AVAILABLE FOOD SUPPLY IN ISRAEL 1950/51–1966/67, AND IN IRAN, 1960, IRAQ, 1960–62, AND JORDAN, 1964

| | Grams per Day | | | | | | | Calories per Day | | Protein |
	Cereals	Pota-toes, etc.	Sugar	Pulses, Nuts & Seeds	Meat	Milk	Fats & Oils	Total	% of Animal Origin	Grams per Day
Israel										
1950/51	365	124	65	26	42	426	42	2,680	20	88
1954/55	384	128	81	28	57	426	44	2,860	17	88
1957/59	337	113	91	23	81	406	45	2,770	18	83
1960/62	318	103	94	26	109	388	48	2,810	18	84
1964/65	278	98	106	27	128	391	49	2,820	20	86
1966/67	304.5	92.8	92.6	23.6	144.1	249.2	54.3	2,925	19.2	89.2
Iran 1960	394	10	52	11	44	176	18	2,050	12	60
Iraq 1960–62	355	15	81	15	55	207	10	2,140	14	62
Jordan 1964	320	31	52	31	21	122	54	2,390	7	59

Sources: *United Nations Statistical Yearbook 1967*, New York, 1968; *Statistical Abstract of Israel 1968.*

Aviv" could boast, has become a commonplace not only in offices, restaurants and places of public gatherings, but also in private homes. The only problem, as far as the middle-class consumer is concerned, is the cost. Because Israel must spend a very high percentage of her gross national income on armaments, the maintenance of an army and military preparedness, it must tax its citizens at a considerably higher average rate than is the case, e.g., in the United States. One way of levying taxes is to impose high duties on appliances imported and equally high taxes on appliances manufactured in Israel. As a result of this situation the Israeli citizen pays much higher prices for radios, TV's, toasters, irons, electric fans, refrigerators, air conditioners, etc. Nevertheless, as seen in the table below, the percentage of families possessing such appliances showed a remarkable increase in the 1958–67 decade and had, by 1967, reached a level found only in the Western world. The only "hardware" not yet used as widely in Israel as in some Western countries was the private car, whose price was nothing short of prohibitive.

JEWISH FAMILIES POSSESSING APPLIANCES BY CONTINENT OF BIRTH OF HEAD OF FAMILY IN PERCENTAGES OUT OF ALL FAMILIES

		Born in Asia & Africa	Born in Europe & America
Electric Refrigerator			
	1958	8.2	51.4
	1960	17.3	68.6
	1965	66.9	93.4
	1966	72.1	95.3
	1967	78.3	95.2
Gas Range			
	1958	14.0	48.9
	1960	43.0	75.3
	1965	85.0	92.4
	1966	84.5	89.6
	1967	86.6	89.6
Electric Washing Machine			
	1958	3.1	12.0
	1960	8.5	20.9
	1965	22.8	32.7
	1966	25.3	33.0
	1968	30.3	33.5
TV Set			
	1965	1.9	2.5
	1966	3.5	3.2
	1967	5.2	4.4

One Radio Set			
	1966	78.3	84.8
	1967	73.4	80.7
Phonograph			
	1959	8.9	14.5
	1960	9.5	17.2
	1965	19.5	26.0
	1966	16.2	25.3
	1967	18.4	31.4
Vacuum Cleaner			
	1964	1.2	18.1
	1965	2.7	22.7
	1966	3.1	24.1
	1967	4.9	30.9
Private Car			
	1962	—	6.1
	1965	1.8	9.9
	1966	3.8	14.2
	1967	5.1	18.7

Source: *Statistical Abstract of Israel 1968.*

The table shows not only the overall increase in the possession of appliances in Israel, but also the speed at which the Afro-Asian families catch up with the Euro-Americans in this field. While by 1967 equality with the European-American families was not yet achieved by the Asian-African families with regard to any of the appliances, the progress evinced by the latter was conspicuous. For instance, in 1958 only 8.2 per cent of the Asian-African families had electric refrigerators; in 1967, 78.3 per cent. As to TV, the higher percentage of Asian-African families owning sets in 1967 (5.2 per cent) as against European-American families (4.4 per cent) is due to the fact that in 1967 Israel had as yet no TV transmitting station, and that the transmissions receivable from neighboring countries were mostly in Arabic, a language understood by many Middle Eastern Jews, but not by Jews of European or American extraction.

What is noteworthy in the development illustrated by the table is not so much the improvement in the economic conditions of the Afro-Asian immigrants in Israel to which it testifies as the Westernization of which it is evidence. For not only did most of the Oriental Jews not possess these appliances in their Asian and North African home countries, many of them never saw, never even heard of, such things. Therefore, after their immigration to Israel, they not only had to acquire the means to buy these appliances, but also had to develop a taste for them to a sufficient degree to spend on them their hard-earned money instead of buying those things which in their old countries were valued as desirable and prestigious possessions. Since a considerable transvaluation of values in the Western direction had to precede the acquisition of these appliances by all Oriental families who could somehow afford them, the foregoing table is an eloquent additional witness to the appeal the technological aspect of Western culture had for all Afro-Asian immigrants in Israel.

P. 147. Note 1. See note to 131.

P. 147. Note 2. *Transportation*. By the 1960s, the problems of transportation had largely been solved. Israel received modern trains as part of the reparations payments rendered by Germany and was able steadily to improve and modernize its fleets of taxis and buses.

P. 149. *Food Consumption*. See note to p. 139 as to the general improvement of food supplies. With regard to ethnic differences in food consumption patterns, the following findings of a study based on 1956/57 data but published only in 1964 are relevant: European immigrants spent 30 per cent less on bread and cereals, 15 per cent less on vegetables and 10 per cent less on fats than Asian immigrants. However, with time there was a reduction of the differences in the consumption of bread, cereals, milk and meat, but not in the consumption levels of eggs and cereals. Cf. Nissan Liviatan, *Consumption Patterns in Israel*, Jerusalem, 1964, as summarized in the Falk Project for Economic Research, *A Ten Year Report* 1954–63, Jerusalem, 1964, p. 57.

P. 150. *Water Supply*. The water supply in the entire country has greatly improved with the completion in 1964 of the National Water Carrier, which brings water from Lake Kinneret in the Galilee to the coastal plain near Tel Aviv. From there the water is carried in the pipe system of the Yarkon-Negev line farther south for distribution in the Lakhish Region and the northern Negev.

P. 151. Note 1. *Clothing*. A study based on 1956/57 data found that Asian immigrants spent more on clothing than European immigrants, and interpreted this "as a kind of 'conspicuous consumption' which is a psychological reaction to their lower status in Israel society." The same study also found a general tendency among Asian immigrants to change their expenditure pattern in the direction of European standards. However, since the European immigrants simultaneously change their consumption patterns (excluding food) in the same direction, the gap between the two divisions of Jewish immigrants does not diminish. Cf. Nissan Liviatan, op. cit.

P. 151. Note 2. *Average Family Income*. The standard of living has consistently improved from the mid-1950s. As far as appliances are concerned, this is shown graphically in the table contained in note to p. 146. The monthly expenditure on consumption by the average Jewish urban employee's family increased from I£. 510.40 in 1959/60 to I£. 671.50 in 1963/64 (both figures calculated at 1963/64 prices). However, differences between the average income of an Afro-Asian family and of a Euro-American family persisted, the former amounting in 1963/64 to only two-thirds of the latter.

A contributing cause of this difference was found in the fact that considerably fewer Oriental women in relation to men worked, and thus augmented the family income than was the case among Ashkenazi Jews. In 1954, for instance, among Jews born in Asia and Africa and aged 14 and over, only 15 per cent of the women were gainfully employed, as against 24 per cent of the women born in Europe and America, and 27 per cent of the women born in Israel (cf. The Falk Project for Economic Research in Israel, *Second Annual Report 1955*, Jerusalem, 1956, p. 19).

Yet, with all the differences between the income levels of Ashkenazi and Oriental Jews, one must not lose sight of the fact that income levels show a definite correlation also with period of immigration. The veteran settlers have higher incomes than the new immigrants (cut-off point: 1948); even veteran settlers born in Asia and Africa have higher incomes than new immigrants born in Europe and America. In 1959/60 the monthly income (in Israeli pounds) of the urban wage and salary earner's families in the four groups was as follows:

Veteran settlers born in Europe and America:	I£ 478.20
Veteran settlers born in Asia and Africa:	381.40
New immigrants born in Europe and America:	343.30
New immigrants born in Asia and Africa:	259.60

(Source: Giora Hanoch, "Income Differentials in Israel," in The Falk Project for Economic Research in Israel, *Fifth Report 1959 and 1960*, Jerusalem, p. 68.)

P. 152. *Rural-Urban Distribution*. With the improvement in economic conditions went industrialization and urbanization resulting in a gradual reduction of the rural population in relation to the urban sector. By 1967 the total rural population of Israel (located in *kibbutzim, moshavim* and other types of rural settlements) was 274,500, or 11.4 per cent of the total Jewish population, which in that year reached 2,383,600.

P. 153. Note 1. *Ma'abarot*. On the disappearance of *ma'abarot* and other temporary housing aggregates see above note to p. 72.

P. 153. Note 2. *Unemployment*. Unemployment remained low in subsequent years. The daily average of the unemployed registered in the labor exchanges decreased from 17,680 in 1953, to 10,738 in 1955. In 1957 it again increased to 12,513, only to decrease gradually to 3,200 in 1965. In 1967 unemployment again shot up to 13,525. In evaluating these figures one must take into account that the population of Israel constantly increased in the years in question, so that in 1967 the 13,525 unemployed represented a much lower percentage of the country's manpower than the 12,513 did in 1957 (Source: *Statistical Abstract of Israel 1968*).

In percentages, unemployment steadily decreased from the high of 11.3 per cent (of the civilian labor force, Jewish and non-Jewish), in 1953, to 4.7 per cent in 1960 (cf. Avner Hovne, in The Falk Project for Economic Research in Israel, *Fifth Report 1959 and 1960*, Jerusalem, 1961, p. 137).

P. 154. The marked improvements in standards of food, housing and clothing after 1952 are dealt with in notes to pp. 121, 131, 139.

P. 159. *Oriental Jewish Organizations*. The prediction that the patriarchal religious community organization of the Oriental Jews in Israel is on its way out has been largely borne out by subsequent developments. By the 1960s, inasmuch as Oriental Jewish organizations based on country of origin still existed, they were run along more or less bureaucratic institutional lines. The most effective and influential of these organizations was the Council of the Sephardi Community in Jerusalem, which published a monthly bulletin of news and comments entitled *Israel's Oriental Problem* (since October, 1965). Cf. also Walter P. Zenner, "Sephardic Communal Organizations in Israel," *The Middle East Journal*, Spring, 1967, 173–86.

p. 161. *The Histadrut*. Late in 1964 the *Histadrut* had a membership of 871,718. The members and their dependents numbered 1,440,527, of whom 1,359,285 were Jews. The total Jewish population of Israel at the time was 2,239,200, of whom 62 per cent were *Histadrut*-affiliated. In the same year, of the Arab population of Israel (286,400) 82,054, or 28.7 per cent, were members of the *Histadrut*.

Also, in 1964 the labor organization of *Hapo'el HaMizrahi* had 84,786 members, and that of the *Agudat Israel*, 11,040 members.

p. 162. *The Kuppat Holim*. The continued growth of the *Histadrut*'s Sick Fund can be seen from the following figures: In 1964 the number of *Kuppat Holim* members (including dependents) reached 1,860,000, or 71 per cent of the total population of Israel. It employed 2,610 doctors, had 998 clinics located in 844 (of a total of 873) places of settlement. Its 14 hospitals had a total of 3,000 beds; its 18 reconvalescent homes, 2,130 beds. On the average, every Israeli individual received 9.3 times a year some kind of medical service from the *Kuppat Holim*'s institutions..

p. 168. *Music*. The influence of popular Oriental Jewish (and especially Yemenite) music has remained strong until the present day.

p. 169. *Painting and Sculpture*. There has been no notable increase from 1952 to 1969 in the participation of Oriental Jews in painting and sculpture.

p. 171. *Art Crafts*. The Yemenite predominance in Israeli silver filigree work, embroidery and basketry has continued to the present day.

p. 173. *Fashions*. With the general improvement in economic conditions, an Israeli fashion industry has made its appearance. The women, who became increasingly conscious of style, preferred, by and large, French, Italian and United States fashions. However, Israeli fashion designers have gradually emerged, and by the late 1960s their designs found good reception both in Israel and abroad.

p. 175. Note 1. *Daily Papers*. The number of daily papers has not increased significantly in Israel since 1952, but the circulation of the newspapers has. In 1963, 13 dailies were published with a total circulation of 339,000, or 143 copies per 1,000 inhabitants. In 1967 the number of dailies was 24, of which 15 were in Hebrew. As a comparison it might be mentioned that Iraq in 1963 had 8 papers with a total circulation of 85,000, or 12 copies per 1,000 inhabitants (Sources: *Statistical Abstract of Israel 1968; United Nations Statistical Yearbook 1967*, New York, 1968). The newsprint consumption has increased correspondingly from 6.6 pounds per capita annually in 1955–59 to 15.4 pounds in 1966 (as compared to 92.18 pounds in the United States, 25.75 in France, 15.62 in Italy and 0.44 in Iraq).

p. 175. Note 2. *Books Published.* The number of books published increased after 1950. As against the 920 titles published in 1950, 1,038 were published in 1964, and 1,471 in 1966/67. Of the titles published in 1964, 453, and of those issued in 1965, 499 were translations from more than 10 European languages, indicating the continued interest of the Israelis in the literary products of world culture. By comparison, of the 286 titles published in Iraq in 1964, only 18 were translations from foreign languages. (Sources: *Statistical Abstract of Israel 1968; United Nations Statistical Yearbook 1967*, New York, 1968).

p. 179. *War Experiences.* The common experiences in the Sinai Campaign of 1956 and the Six Day War of 1967 obliterated much of the distinction between those who fought the War of Independence in 1948 and those who immigrated after it.

p. 194. *Number of Yemenite Jews in Israel.* It is even more difficult to estimate the number of Yemenite Jews in Israel in 1969 than it was in 1950. However, since in 1938–40 it was found that the net rate of reproduction of Yemenite women in Palestine was 2.92 (see above, p. 85), and since, as a result of acculturation in Israel, the fertility of Yemenite women gradually decreases, we may assume that their net rate of reproduction in the period in question was about 2.00. This means that the number of Yemenites increases by 100 percent in one generation. If we take the roughly 20-year period from 1950 to 1969 as two-thirds of a generation, we can expect that by 1969 the number of Yemenite Jews increased by two-thirds of 100 per cent, or by 66.66 per cent. In that case, the 112,670 Yemenites who lived in Israel in 1950 would have increased to 187,775 by 1969. This is undoubtedly a low estimate considering that the *Projection of Population in Israel up to 1985* (Central Bureau of Statistics, Special Series no. 242, Jerusalem, 1968) expects a 65.14 per cent increase of the Afro-Asian Jewish population in Israel from 1967 to 1985 (17½ years).

p. 204. Note 1. *Yemenites in Agriculture.* The prediction that the Yemenite Jews would "constitute one of the most important ethnic elements in the agricultural sector of Israel" has been borne out by the developments since these lines were written. Of all the immigrants who arrived in Israel in the 1949–58 decade, only 5 per cent were Yemenite Jews. Yet of all those 1949–58 immigrants who became engaged in farming in Israel no less than 13.4 per cent were Yemenite (calculated on the basis of data in the *Sh'naton HaHistadrut* 1964/65).

p. 204. Note 2. *Yemenites in the Knesset.* In the third and subsequent Knessets the Yemenites no longer had a separate representation.

p. 206. *Post-Primary Education.* As stated below (note to p. 328), the four educational trends were abolished in 1952, and since that time the Yemenite schools have been under the control of the state religious education system. However, what is more significant for the socio-cultural future of the Yemenites and the other Oriental Jewish ethnic groups in Israel is the fact that in spite of the spread of post-primary education among them, there still remains a considerable gap in this respect between them and the Ashkenazi Jews. The following table shows this very clearly.

RATES OF POST-PRIMARY SCHOOL ATTENDANCE PER 1,000
JEWISH YOUTH AGED 14–17 BY CONTINENT OF BIRTH
1956/57–1966/67

Of Every 1,000 Born	Attended Post-Primary Schools in School Year		
	1956/57	1961/62	1966/67
In Israel	580	590.5	637.6
In Europe-America	408.8	550.5	685.8
In Asia-Africa	130.3	262.2	378.6
Irrespective of place of birth	352.2	465.2	529.3

Source: *Statistical Abstract of Israel.*

P. 217. In 1968 the Christian communities in Israel (including East Jerusalem) had the following membership (estimates):

Church	Members
Greek Orthodox Church	37,000
Latin	22,000
Greek Catholic (or Melkite)	26,500
Maronite	3,000
Chaldean (Assyrian Catholic)	150
Syrian Catholic	150
Armenian Catholic	150
Armenian Orthodox	2,600
Syrian Orthodox (Jacobite)	150
Coptic	200
Ethiopian	100
Protestants	8,000
Total	100,000

P. 223. *School Attendance in Arab Countries and in Israel.* The percentage of children attending school has increased since 1952. By 1965 their percentage in the Arab countries around Israel was as follows.

PERCENTAGE OF CHILDREN AGED 6–14 ATTENDING SCHOOL, 1965

	Total	Males	Females
Lebanon	72	—	—
Egypt (UAR)	54.94	64.73	44.36
Syria	56.36	72.67	37.90
Jordan	70.78	78.68	62.13
Iraq	59.71	81.10	36.69

Cf. Patai, *Golden River to Golden Road,* op. cit. See also above, note to p. 14.

The atmosphere of high priority to education that prevails in Israel and engulfs the Middle Eastern immigrants contrasts with the smaller attention devoted to education in the countries from which they came. This contrast can also be illustrated by comparing the total and per pupil expenditures on education in Jordan (next-door neighbor to Israel), Iraq (from where some 120,000 Jews immigrated to Israel) and Israel.

In Jordan, of a total population of 2,000,000 in 1965, 416,851, or 20.84 per cent, were pupils and students attending all educational institutions. The total annual expenditure on education was 4,145,000 dinars, or 10 dinars (or $28) per pupil. In Iraq, in the same year, of a total population of 7,000,000, 1,262,495, or 18.07 per cent, were pupils and students. The total annual expenditure on education was 28,566,000 dinars, or 22.62 dinars (or $63) per pupil. In Israel in the same year, of 2,561,400 total population, 698,875, or 27.28 per cent were pupils and students. The total annual expenditure on education was I£. 236,678,000, or I£. 338, or $113 per pupil.

A comparison of the three countries indicates not only that in Israel (in spite of its lower fertility) a much higher percentage of the population attended schools, but also that the per capita expenditure on each pupil was four times as high as in Jordan and almost twice as high as in Iraq.

P. 224. *Demographic Rates of Non-Jews in Israel.* The demographic rates of the non-Jews (mainly Arabs) in Israel developed from 1951 to 1967 as follows:

All Non-Jews (Mainly Muslims)	Birthrate	Death Rate	Natural Increase	Infant Mortality
1951	46.5	8.8	37.8	48.8
1955	46.0	8.6	37.4	62.5
1960	50.3	7.5	42.8	48.0
1965	50.7	6.1	44.5	43.4
1967	49.7	6.3	43.4	46.1
Christians				
1967	29.3	6.3	23.0	32.9
Druzes				
1967	39.8	5.9	33.9	43.8

Source: *Statistical Abstract of Israel 1968.*

P. 235. *Samaritans.* The Samaritans in Israel numbered in the 1960s about 160. They lived in Holon, near Tel Aviv. Another 200 lived in Nablus, in the West Bank area occupied in the Six Day War of 1967 by Israel. In Holon, intermarriage between Samaritans and Jews became more and more frequent, so that it could be foreseen that their days as a separate religious ethnic group in Israel were numbered.

Karaites. In 1968 there were some 5,000 Karaites in Israel, living mainly in Afakim, Akko, Ashdod, B'er Sheva', Matzliah, Ramle and Ranen.

P. 237. According to the 1961 census, the Bedouins in Israel numbered 27,012, of whom 17,745 lived in the Negev, and the rest in the Galilee.

P. 241. See note to p. 131.

P. 247. *Increase of the Non-Jewish Population in Israel.* The non-Jewish population in Israel showed the following development from 1949 to 1967:

NON-JEWISH POPULATION OF ISRAEL 1949–67

Year	Muslims	Christians	Druzes and Others	Total
1949	111,500	34,000	14,500	160,000
1950	116,100	36,000	15,000	167,100
1955	136,300	43,300	19,000	198,600
1960	166,300	49,600	23,300	239,200
1965	212,400	51,100	29,800	293,300
1966	223,000	58,500	31,000	312,500
1967	286,600	70,600	33,100	390,300*

*Includes the population of East Jerusalem (about 66,000). Source: *Statistical Abstract of Israel 1968.*

P. 248. *Nazareth.* In 1968 Nazareth had a population of 30,900. In 1957 a Jewish urban settlement, Notzrat 'Ilit (or Upper Nazareth) was established on the outskirts of Nazareth. In 1968 it had 11,400 inhabitants, all of them new immigrants.

P. 254. *Arabs and Druzes in the Knesset.* The Knesset representation of the Arabs and Druzes in Israel in the Sixth Knesset (1965) was 7, of whom 4 represented the Arab Parties, 2 the New Communist Party, and one Mapam. (Three of the above were Muslim Arabs, 3 Christian Arabs, and one Druze).

P. 254. Note 2. By 1964 the Arab membership in the *Histadrut* grew to 82,054 (members and their families), representing 29 per cent of the total Arab population in the country.

P. 267. While the great majority of the *Yishuv* continued in its attitude of indifference to religion, American Conservative and Reform organizations initiated efforts to introduce non-Orthodox religious forms into the country, including the establishment of a few Conservative and Reform synagogues. Also, under American Jewish sponsorship, a "League for the Abolishment of Religious Coercion in Israel" was established in 1964.

P. 268. *National Service for Religious Girls.* In 1953 the Knesset passed the National Service Bill in an amended form, exempting girls from Orthodox homes from military service, and instead imposing upon them a two-year labor service in new immigrants' camps, religious *kibbutzim*, or hospitals. However, girls from ultra-Orthodox homes, who ordinarily would not be allowed to leave their parents' home at all prior to marriage, were exempted altogether.

P. 269. *Religious Parties in the Knesset.* In the third Knesset (1955), *Mizrahi–HaPo'el HaMizrahi* obtained 11 seats and Agudat Israel 6; in the fourth (1959), *Mizrahi–HaPo'el HaMizrahi* had 12 seats and *Agudat Israel–Po'ale Agudat Israel* 6; in the fifth (1961) the *Mizrahi–HaPo'el HaMizrahi* retained its 12 seats, the *Agudat Israel* obtained 4, and the *Po'ale Agudat Israel* 2; in the sixth, the National Religious Party (known as *Mifdal*, i.e. *Miflaga Datit L'umit*, and comprising *Mizrahi* and *HaPo'el HaMizrahi*) obtained 11 seats, *Agudat Israel* 4 and *Po'ale Agudat Israel* 2. In sum, the votes obtained by all the religious parties increased slowly from 12.19 per cent in 1949 to 15.44 in 1961, and then decreased to 14.56 in 1965.

P. 275. *Public Transportation on the Sabbath.* The issue of public transportation on Saturdays and holidays remained unsolved in 1969. Trains and inter-city bus lines still did not operate, and intraurban buses also remained in-operative. The Haifa subway line (the so-called Carmelit), built in 1959 and running from the port to Mount Carmel, was working on Saturdays.

P. 279. *Secularization.* The "battle for the immigrants" waged by the religious parties has, in fact, made very slow headway—this, at least, is the conclusion one can reach from the admittedly insufficient data available on the subject in 1969. In the Knesset elections, as we have seen above (note to p. 269), following a gradual increase to 15.44 per cent of total votes cast in 1961, there followed a decrease to 14.55 per cent in 1965. In education, the percentage of children attending state religious schools slightly increased from 1953/54 to 1967/68, as shown in the Note 1 to p. 328.

To the above can be added the results of a study conducted by E. E. Gutmann and Judah Matras after the 1961 elections to the Knesset. On the basis of data gathered, Dr. Matras estimated that among immigrants born in Iraq, the religious parties received almost twice the support received by Herut, with only insignifi-cant fractions voting for parties other than these two. Among North Africans, Mapai received as many votes as the religious parties and Herut combined, again with only negligible votes going to parties other than these three (cf. Judah Matras, *Social Change in Israel*, op. cit., pp. 113ff.). Thus it appears that the success of the religious parties in capturing the votes of the Middle Eastern immigrants varied considerably from ethnic group to ethnic group, with the overall picture as yet far from being clear. However, numerous other indicators point to a definite shift among the Oriental Jewish immigrants "in the direction of diminished religious observance" (cf. Matras, op. cit., p. 103). Moreover, Matras found that there was a definite correlation between education and shift away from religious observance: the higher the educational attainment (mea-sured in years of school attendance), the higher the percentage of those who moved into the "partially observant" or "non-observant" categories (pp. 105–06). Another factor making for change in the same direction is length of residence in Israel: the more years pass after the arrival of the Oriental Jewish immigrant in

Israel, the more frequent the change in religious observance (p. 107). All this is interpreted by Matras as representing "profound secularization trends or perhaps even the breakup and end of ... traditional Oriental Jewish societies" (p. 109). Whether we agree with this interpretation or not, one thing is clear: the political coalition hoped for by the religious parties between them and the Oriental Jews, which would have resulted in an Ashkenazi religious-Oriental Jewish majority dominating the Knesset and thus the government and the country, has not materialized, and cannot materialize in the future.

p. 289. *American Immigrants to Israel.* Immigration from America increased dramatically in the wake of the Six Day War of 1967. For several years prior to the war the number of American Jewish immigrants to Israel was around 1,700–1,800 (1964: 1,704; 1965: 1,778; 1966: 1,735; 1967: 1,777). After the war, it suddenly jumped up to 4,298. Equally important was the change that occurred in the demographic and professional characteristics of the immigrants. In comparison with the pre-Six-Day-War immigrants, those who made their *'aliya* after the war, were younger, had larger families, comprised more professional and fewer retired people, and, in general, were more representative of the occupational distribution characteristic of the American Jewish community.

p. 290. *Re-emigration from Israel.* The statement about re-emigration of Oriental Jews was based on the incomplete information available at the time. Additional information that has become available since, as well as subsequent developments from 1952 on, show that of the three major population groups in Israel, those born in Israel, in Europe and America, and in Asia and Africa, it is precisely the last mentioned whose share in the re-emigration is the smallest.

As to the countries of origin of the emigrants, the following table gives some data:

EMIGRANTS FROM ISRAEL BY CONTINENT OF BIRTH IN PERCENTAGES

Period	Born in Asia and Africa	Born in Europe and America	Born in Israel
1948–51	24.6	65.6	9.7
1952–61	15.0	63.7	21.2
1962	18.3	51.3	30.4
1962–65	17.7	49.9	31.4

The table indicates that roughly three times as many citizens of Israel who were born in Europe and America emigrated since the establishment of Israel as Israelis born in Asia and Africa.

Emigration from Israel from 1948 to 1964 is summarized in the following table which also shows the percentage of emigrants to immigrants. The table shows that since 1950 the number of emigrants fluctuated between 9,000 and 13,000 annually, constituting in 1961–64 from 12 to 16 per cent of the immigrants.

JEWISH EMIGRATION FROM AND IMMIGRATION TO ISRAEL

Year	No. of Emigrants (estimate)	No. of Immigrants	Emigration Rate[1]	Immigration Rate[2]	Percentage of Emigrants to Immigrants
1948 (May 15–Dec. 31)	1,040	101,828	1.5	177	1.02
1949	7,207	239,576	8.0	266	3.01
1950	9,463	170,249	8.6	154	5.56
1951	10,057	175,095	7.6	132	5.74
1952	13,000	24,369	9.1	17	53.35
1953	12,500	11,326	8.5	8	110.36
1954	7,000	18,370	4.7	12	38.10
1955	6,000	37,478	3.9	24	16.01
1956	11,000	56,234	6.8	35	19.56
1957	11,000	71,224	6.4	41	15.44
1958	11,500	27,082	6.4	15	42.46
1959	9,500	23,895	5.2	13	39.75
1960	8,500	24,510	4.5	13	34.68
1961	7,330[3]	47,638	3.3	25	15.39
1962	7,664[3]	61,328	3.3	30	12.46
1963	10,866[3]	64,364	4.5	30	16.88
1964	9,121[3]	54,716	3.6	25	16.67

[1] Emigrants per 1,000 population.

[2] Immigrants per 1,000 Jewish population.

[3] These figures include Jewish and non-Jewish emigrants.

P. 291. Note 1. *Exit Permits.* A few years after the above lines were written, the requirement of obtaining an exit permit was abolished. Thereafter, any citizen of Israel was free to leave the country after he had fulfilled his military turn of duty.

P. 291. Note 2. *Indian Jews.* The Indian Jews subsequently actually re-immigrated to Israel. Here, however, they and those who had remained in Israel (a total of some 7,000) were soon to face a problem of a different kind. Rabbis refused to perform weddings between *Bnei Israel* (Indian Jews) and other Jews on the grounds that the ancestry of the Indian groom or bride might have been tainted by ritual blemish, such as the remarriage of a divorced woman without having obtained a *"get"* (letter of divorce). In October, 1961, the Chief Rabbinate removed this stigma from the *Bnei Israel* (who had threatened hunger strikes), by declaring them Jews beyond question, but held that an individual investigation of the ancestry of the Indian groom or bride was necessary. This, the *Bnei Israel* felt, was still discrimination. Things came to a head in the summer of 1964, when the *Bnei Israel* held a sit-down strike in Jerusalem. The Government and the Knesset, at this point, took the matter out of the hands of the rabbinate, decreed that the *Bnei Israel* are Jews and must be treated in every respect as such, and instructed the rabbinate to act accordingly.

P. 298. *Decline of the Negative Stereotype and Rising Oriental Jewish Demands.* By 1969 the shortsighted view that ranged from seeing childish simpletons in the

Oriental Jews to considering them (and especially the Moroccans) inveterate thieves, drunks and fornicators, unable to absorb anything intellectual and characterized by chronic sloth and hatred of work, even for whose children "there is no hope" (above, pp. 295–97), has long since disappeared. Events have shown that it was not "a matter of generations" to raise them "out of the depths of their ethnic existence." The speed with which the young generation of Oriental Jews assimilated to the Ashkenazi-*Sabra* culture of Israel must have greatly surprised those who shared the views quoted above.

What in fact happened was that the living conditions of the Oriental Jews improved rapidly, more and more of them took their places next to Ashkenazi Jews in an ever-wider variety of jobs, their endemic diseases were reduced, their children went to school, and even their housing standards were gradually raised. After the Sinai Campaign of 1956, only rarely did one hear of the "inherent racial inferiority" of the Oriental Jews. The official attitude of nondiscrimination seems by that time to have become, if not accepted, at least acquiesced in, by the great majority of Israel's Ashkenazi population.

In fact, the pendulum has swung in the opposite direction, and numerous well-meaning Israeli observers of the local scene, especially of the Labor Zionist persuasion, began to deny the existence of *any* cultural gap between the Ashkenazi and the Oriental Jews even in the field of technical know-how. An example of the latter view is found in a recent volume, entitled *Israel Today: A New Society in the Making*, edited by Yehuda Gothelf and published in 1967 by the *Ihud Olami-Poale Zion*—Labor Zionist World Movement in Tel Aviv. To this collection of essays Eliahu Agasi contributed a paper, "Towards a United Israeli Society," in which he says, among other things: "The immigrants from Islamic lands brought with them no less education and technical know-how than the members of the First, Second and Third *Aliyot* combined" (p. 192). On the basis of this premise as well as other observations, Agasi reproaches the *Yishuv* for not having taken action on the demand voiced by numerous Israeli spokesmen to the effect that while Israel must absorb and integrate the immigrants, she must also safeguard the traditional cultural values of the various Jewish communities (*loc. cit.*). The significance of this essay, written by a long-time official of the *Histadrut*, and himself an Iraqi Jew, lies in the very fact of its inclusion in a volume published by the Labor Zionist movement, which implies Labor Zionist approval of the ideas and demands expressed in it.

Paralleling these developments, as it often happens when low-status or underprivileged or deprived groups experience an easing of their situation,* the dissatisfaction among the Oriental Jews intensified and surfaced. They increasingly gave expression to their impatience at the slow rate of improvement and chafed at the remaining socio-economic inequalities. Minor incidents occurred repeatedly, and in the summer of 1959 a disturbance of greater dimensions took place in the Wadi Salib quarter of Haifa (cf. Raphael Patai, "Wadi Salib—A

---

* Classical expression to this observation was given by Alexis de Tocqueville (1805–59) who wrote as early as 1856: "A people, which has supported without complaint, as if they were not felt, the most oppressive laws, violently throws them off as soon as their weight is lightened...." Cf. Alexis de Tocqueville, *L'Ancien Régime et la Révolution*, trans. M. W. Patterson, Oxford, 1949, p. 186.

Case History," *Midstream,* Winter, 1960; reprinted in R. Patai, *Cultures in Conflict,* A Seven Star Book, Herzl Press, 1961, pp. 57–77).

Some time thereafter the Council of the Sephardi Community in Jerusalem, assuming the role of patrons and spokesmen of all the Oriental Jews in Israel, began to publish its monthly *BaMaʻarakha* (in Hebrew), and its English bulletin, *Israel's Oriental Problem* (see above, note to p. 159), much of whose contents were devoted to attacks on the Israeli establishment. Both publications repeatedly discussed discrimination practiced by the Ashkenazi against the Oriental Jews in Israel, and "proved" the persistence of such discrimination by lengthy quotations from various authors. (One of the first quoted in the very first issue [October 1965] of *Israel's Oriental Problem* was from the first edition of the present book). Following the Six Day War of 1967, the bulletin stated that "One of the more gratifying results of the Six Day War is that it has torpedoed prevalent prejudices about the 'Second Israel,'" and went on to describe the recognition accorded to Oriental Jewish youth for their outstanding performance in the war, and concluded with the demand that the Prime Minister issue an official assurance to the effect that "all facilities granted to prospective immigrants will be enjoyed by all newcomers regardless of the country from which they hail" (vol. III, nos. 2–3, December 1967–January 1968). In subsequent issues the bulletin continued to castigate "the present East European Establishment in Israel" for its "obstinate refusal . . . to see the country's future in anything but 'Western' terms," and went so far as to say that this official attitude made Israel "a self-styled alien intruder in the area" and "makes all talk of peace with the Arabs practically meaningless," in addition to "alienating and finally antagonizing her own Middle Eastern majority." The bulletin suggested that by changing this attitude "Israel could now exist in the Middle East on the absolutely normal basis that the majority of her inhabitants are Middle Easterners and have never been anything else" (March 1968, p. 6).

p. 306 *Law of Return.* The Law of Return, adopted by the Knesset in 1950, has remained in force to the present, and accordingly every Jew can immigrate to Israel by right.

p. 307. The economic easing up actually materialized soon after the cessation of the mass immigration in 1952.

p. 308. See Postscript 1969.

p. 314. As indicated above, in note to p. 298, since 1952 the negatively weighted stereotype of the Oriental Jews subscribed to by Ashkenazi Jews has become much less negative, while the equally negatively weighted stereotype of the Ashkenazi Jews formed by the Oriental Jews has become sharpened.

p. 318. See note to p. 97 discussing the continued ethnic segregation in residential quarters in Jerusalem, and note to p. 131.

p. 319. *Occupational Differences.* This pattern of concentration of Oriental Jewish immigrants in low-paying unskilled jobs has been gradually weakening, with the result that the occupational structure of the Oriental Jews has come to resemble more and more that of the Ashkenazi Jews. Cf. Note 2 to p. 90.

p. 320. Note 1. *Oriental Jews in Agriculture.* The number of the Oriental Jews in agriculture has actually become considerably greater than their percentage in the Jewish population of Israel. From 1949 to 1958, 24,766 immigrant families settled in 256 rural immigrants' settlements. Of these, 16,179 were still living in the settlements in 1958, another 8,587 families having left them. Of those that remained, 64.7 per cent (or 10,482 families) had come from Asia and Africa, 30.6 per cent (or 4,967 families) had come from Europe and America, and 4.5 per cent (or 730 families) from the Balkans (Sephardi Jews from Greece, Yugoslavia and Bulgaria). (Source: *Sh'naton HaHistadrut 1964/65*, Tel Aviv.)

To take a longer period, and, at the same time, present the issue from a different angle, from 1948 to 1967 a total of 240,000 Jewish immigrants who had come from Asia and Africa became gainfully employed in Israel. Of them, 33,734, or 14 per cent, were employed in agriculture in 1967. In the same period, 223,000 Jewish immigrants who had come from Europe and America became gainfully employed. Of the latter, however, only 15,597, or 6.9 per cent, were employed in agriculture in 1967. Of the total of 49,331 immigrants (from 1948 to 1967) who took to agriculture in Israel, some 69 per cent were Afro-Asian, and about 31 per cent Euro-Americans. (Calculated on the basis of data contained in the *Statistical Abstract of Israel 1968.*)

On the basis of the above figures it is clear that following the establishment of Israel the "Yoke of agriculture" (cf. above, pp. 199–202) has indeed been shouldered by the Oriental Jews to a much greater extent than by the Ashkenazi Jews.

p. 320. Note 2. *Upward Mobility and National Unity.* The prediction that the Jews of European (and American) extraction would "come to form a cultural elite" in Israel has come true within a very few years after the establishment of the state. The mass influx of Oriental Jews and of the survivors of concentration camps and displaced persons camps from Europe accelerated this process by turning the veteran Jewish population of Israel into a group occupying the highest rungs on the social ladder while the newcomers, of necessity, augmented the lowest ranks. Once this general range of status ranks was established, the upward mobility of the low ranks depended to a great extent on their ability to acquire the aptitudes, skills and values of the elite. In this respect, of course, the European immigrants had the advantage over the Afro-Asian immigrants. Soon, therefore, Israeli society consisted of four distinct groups: on the top the Ashkenazi old-timers; beneath them the Oriental Jewish veterans (who, however, were very few in numbers); next came the Ashkenazi new immigrants; and lastly, at the bottom, the Oriental Jewish newcomers. This ranking order is also indicated by the four income groups discussed above in Note 2 to page 151.

Continued residential segregation contributed to both the emergence and perpetuation of this pattern. On the other hand, the occupational segmentation along the same lines soon began to loosen up under the effects of the educational effort. As a result, by the early 1960s, the upward socio-cultural mobility of the Oriental Jewish new immigrants became more and more evident, as shown above in Note 2 to page 90. The growing numbers of Ashkenazi girls who were willing to marry Oriental boys is one of the manifestations of this development. Another is the full share of the Oriental Jewish girls in the school attendance. A third is the complete social and training equality the Ashkenazi and Oriental youth enjoys during the three (or, in the case of girls, two) years in army service. The great feeling of national unity and community of fate that emerged during and after the Sinai Campaign of 1956 (and again, on an even larger scale, in 1967, when mortal threat to the very existence of, not only the nation as a whole, but each and every individual personally, was narrowly averted by the Six Day War) had no small part in bridging the cultural differences that still existed between the young generation of the two halves of Israel. Thus, due partly to the conscious efforts of its leadership, and partly to the pressure from across its frontiers to which all Israelis have been exposed almost uninterruptedly since the country's independence, internal differences have tended to diminish to the extent that by 1969 the danger of "ethnic isolation" can definitely be considered a thing of the past.

p. 324. See note to p. 254.

p. 327. Note 1. *Education.* The subsequent development of education in Israel is indicated by the following facts. In 1965 a total of 698,876 pupils and students attended all educational institutions. While post-primary education was still not compulsory, a rapidly increasing percentage of primary school graduates continued their education in secondary day schools (in 1961/62 58.2 per cent of all post-primary school pupils), secondary evening schools, continuation classes, vocational schools, agricultural schools, teachers training schools and other post-primary schools. In 1956/57, 35.22 per cent of all Jewish youth aged 14–17 attended post-primary schools; by 1961/62 this percentage rose to 46.52, and in 1967 to 53 per cent. See also note to p. 206.

p. 327. Note 2. *Arab Education in Israel.* By 1967/68, 70,000 Israeli Arab children attended school, representing about 90 per cent of the total Arab school-age population (6–14) in the country. In none of the neighboring Arab countries was this percentage equalled or even approximated.

p. 328. Note 1. *Religious Education.* The four separate educational trends were abolished in 1952 and their place was taken by a unified but double-branched educational system, comprising state education and state religious education (the State Education Law of 1952). However, the ultra-orthodox *Agudat Israel* and *Po'ale Agudat Israel* parties objected to the new system and continued to maintain independent schools outside it, which are subsidized by the state. The number and percentage of all primary school pupils enrolled in the state religious schools and the independent schools of the Agudat Israel are shown in the table, p. 378.

p. 328 Note 2, and p. 329. *Army Service.* The length of army training and service was subsequently raised to 36 months for men and 24 for women.

p. 337. See Postscript 1969.

PUPILS ATTENDING STATE, STATE RELIGIOUS, AND AGUDAT ISRAEL SCHOOLS, 1953/54–1967/68

	1953/54		1960/61		1967/68	
	Number	%	Number	%	Number	%
Total	219,129	100	361,707	100	385,589	100
State Schools	150,118	68.51	240,970	66.63	248,010	64.32
State Religious Schools	53,573	24.45	96,437	26.67	110,887	28.76
Agudat Israel Schools	15,438	7.04	24,300	6.71	26,692	6.92

Source: *Statistical Abstract of Israel 1968.*

Postscript 1969

In the Introduction (above, p. 6) it was stated that the future of Israel will hinge on the outcome of the "race between the rate at which the population groups of Oriental extraction in Israel will multiply, and the rate at which the institutions of the State will be able to supply them with a Western-type cultural equipment and instill in them the values of their own Western-type culture." These words were written in 1952. By 1969, although the Jews of Sephardi and Oriental extraction had attained the absolute majority in the *Yishuv*—a majority that, within one generation would foreseeably grow to close to three-fourths of the Jewish population of Israel (see notes to pp. 75 and 90)—it has nevertheless become clear that the race has been won by the progress made in imparting Western education, skills, values and other cultural attainments to the Oriental Jewish element in Israel.

That this was actually the case became most apparent if one considered the young generation, the one under 20 years of age, which by 1969 constituted two-thirds of that age group in the country (see above, note to p. 88). But even with reference to the entire Afro-Asian sector of the *Yishuv*, all the economic, social and cultural indices showed that the Westernizing process has indeed reached the point of no return; that is, the stage at which the group in question, like a spaceship travelling between two planets, escaped the gravitational field of the body it left behind and is, instead, pulled with increasing force toward the body in whose direction it has been heading. Let us consider briefly the major manifestations of this development.

The New Demographic Pattern

To begin with, the demographic characteristics of the Oriental (Afro-Asian) sector have shifted considerably in the Ashkenazi (Euro-American) direction. Since the death rate and infant mortality rate of the total Jewish population of Israel were by 1967 as low as, or even lower than, those in any of the most advanced Western countries, one cannot assume that they are the averages of two disparate sets of rates: a high set for the Oriental half, and a low set for the Ashkenazi half of the Jewish population of Israel. This would be impossible, for, in order to counterbalance and average out the higher rate of the Oriental half, it would presuppose such extremely low death and infant mortality rates for the Ashkenazi half, the like of which simply do not exist anywhere in the world. One must therefore conclude that with regard to these vital rates, the Oriental Jews of Israel have already reached, or at least very closely approximated, the extremely low average rates shown in the table contained in the note to p. 84.

With regard to fertility, the Oriental Jews evince rates that are still much higher than those of the Ashkenazi Jews in Israel. However, even as to this rate, which is much more resistant to change than the others, the Oriental Jews of Israel have moved far away from the traditional Middle Eastern profile, and they continue to move closer and closer to the Ashkenazi profile. Thus, demographically, the Oriental Jews are very close to complete Westernization.

Occupations and Residence

As to occupational structure, the shift from a traditional Oriental to a modern Western pattern is well under way (cf. note 2, p. 90), and will accelerate as the children still in school in the late 1960s and early 1970s will mature.

Residential segregation in the late 1960s still showed much of the old patterns (see note to p. 97), but it can be assumed that with more and more housing becoming available, the young generation, which shared schools, army training and war experiences, and which increasingly penetrates into the same occupations, will want to move toward residential integration and succeed before long in doing so.

Intermarriage

The emerging interdivision marriage pattern is not merely an index to the Westernization of the Oriental sector of Israel but also an indicator of the increasing genetic fusion between the two halves of the *Yishuv* (see note to p. 103). If this trend continues, the resulting interbreeding will reinforce cultural intermingling, until the Jews of Israel will not only become one undifferentiated gene pool, but also constitute one people socio-culturally. Of course, when this happens, the fact that the majority of the extant genes in the *Yishuv* came from an originally Afro-Asian stock will have no socio-cultural significance whatsoever, and will be in evidence only in the physical appearance of Israel's Jewish population.

Food, Clothes, and Appliances

As to food consumption, there is little cultural pressure on the Oriental Jews to change their old customs for those of the Ashkenazi Jews. Accordingly, it can be assumed that many descendants of Oriental Jews will continue to cling to their traditional preferences. However, the quantity and variety of the available food already does influence the Oriental Jews, at least to some extent, in the direction of Ashkenazi food habits, and will probably continue to do so in the future.

The abandonment of traditional garb observable among the Oriental Jews results from two factors: practical-material considerations and value associations. In Israel it is easy to obtain both the material for Western-type clothes, and the ready-made Western garments, while it is difficult to obtain the material for Oriental garb and to find the time to sew it, embroider it, etc. Also, Western-type clothes are more practical for work, whether at home or outside. Moreover—and this is the value-associated consideration—they are the most easily visible sign of being part of the Western, prestigious, dominant sector of Israel society. The fact is that one finds no Oriental Jews of the younger age group in Israel, male or female, who would wear any other clothes than the typical, drab, Western, Israeli apparel.

As far as household appliances are concerned, their possession is such a utilitarian matter (in addition to having a strong prestige element) that all Oriental Jews want to, and most of them actually do have them (see above, note to p. 46). It can be easily foreseen that in another few years there will be no difference whatsoever in this respect between Oriental and Ashkenazi Jews.

Reading Habits

Reading habits are a matter more difficult to pinpoint. Yet in this area, too, all signs indicate that shared educational experience results in shared tastes and preferences as far as this facet of cultural consumption is concerned. Most of the Israeli writers and journalists, and certainly almost all the authors of foreign books translated into Hebrew (see above, note to p. 175), are Westerners, Europeans or Americans. But even if the number of native Israeli writers of Oriental extraction should increase, the style of their writing, the literary genres they will use (e.g., the novel, the short story, the essay), will all be Western in origin, form and orientation. Thus, irrespective of the authorship, the very fact of the spread of literary consumption will be conducive to the exposure to and absorption of Western cultural influences by the Oriental sector of Israel.

The Decline of Oriental Culture

These factors and several others (to touch upon which would make this Postscript much too lengthy) leave no doubt as to the outcome of the race referred to above on p. 6. The race, in fact, has been won by the spread of Western-Israeli culture into the growing Oriental majority of the country's Jewish population. And not only has it been won, but won to such an extent that the question is no longer whether Israel will be able to avoid the pitfalls of Levantinization (cf. above, pp. 7–8, 430–33). Those pitfalls have been not only successfully avoided but definitively eliminated. The question that still remains in 1969 is: will there be, or can there be, a synthesis between the modern Western culture brought into Israel and made dominant there, on the one hand, and the Middle Eastern culture that was shared by the Oriental Jews until their immigration to Israel, on the other?

As early as 1952 I observed that in actual practice in Israel the Euro-American culture of the Ashkenazi Jews was gaining the upper hand, but saw at that time indications to the effect that "the end-result of the process is not likely to be the total submergence" of the Middle Eastern culture of the Oriental Jews (above, p. 337). By 1969 it has become evident that this expectation has been fulfilled only to a very minor degree. Indications of this outcome were, of course, present in 1952. Their analysis above in the section entitled "The Fate of Oriental Culture in Israel" (pp. 298–305), led to the conclusion that "under the impact of the modern Israeli scene none of the five crucial complexes of traditional Oriental culture, which were focal concerns in the lives of the Oriental Jewish communities, can stand up," and that, as a result, the Oriental Jews in Israel were going through a cultural crisis.

Surveying the Israeli socio-cultural scene after the Six Day War of 1967 it appears, first of all, that the cultural crisis that buffeted the Oriental Jews in 1952 and for several years thereafter has, by and large, become a thing of the past. Especially in the young generation, the sense of being socially and culturally "declassé" has disappeared, the traditional values of the Jewish variety of Middle Eastern culture have been largely forgotten, and the modern, dominant Ashkenazi culture of Israel has been acquired and internalized to a remarkable extent. If, between discarding the Oriental culture of their fathers and acquiring the Israeli culture of their peers, there was a period of deculturation or Levantinization, it was so brief as to pass almost unnoticed.

Arab Threat—A Unifying Force

There were several factors that have brought this to pass. The instruments of institutionalized Westernization discussed above (pp. 323–32) undoubtedly had a cumulative and increasingly decisive effect in the course of close to two decades. To them must be added the increasing threat from across Israel's borders that proved to be a constant force making for the elimination of internal differences and for the unification of even the most disparate ethnic elements in the *Yishuv*. The Sinai Campaign of 1956, and even more so the Six Day War of 1967, helped crystallize the feeling of being one nation that must remain united if it wants to survive in the midst of an encircling ring of implacably hostile neighbors bent on its destruction. The ever-recurring border incidents, the terrorist attacks in the very midst of the largest population centers, have served as almost daily painful reminders of the imperative need to maintain a strong united stand unweakened by internal dissension. Such events as the secret trial and public hanging of several Jews in Baghdad (in January, 1969) most effectively put an end to any vestigial nostalgia that any of the 150,000 Iraqi Jews in Israel may still have harbored in their hearts for their old homeland, and eliminated the feeling that "it was better there," which usually is a contributing factor to dissatisfaction with the "here and now." The fact that, up to 1969, a much smaller percentage of Oriental than Ashkenazi Jews have re-emigrated from Israel (see above note to p. 290), whatever its contributory causes, indicates that (their more difficult socio-cultural problems in Israel notwithstanding) the great majority of Oriental Jews have settled in Israel for good and thus must have gradually developed the emotional predisposition to make the best of the possibilities within the given institutional, social and cultural framework of the country.

Cultural Synthesis?

Could it, then, be said that the Jewish variant of the traditional Middle Eastern culture has contributed nothing, nor will it in the future be able to contribute anything, to the culture of modern Israel? Has the hope, expressed in 1952, that there would be in Israel a "process of amalgamation," which would eventually lead to a "cultural synthesis between East and West" (cf. above, p. 337), proved vain? The considered answer in 1969 is that this is almost, but not quite, the case. In analyzing the 1969 socio-cultural scene in Israel, one finds that very few elements from the five crucial complexes of traditional Middle Eastern culture discerned above (p. 55) can be considered as having been incorporated into it. It is in the realm of *esthetics* that the clearest indications of such influences are present. Oriental Jewish (and especially Yemenite) folk singing has become well embedded in modern Israel culture, as have Oriental Jewish (again especially Yemenite) arts and crafts (silver filigree work, embroidery, basketry, etc.). In contrast to the permeation of Israeli culture by these minor Oriental arts, no notable contribution has been made in the major art fields either by individual artists of Oriental Jewish extraction or by Oriental art traditions, Jewish or otherwise.

With regard to *religion*, the traditional Oriental Jewish forms have, by 1969, definitely lost their struggle for survival. This, of course, has much to do with the generally secular orientation of modern Israeli culture, which has resulted in an increasing secularization in the outlook and behavior of the great majority of the younger Oriental Jewish generation. However, even in those sectors of the Oriental Jewish component of Israel's population, which continues to adhere to religious observance, the traditional Oriental Jewish forms are being successively replaced by traditional Ashkenazi forms of observance. The reasons for this development lie mainly in the field of education: the control of the religious schools attended by the children of the religiously oriented Oriental Jews, in many cases together with the children of the religiously oriented Ashkenazi Jews, is largely in the hands of religious Ashkenazi Jews. This means that while the Oriental Jews may, and do, augment the numerical strength of the religious sector in Israel, the specific quality of Oriental Jewish religiosity is being replaced by the different quality of Ashkenazi religiosity. This again means that the cultural, as against the numerical, contribution of Oriental Jews to the religious scene in Israel is negligible.

Next, what has become of the "broader outlook on human existence" which as early as 1952, we found had been ignored or rejected by the predominant Western element in Israel? (Cf. above, p. 300.) The answer is that, 17 years later, it has largely shared the fate of religiosity among the Oriental Jewish division of Israel, especially in its young generation. This decline was due not merely to the influence of the Ashkenazi example, precept and attitude, but also, and perhaps to an even greater extent, to the circumstances of Israeli life, and especially its imperative of intensive preoccupation, imposed in equal measure upon all citizens, with the immediate issues of physical survival in the face of sustained Arab hostility. If one suffers privation but lives in relative security, one can find hope and solace in a broader outlook on human life, one of greater detachment from material benefits and greater reliance on the consolation held out by the belief in a better life in the afterworld. But if, even while enjoying creature comforts, one is constantly bombarded by threats of violence and actually witnesses the sudden and violent death of friends and relatives, one will be more inclined to bend one's physical and mental energies to protecting oneself and one's dear ones, and do so with an intense concentration that all but precludes the development of such mental postures as detachment, contentment and serenity.

As to the *extended family*, whose decline among the Oriental Jews in Israel was observed and commented upon in 1952 (see above, p. 302), all that has to be said is that the process, which was well on its way then, has been practically completed by 1969. With the possible exception of a few isolated cases, the classical Middle Eastern extended family of three generations living in one household, headed by the patriarchal grandfather and forming an economic unit, simply is no more. The nuclear family, consisting of father, mother and minor children, is the rule among the Oriental Jews to almost the same extent as among the Ashkenazi Jews. Thus, no Oriental Jewish cultural contribution can be recorded in this area of modern Israeli life.

The same is true with regard to the last complex. If the extended family disappeared, the *composition of larger social units of extended families* must needs have disappeared also. In 1969 very few Israelis still belonged to any social unit or association by strength of their membership in an extended, or even nuclear, family. In general, ascribed status, characteristically found in high frequency in traditional societies, has declined and been replaced by a greater frequency of achieved status, characteristic of modern societies with greater vertical social mobility. In the young generation of Oriental Jews in Israel, as among the Ashkenazi Jews, the position an individual achieves depends primarily on his aptitudes, skills, talents and attitudes. Nothing in this realm has been carried over into modern Israeli culture from the traditional Middle East.

Western Culture Israeli Style

If so little has been saved in modern Israel from the traditional culture of the Middle East, one must recognize that in 1969 it is no longer possible to speak of, or hope for, a true cultural synthesis in Israel between the East and the West. The Oriental half of the *Yishuv* has been so thoroughly Westernized that, in many cases, its younger generation knows of the traditional Middle Eastern culture of its fathers and grandfathers only from hearsay, if at all. Thus by 1969 Israel's cultural physiognomy has become almost as Western as that of any modern country in Western Europe or in North America.

Western culture is, of course, a generalized concept, an abstraction. In actuality, it consists of numerous cultures, each of which shares many features with generalized Western culture and each of which also has several features in which it differs from it. Thus, for instance, while French culture shares the generalized Western cultural pattern described above (pp. 32–39), it differs from that pattern in that its language is French, it has a literature of its own, it places special emphasis on art, cuisine, couture, perfumes, wines, as well as in numerous features in the realm of values.

In a similar manner one can state that modern Israeli culture shares with the generalized Western cultural pattern all its major complexes, and that its own specificity lies in the realms of its Hebrew language, Hebrew literature, the institutionalized forms of Jewish religion (albeit greatly secularized with regard to general religious observance), in the minor arts (with the Oriental Jewish contribution to them), in the socio-economic patterns it developed (the *kibbutz*, the *moshav*, the *Histadrut*), its continued emphasis on education and intellectual excellence, its scientific bent, its preoccupation with its long historical past in its country (including the extraordinary popular interest in archaeology), its intense concern with the fate of Jewish communities in all parts of the world, coupled with the conviction that Israel represents the elite of world Jewry, and the extraordinary élan it evinces in the face of hostile neighbors. The list is a creditable one, and it is indicative of the degree to which Israel by the 1960s has achieved a national identity of its own in spite of the gigantic task of the socio-cultural (as well as economic) absorption of more than a million immigrants.

Self-Criticism

It is a sign of the security Israel feels in having accomplished the implantation of Western culture into its soil that the ubiquitous presence of the cruder aspects of Western culture is being increasingly execrated. As long as one is in the middle of a fight for a cultural (or other) attainment, one is not inclined to criticize it; once it has been achieved, one can (and some usually do) subject it to critical scrutiny. Thus, for instance, a veteran observer of the Israeli scene has recently written:

> One of the more deplorable aspects of our cultural life is its "translated" nature: the imitation of the Western way of life, American or British; the indiscriminate import of films and the worship of film stars, cocktail parties and New Year's parties; foreign behavior patterns and aspirations; fashions; a market flooded with foreign literature; translations of cheap books. . . .°

° Cf. Israel Cohen, "Cultural Life in Israel," in Yehuda Gothelf (ed.), *Israel Today: A New Society in the Making*, Tel Aviv, 1967, p. 171.

For our present considerations it is not at all relevant whether these strictures are justified or not. What is significant is the fact that such a bend of critical attitude could and has emerged, and that its target is not the cultural influences emanating from the Oriental sector of the *Yishuv* but the outgrowths on the body of the Western cultural conglomeration of Israel.

The Case for Cultural Pluralism

Israel has thus succeeded by the late 1960s in making the Western culture of the Ashkenazi veteran settlers the dominant one in the country. It has certainly and definitively escaped the dangers of Levantinization and deculturation. However, by achieving this in a relatively brief period, it has practically excluded the possibility of a true cultural synthesis between East and West. What, then, of the realization that "each culture has complete validity for its own carriers" (cf. above, p. 339) which, of course, is the basic premise of the doctrine of cultural pluralism? Is it still possible, and is it still desirable to introduce this doctrine and all that derives from it, into the Israeli cultural scene? In seeking an answer to these questions, let us consider for a moment the fate of cultural pluralism in the country that gave birth to it, the United States of America.

Cultural pluralism, as it has actually worked out in the United States, means nothing more than the retention, by each non-Anglo-Saxon (or ethnic) group, of a modicum, a very minor residue, of the culture brought along by its immigrant ancestors. In all major aspects, as well as in the overwhelming majority of cultural realms, the American ethnic groups share the dominant Anglo-Saxon culture of the majority. There is also among them an ongoing process of assimilation, albeit at varying rates, to the Anglo-Saxon majority culture. But they are, at the same time, encouraged by the prevailing atmosphere of cultural pluralism to retain, as long as they wish and can, whatever they consider valuable in their own cultural heritage.*

Moreover, in recent years it has clearly emerged in the United States that it is of psychologically great importance for an ethnic group *to have* a cultural heritage of its own. The ethnic groups want to feel that the general environment enables them to familiarize their young generation with their past history and culture and to do so through institutionalized and publicly recognized channels. It was in response to this vocally expressed psycho-cultural need that Puerto Rican, African and Afro-American studies (including the Swahili language) were recently added to the curricula of an increasing number of American high schools and colleges. The same

* Cf. Raphael Patai, *Cultures in Conflict: An Inquiry Into the Socio-Cultural Problems of Israel and Her Neighbors* (A Seven Star Book), New York, 1961, pp. 74 ff.

insight led, many years ago, to the introduction of Hebrew language and literature courses in numerous secondary and higher educational institutions in the United States.

At the same time it is clearly seen in general, and tacitly acknowledged by the ethnic groups themselves, that these and similar manifestations of cultural pluralism do not and cannot constitute even the remotest threat to the sole and complete predominance of Anglo-Saxon, i.e., American, culture. The sub-cultures of the minorities, or, to be more precise, their relatively minor cultural differentiations, fall rather in the same category as the many other sub-cultural varieties in the United States, which are not ethnically correlated but follow from the educational, occupational, economic, social or other stratifications that crisscross this nation of two hundred millions. The primary significance of cultural pluralism is thus found to be not cultural, but psychological: cultural pluralism is upheld in the first place, not because it is assumed that it can lead to a significant enrichment of American culture, but because it has been found to result in psychological satisfactions for the members of the ethnic groups themselves.

Cultural Pluralism in Israel

These observations contain a lesson that Israel would do well to heed. Once the external threats to its existence have subsided, or at least diminished, internal problems, differences and dissatisfactions will inevitably loom larger. A situation may develop in which the very experience itself that Middle Eastern culture has so far contributed very little to the culture of modern Israel may give rise to an increasingly antagonistic reaction among the Oriental Jews to the dominant modern Western culture of Israel and to those traditionally associated with it as a group. The socio-cultural strategy followed and policy advocated by the latter, that, consequently, the Oriental Jews must merge into one cultural entity with the Ashkenazim, since in doing so they would merely give up their backwardness and advance themselves culturally, has not been taken kindly by those towards whom it has been directed. In such a situation it may prove extremely helpful to understand that the purely cultural considerations are best kept in abeyance while steps are being taken to meet the psychological need manifested in the demands of the Oriental sector of the *Yishuv*. Although these demands are couched in cultural terms and can be met only on a cultural level, the desirability of meeting them must be gauged, not on the cultural but on the psychological plane.

This would not be a case of paying mere lip service to the traditional culture of the Oriental Jews. It would be a truly liberal approach to the problem of how to satisfy disparate psycho-cultural needs existing in the socio-economically less advanced sectors of the *Yishuv*. It would be a most desirable supplementation of the great efforts that have been made ever since the achievement of Israel's independence to raise their material, economic, health and educational standards. It would be an effective way, perhaps the only effective way, to raise the low self-esteem characteristic of some of these Oriental Jewish communities that seems to go hand in hand with high criminality and delinquency rates and with a pronouncedly ambivalent attitude towards the dominant Ashkenazi sector, its culture and its values. *

This is not the place to spell out concretely and in detail what exactly can and should be done in order to achieve the above aims. But it can be indicated in a general manner that the steps to be initiated should include the teaching of the history of the Oriental Jewish communities in the lands of Asia and Africa, their contributions (which are by no means few or minor) to the development of Jewish religion, to Hebrew grammar, literature and poetry, to Jewish Philosophy, to medicine, astronomy, mathematics and geometry; their role in the history of the *Yishuv* in Palestine from the Roman exile to the first *Aliya* (a matter of 18 centuries!), and their share in the rise of the great medieval Muslim Arab and Persian cultures from Iran to the Iberian Peninsula. They should also include the encouragement of folk celebrations, annual feasts and commemorative meetings dedicated to traditional events of significance found in the history of every Oriental Jewish community, in which the members of the community in question would be the principals and the Israeli public at large the spectators.

None of this, as can readily be seen, has much to do with the actual value of the indicated procedures for the modern culture of Israel. But then, neither have the celebrations and parades of St. Patrick's Day, Steuben Day, Columbus Day, or Pulaski Day in New York with the enrichment of modern American culture. But, as to the psychological satisfactions, they are a different matter altogether! The pride the ethnic group involved derives from these parades taking place in the public eye of all New York, with the governor, the mayor and all other dignitaries taking the salute from their stands erected along the route, contributes greatly to the self-esteem and self-image of each group. The *basis* of the observances is historical, the *form* they take (what with the national costumes, national music, etc.) is cultural, but their *effect* is psychological.

Similar historical observances in Israel would have a comparable psychological effect, not only on the ethnic group in question, whose

*Cf. op. cit., p. 34.

self-image would greatly improve, but also on the outgroups, who would be inevitably and positively influenced by the public recognition thus accorded them. Both processes could contribute to an easing of the tensions that in 1969 still simmered close to the surface of Israel interethnic relations.

The Oriental Jewish Manpower

In considering the place of an ethnic group within the totality of a nation, there are considerations other than cultural, and it is to one of these that, in conclusion, we now turn. The very physical presence of large numbers of Oriental Jews in Israel almost since the day it achieved independence has made them a most valuable element in the young state. At a time when Israel desperately needed manpower for economic as well as security reasons, the Oriental Jews came and filled the gap. Subsequently, when Israel needed (as it still does) a healthy natural increase, it was almost exclusively the Oriental Jews who supplied this need while the Ashkenazi contingent barely held its own. When the country needed hundreds of thousands of unskilled laborers to till its soil, to stretch roads across its length and width, to erect dwellings and other buildings, it was again mostly the Oriental Jews who filled the demand, although in their home countries they were no more accustomed to this type of work than were the Ashkenazi Jewish immigrants. And when, with the improvement of the economic conditions, Israel needed fewer and fewer unskilled laborers and more and more skilled ones, it was once more the Oriental Jews among whose ranks the manpower could be found to undergo the training and advancement from the first to the second type of occupation.

If, in view of the developments of the last 17 years, it can no longer be expected that a cultural synthesis will take place in Israel between traditional Middle Eastern and modern Western culture, it can now be foreseen that, in another generation, Israel will be a totally Westernized, very highly advanced country, in which all citizens will share the benefits of the most modern technology, medicine and education. The Oriental Jewish element, while still preserving a modicum of its own cultural traditions—fostered by an enlightened policy of cultural pluralism—will be largely acculturated to the country's dominant modern Western culture. Yet, *genetically,* the great majority of the Jewish population will carry an Oriental heritage. The unique combination of a genetically predominantly Middle Eastern but culturally predominantly Western population will show the world that a sustained educational and acculturative effort is capable of transforming culturally deprived populations into peoples of marked cultural excellence.

Index